Provence
& the Côte d'Azur

Provence made to measure

Contents.. 4
A weekend in Nice................................. 5
A weekend in Grasse 6
A weekend in Cannes 7
A weekend around Avignon................. 8
A weekend around Carpentras............. 9
A week on the Côte d'Azur.................. 10
A week on the Provence coast 11
A week in the Arles area 12
A week in Marseille and Toulon........... 13
Two weeks around Luberon
and Ventoux.. 14
Two weeks in the countryside............... 15

Provence à la carte

Contents 16
STREET MARKETS   18
The lemon, fruit of sunny Menton......... 20
The melon, king of Cavaillon 21
Provence in a pinch of
aromatic herbs 22
A TASTE OF PROVENCE   24
Pastis – 'national' drink of Provence..... 26
The olive 28
Sweets and candies............................. 30
Restaurants.. 32
Gourmet Provence............................... 34
LOCAL DISHES   36
Local dishes.. 38
Provençal home cooking 42
VINEYARDS   44
Wines of Provence............................... 46
HOME FURNISHINGS   50
Fabrics and material............................ 52
Wood crafts 53
Glass and glass-blowing...................... 54
Wrought iron 55
Ceramics and pottery.......................... 56
The Provençal crib............................... 57
Ochre pigments................................... 58
Antiques and collectibles 60

CASTLES, 'BORIES' AND HILLTOP VILLAGES   62
Traditional architecture......................... 64
Hilltop villages 66
PREHISTORIC SITES, ROMAN REMAINS AND ROMAN ART   68
Caves and cave-dwellers...................... 70
Roman remains.................................... 72
Monasteries 74
GARDENS AND PERFUMES   76
Flowers.. 78
Lavender.. 80
Perfumes and fragrances...................... 82
SPORTING HOLIDAYS   84
Where to go for sports 86
Pétanque, a national sport.................... 90
HIKES, WALKS AND RAMBLES   92
Gorges and waterfalls........................... 94
Countryside and nature......................... 96
BEACHES AND ISLANDS   98
Days out at the beach.......................... 100
Pony trekking and cycling 101
Leisure parks, aquariums and zoos..... 102
Grand hotels and casinos.................... 104
FESTIVALS, CONCERTS AND THE CINEMA   106
In the footsteps of Provençal writers... 108
Provençal culture 110
Painters and light in Provence............. 112
Cinema on the Côte d'Azur.................. 114
Provençal literature.... 116
Provence on film................................. 117
Nice carnival 118
PLACES OF COMMERCIAL AND SCIENTIFIC INTEREST   120

Provence in detail

Contents... 122
Provence in detail – map.................... 124
THE CAMARGUE   126
Arles... 126
The Camargue 130
Les Saintes-Maries-de-la-Mer 132

THE ALPILLES   134
The Alpilles.................................. 134
Les-Baux-de-Provence................. 136
Saint-Rémy-de-Provence.............. 138

AROUND AVIGNON   140
Avignon...................................... 140
Tarascon and La Montagnette ... 144
Orange 146
Vaison-la-Romaine and
the Haut Vaucluse 148

AROUND CRAU   150
Salon-de-Provence 150
Martigues 152

LUBERON   154
The Petit Luberon....................... 154
The Grand Luberon 156
The Vallée de la Durance 158
Apt and Roussillon 160
Gordes and the Abbey of Sénanque... 162
Cavaillon.................................... 164

COMTAT VENAISSIN   166
L'Isle-sur-la-Sorgue.................... 166
Pernes-les-Fontaines.................. 168
Carpentras.................................. 170
The Mont Ventoux...................... 172

AROUND AIX   174
Aix-en-Provence 174
The Aix district 180

HAUTE PROVENCE   182
Manosque 182
Forcalquier 184
Sisteron 186

AROUND MARSEILLE   188
Marseille..................................... 188
Cassis and Cap Canaille 196
From La Ciotat to Bandol........... 198

TOULON COAST AND THE SAINTE-BAUME   200
From Bandol to Sanary 200
Toulon....................................... 202
The Sainte-Baume range............ 204
The Giens peninsula 206
Hyères 208
Porquerolles 210
Port-Cros and Levant.. 212

THE MAURES   214
Bormes-les-Mimosas and
le Lavandou 214
Saint-Tropez 216
Sainte-Maxime 218
Grimaud, Cogolin and Port-Grimaud ... 220
The Maures range 222

THE ESTEREL COAST   224
Saint-Raphaël and Fréjus 224
The Esterel Coast 226

THE ARGENS   228
Draguignan 228
Deep in the Haut Var....................... 230
The Vallée d'Argens 232

AROUND VERDON   234
The Verdon Gorges............................ 234
The route Napoléon 238

AROUND THE CÔTE D'AZUR   240
Cannes.. 240
The Îles de Lérins 242
Mougins and the Vallée
de la Siagne 244
Grasse and its perfumes 248
The Fayence district 250
Antibes and Juan-les-Pins 252
The Cap d'Antibes 254
Vallauris 256

AROUND VENCE   258
Cagnes-sur-Mer 258
Saint-Paul-de-Vence.......................... 260
Vence 262
Biot 264
The Vallée du Loup 266

AROUND NICE   270
Nice 270
Cap Ferrat....................................... 276
Èze and La Turbie 278
The Paillons Basin 280

AROUND MONACO   282
Monaco 282
Monte-Carlo 286
Roquebrune, Cap-Martin
and Beausoleil.................................. 288
Menton... 290

THE HAUTES VALLÉES   292
The Vallée de la Vésubie 292
The Haute Vallée de la Roya 296

THE PRÉALPES   298
Digne-les-Bains................................ 298
The Hautes Vallées of the Var
and the Verdon................................ 300
Barcelonnette and
the Vallée de l'Ubaye.... 304
Parc du Mercantour 306

Provence made to measure

Two weeks   14

Weekend breaks   5
A weekend in Nice 5
A weekend in Grasse 6
A weekend in Cannes 7
A weekend around Avignon 8
A weekend around Carpentras 9

Two weeks around
Luberon and Ventoux................................14
Two weeks in the countryside............15

A week   10
A week on the Côte d'Azur 10
A week on the Provence coast......... 11
A week in the Arles area 12
A week in Marseille
and Toulon... 13

Spend the next day admiring the work of the two great artists who made Nice their home. Start with the Musée Marc Chagall (p. 274) which contains his monumental work, *The Biblical Message*. For a complete change of mood, visit the Musée Matisse and marvel at the great painter's use of light (p. 274). Matisse lived in Nice for nearly 40 years. Before returning to town, climb up to the Cimiez monastery (p. 274) and see the Roman bath, amphi-theatre, and the monastery's magnificent rose gardens. Your weekend menu should include local dishes such as *salade niçoise*, *ratatouille niçoise* and *pissaladière*.

A weekend in
Nice

Whether you want to luxuriate in its top hotels or discover the simple pleasures of Mediterranean life, Nice will welcome you with open arms. Its extensive beachfront epitomises the French Riviera.

Nice can't make up its mind as to whether it is in France or Italy. Nestling in the Baie des Anges, the city is full of Mediterranean promise with brightly coloured walls, French spoken with an Italian accent and the gentle pace of life. If you want to start soaking up the amosphere immediately, begin the day by strolling through the busy lanes of the old town where craft workshops huddle around the Sainte-Réparate Cathedral (p. 271). Behind its elegant façade, Nice is a bustling market town and fresh flowers, fruit and vegetables are sold on a daily basis (p. 270). In the afternoon, visit the Musée Masséna that tells the story of Nice and its splendid Empire *salons* (p. 273). Then take a stroll along the Promenade des Anglais to the Phœnix Park, where seven different tropical microclimates are recreated in a giant greenhouse (p. 273).

SPECIAL ATTRACTIONS

Party-goers will want to spend their week-end in Nice during the colourful annual carnival in February (p. 275). Art lovers should take an excursion to Saint-Paul-de-Vence (p. 260), the Mecca of contemporary art. Amateur astronomers will be eager to visit the amazing Astrorama on the Corniche d'Èze (p. 278), the scenic road which hugs the coastline between Nice and Menton (p. 278).

A weekend in

Grasse

Lovers of luxurious fragrance and beautiful scenery will find everything they could wish for here. Surrounded by acres of flowers and magnificent countryside, Grasse is famous for perfumes which waft gently throughout the town.

Grasse, the world-famous capital of perfume, has a seductive charm and world-wide reputation. A visit to one of the three great perfumeries which for centuries have been creating the most subtle of French fragrances (p. 248) is an absolute must. You will even be allowed to devise your own perfume. The Villa Fragonard, an elegant country house, will take you back to the voluptuous times of the 18th C. when Grasse became the capital of French perfume after being known solely for its perfumed gloves (p. 249). The fragrant fields of the Domaine de Manon, where, from May to November, you can watch roses and jasmine being picked are just outside the town. You can try the taste of the flowers themselves in the form of candies from Tourettes-sur-Loup, known as 'the city of violets' (p. 266) and in the confectionery factory at the Loup Gorges. The deep, narrow gorges of the Loup (p. 267) and the Château de Gourdon (p. 269) are well worth a visit. The gardens of the Château are perched precariously on the edge of the precipice and were designed by the famous landscape artist Le Nôtre who designed the gardens of Versailles. Those interested in prehistoric sites will enjoy the dark caves of La Baume and the Domaine des Audides (p. 239) where the earliest inhabitants of Provence lived thousands of years ago. Lovers of sport can indulge in abseiling and parachuting.

THE EMPEROR'S ROAD
Grasse is a good starting point for travelling along the route Napoléon (p. 238), so called because it was the road he took to Paris in 1815. The village of Senez which stands beside the road has a splendid Romanesque cathedral decorated with tapestries and wall hangings of the period.

A weekend in
Cannes

With or without the glitz, Cannes exerts a magnetism over people, famous or not. They may be film fans or just want to go scuba-diving; perhaps all they want to do is relax on the beach, or sit at a harbourside café and gaze at the fabulous yachts moored there and the daily pageant of Riviera life.

In Cannes, home of the famous Film Festival (p. 240), you can act like a star. Be photographed on the steps of the Palace (the red carpet is there all year round) and, from behind the sunglasses that keep you incognito, observe the extravagant façades of the grand hotels as you stroll along the Croisette in the late afternoon. Take a trip round the islands; the Îles de Lérins (p. 242) are 15 minutes away by boat from the coast. On Sainte-Marguerite, the mysterious Man in the Iron Mask was incarcerated in the imposing fortress. On the Île Saint-Honorat, the monks still spend their days in a miniature paradise, where they turn the flowers they grow into a liqueur. Spend a day in Mougins (p. 244) where, from the hilltop, you can contemplate the magnificent view over the bay. This ancient fortified village, with its winding, narrow lanes, has been home to many celebrities. Just outside the village, beside the lovely Notre-Dame-de-Vie Chapel (p. 244), is the region in which Pablo Picasso spent his last years and where Winston Churchill learned to paint. The surroundings are bathed in a wonderful light. If you are looking for a place to eat, nothing beats the restaurant located in the old oil press of Mougins which is now one of the best in the area. This is where the stars hang out during the Film Festival (p. 245).

POTTERY

At Vallauris (p. 256), made famous by Picasso when he worked here in the 50s, you can meet potters in their workshops creating the craft earthenware for which the town has become well known. Try throwing a pot of your own or just shop for craft ceramics.

FESTIVAL FEVER

The timing of the Cannes film festival in May is perfect. Film people from all over the world flock to spend a few days in the sun and add even more glitter to the Riviera. Although this festival is synonymous with the town of Cannes (see p. 114), other festivals do take place here. In January the Milia Multimedia Fair comes to town. A much smaller affair, it nevertheless attracts an increasing number of visitors interested in computers, CD Roms and virtual reality.

In between museum visits, stroll down the old streets and linger in the picturesque little squares where you can sit and enjoy a drink. If you want to see sights outside the town, the interesting Val-de-Bénédiction Charterhouse is definitely worth a visit (p. 143). The next day, spend some time in Tarascon (p. 144), the little village made famous by Alphonse Daudet as the home of his fictional anti-hero Tartarin. Try the local delicacy, a rich cake called a Tarasque. Make sure you visit the nearby la Montagnette and the villages of Graveson and Boulbon, and stop at the delightful Saint-Michel-de-Frigolet Abbey which continues the tradition of the 'pastrage' procession of shepherds on Christmas Eve (p. 145). If you plan to go there during the festival, don't forget to book a long time in advance.

A weekend around
Avignon

A magical city, and the cultural centre of Provence for centuries, the ancient town of Avignon is captivating. The Papal Palace stands imposingly on the banks of the Rhône, looking out over the famous bridge.

AN ANTIQUE-HUNTER'S PARADISE

If you like antiques, be sure to visit L'Isle-sur-la-Sorgue (p.166) on a Sunday morning. This little jewel of a village by the water's edge is a paradise for antique and bric-à-brac hunters. Roquemaure also holds antique markets at certain times of the year (p. 142). Look out for Provençal furniture, especially wardrobes.

Avignon is not a large city but it will still take you at least a day to discover all it has to offer, from the imposing Papal Palace to the Pont Saint-Bénezet, subject of a famous French nursery rhyme, to the numerous and interesting museums, such as the Musée Calvet and the Musée du Petit Palais (p. 142).

A weekend around Carpentras

Carpentras contains many architectural and historical treasures as well as plenty of good things to eat. At the foot of Mont Ventoux, the River Sorgue meanders through pretty villages and lovely countryside.

VAISON-LA-ROMAINE

If you take the D938 (B-road) out of Carpentras to the north, you will arrive at Vaison-la-Romaine (p. 148). This is one of the great cities of Antiquity and has some impressive historical remains. The Roman poet Petrarch made it his home.

The first morning of this weekend should be dedicated to exploring the capital of the former province of Comtat Venaissin (p. 170). Its monuments illustrate the numerous influences that have affected the city throughout the ages. Carpentras is a now a busy metropolis with one of the most beautiful markets in Provence. During your stay you can taste the delicious local sweets, such as stripey *berlingots* (humbugs) and crystallised fruits. In the afternoon, wend your way to the picturesque village of Isle-sur-la-Sorgue where you can spend the night. Stop off first at the little town of Pernes-les-Fontaines

(p. 168) and cool down under the so-called *cascatelles*, the 36 fountains after which the town was named. You could even take a detour through Venasque (p. 169) before reaching the Sorgue. The next day, you will have to rise early if you want to find a bargain at the Sunday flea-market. While hunting for antiques, don't forget to look at the pretty houses on the Isle (p. 166). In the afternoon, visit the village of Gordes (p. 162) after a short stop at Fontaine-de-Vaucluse, where you will find the mysterious source of the River Sorgue (p. 167). Visit the beautiful Sénanque Abbey (p. 163), one of the treasures of Romanesque Provence.

A week on the
Côte d'Azur

S ince the beginning of the century, the Côte d'Azur has been the chosen holiday destination of the wealthy. It is also a region with a rich artistic heritage and provides the perfect setting for pursuing all kinds of sports.

Leaving Menton (p. 290), go to Roquebrune (p. 288), a small fortified village perched on the cliff at a height of 1,000 ft and visit its Carolingian fortress which overlooks the Cap-Martin. The peninsula is covered with sumptuous villas (p. 288). Then for a breathtaking experience, try paragliding on the Mont Gros. From Nice explore the beautiful villages in the hinterland behind the Paillons Basin (p. 280). These include Coaraze (the sunniest village in France), Lucéram and Peillon, (reminders of the former Comté de Nice). Then, take the Grande Corniche by La Turbie, where a vast Roman monument awaits you (p. 279). Take a quick look at the Principauté de Monaco from the top of the Tête-de-

Chien, before going down to visit Le Rocher (p. 282) and its famous Musée céanographique (Oceanographical Museum). In the evening, do not miss climbing up to the Astrorama, next to Èze (p. 278) to see the

clearest sky in France. The next day, explore the Cap Ferrat (p. 276) where you can admire the rich Kérylos and Éphrussi villas owned by the Rothschild family. Close to Nice, lies Cagnes-sur-Mer (p. 258) where you can visit the house of the much loved painter, Renoir, or take the family to the huge leisure park of Marineland in Juan-les-Pins (p. 253). Take a final detour by Vence (p. 262), and Saint-Paul-de-Vence (p. 260), home of many contemporary artists, before going to the Cap d'Antibes (p. 254), where you'll see the well-heeled French enjoying this idyllic setting.

A week on the
Provence coast

This is the best place in the Mediterranean to discover water sports. The scenery is stunning: sandy beaches, lush foliage and a myriad colours and scents…

Leaving Cannes (p. 240), drive southwards along the rocky Esterel coast road (p. 226). Walk up to the peak of the Cap Roux, the summit of this splendid 'corniche d'or'. Further south, the sandy beaches of Saint-Raphaël and Fréjus (p. 224) are ideal for a family dip in the sea and in Sainte-Maxime you can get an amazing view of the sea bed in the Aquascope (p. 218). For those who like fishing, the locals will take you fishing *à la palangrotte* (deep line) in the open sea. Then stop for half a day at Port-Grimaud (p. 221), a small town by the sea that looks as though it dates from the 16th-century although it was actually built in 1962. Make sure you visit Saint-Tropez (p. 216), even if only to enjoy an iced coffee at

Sénéquier's. The next day, enter mimosa-country at Bormes-les-Mimosas and Le Lavandou (p. 214), which have 12 beaches, then sample the luxurious lifestyle on the Provence coast in the Edwardian era by taking a walk through the Rayol estate. To end your stay, visit the Presqu'île de Giens (p. 206) – a peninsula which, it is said, is slowly detaching itself from the continent – and

discover its 'double tombolo', a surfers' beach which is of world-wide repute. Not far away, the well-known Bird Park of La Londe (p. 207) adds yet more colour and sound to the landscape. 3 miles (5 km) inland, explore the old fashioned charm of Hyères with its palm-lined streets. At the beginning of the century, the Provence coast had an elegance found nowhere else.

A week in the Arles area

The landscape of the Camargue region is so delightful, it is no wonder that Van Gogh fell in love with it. Arles is an area in which tradition is still very much alive and your week's stay will show you why the people of Arles are so proud of it.

Begin your visit in the coastal areas of the Camargue region. Its wild open spaces are a paradise for horses, pink flamingoes and bulls, (p. 130). Saintes-Maries-de-la-Mer, the home of the Gypsies, lies right on the coast; visit the town itself (p. 132), laze on the beaches or take a boat ride along the waterways of the Rhône Delta.

Or why not hire a bike and ride along the dyke or go for a swim? Next, visit Arles which is the ideal base for a short stay in this delightful region. Arles is full of ancient Roman remains (p. 126). You can also experience the living traditions of Provence by visiting the Museon Arlaten, or by watching a *feria*, a local bullfight. There is an International Photography Conference in July which may provide inspiration for budding photographers in this photogenic city. Leave Arles to visit the Alpilles (p. 134), the foothills of the Alps. Follow the route taken by Van Gogh to Montmajour, where there is a splendid Roman abbey, before going on to Fontvieille. Stop for half a day on the spectacular site

of the Baux-de-Provence (p. 137) to taste the local wine and visit the quarries of the Val d'Enfer (Valley of Hell). The last stop is Salon-de-Provence (p. 150) and the north bank of the Étang de Berre (Berre Pond), where you can stock up on the fragrant soap for which Marseille is famous; or salute the memory of Nostradamus who hailed from these parts.

A week in
Marseille and Toulon

Mingle with the throng in Marseille's crowded streets and drink in the unique character of one of the most ancient ports in the world which is still going strong today. A trip to the atmospheric harbour and its surrounding maze of narrow streets will leave a lasting impression on you.

Marseille (p. 188), has a lot to offer, and will be the star attraction of your stay. Try to spend at least two days there, just enough time for a stroll through the Vieux-Port and to discover the most interesting places and biggest attractions around town. On the third day, the best way to appreciate the beauty of the Mediterranean is by boat. Take a trip to the Îles du Frioul and the legendary Château d'If where the Man in the Iron Mask was incarcerated. In the afternoon, you can laze around on a beach by the Corniche, before setting off to explore the region. Keep a day free for visiting the Blue Coast which lies between Marseille and Martigues (p. 152), on the banks of the

Étang de Berre. There are 15 miles (24 km) of cliffs which offer some magnificent views of Carro, Carry-le-Rouet and Sausset-les-Pins. In Martigues, visit the Musée Ziem, an art museum which has excellent examples of local landscapes – a testimony to the beautiful light of the Midi which has lured so many artists here. The next day, visit the rocky inlets called *calanques* (Morgiou and Sormiou) for breath-taking views. From here, continue to the little port of Cassis (p. 196) and taste the local white wine with its unique bouquet of rosemary, heather and myrtle. From Cassis to Toulon, pleasant seaside resorts, such as La Ciotat (p. 199), Bandol and Sanary-

sur-Mer (p. 200) follow each other in quick succession. The trip ends in Toulon (p. 202), a town of ancient alleyways. The huge belvedere of Mont Faron is also worth seeing. Don't miss the morning market, held in the Cours Lafayette.

Two weeks around
Luberon and
Ventoux

This part of Provence is so magical that it has become famous throughout the world. The fragrant, rocky, sun-drenched landscape is both tranquil and dramatic. From Apt to Mont Ventoux, the Provençal landscape is stunning.

Apt (p. 160) is the ideal starting point for a fortnight spent in the Luberon region. It is well known for its crystallised fruit – which you'll be able to sample – as well as being the headquarters of the Luberon Regional Wildlife Park, which offers numerous opportunities for walks and bike rides. From Apt, take a trip to the ochre quarries where you can see a smaller version of Colorado's Painted Desert (p. 161). Then travel down to Cavaillon (p. 164), capital of the melon trade, from where you can visit the hilltop villages of the Petit Luberon – Ménerbes, Lacoste, Bonnieux and Lourmarin (p. 154). Take a stroll along the banks of the River Durance (p. 158). On its south bank lies the beautiful Silvacane Abbey, (p. 159) medieval home to the members of the Cistercian order. You are

now at the foot of the Grand Luberon (p. 156) where the ruins of ancient castles lie open to the sky. Return to civilisation by spending two days in bustling Aix-en-Provence (p. 174) with its elegant Italianate architecture. From Aix,

travel to Manosque (p. 182), favourite haunt of Marcel Pagnol, author of *Manon des Sources* and *La Gloire de Mon Père*. This is where Haute-Provence begins. The next stop is Forcalquier (p. 184), a headland situated between the Lure Mountain and the Haut Luberon. On your way, stop at the Saint-Michel observatory and visit the beautiful Ganagobie priory, a masterpiece in the Romanesque style. Afterwards, follow the river Durance to Sisteron (p. 186), a breathtaking beauty spot. You are now at the very edge of the mountain region, so complete your trip by returning to Mont Ventoux (p. 172), surrounded by lavender fields and gorges.

Two weeks in the countryside

If the Côte d'Azur no longer holds any secrets for you, the countryside that lies behind it still remains to be explored – magnificent landscapes and breathtaking views await you. From Marseille to the Italian border, this tour shows you the sights behind the glitter of the coast.

The Massif de la Sainte-Baume (p. 204) to the east of Marseille is the most striking feature in the landscape. Start your journey with a pilgrimage to the crest of the rock where Mary Magdalene once took refuge, and admire the basilica and the Royal Convent at Saint-Maximin. Travel deeper into the countryside and stock up on earthenware at the pottery in Moustiers-Sainte-Marie (p. 234), before visiting the natural wonders of the Verdon gorges. Try to spend at least two days there, so that you have time to fish or swim in the Lac de Sainte-Croix or walk along the Sentier de Martel. Afterwards, drive along the Route des Crêtes and the Corniche Sublime, then on through Castellane, and up to the Haute Vallée du Verdon (p. 300). Visit the Fort de Savoie in Colmars which protected the region from Piedmontese attacks in the

17th C. If you're feeling brave try skydiving in nearby Allos (p. 303) from a height of 5,000 feet (1,500m). Eastwards, in the Gorges de Daluis, the Couloir du Var is gouged out of red rock (p. 301). Its a great opportunity to do some canoeing, or try the new sport of canyoning, in these rocky mountains. The next day, take the pretty little 'Train des Pignes' up to the mountain-top citadel of Entrevaux (p. 300). Spend at least three days exploring the Vallée de la Vésubie (p. 292). There are lots of opportunities for

excursions, such as exploring the gorges, climbing up to the site of the Utelle sanctuary from which you can see the sea 15½ miles (25 km) away, lingering in the medieval villages leading to Saint-Martin-de-Vésubie, and relaxing in the Parc du Mercantour (p. 306). To complete the trip, the Haute Vallée de la Roya (p. 296), to the east has two unmissable attractions: the Vallée des Merveilles, with its mysterious rock carvings and a little gem of a chapel – Notre-Dame-des-Fontaines.

Provence à la carte

Street markets 18

The lemon, fruit of sunny Menton ...20
The melon, king of Cavaillon.............21
Provence in a pinch of
aromatic herbs.................................22

A taste of Provence 24

Pastis – 'national'
drink of Provence 26
The olive............................28
Sweets and candies 30

Restaurants 32

Gourmet Provence 34

Local dishes 36

Local dishes....................................38
Provençal home cooking...................42

Vineyards 44

Wines of Provence 46

Castles, 'bories' and hilltop villages 62

Traditional architecture....................64
Hilltop villages 66

Prehistoric sites, Roman remains and Roman art 68

Caves and cave-dwellers...................70
Roman remains................................72
Monasteries.....................................74

Home furnishings 50

Fabrics and materials 52
Wood crafts 53
Glass and glass-blowing 54
Wrought iron...................................55
Ceramics and pottery.......................56
The Provençal crib 57
Ochre pigments 58
Antiques and collectibles 60

Gardens and perfumes 76

Flowers 78
Lavender 80
Perfumes and fragrances 82

Festivals, concerts and the cinema 106

In the footsteps of Provençal writers ..108
Provençal culture 110
Painters and light in Provence 112
Cinema on the Côte d'Azur 114
Provençal literature 116
Provence on film 117
Nice Carnival 118

Sporting holidays 84

Where to go for sports 86
Pétanque, a national sport 90

Hikes, walks and rambles 92

Gorges and waterfalls 94
Countryside and nature 96

Beaches and islands 98

Days out at the beach 100
Pony trekking and cycling. 101

Leisure parks, aquariums and zoos 102

Grand hotels and casinos 104

Places of commercial and scientific interest 120

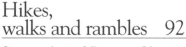

Street markets

People love them for their atmosphere, their colours, their smells and their bargains of course.

Fish markets

1 Marseille (daily).
p. 189.
2 Martigues (Thursday and Sunday).
p. 153.
3 Nice (daily).
p. 271.
4 Saint-Tropez (daily).
p. 216.

Food markets

5 Hyères (Saturday and 3rd Thursday of the month)
p. 209.

Flower markets

6 Aix-en -Provence (daily).
p. 176.
7 Avignon (Saturday).
p. 140.
8 Marseille (Monday).
p. 189.

Specialised markets

These are markets selected by the Conseil des Arts Culinaires for the quality of the wares and the local colour.

9 Apt (Saturday).
p. 160.
10 Cannes (daily, not Monday).
p. 241.
11 Carpentras (Friday).
p. 171.
12 Cavaillon (Monday).
p. 165.
13 Forcalquier (Monday).
p. 184.
14 L'Isle-sur-la-Sorgue (Sunday).
p. 166.
15 Nice (daily).
p. 270.
16 Toulon (daily).
p. 202.

Craft markets

17 Arles (Wednesday and Saturday).
p. 128.
18 Orange (Saturday morning).
p. 146.
19 Sainte-Maxime (daily in summer).
p. 218.
20 Sault (Wednesday).
p. 172.

Carpentras

Avignon

Massif
du Luberon

Manosque ●

Alpilles

Arles

Durance

A54

Camargue

Étang
de Berre

Aix-en-Provence

A55

Marseille

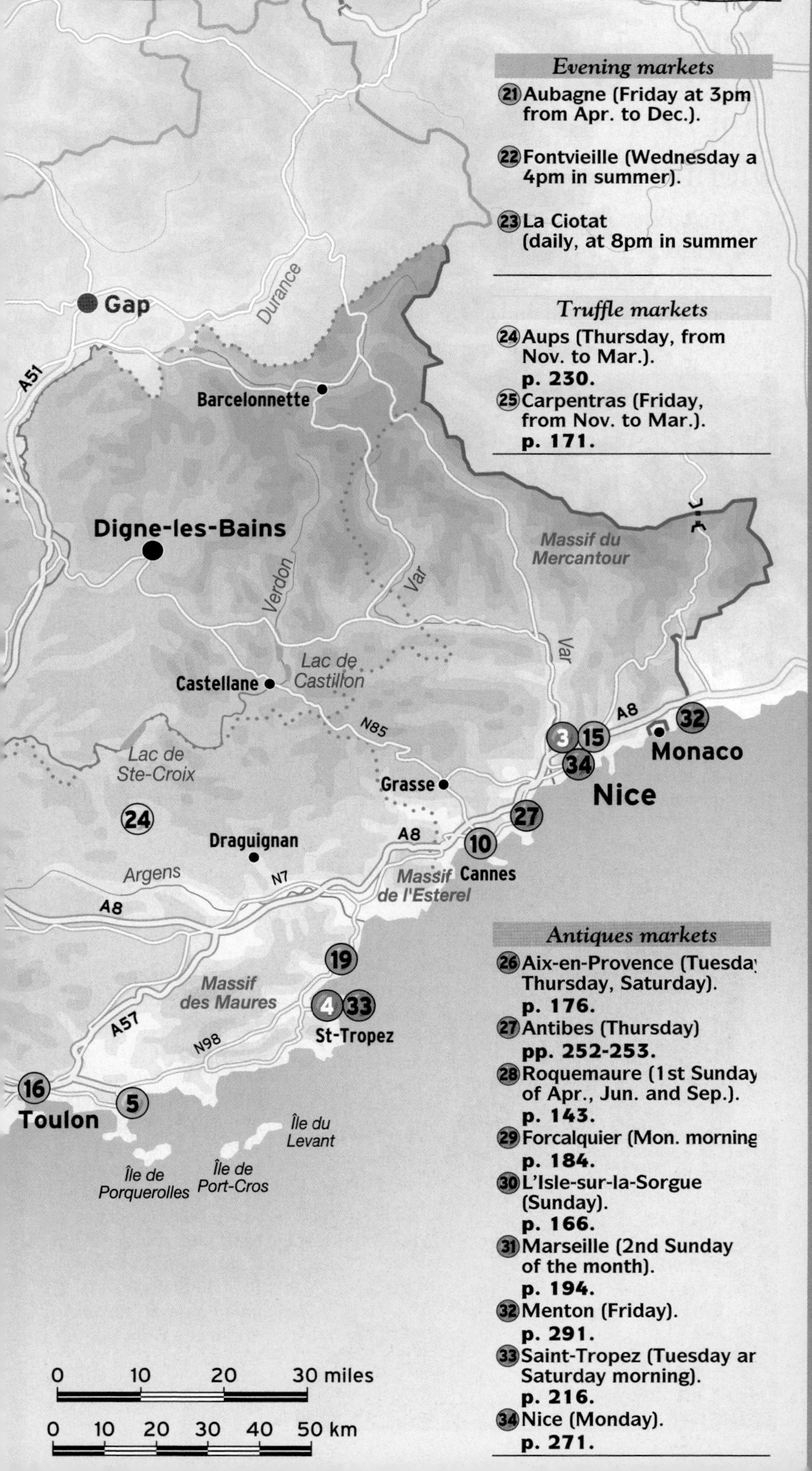

Gap

Durance

A51

Barcelonnette

Digne-les-Bains

Verdon

Var

Massif du
Mercantour

Castellane

Lac de
Castillon

Lac de
Ste-Croix

N85

Var

A8

32

Grasse

3 15

34

27

Monaco

Nice

24

Draguignan

A8

N7

10

Massif
de l'Esterel

Cannes

Argens

A8

19

Massif
des Maures

4 33

St-Tropez

A57

N98

16

5

Toulon

Île du
Levant

Île de
Porquerolles

Île de
Port-Cros

Evening markets
21 Aubagne (Friday at 3pm from Apr. to Dec.).

22 Fontvieille (Wednesday a 4pm in summer).

23 La Ciotat (daily, at 8pm in summer

Truffle markets
24 Aups (Thursday, from Nov. to Mar.).
p. 230.
25 Carpentras (Friday, from Nov. to Mar.).
p. 171.

Antiques markets
26 Aix-en-Provence (Tuesda Thursday, Saturday).
p. 176.
27 Antibes (Thursday)
pp. 252-253.
28 Roquemaure (1st Sunday of Apr., Jun. and Sep.).
p. 143.
29 Forcalquier (Mon. morning
p. 184.
30 L'Isle-sur-la-Sorgue (Sunday).
p. 166.
31 Marseille (2nd Sunday of the month).
p. 194.
32 Menton (Friday).
p. 291.
33 Saint-Tropez (Tuesday ar Saturday morning).
p. 216.
34 Nice (Monday).
p. 271.

0	10	20	30 miles

0	10	20	30	40	50 km

The lemon,
fruit of sunny Menton

S ince 1934, Menton has been famous for its lemons. The Préalpes protect it from cold winds and a blazing sun burnishes it with gold throughout the whole year, allowing the lemon trees to bear fruit and flowers in all seasons.

Lemons in Europe

This citrus fruit, discovered in the Himalayas, was introduced in the Mediterranean region by the Arabs. Used for centuries by women to whiten their teeth or clean their skin, lemons have been grown on the Côte d'Azur from the 15th C. and, by 1480, the lemon trees of

Ollioules were already supplying the court of King René. As its scientific name indicates, the juice of the *citrus medica* was used as a medicine against sore throats in Europe as early as the Renaissance, and later by sailors to prevent scurvy.

The champion of vitamin C

The tree cultivated in Menton is a variety called 'quatre saisons' (four seasons). Lemon trees blossom the whole year round, but their fruit, full of vitamin C and calcium, is only gathered in the winter, the spring and the summer. Don't mistake this tree for the citron tree,

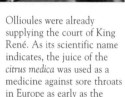

cultivated in the Alpes-Maritimes since 1880, which is larger. In the 1930s, Menton was the largest producer of lemons on the continent with 3,000t. a year; but is now greatly reduced due to competition from the Italians in Piedmont and the harvest does not exceed 400t. Yet Menton still dedicates a festival to the fruit every February (p. 290).

DON'T CONFUSE IT WITH THE *CITRE*
The *citre* is a kind of big watermelon that cannot be eaten raw but makes really good jam. It can weigh more than 22 lb (10 kg) and reaches full maturity in early autumn. Its white flesh is very hard and you can keep it for several months. It is cultivated by some market gardeners in the Bouches-du-Rhône region.

The melon, king of Cavaillon

All over the world, gourmets enjoy the Cavaillon melon because it is the sweetest of the melons with a wonderful flavour and reputation.

The three great varieties

Nowadays, we tend to eat mainly three great kinds of melons: the cantaloupe (or charentais), which is round, flavoured and has an orange flesh; the brodé (or galia), which has a skin like a web; the honeydew melon, which is yellow, oblong, very sweet and has a white and greenish flesh. Some melons are no bigger than a plum, whereas others can weigh up to 65 lb (30 kg). Containing 93% water and 8% sugar, the melon is not very energizing; but it is full of vitamins A and C, and also contains mineral salts.

MELON RECIPES

A versatile fruit, the melon has many uses. You can eat it raw, or cooked, or even drink its juice as a liqueur. There is even a restaurant which uses melon as the main ingredient in its cuisine (p. 41). And what about a melon sorbet? To make 1.75 pt (1 l) of sorbet, you need 32 oz (900 g) of melon flesh, ½ a teaspoonful of salt and some ground pepper, and 3 tablespoons of old port. Pulp the flesh in a food processor to obtain a purée. Mix in the port and pour the mixture into the ice-cream maker. After 20 minutes add the salt and pepper and leave it for another 5 mins. Decorate with mint leaves and slices of fresh fruit.

Melon seasons

From April to May melons are cultivated in heated greenhouses, whereas from May to mid-June they are grown in cool greenhouses. The best melons of all, however, are the ones grown in the fields from mid-June to September. They dominate the market at this time. They are grown on a narrow 2.5 miles wide (4 km) strip of land that borders the Durance river for 4 miles (7 km).

Choosing a melon

Do not choose a melon according to its smell because it could turn out to be too ripe. Weight should be the main criterion for choosing a melon: if it is heavy, the fruit must be full of juice, sun and sugar, and if you notice that its base is cracked, it is even better. Finally, if the *pécou*, or stalk, is easily detached you can be sure you have chosen a good melon.

Provence in a pinch of aromatic herbs

J ust venture into the countryside or stroll through one of the colourful markets, and you will discover the delicious scents and smells so reminiscent of sunny days in the south of France. Provençal herbs are dried, so their fragrance will only emerge when cooked. Once you are back home, they will remind you of your holidays and add flavour to your favourite recipes. However, you need to know how to use them correctly to bring out their full aroma.

Basil

Basil is sold throughout the summer in pots or bunches in the markets. This delicate plant adds vitality to tomato salad, pasta and vegetable dishes. It can be cooked or minced and used to flavour a sauce called *pistou* (a mixture of garlic and basil) which is the essential ingredient in one of the most famous local soups. Make sure a basil plant does not dry out or it will lose its fragrance. In fact, this delicate herb is better when picked at the last minute. Basil is slightly diuretic and is also renowned for its digestive properties.

Garlic *(l'ail)*

Garlic is much used in Provençal cuisine, but don't over indulge or you may scare your friends away. Garlic can be used in many different ways in cooking and adds a delicious flavour to spike a braised or roasted joint, or to flavour courgettes (zucchini). It is also delicious rubbed on a slice of bread and eaten with sliced tomato, olive oil and a sprinkling of parmesan. Garlic is also famous for its curative powers. It is known to reduce high blood pressure, promote sleep, stimulate the digestion and regulate the circulation. Strings and bunches of garlic should be stored in a well-ventilated place, where they will stay fresh the whole winter.

Thyme

An essential ingredient in a bouquet garni, thyme is used in many Provençal dishes, such as *bœuf en daube* (beef stew) and *sauté de lapin* (sauté of rabbit). The strong flavour goes really well with grilled meat, and in pâtés. One sprig is enough to bring out the flavour of fish baked in a foil envelope. Besides its anti-septic properties, thyme can help to relieve the pain of rheumatism.

BOUQUET GARNI

This is a specific mixture of herbs — savory, thyme, bay leaf and rosemary — tied in a bunch, chopped or ground but not reduced to a powder. Be careful of imitations and never store a bouquet garni in a plastic bag. It keeps best in a paper bag or airtight jar. Add part of a bouquet garni at the start of cooking, and the rest before serving the dish to bring out the flavour. If you use the herbs in a bunch, remember to remove them from the dish before serving.

Rosemary

The name derives from the Latin *rosa marina* or sea dew. Rosemary has a pungent odour and needs to be used with care and in moderation.

It goes very well with lamb and in Provence it is added to tomato sauce. Sprigs can be used as fragrant skewers for kebabs. In winter, rosemary oil should be inhaled to help cure a cold.

Bay leaf, savory and others...

Bay leaves are an essential ingredient for a *court-bouillon* (for cooking fish) and for marinades and *ratatouille*. A few leaves added to braised meat will bring out its flavour. Savory, another typically Provençal herb, grows wild in the scrubland. The spicy taste enhances the flavour of broad beans, French beans and fish, and even goat's milk cheeses. Try combining fresh figs, fresh goats' cheese, savory and a drop of olive oil. Other classic herbs that you will find in the street markets of Provence include oregano (or marjoram), another excellent herb for the stewpot; fennel, the aniseed flavour combining excellently with fish and green salads; fresh tarragon, used to flavour roast chicken, and sage, a powerful aroma which combines well with pork and poultry. If you are very familiar with these herbs, you do not even need to buy them, as you will find them growing wild in the countryside.

A taste of Provence

Crystallized fruits, black or white nougat, olive oil, liqueurs, goat's cheese –
just a few of the hundreds of delicious Provençal specialities.

Olives and olive oil

(1) Aups: Montée des Moulins
and its delicious preserves.
p. 231.

(2) Draguignan:
Moulin du Flayosquet,
oils and soaps.
p. 229.

(3) Entrevaux:
oil-press and flour mill.
p. 300.

(4) Gordes:
Moulin des Bouillons
and its ancient oil-press.
pp. 162-163.

(5) Maussane-les-Alpilles :
Cornille windmill.
p. 135.

(6) Nice: Caracoles oil-press
and Alziari olive-press.
p. 271 and p. 274.

Mont Ventoux
6,263 ft
(1,909 m)

(20)

(33)

(10) Carpentras

(16)

(9) Avignon

(4)

(26)

(8)

(31)

Manosque ●

Massif
du Luberon

(22)

(18)

(5) Alpilles

Durance

Rhône

A7

(28) Arles

(17)

A54

(7) Aix-en-Provence

A51

N7

Étang
de Berre

Camargue

A55

Marseille

(14)

A50

Sweets and candies

(7) Aix-en-Provence:
*biscotins, clou de
Cézanne, calissons*
and chocolate.
p. 177.

(8) Apt: excellent
crystallized fruits.
p. 160.

(9) Avignon: oregano
papalines.
p. 143.

(10) Carpentras:
humbugs (*berlingots*)
p. 171.

(11) Cotignac: crystallized quince
p. 233.

(12) Fayence: Provençal honey.
p. 251.

(13) La Garde-Freinet:
patiences.
p. 223.

(14) Marseille: warm and
melting *navettes*.
p. 191.

(15) Nice: Provençal
crystallised fruits.
p. 275.

(16) Pernes-les-Fontaines:
chocolate specialities,
Soleil pernois
and *Esprit Blanchard*.
p. 169.

(17) Saint-Chamas: almonds
and chocolate
pichoulines.
p. 151.

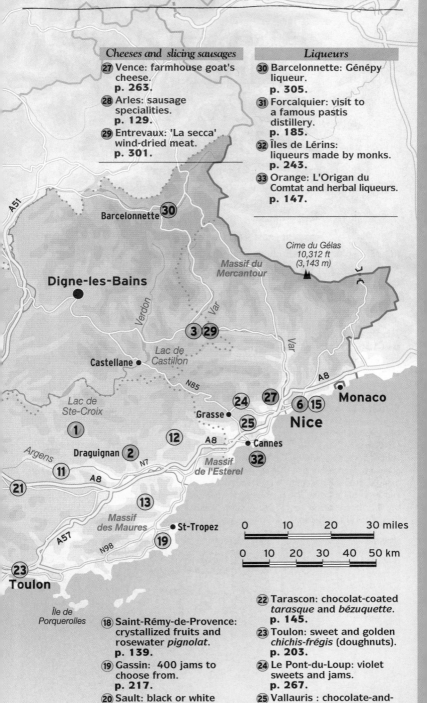

Cheeses and slicing sausages

27 Vence: farmhouse goat's cheese.
p. 263.

28 Arles: sausage specialities.
p. 129.

29 Entrevaux: 'La secca' wind-dried meat.
p. 301.

Liqueurs

30 Barcelonnette: Génépy liqueur.
p. 305.

31 Forcalquier: visit to a famous pastis distillery.
p. 185.

32 Îles de Lérins: liqueurs made by monks.
p. 243.

33 Orange: L'Origan du Comtat and herbal liqueurs.
p. 147.

Cime du Gélas
10,312 ft
(3,143 m)

Massif du
Mercantour

18 Saint-Rémy-de-Provence: crystallized fruits and rosewater *pignolat*.
p. 139.

19 Gassin: 400 jams to choose from.
p. 217.

20 Sault: black or white nougat.
pp. 172-173.

21 Signes: mountain honey nougat.
p. 205.

22 Tarascon: chocolat-coated *tarasque* and *bézuquette*.
p. 145.

23 Toulon: sweet and golden *chichis-frégis* (doughnuts).
p. 203.

24 Le Pont-du-Loup: violet sweets and jams.
p. 267.

25 Vallauris : chocolate-and-orange-flower *pignatines*.
p. 257.

26 Cavaillon : the sweetest melons.
p. 165.

Pastis – national drink of Provence

Pastis is the most popular apéritif in southern France. The term 'pastis' refers to the cloudy mixture obtained when water is added to a clear spirit. Pastis, known locally as *petit jaune*, is deceptively strong, so don't over indulge even if it brings back memories of your holidays and gives you an appetite.

Absinthe, the demon drink

This extremely strong light-green apéritif was prepared by infusing herbs in alcohol. Absinthe was invented in Switzerland by a French doctor named Ordinaire, who gave the recipe to Mr. Pernod in 1797. The aniseed flavour made it very popular in France, but it induced alcoholic poisoning and attacked the brain. It was actually banned in France in 1915, although absinthe can still be drunk legally in Spain.

Star of the bar

Anisé (or pastis) was invented to replace the lethal absinthe. It was flavoured with badian anise, a plant recently imported by merchant seamen from the East. It was an immediate success and by the 1930s a number of brands were available. Nowadays, there are several well-known brands of anisé, anisette, pastis and pernod on the market, all of whom jealously guard their secret recipe.

Some statistics

In France, about 220 million pints (125 million litres) of pastis are drunk annually. The Pernod-Ricard company, which markets the drink under the names Pernod,

DISCOVERING PASTIS

For further information on how to make pastis, you can visit the Henri Bardouin distillery in Forcalquier (p. 185) which produces one of the best brands of pastis in France. You can even sample the different varieties.

a *feuille-morte* (pastis-grenadine-mint), a *goudron* or *gas-oil* (pastis-liquorice water), or a *p'tit vélo* (pastis-orangeade-lemonade). A tiny 1 ml glass of pastis is called a *momie*, but a double contains 4 ml. The normal measure is 2 ml and is called *entier* (whole).

Ricard and Pastis 51, accounts for 50% of the market, whereas Duval, Casanis and Berger account for 10 to 12% each. The market is almost exclusively French and although the greatest consumption is in Provence, the drink is also favoured by northerners.

The recipe

The drink is based on a judicious mixture of herbs. Star anise is now the main ingredient in the anisé and anisette, green aniseed and fennel go into the making of pastis. Cardamom and other herbs and spices are also used. Alcohol, flavoured by maceration or distillation of the plants, is added. The drink is then blended and filtered. It takes more than just plant extracts to make a good pastis: everything depends upon the choice of plants, correct proportions, blending and the quality of the alcohol. Since 1991, pastis has had an *appellation contrôlée*. To be able to call itself 'pastis de Marseille', the liqueur must

be 45° proof and contain 31 grains (2 g) of anethol (the essential oil of anise).

One thousand and one pastis

Pastis can be used to make cocktails in many delicious, attractive and even surprising combinations. If you combine pastis with various cordials, you can make a *mauresque* (pastis and orgeat), a *tomate* (pastis and grenadine), a *perroquet* (pastis and mint),

The best way to enjoy pastis

The first rule is never to refrigerate pastis and to avoid any violent change of temperature: for instance, never add an ice cube to undiluted pastis. The water used to dilute should be cool, around 40°F (4°C), but not iced. Ice cubes are added once the mixture is in the glass. The way to enable the pastis to release all its fragrance is to add a lot of water to the mixture (4 to 6 times the amount of water to pastis).

The olive

P rovence sparkles beneath the silvery green
foliage of the olive tree and its abundant
fruit. Well known for its numerous
virtues, olive oil is the pure essence of golden
sunshine, a cocktail of vitamins that sharpens
the taste buds and enhances the flavours of
other foods. It is worth learning how to choose a fine olive oil so as to fully
appreciate its great finesse.

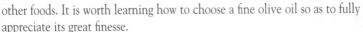

Olives in legend

The olive tree was renowned
in Antiquity. In Greek
mythology, in the duel
between Poseidon and
Athena, the sea-god caused
water to spring from a rock,
but the goddess of wisdom
created the olive tree, laden
with fruit, and thus won the
contest. Romulus and Remus
sheltered in its shade, kings
were anointed with its precious oil to give them authority, power and wisdom. In
the story of Noah's Ark a

dove brings an olive branch
to indicate the end of the
flood. Since then the tree
has symbolised peace and
fecundity.

A little botany

The olive tree belongs to
the same family as jasmine,
lilac, privet and forsythia.
Evergreen and extremely
hardy, it can grow in poor soil
and is recognisable by its
splendid silver-green foliage.
The tree does not fruit until it
is five or six years old, and

only produces a full crop
when it is 30 years old. The
tree flowers between April
and June, and the fruit is
harvested between September
and February.

The fruit of the olive tree

As they ripen, the fruit
becomes richer in oil and
changes colour from green to
black. The olive is very nutri-
tious, containing as much
calcium as milk. There are
several Provençal varieties,
including the *aglandau* and
the *verdale*, used exclusively
for making oil, the green
salonenque, the sweet, black
grossane, and the *bégurette*.
The *caillette* is an aromatic
brown olive that is grown
in the Nice area and is delicious to eat. The largest olive
groves used to be found in
the Alpilles (p. 134), and
Maussane once had many
olive presses, but following
the terrible winter of 1966
only two remain.

the press to be sorted, washed and crushed. The paste is then pressed on mats (called *scourtins*) or mixed mechanically. Finally, the extracted oil (*l'huile*) is purified of any remaining *grignons* (pulp and stone waste) and water (*l'eau*). Olive oil is of such importance in Provence that two festivals celebrate it in Mouriès (p. 134).

Choose your colour

Before the olive, whether green or black, is ready for eating, the bitterness must be removed. This is carried out via several processes (none using chemicals) in the *confiseries*. The green olive, prepared *à la picholine*, is eaten until Easter. The Picholini family invented the recipe in the 18th C. To remove the bitterness, olives are soaked in a paste of wood ash and water, then rinsed in fresh water and preserved in brine (they should be rinsed before eating). Black olives are used to make the olive paste known as *tapenade*, first created in Marseille; the name comes from the Provençal word *tapeno*, meaning 'caper', which is one of its ingredients.

A matter of taste

A good oil depends on its level of acidity: 1% for a superb extra-virgin oil extracted from a single cold pressing; between 1% and 2% for a very good quality virgin oil, and from 2% to 3.3% for good flavour but standard quality. Olive oil is expensive and delicate, it must be protected from heat, cold and light. The best oil for cooking is the *fruité vert* with a scent of fruit and artichokes. The *fruité noir*, whose flavour is woody, is best used as a salad dressing.

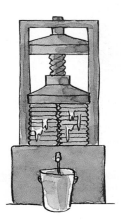

From olive to bottle

Once the fruit has ripened, it is time for the *olivade*, the olive harvest. 11 lb (5 kg) of olives, gathered by hand, are needed for 1¼ pints (1 litre) of oil. They are then brought to

HUILE
EAU

Sweets and candies

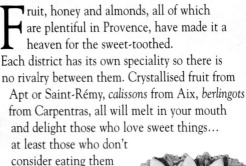

F ruit, honey and almonds, all of which are plentiful in Provence, have made it a heaven for the sweet-toothed. Each district has its own speciality so there is no rivalry between them. Crystallised fruit from Apt or Saint-Rémy, *calissons* from Aix, *berlingots* from Carpentras, all will melt in your mouth and delight those who love sweet things… at least those who don't consider eating them a sin!

Calissons d'Aix

LÉONARD PARLI
Aix-en-Provence

630 g

Crystallised fruit from the Apt region

Apt is without doubt the world capital of crystallised fruit. There are many places from which to buy it (p. 160). The technique is simple but requires great skill. The most perfect freshly-picked fruits are peeled and lightly stewed; they are then plunged into a thick sugar syrup and the mixture is cooked again; finally the fruits are drained and dried. Glacé fruits are as attractive to look at as they are good to eat and are not sticky. If you use them in cakes, it is preferable to buy them just after they have been drained.

Saint-Rémy-de-Provence also has excellent confectionery shops (p. 139).

Sweets and candies

Typical sweets made in Provence are: *berlingots* (humbugs) of Carpentras (p. 171) are dark with white stripes. Avignon has its own speciali-

ty, an oregano-flavoured pink cluster called a *papaline* (p. 143). As for Aix-en-Provence (p. 177), the reputation of its renowned *calisson* (a lozenge-shaped sweet made of ground almonds) is firmly established. Its smoothness is due to the crystallised oranges and melons that go into the paste which is then coated with marzipan and finished with a piece of rice paper. Made in Sault for more than a hundred years (p. 173), nougat contains lavender honey from the slopes of Mont Ventoux and locally-

Honey

Honey is nature's ready-made sweetener. In Provence, it is flavoured with many different scents from the region – lavender, rosemary, thyme and heather. Whether it is garrigue honey or mixed-flower honey, whether made from cultivated or wild flowers, it is always sweet and fragrant.

The star is lavender honey which was granted the appellation *miel du cru* (vintage honey)in 1990. Its consistency is normally runny and its colour pale. Every market has local producers, and each corner of Provence its speciality… it's up to you to find the one that most appeals.

grown almonds. The nougat is white, delicate and very smooth, but there is also a black variety, which the local people prefer (see also p. 205).

The 'thirteen desserts'

The *gros souper* (big supper) is a Provençal culinary tradition, a Christmas feast eaten after the Midnight Mass, which traditionally ends with thirteen desserts. Each

family contributes its personal touch, but certain standard dishes are always included, such as the *pompe à huile* (a thick, rich round-shaped bread),

"BAH, HUMBUG!"

You can make your own Carpentras humbugs at home. Take 18 oz (500 g) of sugar, 7 fl oz (200 ml) of water and one tablespoon of lemon juice. Pour all the ingredients into a heavy-based deep frying pan, bring to the boil and cook, stirring continuously. Pour the pale-yellow mixture on an oiled slab or dish. As soon as it is cool enough to handle, pull it out and cut it into short strips. Then leave to cool further until completely hard.

flavoured with olive oil and orange), white and black nougat, and the *quatre mendiants* ('four beggars') – almonds, dried figs, raisins and walnuts or hazelnuts. There are also winter fruits (dates, oranges and other citrus fruits), quince jam, *calissons* and crystallised fruit. However, it is essential that there be exactly thirteen different desserts on the festive table, to represent Jesus and the twelve disciples.

Restaurants

The restaurants of the great chefs of Provence are highly rated and will enable you to enjoy classic and modern dishes of French haute cuisine. The best restaurants all make use of the delicious, fresh local produce, each in their own way, to create extra-special dishes. Details are given on the following pages, unless there is a note to the contrary.

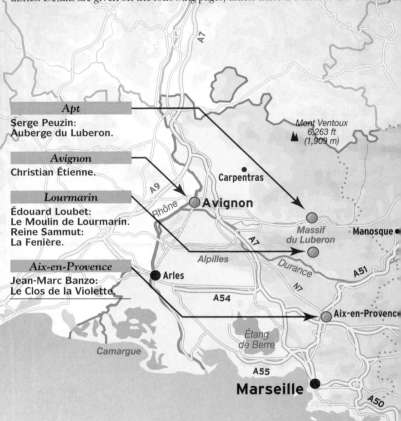

Apt
Serge Peuzin:
Auberge du Luberon.

Avignon
Christian Étienne.

Lourmarin
Édouard Loubet:
Le Moulin de Lourmarin.
Reine Sammut:
La Fenière.

Aix-en-Provence
Jean-Marc Banzo:
Le Clos de la Violette.

Mont Ventoux
6,263 ft
(1,909 m)

Carpentras

Avignon

Rhône

A9

A7

Alpilles

Massif
du Luberon

Manosque

Durance

A51

Arles

A54

N7

Étang
de Berre

Aix-en-Provence

Camargue

A55

Marseille

A50

0   10   20   30 miles

0   10   20   30   40   50 km

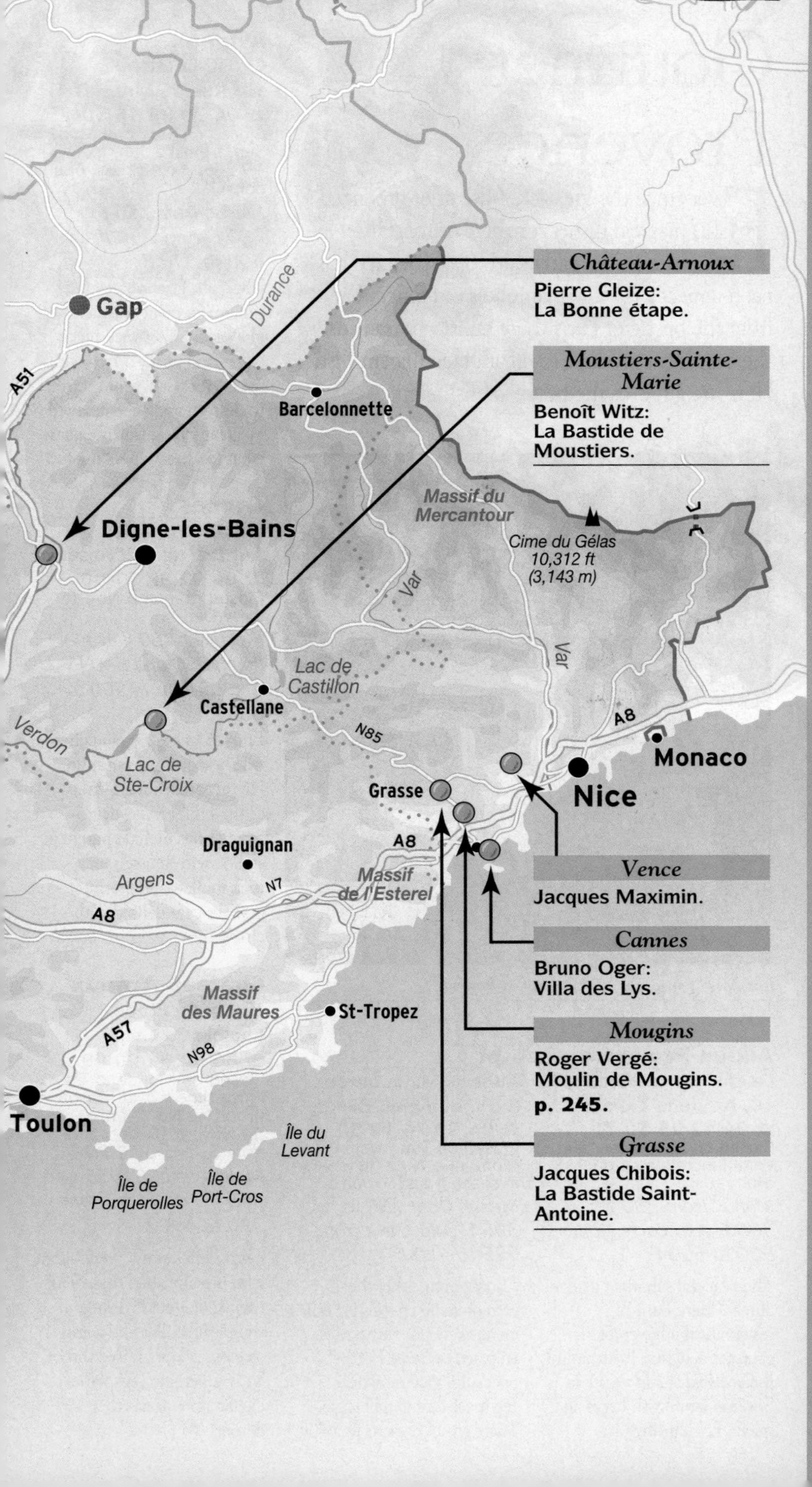

Gap

Château-Arnoux
Pierre Gleize:
La Bonne étape.

Moustiers-Sainte-Marie
Benoît Witz:
La Bastide de Moustiers.

A51

Durance

Barcelonnette

Digne-les-Bains

Massif du Mercantour

Var

▲
*Cime du Gélas
10,312 ft
(3,143 m)*

Lac de Castillon

Castellane

N85

Verdon

Lac de Ste-Croix

Grasse

A8

Nice

A8

Monaco

Draguignan

N7

Massif de l'Esterel

Vence
Jacques Maximin.

Argens

A8

Cannes
Bruno Oger:
Villa des Lys.

Massif des Maures

St-Tropez

A57

N98

Mougins
Roger Vergé:
Moulin de Mougins.
p. 245.

Toulon

Île du Levant

Grasse
Jacques Chibois:
La Bastide Saint-Antoine.

Île de Porquerolles

Île de Port-Cros

Gourmet Provence

Ever since the great chef Escoffier produced his magical dishes for the Carlton Hotel at Cannes in the early 20th C., Provence has been a mecca for the great chefs of France. Far from the bustle of Paris these culinary artists use the best local produce to create magnificent dishes. Here are a few of the best establishments.

Jean-Marc Banzo who works in Aix-en-Provence

Aix-en-Provence

**Le Clos de la Violette,
10, Av. de la Violette,
☎ 04 42 23 30 71.**
Closed on Sun., Mon. and Wed. lunchtime, and in Mar.
Menus from 250 to 500 F. À la carte from 500 to 600 F.

The peaceful suburban garden of Jean-Marc Banzo's restaurant is a haven of gourmet delights. Try sampling the *petits farcis à la niçoise* or Sisteron lamb with herbs and spices. Enchanting.

Apt

**Auberge du Luberon,
8, Pl. du Fg-du-Ballet,
☎ 04 90 74 12 50.**
Closed on Sun. evening, Mon. (only Mon. lunchtime in season) and in Jan.
Menus from 155 to 395 F. À la carte from 225 to 420 F.

Choose from either the extraordinary crystallised fruit menu or the savoury dishes prepared by Serge Peuzin. Specialities are monkfish, cep fricassee and rabbit pie. There are 13 desserts to follow.

Avignon

**Christian Étienne,
10, Rue de Mons,
☎ 04 90 86 16 50.**
Closed on Sun. and Mon., Sun. from 15 Jun. to 15 Sept. (except Jul. open daily).
Menus from 160 to 480 F. À la carte from 400 to 510 F.
Christian Étienne practises simple but great cuisine. His fried mullet with black olives and crispy artichokes speaks for itself. From starter to dessert, and accompanied by great wines, this is exactly what foodies are looking for.

Cannes

**Villa des Lys,
14, Bd. de La Croisette,
☎ 04 92 98 77 00.**
Closed from end Nov. to early Dec.
Menus at 260 (lunch time), 350 and 540 F. À la carte from 500 to 650 F.
Bruno Oger is a young chef with a growing reputation. He prepares subtle dishes at the Hôtel Majestic. Specialities include pumpkin stuffed with mussels and rock mullet, and gratin of oranges caramelised with citrus juice.

Château-Arnoux

**La Bonne Étape,
Chemin du Lac,
☎ 04 92 64 00 09.**
Closed on Mon. and Tue. lunch time out of season (from 1st Nov.), from 30 Nov. to 11 Dec. and from 3 Jan. to 12 Feb.
Menus at 220, 535 and 595 F. À la carte from 290 to 490 F.

The Gleize family's reputation is well established thanks to their home-made dishes, a wonderful cellar and warm welcome. The braised turbot with aubergine (eggplant) caviar alone is worth a detour.

The Gleize family, father and son, owners of La Bonne Étape, in Château-Arnoux

Closed from 4 Jan. to 4 Mar. (except to customers of the hotel). *Only one menu at 260 F.*

Benoît Witz, a talented student of Ducasse, concocts very difficult dishes with style, such as young pigeon stuffed with bacon and sage, served with French beans and pickled tomatoes, or warm waffles with strawberry and rhubarb compote. Together with the subtle decor these dishes make dining here an unforgettable experience.

Grasse

La Bastide Saint-Antoine, 48, Av. Henri-Dunant, ☎ 04 93 70 94 94.
Menus from 230 (lunch time) to 600 F. À la carte from 400 to 500 F.
The great chef, Jacques Chibois, practises Provençal cuisine with subtle hints of Italy in a mansion high above Grasse. Try the Provençal stewed wild boar with polenta, turbot minestrone and coconut purée with olives.

Lourmarin

La Fenière, Route du Cadenet, ☎ 04 90 68 11 79.
Closed on Mon. (lunch time only in season) and in Jan.
Menus from 190 to 490 F. À la carte from 380 to 480 F.
Reine Sammut – a queen of the kitchen – adds a feminine touch to Provençal cuisine. Her saffron flavoured risotto with small squid and her puff-pastry with fruit flavoured with orange-flower water are simply magnificent.

Le Moulin de Lourmarin, ☎ 04 90 68 06 69.
Closed on Tue. and Wed. except in season and mid-Jan. to mid-Feb.

Menus from 180 to 380 F. À la carte 500 F.
Édouard Loubet, pupil of Marc Veyrat, is a talented young chef. His two foies gras with green tomato purée and home-made walnut ice cream are memorable.

Moustiers-Sainte-Marie

La Bastide de Moustiers, La Crisolière, ☎ 04 92 70 47 47.

Vence

Jacques Maximin, 689, Chemin de La Gaude, ☎ 04 93 58 90 75.
Closed on Sun. eve. and Mon. from 9 Nov. to 10 Dec.
Menus from 240 (lunch time) to 500 F. À la carte from 280 to 480 F.

Jacques Maximin creates his dishes daily according to the choicest produce available at the market that morning. His pickled aubergines and duck with garlic and chanterelles are particularly good.

Reine Sammut of Lourmarin

Local dishes

Here is a selection of restaurants where you will be able to taste typically traditional or modern Provençal cuisine.

Unless there is a note to the contrary, all the addresses and comments are listed on pages 38-41.

Vaucluse

1. Avignon: Le Pistou.
2. Cavaillon: Prévôt.
3. Monteux:
   Le Saule pleureur.
4. Sault: Hostellerie
   du Val de Sault.
5. Viens: La Haute Burlière.

Mont Ventoux
6,263 ft
(1,909 m)

● Carpentras

Rhône

① Avignon

Nîmes ●

Massif
du Luberon

Manosque ⑪

Alpilles

Durance

⑥ Arles

A54

Étang
de Berre

Aix-en-Provence ●

Camargue

A55

Marseille ⑦

A50

Bouches-du-Rhône

6. Arles: Le Vaccarès.
7. Marseille: Le Lunch,
   Les Arcenaulx,
   Le Miramar.
   p. 190.

| 0 | 10 | 20 | 30 miles |

| 0 | 10 | 20 | 30 | 40 | 50 km |

Alpes-de-Haute-Provence

⑧ Digne-les-Bains:
L'Origan.
⑨ Lardiers: La Lavande.
⑩ Les Mées:
Le Vieux Colombier.
⑪ Manosque:
Le Mas Saint-Yves.
⑫ Sisteron: L'Iris de Suse.
⑬ Valensole:
Hostellerie de la Fuste.

Cime du Gélas
10,312 ft
(3,143 m)

Alpes-Maritimes

⑭ Biot:
Galerie des Arcades.
⑮ Cannes: La Cave.
⑯ Nice: Barale,
La Méranda, Rive droite.
⑰ Saint-Cézaire-sur-Siagne:
L'Auberge du puits
d'Amon.
⑱ Vescous: La Capeline.

Var

⑲ Ampus:
La Fontaine d'Ampus.
⑳ Bormes-les-Mimosas:
Le Jardin de Perlefleurs.
㉑ Carqueiranne:
Les Santonniers.
㉒ Châteaudouble:
Le Restaurant de la Tour.
㉓ Fox-Amphoux:
L'Auberge du vieux Fox.
㉔ La Londe-les-Maures:
Le Bistrot à l'ail.
㉕ La Môle:
La Ferme du Magnan.

Local dishes

From *tian* to *pissaladière*, not forgetting *bouillabaisse*, Provençal cuisine is rich in delicious flavours. There is an amazing range of local dishes, many of them flavoured with, or cooked in, olive oil. Here is a selection of restaurants in the region which specialise in the best Provençal cooking.

Iced tomato soup by Dominique Bucaille

Alpes-de-Haute-Provence

Digne-les-Bains
L'Origan,
6, Rue Pied-de-Ville,
☎ **04 92 31 62 13.**
Closed Sun. and 15 days in Dec.
Menus from 70 to 185 F.
À la carte from 180 to 240 F.
In a narrow alley deep in the Old Town, you can enjoy *pieds paquets* (pigs' trotters) and scrambled egg with black truffles, in this family restaurant with a cosy atmosphere.

Lardiers
La Lavande,
☎ **04 92 73 31 52.**
Closed in Feb. and in Nov.
Only one menu at 95 F.
This place in the Montagnes de Lure is a real find because prices are so reasonable. Discover Provence through *aïoli* (garlic mayonnaise), *daube* (meat stew), *brandade* (salt cod) and the excellent wine cellar.

Les Mées
Le Vieux Colombier,
☎ **04 92 34 32 32.**
Closed on Sun. eve., Wed. and early Jan.
Menus from 120 to 300 F. À la carte 215 F.
Specialities in this delightful restaurant include a delicious *filet de loup poêlé* (fried bass fillet) and *salade de lapereau au vinaigre de romarin* (rabbit salad with rosemary vinegar).

Manosque
Le Mas Saint-Yves
☎ **04 92 79 31 50.**
Closed Mon. lunch time.
Menus from 89 to 265 F. À la carte from 150 to 310 F.
Excellent meals eaten beneath the trees, prepared by a chef from Brittany who loves to cook local dishes such as tagliatelle *au pistou* (with basil and garlic) and sole fillets. His wines are a delight.

Sisteron
L'Iris de Suse,
☎ **04 92 62 21 69.**
Closed on Sun. eve. and Mon., and Mon. eve. and Tue. in Jul.- Aug.
Menus from 75 to 145 F.
À la carte from 140 to 175 F.
There is something deliciously old-fashioned about this restaurant. Specialities include aubergine flan and pancake with garlic.

Valensole
Hostellerie de la Fuste,
☎ **04 92 72 05 95.**
Closed on Sun. eve. and Mon. and 10 Jan.-10 Feb.
Menus from 250 to 420 F.
Lulled by the Durance river, Dominique Bucaille has turned his restaurant into a haven of peace.This famous chef cooks Sisteron lamb with finesse.

Tagliatelle au pistou by Dominique Le Stanc.

Bouillabaisse by Guy Gedda (see next page)

Alpes-Maritimes

Biot

**La Galerie des Arcades,
16, Pl. des Arcades,
☎ 04 93 65 01 04.**
Closed on Sun. eve. and Mon.
*Menu at 180 F.
À la carte 170 F.*
This little restaurant serves the true cuisine of the South. You must taste the aubergine *tian* and the breaded sardines. Cosy atmosphere.

Cannes

**La Cave,
9, Av. de la République,
☎ 04 93 99 79 87.**
Closed on Sun. and in Jul.
Menu at 140 F. À la carte from 150 to 200 F.
Meals are a veritable hymn to Provence: courgette (zucchini) flower fritters, tripe and a delicious *pissaladière*. Warm, friendly, atmosphere.

Nice

**Barale,
39, Rue Beaumont,
☎ 04 93 89 17 94.**
Closed at lunch time, Sun. and Mon.
À la carte from 150 to 200 F.
The owner of Barale has been delighting the locals of Nice for many years with stuffed vegetables, pies and superb *ratatouille*. Her restaurant has become an institution.

**La Méranda
4, Rue Terrasse,
(no phone number).**
Closed on Sat., Sun., at Christmas and in Feb., also from 20 Jul. to 17 Aug.
À la carte from 130 to 200 F.
Dominique Le Stanc, a talented student of Alain Senderens, is already a great chef who cooks the best pasta with *pistou* sauce in the region.

**La Rive Droite,
22, Av. Saint-Jean-Baptiste,
☎ 04 93 62 16 72.**
Closed on Sun.
Menu at 180 F. À la carte from 150 to 200 F.
The salade niçoise is perfect and the pizza is so good it is as if you were tasting it for the first time. In this restaurant, generosity is paramount and Provençal cuisine is celebrated the way it should be.

Saint-Cézaire-sur-Siagne

**L'Auberge du Puits d'Amon,
2, Rue Arnaud,
☎ 04 93 60 28 50.**
Closed on Sun. eve. and Wed., from late Jan.to early Feb.
*Menus from 90 to 210 F.
À la carte from 170 to 260 F.*
Panoramic view of Cannes. Specialities include the *tartou*, a pie of thyme-flavoured

mullet and leeks, followed by warm macaroons and ice cream. Impeccable cuisine.

Vescous

**La Capeline (near Gilette),
☎ 04 93 08 58 06.**
Closed on Mon. and Tue.
Menus at 108 and 128 F on weekdays; 128 F and 155 F at weekends.
Mme Demas treats you to a wonderful *pissaladière* and unforgettable stuffed rabbit. Provençal cuisine at its best.

Bouches-du-Rhône

Arles

**Le Vaccarès,
9, Rue Favorin,
☎ 04 90 96 06 17.**
Closed on Sun. eve. and Mon., and from Jan. to Feb.
Menus from 98 to 280 F.
The Dumas family offers excellent Provençal menus for all budgets, including such elegant dishes as Mediterranean-style monkfish baked on the bone with baby squid and red peppers. Sheer perfection!

Marseille

**Le Lunch,
La calanque de Sormiou,
☎ 04 91 25 05 37.**
Closed from mid-Oct. to end of Mar.
Menu at about 200 F.
A small hut by the sea. The owner himself cooks the fish fresh from the water and sprinkles them with sweet-smelling herbs. Heaven!

Provençal-style vegetables

**Les Arcenaulx,
25, Cours d'Estienne-
d'Orves,**
☎ 04 91 59 80 30.
Closed on Sun.
*Menu at 135 F. À la
carte from 180 F to
360 F.*

Bibliophiles and food lovers
consume delicious Marseille
specialities next door to a
bookshop (p.189).

Var

Ampus
**La Fontaine d'Ampus,
Pl. de la Mairie,**
☎ 04 94 70 97 74.
Closed on Mon. and Tue.,
in Feb. and 15 days in Oct.
*Menus from 152 to
280 F.*
A tiny place which is always
packed, probably because of
its perfect fried grey mullet,
stewed tomatoes with
oregano and the warm
welcome extended by the
proprietors. One dish
consists solely of truffles.

**Bormes-
les-Mimosas**
**Le Jardin de Perlefleurs,
100, Chemin Orangerie,**
☎ 04 94 64 99 23

Open noon to 2.30pm
and 8 to 11.30pm (last
service). Closed on Sun.
Thanks to his international
reputation, Guy Gedda
treats gourmets from all
over the world to delicious
meals, but he is only in
Provence for three months a
year. His *tian de bouillabaisse*
and *crème brûlée* with chest-
nuts are memorable.

Carqueiranne
**Les Santonniers,
18, Av. Jean-Jaurès,**
☎ 04 94 58 62 33.
Closed on Thu. and Sat
lunchtime, except in
summer.
Menu at 85 F.

Rascasse is beautifully served
and there are many other
generous and carefully
prepared dishes. The subtle
decor adds to the enjoyment.

Châteaudouble
Le Restaurant de la Tour,
☎ 04 94 70 93 08.
Closed on Wed.
*Menu at 90 F. À la carte
from 135 to 180 F.*

Thanks to a magnificent
view overlooking the gorges
combined with a great
choice of simple and
stimulating dishes, you will
want to linger here. A
wonderful find for gourmets.

Fox-Amphoux
L'Auberge du Vieux Fox,
☎ 04 94 80 71 69.
Open all year round.
*Menus from 135 to
250 F. À la carte from
155 to 315 F.*

The restaurant of this
charming hotel serves an
exceptional lamb with herbs,
garlic and spices, and many
other delicious surprises.

**La Londe-
les-Maures**
Bistrot à l'Ail,
☎ 04 94 66 97 93.
Closed on Mon. and in Oct.
*Menus from 135 to
150 F.*

Garlic is obviously the star
ingredient here. But it is used
so creatively that it seems to
taste different in each dish.
The fish is marvellous and
the hosts are charming.

La Môle
La Ferme du Magnan
☎ 04 94 49 57 54.
Closed Tue., and all
winter.
*Menus from 140 to 290 F.
À la carte from 170 to
350 F.*
Just before Cogolin, a tiny
farmhouse serving fresh mussels stuffed with herbs, followed by attractive desserts.

Aigoboulido soup

Michel Philibert is passionate about truffles and cooks them in different ways, much to the delight of truffle-lovers. However truffles do add extra expense, but don't worry, the *pissaladière* (without truffles) is delicious too.

Sault
Hostellerie du Val de Sault, Route de St.-Trinit, ancien Chemin d'Aurel, ☎ 04 90 64 01 41.
Closed from Nov. to Apr.
Menus from 125 to 220 F. À la carte from 250 to 380 F.

Yves Gattechaut's dishes have powerful but harmonious flavours, his masterpiece being lamb cooked with lavender and blackcurrant. You'll want to return again and again.

Vaucluse

Avignon
Le Pistou, 84, Rue Bonneterie, ☎ 04 90 14 60 62.
Closed on Sun. and Mon.
Menus at 85 F (lunch time) and 135 F (evenings). À la carte about 200 F.

Large portions of real home cooking served by charming staff. Stuffed vegetables, fish soup and rabbit with olives. You will ask for second helpings!

Cavaillon
Restaurant Prévot, 353, Av. de Verdun, ☎ 04 90 71 32 43.
Closed on Sun. eve. and Mon.
Menus from 160 to 320 F.
A very unusual restaurant dedicated entirely to the melon. From May to September, there is a wide variety of melon dishes on the menu, with recipes containing raw,

Wedge-shells Camargue style

cooked, dried, crystallised – and even salted or fried melon. A veritable melon fest.

Monteux
Le Saule Pleureur, Quartier Beauregard, ☎ 04 90 62 01 35.
Closed Sun. eve. and Mon., 15 days in Nov. and 15 days in Mar.
Menus from 165 to 320 F. À la carte 240 to 310 F.

Viens
La Haute Burlière, ☎ 04 90 75 25 13.
Open all year round.
Menus from 100 to 150 F.

The village of Viens is quaint and typically Provençal, as is the restaurant itself, where the menu is written in the local Provençal dialect. Cicadas will serenade you as you taste the delicious *pieds et paquets* (pigs' trotters), *broufado* (pickled beef stew with gherkins) and crystallised fruit.

Provençal home cooking

P rovençal home cooking is plain, hearty and tastes of the sun. It has produced great classics which are world-famous, including *bouillabaisse*, which is very hard to make well outside Provence, *daube provençale*, *pissaladière*, *tapenade*, *anchoïade* and *aïoli*. However, there are still many dishes awaiting discovery, or rediscovery, which are all distinctly Provençal.

The art of soup

The *aïgo boulido*, a great classic Provençal soup, combines the tastes of garlic and herbs and is really ideal as a pick-me-up after a heavy night out. Add 10 crushed garlic cloves to 1¼ pints (1 litre) of light stock with thyme, bay leaf and cooking salt. Bring the mixture to the boil, throw in some sage leaves (a whole sprig),

then turn off the heat and poach one egg per person in the soup. To serve, put a slice of local toasted bread in each soup plate, add the poached egg, a drizzle of olive oil, a little freshly ground pepper and some grated cheese. Then pour the soup over this preparation. Delicious.

In all simplicity

For summer walks, picnics, or after a swim, indulge in a genuine *pan bagnat*, local bread rubbed with garlic and generously filled with tuna, tomatoes and peppers. Or try a *crespeou*, an omelette which is topped, but not filled, with vegetables, herbs, or small fish. Served cold, in layers, it tastes as good as it looks.

Olives and capers, in every sauce

Compared to the famous *aïoli* (garlic mayonnaise), *raïto* is a sauce that tends to be forgotten. However, it is delicious and easy to make. Finely chop and shallow-fry a large red onion. When it turns golden, add a tablespoon of flour, then pour on 9 fl oz (30 cl) of hot stock. When the liquid comes to the boil, add 16 fl oz (50 cl) of red wine (such as Côtes-de-Provence). As soon as the liquid returns to the boil, add two crushed garlic cloves, 1 tablespoon of tomato purée and a bouquet garni. When the mixture has reduced by two-thirds, blend it in a food processor or vegetable mill.

Add capers and bitter olives before reheating. Serve with poached fish or steamed potatoes.

Fish and vegetables reign supreme

Fish and vegetables are the main ingredients of a great number of recipes. Vegetables may be raw or steamed, served with an *aïoli* or an *anchoïade*, stuffed with minced meat or deep-fried and served with a tomato sauce. The Mediterranean is full of fish which may be served in many ways (grilled, poached, or cooked in foil envelopes). The most popular fish is definitely bass (*loup*), though another firm favourite with the locals is mullet (*rouget*), which the gastronome Brillat-Savarin used to refer to as 'sea woodcock' because, like the game bird, connaisseurs eat it 'unplucked' and ungutted. As a special delicacy, the *rouget* innards are cooked and spread on large slices of toast. Watch out for bones!

An alternative to olive oil

In the Préalpes, the foothills of the Alps, people tend to use lard, or pork fat in their cooking, in preference to olive oil. The rest of the cuisine is different here, too. Soups are thick, and enriched with bacon. Many dishes contain dried beans and other pulses, or game (rabbit, hare and wild boar).

The local food is inspired by ingredients provided by the mountains and forests. Classic dishes from this region include the delicious *ravioles*, a type of ravioli, based on potatoes or chopped green vegetables and cheese. Many imaginative dishes use the local mountain lamb.

A TRUE SALADE NIÇOISE

The version served in bistrots nowadays has become pretty bland. The vegetables are wilted, the French beans frozen, the tuna is tinned and the vinaigrette is cloudy. The real recipe is full of energising freshness. It consists of a few lettuce leaves, lots of tomatoes cut into quarters, finely chopped pearl onions, sliced green pepper, hard-boiled eggs, and a few radishes and olives from Nice. The dressing is a simple combination of a trickle of olive oil and chopped tinned anchovies. Cold cooked rice can be added if you wish.

Vineyards

The rosé wines of Provence are not the only ones to benefit from the warm sun of the Midi. You should also try the reds and the whites and use your trip to visit some of the larger vineyards.

Vaucluse

1 **Châteauneuf-du-Pape (Côtes-du-Rhône villages). p. 146.**

2 **Gigondas/Vacqueyras (Côtes-du-Rhône villages). p. 149.**

Bouches-du-Rhône

3 **Mas de Rey (Coteaux-des-Baux). p. 129.**

4 **Château Simone (Palette). p. 179.**

5 **Clos Sainte-Magdeleine (Cassis). p. 197.**

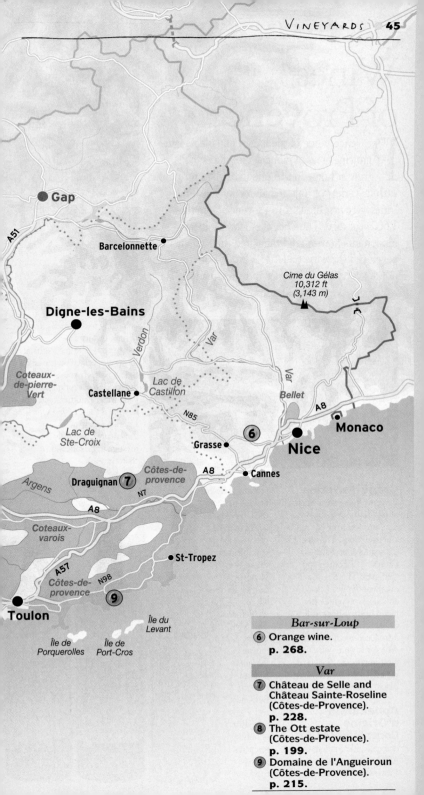

Gap

Barcelonnette

Cime du Gélas
10,312 ft
(3,143 m)

Digne-les-Bains

Verdon

Var

Coteaux-
de-pierre-
Vert

Lac de
Castillon

Var

Bellet

Castellane

N85

A8

Monaco

Lac de
Ste-Croix

⑥

Grasse

Nice

Argens

Draguignan ⑦

Côtes-de-
provence

A8

Cannes

N7

Coteaux-
varois

A57

A8

St-Tropez

Côtes-de-
provence

N98

⑨

Toulon

Île du
Levant

Île de
Porquerolles

Île de
Port-Cros

Bar-sur-Loup

⑥ Orange wine.
p. 268.

Var

⑦ Château de Selle and
Château Sainte-Roseline
(Côtes-de-Provence).
p. 228.
⑧ The Ott estate
(Côtes-de-Provence).
p. 199.
⑨ Domaine de l'Angueiroun
(Côtes-de-Provence).
p. 215.

Wines of Provence

Provence is one of the largest and oldest wine-growing areas of France. The grapevine is truly at home in this undulating landscape, with its variety of soils and abundant sunshine. Vines were first brought to Provence more than 2,600 years ago. The Greeks taught the local inhabitants how to tend them and the Romans developed the wine trade. The Provençal vineyards nowadays offer a wide range of wines, many of which deserve to be better known.

belonging to the small growers of high-quality wines. The more precise the geographical location specified on the label, the more likely you are to be drinking an exceptionally good wine. Another grade of wine is the VDQS (Vins Délimités de Qualité Supérieure), a slightly less prestigious classification than the AOC.

Grape varieties

Provence has a great number of traditional grape varieties that are used to create red and rosé wines. They include Cinsault, Mourvèdre, Grenache, Tibouren and Carignan. There is also some excellent Syrah stock, although it is more often found in the Rhône valley. Cabernet-Sauvignon was introduced more recently. As regards white wines, the most important Provençal varieties are Clairette, Ugni Blanc, Rolle and Sémillon.

Appellation d'Origine Contrôlée (AOC)

French legislation uses the AOC to indicate the origin of a wine, as well as the grape-growing and wine making methods used to produce it. All of these processes are controlled by the Institut National des Appellations d'Origine. The AOC covers territories that may be large (e.g. the Burgundy region), or consist of only a few acres, such as those

Alpes-Maritimes
Bellet

This appellation dates from 1941 and plantings cover 122 acres (45 ha), although the appellation area covers 1660 acres (650 ha). The red wine comes from the Nice area and has a strong cherry bouquet. The rosé wines are flowery and the white wines have a delicate lime-blossom fragrance. The Château de Bellet and the Mas Crémat are the finest Bellet wines.

Bouches-du-Rhône
Les Coteaux d'Aix-en-Provence

This appellation used to be known as Les Coteaux du Roy René, in honour of the king who brought the wines of Provence to the royal table in the 15th C. These wines, which come from the slopes around Aix-en-Provence, received the VDQS appellation in 1959, and the AOC in 1977. The 8,648 acre (3,500 ha) vineyard covers an area which includes some 49 towns and villages. The robust and fruity red wines should be drunk when they are 2 to 4 years old. The rosé wines are supple and fruity, and the white wines (6% of the production) are well flavoured. Châteaux Vignelaure and La Coste are among the best vineyards.

WINE AND SPIRITS MUSEUM
Open Apr. to Sep., 10am-noon and 2-6pm. Closed Wed.

Bendor, an island off Bandol, was bought by Paul Ricard in 1950. The museum on the island contains 10,000 bottles from fifty-one countries.

Les Coteaux-des-Baux

The soil of Les Baux produces a wine which has benefited from an AOC since 1995. The soil and microclimate in this area are particularly good for grapes. The stocks used are Cabernet-Sauvignon and Syrah. The wines produced in Les Baux are the result of a happy combination of mistral wind and sun. White and rosé wines should be drunk young, the reds are ready after 5 or 6 years. Château Havette and the Mas de la Dame Blanche are the best. (Visit the Mas de Rey, p. 129.)

LA VIE EN ROSÉ

There are two ways of obtaining a rosé wine: they are known as saignée and pressurage. The saignée process, which is the more difficult, results in a fruitier wine. It is made from white-fleshed, red-skinned grapes from which a pink juice is extracted. The grape juice is left in contact with the skins for a single night only, before being separated for fermentation. The rest of the vat is used to make red wine. Pressurage rosé is made with the same grapes, but they are pressed to a maximum.

Palette

This small AOC dating from 1948 is near Aix-en-Provence and Tholonet and Meyreuil. It is planted over 42 acres (17 ha) and produces one of the greatest white wines in the region. Most of the vines are grown by the Château-Simone (visit on p. 179) and the Domaine de la Crémade. The red wines are pleasantly hearty. Palette also produces a traditional Provençal liqueur wine. You can taste and buy these wines at the old farmhouse where Cézanne used to paint (Caves de la Palette, ☎ 04 42 66 90 23).

Cassis

This is the oldest appellation in Provence, dating from 1936, and its dry, fruity white wines compete with Palette as the best for serving with fish. The vineyard covers 395 acres (160 ha) and is divided among 12 wine growers. Do not store these wines at too low a temperature as this could spoil their flavour. The finest are Clos Sainte-Magdeleine (visit on p. 197) and Ferme blanche.

Var

Côtes-de-Provence

The AOC dates from 1977 and covers a huge area of 43,242 acres (17,500 ha). The rosés are quite neutral and a very suitable accompaniment to Provençal cuisine. The appellation is mainly known for its powerful reds. There are many producers of quality wines, including La Courtade, Les Châteaux de Selle (visit on p. 228), Sainte-Marguerite, and the Clos Mireille. The few, but delicious, white wines in this area are to be found not far from Le Lavandou, in the Domaine de l'Angueiroun (visit on p. 215). The Coteaux-de-Pierrevert which covers the area around Manosque deserves a mention. Its whites and rosés taste much like Côtes-du-Rhône.

Bandol

One of the oldest AOCs (1941). Vines are grown on little hillside terraces called *restanques*. Bandol covers 2,471 acres (1,000 ha) on soil that is full of shells. The wines are powerful and faintly spicy. The great wines age extremely well and compete with the best of vintage wines in France: they can be kept for twenty years. There are many great Bandol wines, but if you want to obtain the best, visit the Maison des Vins in Bandol (p.201). (See also the Domaine Ott, p. 198.)

Coteaux-Varois

These extend around Brignoles, in the centre of the region, right to the foothills of Sainte-Baume. This appellation, granted in 1993, has slightly more rosé (60 %) than red wines. The 42,000 acres (17,000 ha) of vines produce a light, fresh wine whose popularity is increasing. It goes well with Provençal cooking. Recommendations include the Domaine des Trians and the Château Thuerry.

Vaucluse

The Côtes-du-Luberon

This vineyard received its AOC in 1988. It covers 7,907 acres (3,200 ha) divided into 36 communes. It produces mainly sophisticated reds which go particularly well with meat, since they have a special fragrance of berries, a hint of peppers and a whiff of truffles and undergrowth. The 1995 Prestige vintage of the Château de l'Isolette is particularly good (Route de Bonnieux, Apt,

☎ 04 90 74 16 70 except Sun. and public holidays). The Châteaux de La Canorgue and de Val Joanis, the Domaines Mayol and Fontenille all maintain the standard very well.

The Côtes-du-Ventoux

This appellation is istuated next to well-known Côtes-du-Luberon. Some villages, such as Apt, Bonnieux, Gargas, Gordes, Goult, Murs and Roussillon, grow under both appellations, though the wines are very different because of the different soil types and grape varieties. The Côtes-du-Ventoux appellation extends from the south to the west of the Ventoux. The grapes are grown at altitudes of between 333 and 1,400 ft (100 and 400 m) and produce a wide variety of light, fruity wines (89% red wines), which should be drunk young. The Domaines Aymard (Carpentras) and Fondrèche (Mazan) are recommended.

The Vallée du Rhône

The wines of the Haut-Vaucluse are covered by the general appellation of Côtes-du-Rhône, which includes 163 communes. The Vallée du Rhône, the gateway to Provence, is represented by three internationally famous wines – Châteauneuf-du-Pape, Gigondas and Vacquerays (visit on p. 149). Of the 77 communes of the Côtes-du-Rhône Villages, 16 produce AOC wines which are among the best in the region.

Many great wines of this appellation are produced in the Vaucluse, among which are the famous muscat of Beaumes-de-Venise, Cairanne the great red wine of Rasteau, and the wines of Roaix, Sablet, Séguret, Valréas and Visan.

(visit on p. 149).

WINE TASTING

Here are a few hints and tips for those who want to taste and appreciate wine as the French do. Do not forget to taste a wine before you eat. Never do so after smoking. You must hold the glass by its stem in order not to modify the wine's temperature. A perfectly balanced red wine is obtained by finely judging the amount of acidity, mellowness and tannin it contains. Finally, the older the vine, the better the wine is likely to be. One of the great vintages of the southern wines is 1990, while 1995 and 1996 also look extremely promising.

Home furnishings

Wrought iron balustrades, fine china plates, glazed terracotta jars, carefully crafted souvenirs, traditional fabrics … Provençal decor is always in vogue so you are in the right place!

① **Apt**
Traditional earthenware.
p. 160.

② **Jonquières**
Old-fashioned Provençal furniture.
p. 53.

③ **Avignon**
Boutis fabrics.
p. 143.

④ **Tarascon**
Souleïado fabrics.
p. 145.

⑤ **Saint-Étienne-du-Grès**
The Olivades fabrics.
p. 52.

⑥ **Fontvieille**
Wrought iron housewares.
p. 135.

⑦ **Aix-en-Provence**
Painted furniture and traditional *santons*.
p. 178.

Marseille
⑧ Pipes and earthenware.
p. 56.
⑨ Traditional *santons*.
p. 193.
⑩ Picture frames.
p. 195.

⑪ **Aubagne**
Garden pottery and Provençal *santons*.
p. 197.

⑫ **Théoule-sur-Mer**
Stained-glass windows.
p. 227.

A7

② Mont Ventoux
6,263 ft
(1,909 m)

Carpentras

③ Avignon

Rhône

A9

④
⑤
⑥

Arles

A7

① Massif du Luberon

Manosque ●

Durance

N7

A51

Alpilles

A54

⑦ Aix-en-Provence

Camargue

Étang de Berre

A55

Marseille ⑧ ⑨ ⑪
⑩

A50

Fabrics

Furniture

Terracotta & santons

Glasswork

Other crafts (stonework, picture frames, wrought iron, wax)

Gap

(21) Barcelonnette

Digne-les-Bains

Massif du
Mercantour

Cime du Gélas
10,312 ft
(3,143 m)

Verdon

Var

Var

Lac de
Castillon

Castellane

N85

A8

(14)

Lac de
Ste-Croix

Grasse

(16)

Monaco

(13) (15)

Nice

Cannes

Argens

(20) Draguignan

A8

N7

(12)

Massif
de l'Esterel

(19)

A57

Massif
des Maures

(17) (18) St-Tropez

N98

Toulon

Île du
Levant

Île de
Porquerolles

Île de
Port-Cros

A51

| (13) | **Mougins** |
Craft candles and
pottery.
pp. 246–247.

| (14) | **Moustiers** |
Fine ceramics from the
Ségriès workshop.
p. 235.

| (15) | **Vallauris** |
Pottery.
pp. 256–257.

| (16) | **Biot** |
Traditional glassware.
p. 265.

(17) **Grimaud/Cogolin**
Carpets and pipes.
pp. 220–221.

(18) **Saint-Tropez**
Boutis prints and fabrics.
p. 52.

(19) **Sainte-Maxime**
Terracotta *santons* and
olive wood carvings.
p. 219.

(20) **Salernes**
Traditional terracotta
floor tiles.
p. 231.

(21) **Barcelonnette**
Sundials.
pp. 304–305.

0   10   20   30 miles

0   10   20   30   40   50 km

Fabrics and material

Whether you just want fabric for a skirt or wish to decorate your whole house with the colours of the Midi, you are bound to be tempted by the beautiful flowered cottons or printed calicos of Provence that are reminiscent of cloth from the Orient.

The printed calico tradition

In the 17th C., the Court of the Sun King, Louis XIV, went into raptures over the printed fabrics imported from India and Provençal manufacturers soon began printing cottons, originally in Marseille. However the silk merchants of Lyon, anxious in the face of new competition, managed to have the printed calico trade in France banned in 1686. The cotton factories therefore moved to Avignon, a papal state which was not subject to French royal authority.

ROLLER PRINTING
The fabric passes between the press and the engraved roller which is fed with ink by an inking roller.

If the fabric is printed in several colours, there will be as many rollers as there are colours to be printed.

Manufacture

The technique called *au cadre plat* was the first to be used. It employed one printing frame per colour. Nowadays, the fabric is fed between the press

and the patterned ink roller. It is then dried and passed through a vat of steam (to fix the colours) before being washed. The Municipal Museum in Orange traces the history of printed cotton manufacture (p. 146).

Multi-coloured designs

The brightly coloured printed cotton designs are really irresistible. Traditionally used for the shawls which all Provençal women wore, they are now used a great deal in interior decoration and may also be bought with a protective *plastifié* finish.
The best fabrics in the purest Provençal tradition are to be found at Souleïado's (p. 145). The fabrics from the Olivades (Chemin des Indienneurs, St.-Étienne-du-Grès ☎ 04 90 49 19 19), are exclusively printed on the spot.

BOUTIS

The *boutis* technique requires patience and skill as motifs are quilted onto the fabric using appliqué techniques. These elegant materials can be found at La Maison des Lices, in Saint-Tropez (18, Bd. Louis-Blanc ☎ 04 94 97 11 34, from Tue. to Sat.) and in Avignon.

Wood crafts

From walnut to olive wood, which is used for hand-crafted kitchen utensils, there are enough types of woodwork here to appeal to everyone's tastes. Reeds for musical instruments are cut from the marshes near Cogolin and the bark of the cork oak is harvested from local forests to provide corks for bottles of all shapes and sizes.

History of wood

The classic Arles bread bin was in everyday use as early as the 13th C. Provençal-style furniture was made popular by the court of King René. In the 16th C., joiners decided to use the dark hardwood of the walnut tree which gradually replaced white wood. Provençal furniture moved upmarket, becoming as decorative as it was practical. Whether carved or painted (in Aix, p. 178), the symbolic decorations of wedding wardrobes or the floral patterns on sideboards make them delightful pieces of everyday furniture.

Country seats

Chair designs, originally from Italy, took on a trapezoid shape in Provence. Made of walnut, beech, limewood, oak or mulberry, they had fluted feet and openwork or crosspiece-decorated backs. The Laffanour workshops still make chairs in the traditional way, as they have done since 1840 (91, Bd de la Libération, 84150 Jonquières, ☎ 04 90 70 60 82, open daily except Sat. morning and Sun.). They also sell rush-seated settees, painted armchairs and polished wooden chairs.

Musical reeds

Cogolin is certainly famous for its briar pipe factories (p. 220), but the village has also made a name for itself among musicians worldwide, thanks to its reed workshop for wind instruments. The small wooden mouthpieces produced here from locally grown reeds are in great demand among world-famous international orchestras.

CORK AND BOTTLE

Only cork oak can be used to make corks for bottles, and the tree must be at least 25 years old before it can be harvested. The cork, which is actually the tree bark, is cut and left to stand for four weeks, after which it is dried and boiled in order to make it more supple. The cork is then cut up into manageable blocks before the individual corks are punched out by machine. For more information about cork, visit the Écomusée du Liège in Gonfaron (p. 223).

Glass and glass-blowing

B iot, which has long been famous for its earthenware containers for olive oil, first became known for glass-making in the 1950s. Tumblers, oil jugs and vinegar bottles, as well as *porrons* (Provençal carafes) are now made from blown glass and the result is spectacular.

Blown or bubble glass?

In the 1950s, a ceramics expert from the Sèvres school, assisted by a former glass-maker and a glass-blower, rediscovered the technique of making bubble-glass. He turned what was once a flaw in the glass into a genuine art. In 1956, he created the Verrerie de Biot (Biot glassworks, p. 265) which attracts thousands of visitors every year and which has the only registered trademark of its name.

Glass dust

Nature provides the raw materials (sand and limestone) to which are added sodium silicates, potassium, calcium and lead. The mixture fuses into glass at temperatures of 2,550-2,730°F (1,400-1,500°C). When sodium carbonate is sprinkled over glass during the fusion process it makes pretty bubbles. Metallic oxides may then be added to obtain various colours (cobalt for blue, chromium and copper for green, charcoal dust for yellow).

These wooden sticks are used to shape the incandescent ball before the master glass-maker gets to work refining the shape.

Skilful work

Glass-making is the result of teamwork. The apprentice 'picks' some red-hot glass out of the kiln, then rolls it on a cast-iron table (the marble). A little red blob is formed which an assistant coats with another layer of glass, before rolling it into a large wet crucible (using a wooden stick) and shaping it with a pair of pliers. Every now and then, the assistant blows into the vase to expand it, but the finishing touch is added by the master glass-maker. Quick as a flash, he blows skilfully into the piece to give it the distinctive shape which is his hallmark.

Wrought iron

I ron transformed into works of art… For many years, Provençal ironsmiths have created both useful and decorative objects. In contemporary workshops, copies of antique items are placed side by side with new designs and creations.

Iron objects

Nowadays, craftsmen working in metal are few and far between. It is hard, physical work, but considerable skill is needed to shape and work the metal while it is red-hot. Craftsmen in iron produce many different kinds of objects from keys, candlesticks, chandeliers, tablebases, and the frames for four-poster beds to doorknockers, chairs, garden tables, gates, and so on for the outdoors.

Provençal ironwork

Much wrought iron is to be seen in the decoration of farmhouses and mansions. You can see balcony railings displaying intricate iron lace-work and finely worked weather vanes perched on rooftops, at the mercy of the *mistral* winds. To find out

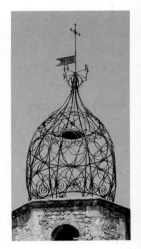

more about Provençal ironwork, visit the Noël-Biret collection at the Musée Calvet in Avignon (p. 142). If you want to buy ironwork, you can find many examples in Fontvieille (p. 135).

Iron in Antiquity

Iron is said to have been invented by the Chinese Emperor Fou-Hi (3,000 BC). It has been known in Europe since Antiquity, but reached its zenith as a building material in the Middle Ages. Every example of the smith's craft of that period is a work of art. Iron was in daily use everywhere, in jewellery, weaponry and religious artefacts, until the 19th C. It was embossed, engraved and sometimes had added reliefs. The industrial revolution then arrived and with it the invention of cast iron which became the most widely used material.

Ceramics and pottery

Tiles, floor-tiles, jars or decorated earthenware… everything created by Provençal potters is inspired by traditional designs. This art, which began in the 17th C., still has a bright future much to the delight of pottery lovers.

Shaping the clay

Clay needs to go through several stages – crushing, filtering, clarifying and fermentation – to produce a piece of earthenware. Terracotta tiles also need to be mixed, dried and cut to size before firing. Besides floor-tiles, Provence uses terracotta for its famous garden containers, jars for oil, garlic and herbs, and for the kitchen pots and casseroles which have given their name to traditional dishes (such as *tian*).

Tile-making in Salernes

Since the last century, the floor-tile industry has made Salernes the capital of traditional tiling. The soil around the village contains a clay rich in iron oxide which produces very strong and hard tiles. You can find a good selection of tiles in the numerous workshops situated between Salernes and Draguignan (p. 231), in Aubagne (p. 197) or in Apt (pp. 155 and 160).

On the right: typical Vallauris earthenware.

The history of faïence

Faïence (earthenware dipped in silica-based glaze) has been made in Provence since the 17th C., when the local ceramics industry became a floor-tile industry centred mainly on Marseille. This golden age later reached Apt and Castellet where 'fine' tin-glazed earthenware was produced. The glaze used was almost transparent and coloured in warm hues (usually yellow, orange and green).

THE PIPE-SMOKER'S DREAM

In the past, clay pipes were used by tobacco lovers in order to taste the tobacco better. They are hard to find nowadays, but are still made near Marseille, thanks to Jean-Michel Coquet (quartier Les Jas, 13116 Vernègues, ☎ 04 90 59 30 85). This talented local craftsman specialises in hand-decorated faïence.

The Provençal crib

The Christmas period in Provence lasts from December 4 to January 6. Midnight Mass and the Thirteen Desserts are just some of the local customs to which the region is firmly attached. The tradition of making *santons* (small clay figurines) is probably the best-known.

The unbaked clay is pressed between two plaster moulds. The character thus created is then dried before being painted. Some santons *have accessories that are moulded separately and attached to the body at a later stage.*

Santon FAIRS

Numerous Provençal towns and villages organise *santon* fairs before Christmas. The largest ones are in Aix (p. 178) and in the Alpilles (p. 135) but they are also held in Apt, Arles, Carpentras, Salon and Tarascon. There is an extensive choice at the Marseille fair where you can find Carbonel and Jacques Flore *santons* (p. 193).

Provençal figurines

All the typical inhabitants of the village are gathered around the Holy Family: the shepherd (*lou pastre*), the angel Boufareu blowing his trumpet, the sleepy miller in his nightcap, the *boumian* with his bear, the *tambourin*-player who carries nothing since he owns nothing, the mayor, the woodcutter, the blind man and his son, the loveable bourgeois Roustido with his red umbrella, the incorrigible drunkard Bartomiou and his tall cotton cap. All are characters in the Pastorale, the Christmas play performed in Provence.

Born in Italy

In 1223, in a cowshed in the Abruzzi, St. Francis of Assisi created the Nativity scene with live animals and people. The name *santon* derives from the Provençal word *santoun*, meaning 'little saint'. The figures were first created in the 16th C. but started to become popular during the Revolution, when midnight mass and the crib were banned. A Marseille potter therefore had the idea of creating this series of little terra-cotta figures.

Choosing *santons*

The figurines shaped in the clay of Aubagne (p. 197) are still dressed in the Provençal costumes of the Restoration. They are moulded between two plaster casts, and are then dried, trimmed and painted with gouache after firing. You will find *puces* of 1-1¼ ins (1-3 cm), costing 25-30 F, *cigales* at about 30 F, *santons* of around 2¾ ins (7 cm) at about 50 F and larger ones of almost 8 ins (20 cm) from 100 F upwards.

Ochre pigments

In Provence, nature is often dramatic.
The deep gorges and jagged silhouettes of the
Apt region resemble a miniature Colorado
Desert, with a palette of colours ranging from
white to brightest red, and from yellow to purple. Man
has left his mark in the ancient open-cast ochre quarries,
and erosion has done the rest, creating extraordinary rock
formations – mounds, knolls, cliffs and chimneys.

A sad story

It is said that Dame
Sermonde, wife of a certain
Raimond d'Avignon, fell
in love with a troubadour.
Her jealous husband took
his rival hunting and stabbed
him. Back at the castle, he
ordered the cook to bake
his victim's heart in a tasty
dish for his wife. But when
Raimond revealed what was
in the dish she had just eaten,
Sermonde threw herself over
the cliff and the ground took
on the colour of her blood.

The origins of ochre

There is a more down-to-
earth reason for the origin of
ochre than this tragic tale.
The area lay underwater
for 120 million years
and when the sea
retreated, heavy rains followed, creating ochre sand
and pigments from the green
sand left behind. Ochre was
first quarried by the Romans,
then rediscovered during the
Revolution. Production
peaked between 1919
and 1940. But since the
discovery of chemical
pigments, ochre quarrying
has fallen off considerably
despite it being more
stable and less expensive
than its man-made
substitutes. The Société
des Ocres de France remains

the only quarrier, producing
2,000 tons a year.

Manufacture

Ochre is a mixture of clay and iron-oxide coloured sands. The first step consists of separating the sands (80%) from the oxides. The ore is then blended and washed before draining into vats as it dries. It is left to dry for a month, and is then ground to a fine powder. If the powder is baked in a kiln at 1,022°F (550°C) yellow ochre will turn into red ochre.

The ochre festival

Every year, on the second weekend of August, the shop-keepers of Rustrel organise an ochre festival. It consists of a typical and welcoming Provençal market and visits to the ochre quarries (information available at the town hall, ☎ 04 90 04 91 09). Apt (p. 161) is an important ochre centre that can be visited all year round.

The ochre tour

Departure from Rustrel, 5 miles (8 km) from Apt along the D22.

Three tours are available, each taking an hour: the Sahara, or Cirque de Bouvène, called the White Route; the Belvédère tour or fairy walk, called the Green Route; the Cirque des Barries tour, the Red and White Route of the GR (Grande Randonnée walk).

Entrance fees are charged. This long vein of ochre, dubbed 'Provençal Colorado' in 1935 by a native of Apt, offers a wide choice of excursions and colourful landscapes. This landscape is very fragile, so take care not to do any damage during the walk.

ART AND DECORATION

Ochre is used mainly by artists, but it is also effective as a house-paint on a dark wall or a dull facade. By thinning one of these natural pigments — there are more than 20 shades of natural ochre — with water and adding an acrylic or vinyl binding agent, you will obtain a colour that will fix on any material. It is ideal for patinas and colourwashing. To cover 377 sq. ft (35 m²), you will need a pot of *gel chiffonné*, 150 F for 1.4 pt (2.5 l), 5.3 oz (150 g) of pigment, 13 to 25 F for 8.8 oz (250 g). All these products are sold in the Maison Chauvin (Av. de Viton, Apt, ☎ 04 90 74 21 68).

Antiques and collectibles

The antique dealers of Provence collect what remains of daily life from the old country houses, called *bastides*. Rush-bottomed chairs, antique furniture, decorative objects, kitchen utensils; whether made of wood or clay, iron or stone – traditional Midi workmanship still exists and you can find examples in the local markets. If you want to take an elegant souvenir back home or serve Provençal food on local plates, you will find whatever you're looking for in the antique markets.

Antiques and secondhand goods dealers

Whether they are non-specialised, or chic and expensive specialist antique dealers, most offer items of regional heritage that range from yellowing postcards to authentic dressers. Antique dealers hoard objects with a passion reminiscent of museum curators. Secondhand goods dealers offer more reasonably priced bric-à-brac, and objects of more modest origin. Both types of dealer are to be found grouped in 'villages' (on L'Isle-sur-la-Sorgue, p. 166), or in Apt (antique fair in July), Avignon (rue Petite-Fusterie), Roquemaure (p. 143), Ménerbes, Arles, Marseille (cours Julien, p. 194), Aix-en-Provence, Puyricard, Toulon, Saint-Tropez (p. 216), Montauroux (p. 247), Salernes, Sanary-sur-Mer and Fayence (see also map on pp. 18-19).

Traditional furniture

Specifically Provençal items such as the bread bin, meat-safe (*manjaou*) and dresser have gone upmarket and become more elaborately carved over time. Real finds

include the *estagnié*, for storing pewterware, the *veiriau* for glasses, or the *coutelier* for knives. A wedding wardrobe makes a handsome piece of

furniture, with a typical decoration of intertwined hearts, ears of wheat or doves.

Terracotta

In Provence, red clay tiles have been used for flooring since the 17th C. Genuine antiques have become rare because terracotta is so easily breakable. You can still find tiles at potteries, alongside tableware, traditional tureens and casserole dishes, vases and lamps. Beautifully decorated tin-glazed earthenware (*faïence*) in warm, bright colours, as well as Provençal *santons*, can still be found for sale in antiques markets throughout the region (see p. 56).

Provence stonework

You can find sundials, fountains, garden benches, romantic statues or even mantelpieces in local stonemasons' workshops. Like their ancestors, they make use of the wide range of regional stone, some even creating mosaics to combine them all – the pink marble of Brignoles, the stone of the Luberon (used to build the Palais des Papes at Avignon), the stone of Cassis, of Fontvieille or of Rognes. The traditional Provençal farmhouse, made of sunbleached stone and red roof tiles is called a *mas*.

Fabrics

Provençal cottons, linens and silks are patterned in traditional designs, inspired by their distant oriental origins. The 'printed calico' tradition was enriched by modern designs which tastefully decorate tablecloths, napkins, curtains, bedspreads, hangings, clothing and wedding dresses. You will find the most beautiful examples of this craft at two famous firms, Souleïado (p. 155) and Les Olivades (p. 52).

A PASSION FOR RARITIES

Holidays are ideal for finding that book you have been seeking for ages, discovering an unknown author or finding some ancient tome about Provence. In Aix-en-Provence, there is a bookshop called Rue des Bouquinistes Obscurs (Street of Obscure Booksellers) (2, rue Boulegon, ☎ 04 42 96 03 19, closed on Sun.), where you may well find what you are looking for. Further along the street, L'Abécédaire stocks rare editions and there is even a little reading space and play area for children. There is also a Provençal bookshop in Apt called Librairie Dumas, (Pl. Gabriel-Péri, ☎ 04 90 74 23 81).

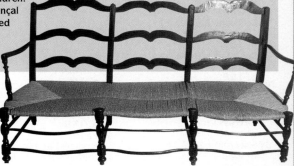

Castles, 'bories' and hilltop villages

Provence is studded with solid stone testimonies to its rich past. They are so numerous that only the most outstanding are given here.

Castles

1. **Ansouis:** Renaissance architecture and French-style garden. **pp. 156-157.**
2. **Bonnieux:** a former Roman fort. **pp. 154-155.**
3. **Cagnes-sur-Mer:** feudal castle. **p. 258.**
4. **Cannes:** the Château-musée de la Castre. **pp. 240-241.**
5. **Château-Arnoux:** Renaissance mansion. **p. 187.**
6. **Entrecasteaux:** Castle and gardens. **p. 233.**
7. **Entrevaux:** fortified citadel. **p. 300.**
8. **Gordes:** Renaissance-style castle. **p. 162.**
9. **Gourdon:** Medieval house and museum. **pp. 228-229.**
10. **Grimaud:** medieval ruins. **p. 220.**
11. **Hyères:** the Castel Sainte-Claire. **p. 209.**
12. **Îles-de-Lérins:** prison of the Man in the Iron Mask. **p. 242.**
13. **Le Tholonet:** view of Cézanne country. **p. 180.**
14. **Lourmarin:** Renaissance castle. **p. 156.**
15. **Marseille:** the Château d'If. **p. 192.**
16. **Roquebrune:** Carolingian fortress. **p. 288.**
17. **Sisteron:** military citadel. **p. 186.**
18. **Tarascon:** castle. **p. 144.**
19. **Vaison-la-Romaine:** one of the castles of the Counts of Toulouse. **p. 148.**
20. **Vence:** medieval architecture and contemporary paintings. **p. 262.**

Mont Ventoux
6,263 ft
(1,909 m)

Carpentras

Rhône

Avignon

8 21

2

Manosque

14 1

Massif du Luberon

Durance

Alpilles

Arles

A54

Étang de Berre

Camargue

A55

Marseille

15

Aix-en-Provence

13

Bories

21 Gordes:
village of the 'bories'.
p. 163.

Hilltop villages

The pink areas on this map
indicate the areas of the
Alpes-de-Haute-Provence,
the Bouches-du-Rhône,
the Luberon, the Var, the
hinterland of Nice, on the
Plateau du Vaucluse and
around the Ventoux, which
contain numerous hilltop
villages.

pp. 66-67.

22 Biot: overlooks the Vallée
de la Brague.
pp. 264-265.

23 Entrevaux: fortified city in
the clouds.
p. 300.

Massif du
Mercantour

Cime du Gélas
10,312 ft
(3,143 m)

Gap

Barcelonnette

Digne-les-Bains

Verdon

Var

Var

Lac de
Castillon

Castellane

N85

Lac de
Ste-Croix

Grasse

Cannes

Monaco

Nice

A8

Draguignan

N7

Massif
de l'Esterel

Argens

A8

A57

Massif
des Maures

N98

St-Tropez

Toulon

Île du
Levant

Île de
Porquerolles

Île de
Port-Cros

24 Èze: on the cliff top.
p. 278.

25 Gourdon:
at 2,500 ft (760 m).
p. 268.

26 Moustiers-Sainte-Marie:
sheltered by the Verdon
Gorges.
p. 234.

27 Saorge:
amphitheatre village.
p. 67.

28 Touët-sur-Var: suspended
over the gorges.
p. 67.

29 Tourrettes-sur-Loup:
carved into the
limestone.
p. 266.

0   10   20   30 miles

0 10 20 30 40 50 km

Traditional architecture

Two types of classic country residence characterise Provence: the *mas* or farmhouse, and the *bastide* or country house. Even the words evoke the very essence of Provence – its colours, space, atmosphere and way of life. But they conceal a harsh reality. The inhabitants struggled for many years to learn the best way to build their homes in order to mitigate the effects of the bitter *mistral* winds, the long, scorching-hot summers and the harsh winters. The traditional *mas* and *bastide* of Provence are the result of this long learning curve, offering protection from the extremes of weather.

In harmony with nature

The Provençal house is simple in shape, built from beautiful but sturdy materials and protected from the northern *mistral* wind by a solid wall. It has also been designed to resist the worst of the scorching heat, with thick, brightly-coloured walls and shutters at the windows. Inside, arched doors, white stone vaulted ceilings, window embrasures, terracotta floor-tiles and ceramics add the finishing touches to this delightful country home.

Tiles and stones

Characteristically, the roof-tiles are semi-circular Roman tiles, made of baked clay and shaped like guttering on a wooden mould (or sometimes on the thigh). The stones are used to build walls, and as paving-stones, when they are known as *calades* (from the Provençal word *calado*, small rounded pebbles from streams). These paving-stones are

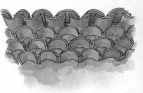

typical of the hilltop villages which are dotted all over Provence.

The *mas*

These farmhouses were built facing south so that they were protected from rain from the east and the *mistral* from the north.

Left: Channel tiling
Above: Genoa tiling

They were L-shaped or closed around a courtyard, and consisted of the main building and outhouses (sheepfold, barn, *magnanerie* for breeding silkworms, well and oven). In the Vaucluse, smaller farms are called *campagnes*, *granges*, or *ousaus*.

The *bastide*

Dubbed the 'cabanon des riches', the *bastide* or country mansion looks like a fortification with an imposing facade and formal garden. Once the home of the local landowner, the *bastide* is bigger than the *mas* and is one or two storeys high.

There are also some *bastidons*, one-room constructions of ancient origin.

The *cabanon*

The whole family would gather to eat *bouillabaisse* (fish soup) in these little huts. Hidden away in the shade of an olive tree or a cleft in the rock, these little cottages or huts are only for those who are resolutely Provençal to the core. To live in a *cabanon* you need to know how to do nothing at all without the slightest twinge of conscience. The little huts are sometimes seen in the vineyards and are used to store tools. They are also called *cabanons* or *bastidous*.

The *cabane Camarguaise*

The Camargue hut is where the herdsman (*gardian*) lives. The interior is very simple, consisting of a kitchen and a bedroom separated from each other by a reed partition. The rectangular shape is rounded at the back so that the wind slides over it, and the opposite side is open to the elements. It is built of inexpensive materials, with low walls and a thatched roof.

The *bories*

Drystone walls, ending in a conical roof, and judiciously constructed to stay in place without mortar, are the basis of these strange little shelters (*photo above*). They are a common sight in Provence (there are more than 5,000, of which 1,610 are in the Vaucluse), particularly in the Forcalquier district and the Lure mountains, where there is no lack of stones. The most attractive are situated in the Gordes area (p. 163). *Bories* were used mainly as temporary shelters, sheepfolds, *cabanons* or huts. Nowadays, they may be quite luxuriously and elegantly appointed.

Les Baux-de-Provence, in the Bouches-du-Rhône

Hilltop villages

Whether situated on top of a peak or encircling a hill, the origins of hilltop villages can be found in ancient history. Often fortified and topped by a castle or church, the villages balance precariously on the rock and are not easily accessible. But the climb is well worth it because from the highest point you can look down on a mosaic of overlapping roofs, a maze of steep lanes and magnificent views over the surrounding landscape.

Vertiginous citadels

These vestiges of the Middle Ages are evidence of the concerns of their earliest inhabitants. It was vital to be protected from the unhealthy air of the floodplains and from the incessant wars. From the top of a rock the enemy could be seen approaching and protective measures taken. Although nowadays one can take pleasure in the view from the summit of these hilltop villages, bear in mind that the inhabitants chose to live here in order to survive despite the difficulties (the water supply, for instance).

Villages revived

From the 16th C. onwards, the villagers tended to abandon their austere and isolated homes and return to the plains, where communication was better and farming more productive. Over the years, some villages became completely deserted while others struggled to survive. Now that they have been restored, many hilltop villages have won a new lease of life thanks to their many enthusiastic visitors.

Moustiers-Sainte-Marie

In the Alpes-de-Haute-Provence

The landscape of this region is dotted with more than 100 hilltop villages. The most famous are Moustiers-Sainte-Marie (p. 234), Entrevaux (p. 300), Thoard, Saint-Vincent-les-Forts, Simiane-la-Rotonde, Banon (p. 286), Dauphin, Montfort and Lurs (p. 184). Others, less well-known, wait to be discovered. They include Villevieille, Rougon, Montfuron, Montjustin, Vachères, Montsallier, Oppedette and Le Rocher-d'Ongles.

A lane in the village of Peillon

In the Alpes-Maritimes

Here, the villages hug the natural reliefs of the landscape. Villages worth seeing include Touët-sur-Var (between the Gorges de la Mescla and the Gorges de Cians), Saorge, laid out like an amphitheatre at 333 ft (100 m) above the Vallée de la Roya, (p. 296), Gourdon (behind the Côte d'Azur) at a height of 2,533 ft (760 m) above the Vallée du Loup, (p. 268), Tourrettes-sur-Loup (p 266), Bonson, Auribeau-sur-Siagne (p. 246), Peillon (p. 281), Sainte-Agnès, Coaraze (p. 280) and Lucéram (p. 280) in the Nice hinterland.

In the Bouches-du-Rhône

There are only a few hilltop villages in this area, being a region of low relief. The most beautiful are in the Alpilles. They include Eygalières which overlooks the Plaine de Saint-Rémy, and Les Baux-de-Provence (p. 136), balanced on the edge of a rocky peak. The panoramic views more than make up for the climb.

TOPOGRAPHY OF THE VILLAGES
The characteristics of the particular site were used to their best advantage for the construction of each settlement. The village may occupy an entire hill, coiling around the château like a snail shell. It may also be hidden on a plateau protected by a rocky ridge or attach itself to a ledge halfway up the slope. The buildings are always huddled together to produce as much cool shade as possible, and the houses are all built of local freestone.

In the Var

The highest village of the Var is Bargème, perched at an altitude of 3,657 ft (1,097 m). Nearby Mons (p. 251) and Seillans (p. 251) are also as high up as possible. Towards the centre, Cotignac (p. 233) and Barjols (p. 232) are perched on the mountainside. Above Bandol, La Cadière-d'Azur (p. 198) faces Le Castellet (p. 198), Le Beausset (p. 199) and Évenos overlook the Gorges d'Ollioules. In the Massif des Maures, Collobrières (p. 222), Grimau (p. 220) and La Garde-Freinet (p. 223) reach for the sky, while Gassin (p. 216) and Ramatuelle, nearest to the coast, overlook a sheer drop.

In the Vaucluse

Hilltop villages were also built around the Mont Ventoux (Bédoin, Crillon-le-Brave, Le Barroux, Brantes and Aurel), or the Plateau du Vaucluse, such as Vénasque (p. 169), Gordes (p. 162), Roussillon (p. 161), Goult (p. 161), Murs, Cazenenve and Viens. In the Luberon are Ménerbes, Oppède-le-Vieux, Lacoste, Bonnieux, Buoux, Saignon and Ansouis (pp. 154 to 157).

The snail-shell structure of Ramatuelle, on the Saint-Tropez peninsula

Prehistoric sites, Roman remains and Roman art

Painted caves, Roman arenas, Romanesque abbeys with silent cloisters, remote priories in lavender fields – here are ideal opportunities for calm and contemplation.

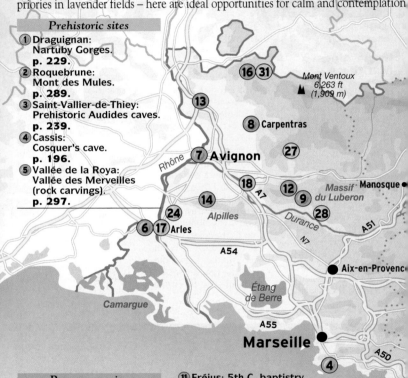

Prehistoric sites

① Draguignan:
Nartuby Gorges.
p. 229.

② Roquebrune:
Mont des Mules.
p. 289.

③ Saint-Vallier-de-Thiey:
Prehistoric Audides caves.
p. 239.

④ Cassis:
Cosquer's cave.
p. 196.

⑤ Vallée de la Roya:
Vallée des Merveilles
(rock carvings).
p. 297.

Roman remains

⑥ Arles: Necropolis of the Alyscamps.
p. 126.

⑦ Avignon: antiquities in the Musée Calvet.
p. 142.

⑧ Carpentras:
1st C. Triumphal arch.
p. 170.

⑨ Céreste: Medieval village.
p. 157.

⑩ La Turbie:
Trophy of the Alps.
p. 279.

⑪ Fréjus: 5th C. baptistry and Porte des Gaules.
p. 224.

⑫ Bonnieux: 3rd C. bridge.
p. 154.

⑬ Orange: Arc de Triomphe and amphitheatre.
pp. 146-147.

⑭ Saint-Rémy-de-Provence:
Glanum (Roman city).
p. 139.

⑮ Senez:
12th C. cathedral.
p. 238.

⑯ Vaison-la-Romaine:
Roman theatre
and Maison des Messii.
p. 148.

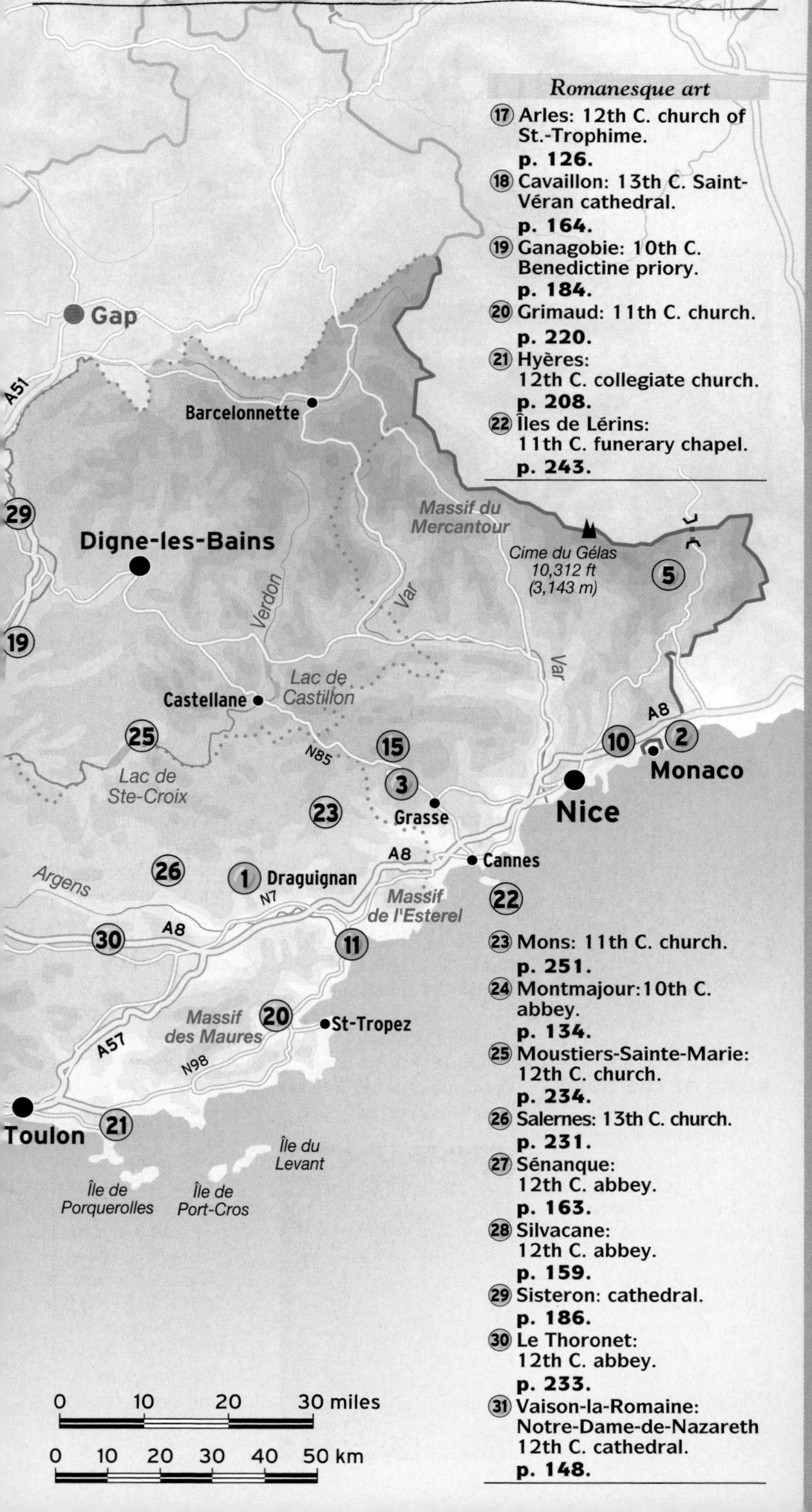

Romanesque art

17 Arles: 12th C. church of St.-Trophime.
p. 126.

18 Cavaillon: 13th C. Saint-Véran cathedral.
p. 164.

19 Ganagobie: 10th C. Benedictine priory.
p. 184.

20 Grimaud: 11th C. church.
p. 220.

21 Hyères: 12th C. collegiate church.
p. 208.

22 Îles de Lérins: 11th C. funerary chapel.
p. 243.

Gap

Barcelonnette

A51

29

Digne-les-Bains

19

Massif du Mercantour

Cime du Gélas
10,312 ft
(3,143 m)

5

Verdon

Var

Var

Castellane

Lac de Castillon

25

N85

15

3

23

Grasse

10

A8

2

Monaco

Nice

Lac de Ste-Croix

Argens

26

1 Draguignan

N7

A8

Cannes

22

30

A8

11

Massif de l'Esterel

A57

Massif des Maures

N98

20

St-Tropez

Toulon

21

Île du Levant

Île de Porquerolles

Île de Port-Cros

23 Mons: 11th C. church.
p. 251.

24 Montmajour: 10th C. abbey.
p. 134.

25 Moustiers-Sainte-Marie: 12th C. church.
p. 234.

26 Salernes: 13th C. church.
p. 231.

27 Sénanque: 12th C. abbey.
p. 163.

28 Silvacane: 12th C. abbey.
p. 159.

29 Sisteron: cathedral.
p. 186.

30 Le Thoronet: 12th C. abbey.
p. 233.

31 Vaison-la-Romaine: Notre-Dame-de-Nazareth 12th C. cathedral.
p. 148.

0	10	20	30 miles

0	10	20	30	40	50 km

Caves and cave-dwellers

The mountains of Provence possess an incredible prehistoric heritage; a hidden treasure called the Vallée des Merveilles. At a height of 6,667ft (2,000m) tens of thousands of rock carvings testify to the presence of Bronze Age inhabitants who lived there thirty-seven centuries ago. Even today the carvings have barely begun to reveal their mysterious message.

Early theories

It was only in the early 19th C. that the first rational explanations for the carvings were provided. In 1821, an historian claimed that they had been made by Hannibal's Carthaginian troops in 237BC. A second researcher spoke of 'Phoenician patterns' made four centuries earlier. A third historian claimed that these were mere patterns in the chalk grooves. Bronze Age man, the true creator of these wonderful carvings, was finally given the credit in 1882.

A site survey

To enable the rock carvings of the Vallée des Merveilles to be properly understood – they often overlapped and were jumbled (p. 297) – they had to be isolated, inventoried and classified. Clarence Bicknell, an English botanist, was the first to embark on this mammoth task. Over 12 laborious summers, starting in 1878, he counted 14,000 of them, some dug out from 12 to 20 ins (30 to 50 cm) below the surface. Between 1927 and 1939, an Italian, Carlo Conti, discovered 36,000 more carvings. Recently, Professor de Lumley, from the University of Marseille,

Signs of the devil

Until their identification, these thousands of drawings covering the rock face were believed to be the work of the devil. In the Middle Ages, the Church tried to make them disappear and sent a delegation of monks to purify this satanic area. It was out of bounds and cursed until the 19th C., and was said to be home to Satan himself, who changed hapless wanderers into larch trees during violent thunderstorms.

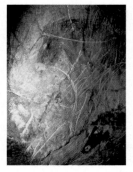

cataloqued more than 100,000 carvings! But even this total is likely to be provisional.

The designs

Horned animals feature most frequently in the drawings and carvings (60%), and their shape is very stylised. Also featured are weapons and tools (daggers, sickles, harnesses), simple geometrical figures, and some human figures which discoverers have nicknamed – e.g. 'the

dancer', 'the Christ' or 'the sorcerer'. It is now thought that the site was inhabited and the carvings produced in the rocks between 1700 and 1000BC.

The carving technique

All the rock carvings (or petroglyphs) were stippled. In other words their creators made dotted lines in the rock with a sharp tool made of flint or metal. Two techniques were used: carving directly into the rock with a stone; or chiselling, which produced a more precise line,

especially in the design of the horns of the animals, which were always meticulously represented in great detail.

Why?

This is the great enigma which is far from being solved. Perhaps the area was inhabited by hunter-warriors because many weapons are depicted. The horned animals represented in the carvings may also refer to the cattle that prehistoric man placed under the protection of a bull-god.

Mont Bégo, which overlooks the Vallée des Merveilles, may thus have been chosen for its resemblance to such a divinity (the sharp peak could symbolise the tip of a horn). This hypothesis is given extra weight by the fact that the river flowing down it used to be called the 'Rivière des Bœufs' ('Ox River').

BEFORE THE VALLÉE DES MERVEILLES

The presence of mankind in Provence is visible even before the Bronze Age. On the site of Terra Amata in Nice, archaeologists found evidence of the old Palaeolithic Age (400,000 years ago). Numerous caves reveal the existence of man and his artistic creativity, especially in Saint-Cézaire-sur-Siagne, (p. 245). One of the most recent discoveries was the splendid wall paintings in the cave of Cosquer (p. 196), in Sormiou off Cassis, which can only be seen by the general public on CD-Rom, in order to preserve and protect its natural beauty.

Roman remains

The Roman baths in Nice

The arena at Arles

The Romans, who in 125BC came to the rescue of Marseille threatened by the Franks, acquired a taste for Gaul and settled there. Anxious to control communications between Spain and Italy, they created Provincia and began a major romanisation of the region. Roman veterans came to live there, bringing with them the artistic and social genius of the Empire. Traces of these fundamental influences on the development of the region are still visible in numerous sites.

The Roman bridge across the River Ouvèze at Vaison-la-Romaine

In the days of the Pax romana

The territories conquered by the Romans were subject to their authority, but these shrewd strategists understood the importance for the native populations of retaining their own rituals and customs. The Romans imposed their hierarchy and social organisation by tolerating ancient traditions. Their civil engineering and town-planning skills were responsible for the foundation of cities such as Orange, aligned on the north-south axis road, the *cardo*, and the east-west axis road, the *decumanus* (p. 148). Living conditions in the towns and cities were improved and the communications network expanded. Roads such as the Via Agrippa, the Via Domitia, the Via Julia Augusta and the Via Aurelia were built and new ports created on the Rivers Rhône and Durance.

The *villae*

The Gauls were a nation of farmers. They found the Roman inventions very useful for increasing production and making their region prosper through trade. At first, they were reluctant to adopt the new Roman way of life but they soon changed, especially with regard to the farmhouses, or *villae*. A *villa* is a large group of buildings, including the owner's house (*pars urbana*) and outbuildings (*pars agraria*); it became the model for the Provençal *bastide*. The *villae* of Provence were very original and richly decorated with mosaics, marble, frescoes and statues.

Augustinian trophy, La Turbie

Traditionally, Roman baths are divided into three distinctive zones: the warm bath (caldarium), the tepid bath (tepidarium) and the cold bath (frigidarium). The caldarium was heated by a hypocaust, that is to say by an ingenious system of warm air, fed by a furnace and circulated under the floor through ducts made of fire-bricks.

PUBLIC BUILDINGS

The public buildings are the best evidence of how thoroughly the Roman way of life was adopted in Provence. There are aqueducts and public baths at Vaison-la-Romaine (p. 148), theatres at Orange and Arles, triumphal arches at the site of Glanum, near Saint-Rémy (p. 139). Many buildings disappeared when subsequent generations re-used the stone for private purposes.

Saint-Rémy-de-Provence: the remains of Glanum

Roman amusements and leisure

The Romans were brave soldiers and good citizens. Games and spectacles played a very important part in their daily lives because they believed that entertaining the gods would make them benevolent. Horse-races and chariot-races were staged in the amphitheatres; tragedies and comedies accompanied by singing and miming were performed in theatres. In the amphitheatres, human sacrifices were soon replaced by gladiatorial combat. The Romans created leisure areas and each colonised city had gardens and lakes, porticos (arcades or galleries), and public baths where citizens could relax and exercise.

The supremacy of Arles

Whereas Avignon and Apt were merely influenced by the Romans, Arles (p. 126) was completely romanised. The city, called the 'Rome of the Gauls' by the poet Ausonius, is full of splendid remains including Constantine's public baths, a theatre, arenas and the Alyscamps necropolis, to name but a few. Arles was the regional capital from the 4th to the 5th C. Several Roman emperors made their home in the city and set up mints for coining local currency. Nearby Aix-en-Provence (Aquae Sextiae), the first town to be founded by the Romans in 122BC, subsequently became the main administrative centre of Provincia.

Aix-en-Provence: the oppidum of Entremont

Monasteries

The landscapes of Provence positively invite calm and contemplation. There are many ancient ruins as well as Roman works of art and the monastic orders still take an active part in everyday life. Several religious communities keep these historic sites alive and sell their own produce to help fund their good works. Devoted to God but open to the world, monks and nuns often welcome those who wish to go on retreat to a monastery or convent.

The Abbey of Sénanque

The Benedictines

Benedict of Nursia (c. AD 480-547) founded his order in Subiaco, Italy. The order was an open one, and reached its zenith when the foundation of Cluny was created in 910. Its members are called the 'black friars' because of their dark-coloured habits. The Benedictine Abbey of Ganagobie overlooks the beautiful Vallée de la Durance (p. 184) north of Manosque, and has a pretty Romanesque church containing 12th C. mosaics. Retreats last a week.

Bethlehem

This recent order (1951) was inspired by the strict rule of the Carthusians, the order

created by Saint Brian in 1084. They lead the lives of hermits, devoted to study and meditation. This community breathed new spiritual life into two important religious centres: Le Thoronet (p. 233), a silent order of Cistercians which offers a few retreats, and the Charterhouse of La Verne (p. 222), an architechtural jewel deep in the countryside which does not allow retreats.

The Cistercians

These monks strictly observe the rule of Saint Benedict of Nursia which is extremely ascetic. Robert of Molesme created the order in 1075.

Cîteaux and Clairvaux were great Cistercian centres and these enlightened minds conceived the most beautiful Romanesque monuments. Their cream-coloured habits distinguish these monks from the Benedictines. In 429, the Monastery of Lérins (p. 242), built around 410 by Honoratus, was one of the most famous in the West. It became Cistercian in 1073. After the Revolution, it was revived in 1869 thanks to the monks of Sénanque. The Romanesque Abbey of Sénanque (p. 163) was built in 1148. The monks, who had been expelled and moved to Lérins, returned to the abbey in 1988.

Barrel vault

Saint-Rémy-de-Provence: cloister of the monastery at Saint-Paul-de-Mausole

The Franciscans

Francis of Assisi created his mendicant order in 1209 as a reaction against ecclesiastic excesses. The monks, who wear a coarse serge robe tied by a simple piece of rope at the waist, take vows of poverty. They are represented in Provence by the splendid Monastery of Cimiez (p. 274).

The Premonstratensians

This order, also known as the White Canons, observes the rule of Saint Augustine. It was created by Norbert, a German prelate, in 1120 at Prémontré. Canons take monastic vows but enclosure is not as strict as in other orders. In 1858, Father Edmond Boulbon chose Saint Michel-de-Frigolet Abbey (p. 145), founded in 1133 by a community of Canons, to restore the order that had disappeared after the Revolution. Retreats are permitted.

Ribbed vault

Romanesque entrance

ROMANESQUE ART IN PROVENCE

Between the 11th and 13th C., stone buildings inspired by the Romans replaced the fragile wooden chapels. Known as the three sisters of Provence, Le Thoronet, Sénanque and Silvacane Abbeys are the most beautiful examples of the Romanesque style, which aimed at the monastic ideals of peace, retreat, silence, simplicity and purity of form. Silvacane (p. 159), which was built after Le Thoronet and Sénanque, contains allusions to the later Gothic style in its splendid chapter-house. In Arles, the church of Saint-Trophime (p. 126) is typical of the Provençal Romanesque style with its ornate entrance and austere interior. Montmajour Abbey has a Romanesque cloister (p. 134). It is also worth going to Languedoc-Roussillon to see the most beautiful Romanesque sculptures in the region, at Saint-Gilles-du-Gard, 10 miles (16km) west of Arles.

Digne: Notre-Dame du Bourg cathedral

Roman apse with radiating chapels

Gardens and perfumes

The gardens of Provence are resplendent with oleanders, dark cypresses, succulents and century-plants, bowers of rambling roses and jasmine and fields of lavender. It is no wonder that Provence is the centre of the perfume industry.

Gardens

1. Aix-en-Provence: Albertas Gardens. **pp. 178-179.**
2. Antibes: Jardins Thuret. **p. 254.**
3. Arles: Summer Gardens. **p. 128.**
4. Avignon: The Doms Rocks and Tropical Flower Park. **pp. 142-143.**
5. Bandol: exotic gardens. **p. 201.**
6. Biot: bonsai trees. **p. 264.**
7. Glorious gardens: Rayol: Canadel. **p. 215.**
8. Cagnes-sur-Mer: Vaugrenier Park. **p. 259.**
9. Èze: exotic gardens. **p. 279.**
10. Gémenos: Parc de Saint-Pons. **p. 205.**
11. Gourdon: jardin du château **p. 269.**
12. La Ciotat: Parc du Mugel. **p. 199.**
13. La Gaude: knot garden. **p. 179.**
14. Menton: jardin Biovès. **p. 291.**
15. Monaco: exotic gardens. **p. 284.**
16. Monte-Carlo: Japanese gardens. **p. 287.**
17. Mougins: Park Caillenco and bamboo plantation. **p. 247.**
18. Nice: Parc exotique Phœnix. **p. 270.**
19. Oppède-le-Vieux: hilltop terraces of Sainte-Cécile. **p. 165.**
20. Orange: Jardins de l'Harmas. **p. 147.**
21. Prieuré de Salagon: ethnobotanical gardens. **p. 185.**
22. Saint-Jean-Cap-Ferrat: Villa Île-de-France and botanical gardens. **pp. 276-277.**
23. Saint-Zacharie: Parc du Moulin-Blanc. **p. 205.**
24. Vence: Gardens of Notre Dame-des-Fleurs. **p. 262.**

Mont Ventoux 6,263 ft (1,909 m)

● Carpentras

Avignon

Rhône

Alpilles

Arles

Camargue

A54

Massif du Luberon

Durance

Manosque ●

Étang de Berre

A55

A50

A51

Marseille ●

Aix-en-Provence

Gap

Barcelonnette

Digne-les-Bains

Verdon

Castellane

Lac de Castillon

Massif du Mercantour

Cime du Gélas
10,312 ft
(3,143 m)

Var

Var

Lac de Ste-Croix

N85

(11)

(24)

(14) (30)

(9)

(15) (16)

Grasse (28)

(8) (18) (22)

Monaco

(17) (6)

Nice

(2)

A8

Draguignan

Cannes

N7

Massif de l'Esterel

Argens

A8

Massif des Maures

N98

St-Tropez

A57

(7) (26)

0   10   20   30 miles

Toulon

(29)

0 10 20 30 40 50 km

(27)

Île de Port-Cros

Île du Levant

Île de Porquerolles

Perfumes

(25) **Apt:** Chemin
de la Roche-Redonne.
p. 161.

(26) **Bormes-les-Mimosas:**
mimosa nursery.
p. 214.

(27) **Giens:**
Decugis nursery.
p. 207.

(28) **Grasse:**
Domain de Manon.
p. 249.

(29) **Hyères:**
jardin Saint-Bernard.
p. 209.

(30) **Menton:**
gardens and exotic
perfumes of Val Rameh.
p. 291.

(31) **Sault:**
lavender gardens.
p. 173.

(32) **Tarascon:** perfumed
gardens of Graveson.
p. 145.

Flowers

Lavender, mimosa, carnations, tulips, roses, violets and orange blossom cover Provence with a sweet-scented carpet. The Var region produces one third of the entire production of commercial flowers in France. Whether classic flower scents or new varieties, horticulturists have been experimenting for two centuries and are now aiming at increasing longevity.

Lavender

Lavender is undoubtedly the queen of Provençal flowers. The perfume of both wild and cultivated lavender pervades the region, especially in mid-summer when the scent is strongest. There are traditional processions of floral floats to celebrate the lavender harvest in Valréas and Sault (p. 172). The lavandin hybrid is very popular with bees which use it to make particularly delicious honey (p. 31 and p. 172).

Mimosa

This small shrub from Australia was first planted in Provence in 1880, when a gardener from Cannes gave a local horticulturist one of the first mimosa plants brought back from Australia by his master. The horticulturist carelessly threw the small branch on a compost-heap, and the next morning, he discovered with astonishment that the plant was covered in bright yellow blossoms! He decided to begin experimenting with a forcing technique whereby branches which have not yet flowered are kept in a hot, humid environment, in order to make them flower early. This technique still helps to extend the season for mimosa. In February, when the small yellow buds open out, mimosa is celebrated in Bormes-les-Mimosas (p. 214), in Saint-Raphaël, Fréjus, Ollioules and in Le Lavandou. It looks wonderful against the red of the Massif de l'Esterel and continues to flower until March.

Carnations and tulips

83% of French carnations are grown on the Côte d'Azur. Although they are mostly cultivated in the terraced gardens surrounding Nice, they are also found at Cagnes-sur-Mer and in Saint-Laurent-du-Var. Carqueiranne cultivates tulips from October to March and is famous for a giant variety known all over the world. You can buy tulips at bargain prices at ASO Fleurs (D 559, next to the town stadium, open daily except Sun. from 8 am to 5.30 pm).

The rose

The rose makes the most of the exceptional sun of the Côte d'Azur like no other flower. After World War II, Antibes became the capital of the rose thanks to local research carried out by the Institut National de Recherche Agronomique (INRA), and to the work of the creators of new varieties. 63% of French roses are produced in Provence. In the region of Grasse the May rose is used in perfumery. The most popular roses in the world, the Baccara and the Sonia, come from the Meilland nurseries (☎ 04 93 95 96 23) which produce one third of roses worldwide. Also have a look at Astoux's (p. 255).

The violet

Tourettes-sur-Loup (p. 266), north of Cannes, is the violet-growing region. This village, which is the premier producer in France (outstripping Toulouse), regularly supplies the markets of Paris, Nice and Antibes. Violets, which are gathered individually and manually, are always sold in a bunches of 25. They are grown from March to October in the surrounding terraced gardens. The petals are used in confectionery and the leaves in perfumery.

Orange blossom

Orange blossom is now something of a rarity. It is grown in Bar-sur-Loup in the Alpes-Maritimes. Orange blossoms are picked by hand in May. They are distilled and made into neroli essence for the perfume trade (see Vallauris, p. 257) or into orange flower water for use in confectionery. Green bitter oranges are picked in November and sold to perfumeries to make essential oils (the Musée des Arômes in Saint-Rémy explains the various stages p. 138).

TOURS OF GARDENS

Provence has some magnificent gardens to visit. If you thrive in tropical climes, there are two in particular not to be missed: the tropical forest of Barbentane (p. 143) and the Parc de Menton (p. 291). There is also a pretty, fragrant garden in Goult (p. 161). Do not forget to visit the gardens of L'Harmas, in Sérignan (p. 147), the Priory of Salagon, in Mane (p. 185), and the forest park of Mont-Boron, in Nice (p. 274). Finally, the sumptuous Italianate garden of La Gaude (p. 179) will leave you speechless.

Lavender

Lavender, which belongs to the same family as thyme, rosemary and savory, is a hardy plant that grows wild in Provence. Its name may come from the Latin word *lavare* (to wash). Lavender, used in perfumery, confectionery, and as a room freshener, is a wonderful plant. Its scent and colour pervades Provence, where it grows abundantly.

A touch of botany

There are three varieties of lavender: spike-lavender, which is no longer grown because it is too expensive and has a poor yield; the 'real' or 'fine' lavender, about 12 in (30 cm) tall, which grows at high altitude and produces a strong essence, which is much sought-after. It is also the most expensive type of lavender. Finally, lavandin, a larger, coarser hybrid of true lavender and spike-lavender, which is cultivated in the plains and propagated by taking cuttings. It is used for perfuming toiletries.

Gathering and distillation

Lavender blossoms in July and is mechanically harvested. In the past (as recently as 1960), a dozen people could cut 1,100 to 1,760 lb (500 to 800 kg) of blooms a day and were paid 10 centimes for 2.2 lb (1 kg). Lavender is then tied in bundles and sent to the distillery. There, micro-droplets of aroma contained inside the flower will burst under the pressure of steam. The water, which is heavier, is then separated from the essence through refrigeration. To obtain 2.2 lb (1 kg) of lavender essence, 264 to 286 lb (120 to 130 kg) of plant matter needs to be distilled. Lavandin has a higher yield: up to 110 to 132 lb (50 to 60 kg) is enough to produce 2.2 lb (1 kg) of lavender essence. At the moment, the price of lavender essence is about 350 F per 2.2 lb (1 kg), whereas the price of lavandin essence is dramatically cheaper at 65 F on average.

Uses of lavender

Used in wardrobes and closets, lavender perfumes linen and drives away moths. It is used to make perfumes, colognes, perfumed soaps and deodorants. The craftsmen of L'Occitane have even created a lavender water for linen which makes ironing more pleasant! Lavender honey is famous here and is still cold-extracted. Lavender wine is not as well-known, but is still produced.

The lavender road

The annual lavender festival, held on 15 August in Sault, has a pretty 'lavender road' (p. 173). Digne-les-Bains is also a major production centre (p. 298). Lavender enthusiasts should follow its trail in the Apt district. At the Garde-d'Apt, the Château du Bois (☎ 04 90 76 91 23, open in summer 9am-7pm) welcomes visitors to its lavender-producing domain. Harvesting and making essential oil are demonstrated. There is also a Musée de la Lavande (Lavender Museum) at Coustellet (open daily except Mon., 10am-noon and 2-6pm, and until 7pm in Jul.-Aug.). If you want to discover the secrets of the distillation, make an appointment at Lavande 1,100, which is also in Apt (M. Fra, ☎ 04 90 75 01 42, open daily 10am-6pm, from 25 Jul. to 25 Aug.).

OLD WIVES' TALES

Lavender is the most popular of aromatic herbs as well as one of the most beneficial. Its healing and disinfectant properties (for use on cuts, burns and bruises) are well-known, but it has other therapeutic virtues. For instance, three small stems of lavender drunk as an infusion are said to have indisputable sedative, diuretic and anti-rheumatic powers.

Lavender stems, which are cut and then dried, are packed into a container which is plunged into a double boiler heated to a high temperature. Under the pressure of the heat, the steam passes through the plant matter to be distilled; the result is a mixture of water and essence. This mixture goes through a distiller placed inside a refrigeration unit. As it cools, the mixture produces liquid droplets which are stored in the essence-maker; once it has settled, the essence rises to the top because it is lighter than water.

Perfumes and fragrances

T he perfumes of Grasse are world-famous. The capital of fragrance has been blending rose, jasmine, violet, lavender, mimosa, orange flower and other scents in its 30 factories for two centuries. Originally used to hide the smell of the local tanneries, these 'wonderful waters' ('eaux') start life on layers of grease yet end in valuable flasks of pure essence.

Hiding the smell of the tanneries

Grasse was famous in the Middle Ages for its tanneries and its glove-making industry. The perfume industry was developed in order to neutralise the strong smell emanating from the leather. With the approval of Catherine de Médicis, who adored the fashion for perfumed gloves, glove-makers became perfumers as well. By the late 18th C. they were devoting themselves exclusively to making perfume. The whole industry developed in Grasse purely as a by-product of the leather industry.

The extraction

Solvent extraction is the technique most often used nowadays to extract floral essences. It is the quickest and the most effective method. The flowers are washed several times with benzene or hexane, to release their fragrances in a series of difficult operations such as evaporation of the solvent, filtering, freezing and pressing. Finally, the 'absolute' concentrate is extracted and stored.

Distillation

Flowers whose fragrances might be affected by solvents are treated with steam. The flowers are placed in a boiler with one to five times their weight of water, and their essences are extracted by steam. The steam is cooled by refrigeration, and the condensation produces a mixture of water and essential oil. These can be immediately separated in an *essencier* due to the difference in their density. The essential oil, which is not as pure as a distillate, is called a *concrète*.

The flowers are placed in a boiler. Their essences evaporate and are condensed.

The mixture of water and oil is then separated.

Price of the essence

Flower essences cost more than gold. To obtain 2.2 lb (1 kg) of jasmine essence, a picker would have to work two thousand hours to gather 1 million flowers by hand. Then the costs of extraction must be added. So 1¾ pt (1 litre) of pure essence can cost 120,000 to 150,000 F! But as this essence will contribute to the production of 5,263 pt (3,000 l) of perfume, it all becomes relative. If a designer name is associated with the perfume, then naturally the price increases rapidly.

THE GREAT PERFUMES OF GRASSE

The great 'noses' of Grasse are famous for creating legendary perfumes. In the early twenties, Ernest Baux produced the classic Chanel No. 5. His discovery was that the addition of alde-hydes increased the power of the Grasse jasmine. Later, Jean Carles mixed the Bulgarian attar of roses with the same jasmine to make Joy by Jean Patou. In the mid-1960s, Edmond Roudnitska, a brilliant 'nose', created Eau Sauvage and Diorella for Christian Dior. This great master of perfumery confessed that he had been thinking about this perfume for at least two years before creating it.

A question of 'nose'

The creation of a perfume is the work of a 'nose', or a master of fragrances, who is the key staff member of every perfumery. Surrounded by computers and chemical formulae, he is able to recognise thousands of different smells. He mixes scents all year round and produces subtle mixtures which take into account both his own creative impulse and current trends. A 'nose' is born, not made and produces a maximum of three to four perfumes a year.

Millions of petals

The perfume of delicate flowers, such as jasmine and hyacinth, is extracted by arranging the petals on a thick layer of pork or beef fat which slowly absorbs the scent until it reaches saturation point. The result is then washed with alcohol to provide the raw material of the perfume. 1,540 lb (700 kg) of flowers (about 5 million petals) are needed to obtain 2.2 lb (1 kg) of 'absolute' concentrate.

Sporting holidays

Gliding, diving, tennis, climbing, parascending, sailboarding, golf, skiing or potholing – it's up to you! All the information you need is on the following pages. For information about hiking, rambling and pony-trekking, see pp. 92-93.

Water sports

1. **Vallée de l'Argens:** fishing at the Lac de Carcès. **p. 232.**
2. **Barcelonnette:** rafting and swimming. **p. 305.**
3. **Cagnes-sur-Mer:** windsurfing, water-skiing and bare-foot water-skiing. **p. 259.**
4. **Estérel:** Scuba-diving courses. **p. 227.**
5. **Giens:** fishing and windsurfing at the Tombolo. **pp. 206-207.**
6. **Gorges du Loup:** canyoning in the Cascades. **pp. 267-268.**
7. **Gorges du Verdon:** canyoning. **p. 301.**
8. **Grimaud:** windsurfing and pedalo. **p. 221.**
9. **L'Isle-sur-la-Sorgue:** canoeing and fishing along the River Sorgue. **p. 167.**
10. **Istres:** Canoeing on the Étang de Berre. **p. 151.**
11. **La Ciotat:** diving off Saint-Cyr-sur-Mer. **p. 199.**
12. **Marseille:** diving, sailing and mountain-biking. **p. 88 and p. 193.**
13. **Monaco:** diving at the foot of the Rock. **p. 285.**
14. **Monte-Carlo:** water-skiing and jet-skiing. **p. 287.**
15. **Moustiers-Sainte-Marie:** canoeing on the River Verdon or on the Lac Sainte-Croix. **p. 235.**
16. **Port-Cros:** diving at the Iles d'Or. **p. 212.**
17. **Roquebrune:** windsurfing. **p. 289.**
18. **Vallée de la Roya:** rafting and kayaking. **pp. 296-297.**
19. **Saint-Jean-Cap-Ferrat:** sailing and windsurfing. **pp. 276-277.**
20. **Sainte-Maxime:** fishing. **pp. 218-219.**
21. **Saintes-Maries-de-la-Mer:** canoeing on the Petit Rhône. **pp. 132-133.**

Mountain sports

22. **Vallée de l'Argens:** potholing in the Vallon Sourn. **p. 232.**
23. **Baux-de-Provence:** climbing in the Alpilles. **p. 137.**
24. **Cassis:** climbing in the Calanques. **p. 86.**
25. **Cavaillon:** climbing the hill of Saint-Jacques. **p. 164.**
26. **Vallée du Loup:** skiing at Gréolières-les-Neiges. **p. 86.**

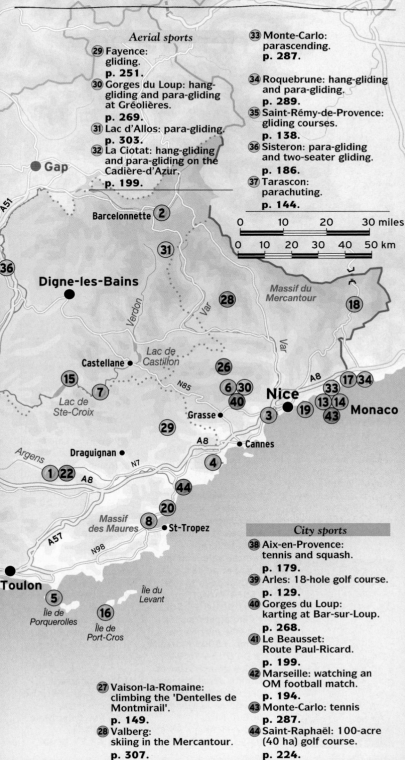

Aerial sports

29 Fayence:
gliding.
p. 251.

30 Gorges du Loup: hang-
gliding and para-gliding
at Gréolières.
p. 269.

31 Lac d'Allos: para-gliding.
p. 303.

32 La Ciotat: hang-gliding
and para-gliding on the
Cadière-d'Azur.
p. 199.

33 Monte-Carlo:
parascending.
p. 287.

34 Roquebrune: hang-gliding
and para-gliding.
p. 289.

35 Saint-Rémy-de-Provence:
gliding courses.
p. 138.

36 Sisteron: para-gliding
and two-seater gliding.
p. 186.

37 Tarascon:
parachuting.
p. 144.

0   10   20   30 miles

0   10   20   30   40   50 km

27 Vaison-la-Romaine:
climbing the 'Dentelles de
Montmirail'.
p. 149.

28 Valberg:
skiing in the Mercantour.
p. 307.

City sports

38 Aix-en-Provence:
tennis and squash.
p. 179.

39 Arles: 18-hole golf course.
p. 129.

40 Gorges du Loup:
karting at Bar-sur-Loup.
p. 268.

41 Le Beausset:
Route Paul-Ricard.
p. 199.

42 Marseille: watching an
OM football match.
p. 194.

43 Monte-Carlo: tennis
p. 287.

44 Saint-Raphaël: 100-acre
(40 ha) golf course.
p. 224.

Gap

Barcelonnette

Digne-les-Bains

Verdon

Var

Massif du
Mercantour

Castellane

Lac de
Castillon

N85

Nice

Monaco

Grasse

A8

Cannes

Lac de
Ste-Croix

Draguignan

N7

Argens

A8

Massif
des Maures

St-Tropez

A57

N98

Toulon

Île du
Levant

Île de
Porquerolles

Île de
Port-Cros

Where to go for sports

(Also see the index under 'sports').

Alpine skiing

The resorts of the Southern Alps are renowned for their heavy covering of snow (in some years the slopes are open from the end of November) and for the mildness of the climate. Of course, there are always some sunny days...

SKI SCHOOLS
• Isola 2000, Office de Tourisme,
☎ 04 93 23 15 15.
École du ski français,
☎ 04 93 23 28 00.
• Auron, Office de Tourisme,
☎ 04 93 23 02 66.
École du ski français,
☎ 04 93 23 02 53.
• Valberg (three sites): Valberg, the Launes and Beuil), Office de Tourisme,
☎ 04 93 23 24 25.
École du ski français,
☎ 04 93 02 51 20.

Potholing

Thanks to the large network of caves and potholes, especially on the Plateau d'Albion, the Midi is a great place for cave exploration. The deepest gorges are not accessible to potholers but there are numerous 'initiation' caves to build up your confidence.

USEFUL ADDRESSES
• Fédération française de spéléologie,
130, Rue Saint-Maur, 75011 Paris,
☎ 01 43 57 56 54.

Mountain sports
Rock-climbing

The region possesses natural sites of great beauty for rock-climbing. The rock is mainly limestone. Two sites are particularly attractive: the Baou de Saint-Jeannet for different routes to the summit, and La Loubière where climbers can tackle very

difficult limestone cliff faces overlooking the sea, above Cap Ferrat (p. 276). Climbing in the Calanques is an unforgettable experience (information in Marseille p. 195).

MOUNTAINEERING AND ROCK-CLIMBING ASSOCIATIONS
• Centre d'informations de la Fédération française de la montagne et de l'escalade, 8, Quai de la Marne, 75019 Paris,
☎ 01 40 18 75 50.
• Club alpin français, 12, Rue Fort-Notre-Dame, 13005 Marseille
☎ 04 91 54 36 94.
• Club grimpe Azur et Comité départemental des Alpes Maritimes, 45, Bd de la Madeleine, 06600 Nice,
☎ 04 93 96 17 43 and 04 93 96 14 33.

• Adventure centre on the Ubaye, the river with 30 rapids, at Barcelonnette.
Eau vive évasion rafting, Pl. Reuilly,
04240 Annot,
☎ 04 92 83 38 04.
• Guillaumes Centre in the southern Alps (Var, Verdon, Ubaye, gorges de Daluis),
Association montagne et rivière,
19, Rue du Mitan,
04120 Castellane,
☎ 04 92 83 73 57,
fax: 04 92 83 677 24.

Angling

There is an enormous choice of

• Accueil spéléologique du plateau d'Albion,
Rue de l'Église, 84390 Saint-Christole-d'Albion,
☎ 04 90 75 08 33.

Water sports

Rafting, canoeing and kayaking

Provence is the ideal place for these sports, since the scenery is so magnificent – for example the Verdon Gorges (p. 234) – and there is plenty of white water. Many clubs offer rafting, canyoning, canoeing, kayaking and white water swimming (about 200 F for a 1½ hour session).

USEFUL ADDRESSES FOR WATER SPORTS:
• Fédération française de canoë-kayak,
57, Quai de la Marne,
94333340 Joinville-le-Pont,
☎ 01 45 11 08 50.
• Maison du canoë-kayak et du rafting river,
Le Four à chaux,
04340 Méolans,
☎ 04 92 85 53 99.

excellent freshwater sites, such as reservoirs, mountain lakes and major and minor rivers. The catch is mainly trout, pike and arctic char. It is important to contact the French angling associations to get a list of permitted fishing spots and learn the rules, which are strictly enforced all over France. The mountain lakes of Sainte-Croix (p. 235), Serre-Ponçon, and the River Sorgue (p. 166) are exceptional fishing sites for the quality of the water and the wildlife.

ADDRESSES OF ANGLING ASSOCIATIONS IN VARIOUS PARTS OF PROVENCE
• Alpes-de-Haute-Provence:
Av. du Levant,
04000 Digne-les-Bains,
☎ 04 92 32 25 40,.
• Alpes-Maritimes:
34, Av. Saint-Augustin,
06200 Nice,
☎ 04 93 72 06 01.
• Var:
B.P. 104,
83170 Brignoles Cedex,
☎ 04 94 69 05 56.
• Vaucluse:
5, Bd Chamfleury,
84000 Avignon,
☎ 04 90 86 62 68.
• Bouches-du-Rhône:
Rue Mahatma Gandhi,
13084 Aix-en-Provence,
☎ 04 42 26 59 15.

THREE TYPES OF FISHING

For heavy catches, an immense net 1¼ miles by ⅛ mile (2 km by 0.2 km) called a turning seine is used. One end is attached to a stationary boat, the other to a small trawler which moves in a large circle and imprisons the shoals of tuna and *liche*, a relative of the pilot fish. The trawler line is reserved for conger, bronze bream, sea bream and bass. It consists of a series of hooks attached every 17 ft (5 m) to a main line, either on the surface or on the sea bed. Sardine and anchovy fishing by lamplight is practised from February to April. A net is thrown into a patch of vegetation on the sea bed and pulled up by hand. At sites where this technique is not permitted, rod-and-line fishing is practised at night using a light source to attract the prey.

Diving

There are more than forty sites for diving along the coast where red coral, unique to the Mediterranean, can be admired. There are also excellent chances of being able to watch schools of dolphins.

USEFUL ADDRESS
• Fédération française d'études et de sports sous-marins,
24, Quai de Rive-Neuve,
13284 Marseille
Cedex 7,
☎ 04 91 33 99 31.

Water-skiing

There are about thirty clubs serving the entire region. Most are situated by the sea but you can also water-ski on certain lakes.

USEFUL ADDRESSES OF WATER-SKIING ASSOCIATIONS
• Ligue Méditerranée-Côte d'Azur,
22, Rue du 11-Novembre,
06400 Cannes,
☎ 04 93 38 64 85.
• Ligue Alpes-Provence,
38, Route des Trois-Frères,
13220 La Mede,
☎ 04 42 40 33 02.

Aerial sports
Parachuting

If you want to experience a real thrill high above Provence, try the big jump. It will cost you 850 F for an initiation jump, 2,600 F for individual training and 1,000 F for a tandem jump (with the instructor), which includes 40 seconds of skydiving.

USEFUL ADDRESSES
• **Ligue de parachutisme sportif,**
122, Corniche des Oliviers,
06000 Nice,
☎ **04 92 09 88 07.**
• **Ligue de Provence de parachutisme,**
84, Chemin de Morgiou,
13009 Marseille,
☎ **04 91 40 46 60.**

Para-gliding, hang-gliding, skydiving

These sports are becoming ever more popular and fashionable. The prices for an initiation flight are reasonable (between 300 F and 500 F for a two-seater flight). If you want to practice the cost is higher. The set price for one week is between 2,500 F and 3,500 F. The sites of Roquebrune, Gourdon and Colmiane are particularly lovely from a bird's eye view.

USEFUL ADDRESSES
• **Fédération française de vol libre,**
4, Rue de Suisse,
06000 Nice,
☎ **04 93 88 62 89.**

• **Ligue de vol libre du Sud-Est,**
20, Av. du Loup,
06270 Villeneuve-Loubet,
☎ **04 93 73 16 99.**

City sports
Tennis

There are many places in the area to play tennis, as Provence has more than 336 clubs. In summer, however, due to high demand, court reservations well in advance are highly recommended if you want to play at a particular time of the day. Due to the summer heat, early morning and early evening sessions are quickly booked up.

USEFUL ADDRESSES
• **Ligue de Tennis de Provence,**
Château Creissauds,
Clos Rufisque,
13400 Aubagne,
☎ **04 91 35 82 45.**
• **Ligue de tennis de la Côte d'Azur,**
66, Rte de Grenoble,
06200 Nice,
☎ **04 93 18 00 95.**

Golf

There are about twenty golf clubs in the region. The weekday green fee for an 18-hole course is between 200 F and 300 F and more at weekends (between 250 F and 350 F).
A list of clubs is available at the regional Ligue de Golf.

• **Ligue de golf Provence-Alpes-Côte d'Azur,**
Domaine Riquetti,
13290 Les Miles,
☎ **04 42 39 86 83.**

Karting

• **Karting Dellaroli (70 F for 10 mins.),**
Zone industrielle (by the roadside),
04400 Barcelonnette,
☎ **04 92 81 90 44.**
• **Karting Location (50 F for 5 mins.),**
Rte de Gourdon,
06620 Le Bar-sur-Loup,
☎ **04 93 42 48 08.**

HIKING

See the index under 'hiking' and 'footpaths' and the map on pages 92-93. For further information, apply to: Centre d'informations de la Fédération française de randonnées pédestres, 14, Rue Riquet, 75019 Paris, ☎ 01 44 89 93 93. For horse-riding, pony-trekking, biking, boat rides and trips out to sea, see pp. 101-102.

Pétanque
a national sport

O n fine days, everyone in Provence gathers on the *terrain de pétanque* and, for the first weekend of July, the Borély Park of Marseille becomes the Wimbledon of pétanque or *boules*. Hardly surprising then, that France has the record for being the most successful *boules*-playing country in the world. You too can become a real expert, or at least discover why the people of Provence are so enthusiastic about pétanque.

Short history of the game of 'boules'

Boules has been played since Antiquity. The Greeks played with coins whilst the Romans used pebbles. In the 19th C., Provence updated the game and renamed it 'Provençale' or 'Longue'. The bowls used at that time were made of boxwood toughened with nails.

Longue or pétanque?

Do not dare to confuse these two games, or you face a strong risk of being written off as a foreigner! Longue is played on a surface at least 83 ft (25 m) long and the jack (or *bouchon*) is placed at a distance of between 50 and 70 ft (15 to 21 m) from the players. The players rolling the bowls are not allowed to take more than one step to bowl, but those who throw it are allowed three small jumps out of the playing circle. In 1910 at La Ciotat, Jules le Noir, a famous player of Longue, was unable to take the traditional three steps because he suffered from rheumatism. He decided, therefore, to throw his

bowls from a stationary position, his 'pieds tanqués' (i.e. his feet were together and flat on the ground). This expression gave the word *pétanque* to the new game he had just invented.

Rules of the game

Pétanque is a game of two players or two teams. Each player plays three times and the bowls have to get as close to the *bouchon* as possible. They are thrown at a distance of between 20 and 33 ft (6 and 10 m). A game consists of 13 points and everything is

Choosing your technique

Players rolling the bowl should use a middle-sized, slightly heavy bowl, with a diameter of 2.8 to 2.9 in (72 to 73 mm), and weighing between 25 and 26 oz (710 to 740 g)) with one or more grooves. Players throwing the bowl will prefer a smooth bowl with a larger diameter, 3 to 3.1 in (76 to 78 mm)) and weighing 24 to 25 oz (680 to 710 g). It is worth knowing that stainless steel bowls are more easily thrown because the metal is more polished; on the other hand, carbon bowls become dulled when used, which makes them easier to grasp.

LA BOULE BLEUE
Montée de Saint-Menet, Z. I. La Valentine, Marseille (XIe arr.),
☎ **04 91 43 27 20.**
Open 7.30am - 4.30pm, except weekends.
Founded in 1904, this is the last remaining crafted bowls company in the region. Each set of bowls can be personalised with your name, favourite number, and so on, and made to measure (weight, diameter, number of grooves). You will be given advice on the best material for your bowls and whether they need anti-bounce treatment. A set of three competition-quality bowls comes with a 5-year guarantee, and costs 290-950 F. The jacks cost 10 F for 4, the *bisou boule* 40 F, and the measuring stick 120 F for the iron version, 60 F in plastic. Made-to-measure bowls should be ready for collection in five days.

a question of curves. Swing your arm in a controlled way, holding the bowl in the hollow of your hand, the fingers loosely closed. Depending on the type of throw chosen, you will have to stand, kneel or flex your knees and crouch. Pétanque requires keen observation and careful tactics. You have to study the ground and the positions of the other bowls, choose the angle, and decide whether to throw or roll the bowl.

A true sport

Far from just being a pastime, *boules* is a world-class sport; 43 countries are members of the International Federation. There are 460,000 licensed players in France. Yet even though the Pétanque Federation is the fourth largest sports association in France (after football, tennis and skiing), pétanque is still not recognised as an Olympic sport. Of course, it could change at future Olympics, you never know…

Hikes, walks and rambles

The region offers all sorts of walking possibilities – family walks, all-day rambles, hikes lasting several days. Here is a good selection.

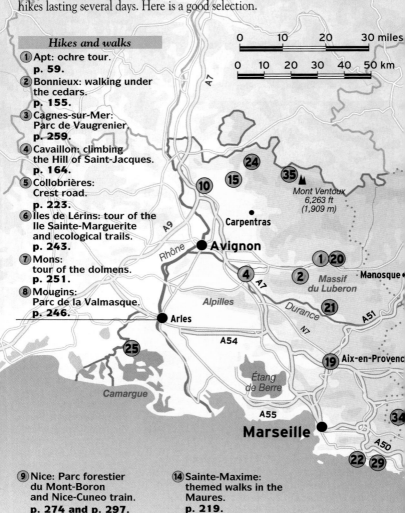

Hikes and walks

① Apt: ochre tour.
p. 59.

② Bonnieux: walking under the cedars.
p. 155.

③ Cagnes-sur-Mer: Parc de Vaugrenier.
p. 259.

④ Cavaillon: climbing the Hill of Saint-Jacques.
p. 164.

⑤ Collobrières: Crest road.
p. 223.

⑥ Îles de Lérins: tour of the Île Sainte-Marguerite and ecological trails.
p. 243.

⑦ Mons: tour of the dolmens.
p. 251.

⑧ Mougins: Parc de la Valmasque.
p. 246.

⑨ Nice: Parc forestier du Mont-Boron and Nice-Cuneo train.
p. 274 and p. 297.

⑩ Orange: botanical path du Mont-Serein.
p. 147.

⑪ Porquerolles: paths in the *maquis*.
p. 211.

⑫ Port-Cros: protected National Park.
p. 213.

⑬ Saint-Paul-de-Vence: along the canal road.
p. 261.

⑭ Sainte-Maxime: themed walks in the Maures.
p. 219.

⑮ Vacqueyras: botanical area of the Coste de Coa.
p. 149.

⑯ Vallée de la Roya: Nice-Cuneo train.
p. 297.

⑰ Vallée du Var: mountain train in the Pignes.
p. 302.

⑱ Vence: Col de Vence and botanical tour.
p. 263.

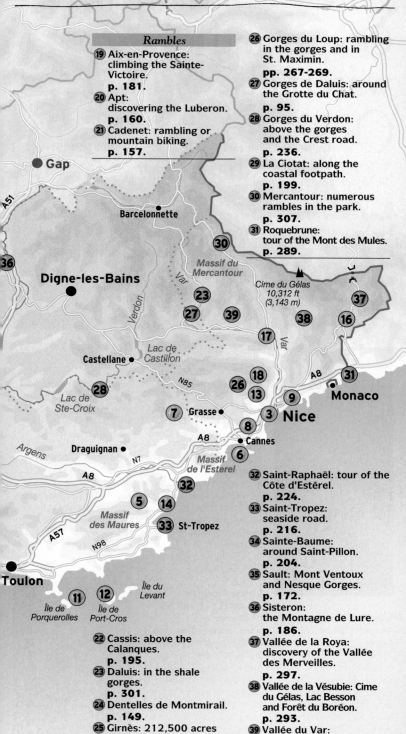

Rambles

19 Aix-en-Provence: climbing the Sainte-Victoire.
p. 181.

20 Apt: discovering the Luberon.
p. 160.

21 Cadenet: rambling or mountain biking.
p. 157.

26 Gorges du Loup: rambling in the gorges and in St. Maximin.
pp. 267-269.

27 Gorges de Daluis: around the Grotte du Chat.
p. 95.

28 Gorges du Verdon: above the gorges and the Crest road.
p. 236.

29 La Ciotat: along the coastal footpath.
p. 199.

30 Mercantour: numerous rambles in the park.
p. 307.

31 Roquebrune: tour of the Mont des Mules.
p. 289.

32 Saint-Raphaël: tour of the Côte d'Estérel.
p. 224.

33 Saint-Tropez: seaside road.
p. 216.

34 Sainte-Baume: around Saint-Pillon.
p. 204.

35 Sault: Mont Ventoux and Nesque Gorges.
p. 172.

36 Sisteron: the Montagne de Lure.
p. 186.

37 Vallée de la Roya: discovery of the Vallée des Merveilles.
p. 297.

38 Vallée de la Vésubie: Cime du Gélas, Lac Besson and Forêt du Boréon.
p. 293.

39 Vallée du Var: Gorges de Cians.
p. 302.

22 Cassis: above the Calanques.
p. 195.

23 Daluis: in the shale gorges.
p. 301.

24 Dentelles de Montmirail.
p. 149.

25 Girnès: 212,500 acres (86,000 ha) in Camargue.
p. 130.

Gorges and waterfalls

Over millennia, the raging torrents of the Alps have cut into the soft rock of Provence in their rush towards the Mediterranean Sea, where all the rivers end. Southern Provence is criss-crossed by these wild waters which can still be dangerous at times. They have carved out deep clefts and furrows, which are beautiful scenic spots for walks and a variety of sports.

Along its 106 miles (170 km) the River Verdon is cluttered with fallen rocks and rock piles, making navigation dangerous.

a height of between 833 and 2,500 ft (250 and 750 m). Europe's answer to the Grand Canyon is surrounded by two large lakes (Castillon and Sainte-Croix, p. 234) whose calm surfaces are suitable for every kind of water sport. Explore the gorges by following the river, taking a circular tour on both banks. Stop at the pretty villages of Rougon, La Palus, Moustiers-Sainte-Marie and Aiguines.

Loup Gorges
7½ miles (12 km) NE of Grasse

These are the shortest gorges and the nearest to the coast (p. 267). Over a distance of less than 6¼ miles (10 km), the River Loup split open the enormous limestone cliff that barred its way to the Mediterranean Sea. It also took a few spectacular short cuts. The Courmes waterfall, half-way

along, creates a 133 ft (40 m) drop. A winding road overlooks these incredible gorges, which lie midway between the pistes of the ski-resort of Gréolières-les-Neiges, 4,666 ft (1,400 m) and the beach of Cagnes-sur-Mer.

Vésubie Gorges
15 miles (24 km) N of Nice

22 miles (35 km) from the sea, the River Vésubie cut through the limestone rock which separated it from the River Var (p. 294). Take the twisting

Verdon Gorges
44 miles (70 km) S of Digne

These gorges are unique because of their length and unbelievable beauty. They extend for more than 12½ miles (20 km) and their waters are a brilliant blue-green. They flow in a deep cleft in the rock which rises to

Nesque digs deep into the limestone, following a tortuous route beside the Plateau du Vaucluse and disappears under-ground for more than 1,333 ft (400 m) (p. 173). This deep canyon shows signs of ancient human life, traces of occupation have been dis-covered in the caves dating from the Paleo-lithic to the Middle Ages. The Corniche road, which follows the course of the river, is a scenic route in most places but it is roofed over with tunnels in parts.

NARTUBY WATERFALL
(CASCADE DE LA NARTUBY)

road which winds above the deep gorges and admire the colours (from brilliant white to grey streaked with infinite shades of green). Sumach trees, the sap of which was used by the Romans to dye fabrics a brownish-green, still cling to the sides of the gorges.

The Red Gorges
44 m (70 km) NW of Nice by N 202
On the map, the Red Gorges are called the Daluis Gorges (p. 301). The upper valley of the River Var cuts through the red schist of the cliff, opening a brightly coloured path, which is a striking contrast to the green vegetation and the blue of the sky.

The 3 mile (5 km) winding road, attached to the rock face like a corniche or a balcony, overlooks this brilliantly coloured canyon. Where the gorges start there is a feudal castle, and, at the end, the Grotte du Chat, the largest cave in the Alpes-Maritimes region. The *gorges supérieures* du Cians, which are not far to the east, are even narrower and redder (p. 302).

Nesque Gorges
12½ miles (20 km) E of Carpentras
According to the scientists, these gorges at the foot of Mont Ventoux are 'one of the beautiful hydro-geological spaces in the Midi'. The river

Just 2½ miles (4 km) outside Draguignan (see also page 229), the River Nartuby starts off with a series of pretty waterfalls, large and small, until it reaches Trans-en-Provence. It continues for 3¾ miles (6 km), and suddenly takes a huge drop of 117 ft (35 m) at Saut-de-Capelan, near La Motte. It is said that this spectacular beauty spot was named after a local priest who was pushed off the cliff by the Revolutionaries and miraculously found himself alive at the bottom.

Countryside and nature

Provence has a delightful countryside with richly diverse vegetation. Apart from the familiar plants such as lavender, olive trees, wild herbs, mimosa and violets, the region possesses many other natural treasures. Here is some information about typical trees and shrubs you might see during your walks.

the most beautiful woods used in furniture-making, while the delicious nuts are always popular.

Pine trees

There are three main varieties of pine in Provence. The maritime pine has a dark foliage with blue reflections and a beautiful purplish-red bark. The umbrella pine grows in isolation and can be easily spotted by its unique shape. The Aleppo pine grows on chalky soil. It has a gnarled trunk, grey bark and is often found growing beside an evergreen oak.

The *garrigue*

Originally the *garrigue* was the name for the sun-scorched limestone hills at the foot of the Cévennes, criss-crossed dry river beds and mountain streams and dominated by evergreen oaks and fragrant herbs. By extension, it is now used to refer to any arid scrubland with a limestone subsoil, covered with rosemary, thyme and juniper. *Garrigues* are found all over Provence at an altitude of 670 ft (200 m). The Kermes oak, a dwarf tree with spiny leaves is typical and can grow on poor soil.

The walnut tree

The rich, dark wood of the walnut has been the delight of furniture-makers for centuries. The walnut tree is accorded mysterious powers in Provence. It cannot grow in a forest because its deep roots contain a toxic substance (juglone) which destroys the surrounding species. The foliage is also impregnated with this substance, and anyone taking a nap under a walnut tree risks waking up with a terrible headache. Walnut wood is still one of

Larch

A delicious wild mushroom

The blood-red milk-cap (*Lactarius sanguiflluu*) grows in the coniferous woods of Provence in spring and autumn. This milk-cap with red milk is highly recommended in Provençal cuisine and can be used in numerous recipes. It is either grilled, deep-fried in batter, dried or preserved in a mixture of olive oil, vinegar and aromatic herbs.

Wild strawberry bush

The Austrian black pine and the hook pine grow in the Montagnes de Lure. The black pine has a very straight trunk, a dark brown bark and can grow to 117 ft (35 m). The hook pine is a mountain tree with dark foliage which takes its name from the curved hooks on its cones.

Scots pine

Cypress

The almond tree

The almond originated in Asia, and was first brought to France in the 16th C. It belongs to the *Rosaceae* family and is in its element in the Mediterranean region. The tree looks something like a peach tree; the skin around the nut is light-green as well as downy. It flowers very early in the year, producing magnificent white blossom in January and February.

The evergreen oak

This tree is also called the holm-oak and does not shed its leaves in winter. It is very common in Provence, with low branches as spiky as holly. It can grow to 67 ft (20 m) tall and is very resistant to the dryness of the Mediterranean soil.

White oak

FORESTS: AN ASSET IN NEED OF PROTECTION

Provence has 4,299,540 acres (1,740,000 ha) of trees, and no less than 227,678 acres (92,140 ha) have been destroyed by forest fires over the past ten years. In 1989 and 1990 alone, 175,441 acres (71,000 ha) were destroyed. More than 200,000 trees were replanted, but long-term vigilance will be essential to prevent the soil remaining barren. In order to respect this fragile, dry environment, so much at risk from the *mistral* wind, here is a code of conduct. Do not light fires, barbecue or camp stoves in the wild; avoid smoking or you will not smell the delicious fragrances of the *garrigue*; if you must smoke, do not throw cigarette butts out of the car window; always keep the forest clean (a piece of broken bottle could start a fire through the sun's reflection); do not pick the wild flowers; obey the rules which permit or forbid access to particular areas. You will be helping in the fight to maintain the forests.

Cork oak

Beaches and islands

Whether they are sandy or pebbly, wild or protected, private or crowded, the beaches of the Côte d'Azur have made the region what it is today. As for its islands, they still have many surprises in store for those who want to explore them

- Beaches
- Islands

Mont Ventoux
6,263 ft
(1,909 m)

Carpentras

Avignon

Nîmes

Rhône

Massif du Luberon

Manosque

Alpilles

Durance

Arles

A54

N7

Aix-en-Provenc

Camargue

Étang de Berre

A55

Marseille ③

④

⑤

Camargue
① Piémançon beaches.
 p. 130.

Martigues
② Côte Bleue.
 p. 153.

Marseille
③ Îles d'If, Pomègues and Ratonneau.
 p. 192.
④ Prado beach.
 p. 191.

Bandol
⑤ Îles de Bendor and des Embiez.
 p. 201.

Giens Peninsula
⑥ Tombolo beaches.
 p. 206.
⑦ Porquerolles beaches.
 p. 211.
⑧ Îles d'Or beaches.
 p. 213.

Le Lavandou
⑨ Saint-Clair beach.
 p. 214.

Les Pradels
⑩ Cavalière beach
 p. 223.

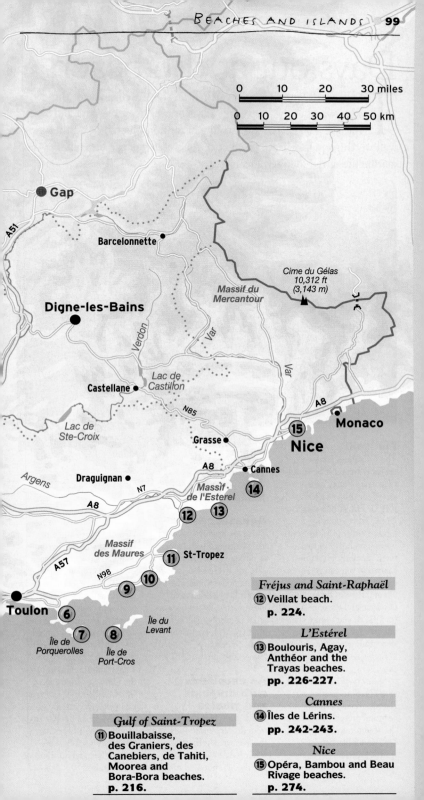

Cime du Gélas
10,312 ft
(3,143 m)

Massif du
Mercantour

Gap

Barcelonnette

Digne-les-Bains

A51

Verdon

Var

Var

Castellane

Lac de
Castillon

N85

Lac de
Ste-Croix

A8

Grasse

⑮ **Nice**

Monaco

Argens

Draguignan

N7

A8

● **Cannes**

⑭

Massif
de l'Esterel

⑫ ⑬

A8

**Massif
des Maures**

A57

⑪ **St-Tropez**

N98

⑩

⑨

Île du
Levant

Toulon

⑥

⑦

⑧

Île de
Porquerolles

Île de
Port-Cros

Fréjus and Saint-Raphaël
⑫ **Veillat beach.
p. 224.**

L'Estérel
⑬ **Boulouris, Agay,
Anthéor and the
Trayas beaches.
pp. 226-227.**

Cannes
⑭ **Îles de Lérins.
pp. 242-243.**

Nice
⑮ **Opéra, Bambou and Beau
Rivage beaches.
p. 274.**

Gulf of Saint-Tropez
⑪ **Bouillabaisse,
des Graniers, des
Canebiers, de Tahiti,
Moorea and
Bora-Bora beaches.
p. 216.**

Days out at the beach

The Côte d'Azur offers many delightful short excursions for those who, whether they are good sailors or not, like adventure and love the sea. The islands are usually not far from the coast and they are well worth seeing. Beneath the blue of the water, you can also observe the marine life of the Mediterranean.

Full sail!

The Calanques ramble is probably the most beautiful (departure from Cassis, p. 197, or from Marseille, p.195). The sailing-ship *Hoëdic* leaves from Le Lavandou (p. 215), welcoming you on board in true maritime tradition. From Marseille, you can go and explore the famous Château d'If and the Îles du Frioul, Pomègue and Ratonneau (p. 192). If you want to find out about the Man in the Iron Mask, go to the Îles de Lérin (p. 242). There are also excursions to San Remo or to Saint-Tropez from Nice (p. 272). Porquerolles, off Hyères, is one of the most beautiful protected islands in the Mediterranean (p. 210). Off Bandol lies Bendor (p. 201), perhaps the most civilized island in Provence.

Aquascopes

These are brightly-coloured glass-bottomed boats which, in optimum conditions, enable you to see what is happening under water. The trip usually lasts half an hour; the most interesting sea beds are at Le Lavandou (p. 215), Nice (p. 272), Port-Cros (p. 212), Agay (p. 226) and Sainte-Maxime (p. 218).

An encounter with dolphins and whales

The Ligures basin extends from Provence into Italy and the average depth of its water is 8,333 ft (2,500 m). Nearly one thousand rorquals – whales that are between 26 and 30 ft (8 and 9 m) long, and weigh between 6 and 8 tons – can be seen there. In April and May, they are found between Corsica and the Provençal coast. Sperm-whales and dolphins remain in this area all year round. You can set off from Toulon and watch them on a trip lasting 3 to 7 days (information from the Office de Tourisme, ☎ 04 94 18 53 00, or from Europe Conservation, ☎ 02 54 58 22 22. But be careful, these interesting excursions on a boat are quite tiring, and not relaxing ocean cruises!

Pony trekking and cycling

This is the best way to discover the Camargue and the Rhône delta. Whether you ride on your own or take an accompanied trip lasting several days, pony trekking will give you the chance to experience the pleasures of the countryside at leisure. Expect to see some magnificent scenery.

Nice (p. 274), in the Grand Luberon (p. 157) and on the Valensole plateau (p. 183).

The Camargue horse

The Camargue horse is said to be descended from those that live on the steppes of Central Asia. This freedom-loving, swift but easy-to-handle horse is unlike any other. They have grey coats, square heads, short necks and thick manes. This horse is the herdsman's closest friend, helping to guard cattle in marshes that cannot be accessed by road. It is particularly well-adapted to swamps, extremes of temperature and, best of all, appears to be impervious to mosquito bites.

In the saddle

You will find addresses of livery stables at the Office de Tourisme (p. 131). Florian Colomb had the brilliant idea of offering riding excursions from his Hostellerie de Cacharel, in Saintes-Maries-de-la-Mer (☎ 04 90 97 95 44). This typical Provençal farmhouse (*mas*) is situated deep in the country, surrounded by 150 acres (70 ha) of glorious countryside. The owner accompanies groups of 5 or 6 people, and shares his passion for the Camargue with his visitors. You can also go horse riding in Mougins (p. 247),

How about a bike ride?

If horse riding is not your thing, bicycles never go out of fashion and you can take delightful rides through the flatter parts of Provence. This mode of transport will enable you to discover secret places which are inaccessible by car. You can hire bicycles in Porquerolles (p. 211), Giens (p. 206), Pernes-les-Fontaines (p. 169), Grasse (p. 249), in Camargue (p. 131), in Lauris (p. 157) and even in Marseille where they ride hydrocycles (p. 193).

Leisure parks, aquariums and zoos

Watch the birds, sail down a flume, discover underwater fauna or even visit a llama rearing farm. There is certainly plenty of choice.

Aquariums

1 **Antibes: Marineland.**
   p. 253.
2 **Fréjus: Aquatica.**
   p. 225.
3 **Île des Embiez: Fondation océanographique.**
   p. 201.
4 **Monaco: Musée océanographique.**
   p. 282.
5 **Sainte-Maxime: Aquascope.**
   p. 218.
6 **Toulon: Aqualand.**
   p. 203.

Leisure parks

7 **Brignoles: Mini-France.**
   p. 233.
8 **Cuges-les-Pins: OK Corral.**
   p. 205.
9 **Châteauneuf-les-Martigues: El Dorado City.**
   p. 195.

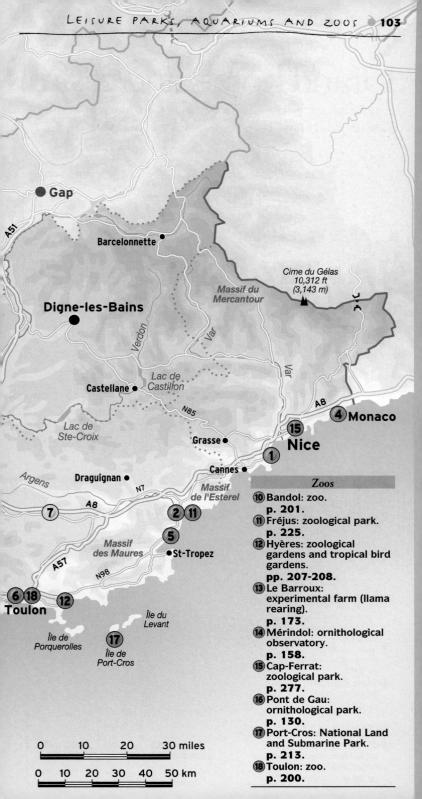

Gap

Barcelonnette

Cime du Gélas
10,312 ft
(3,143 m)

Massif du
Mercantour

Digne-les-Bains

Verdon

Var

Lac de
Castillon

Castellane

Var

N85

A8

Lac de
Ste-Croix

Grasse

④ Monaco

⑮

Argens

Draguignan

N7

Massif
de l'Esterel

Cannes

① Nice

A8

⑦

② ⑪

⑤

Massif
des Maures

St-Tropez

A57

N98

⑥ ⑱

Toulon

⑫

Île du
Levant

Île de
Porquerolles

⑰

Île de
Port-Cros

Zoos

⑩ Bandol: zoo.
p. 201.

⑪ Fréjus: zoological park.
p. 225.

⑫ Hyères: zoological gardens and tropical bird gardens.
pp. 207-208.

⑬ Le Barroux: experimental farm (llama rearing).
p. 173.

⑭ Mérindol: ornithological observatory.
p. 158.

⑮ Cap-Ferrat: zoological park.
p. 277.

⑯ Pont de Gau: ornithological park.
p. 130.

⑰ Port-Cros: National Land and Submarine Park.
p. 213.

⑱ Toulon: zoo.
p. 200.

| 0 | 10 | 20 | 30 miles |

| 0 | 10 | 20 | 30 | 40 | 50 km |

Grand hotels and casinos

From the baccarat tables to luxurious swimming pools, from horse races to grand hotels, the Côte d'Azur is also the kingdom of millionaires.

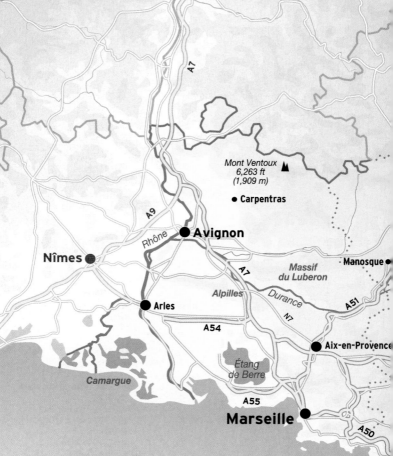

Mont Ventoux
6,263 ft
(1,909 m)

● **Carpentras**

● **Avignon**

Rhône

Nîmes ●

A9

A7

Massif du Luberon

Manosque ●

Alpilles

Durance

A51

● **Arles**

N7

A54

● **Aix-en-Provence**

Étang de Berre

Camargue

A55

● **Marseille**

A50

Casinos

① **Cannes: the Carlton, ultimate luxury.**
p. 241.
② **Monte-Carlo: the largest casino.**
p. 287.
③ **Saint-Raphaël: an institution.**
p. 225.

Races

④ **Cagnes-sur-Mer: night-time horse-racing and entertainment.**
p. 259.

0   10   20   30 miles

0 10 20 30 40 50 km

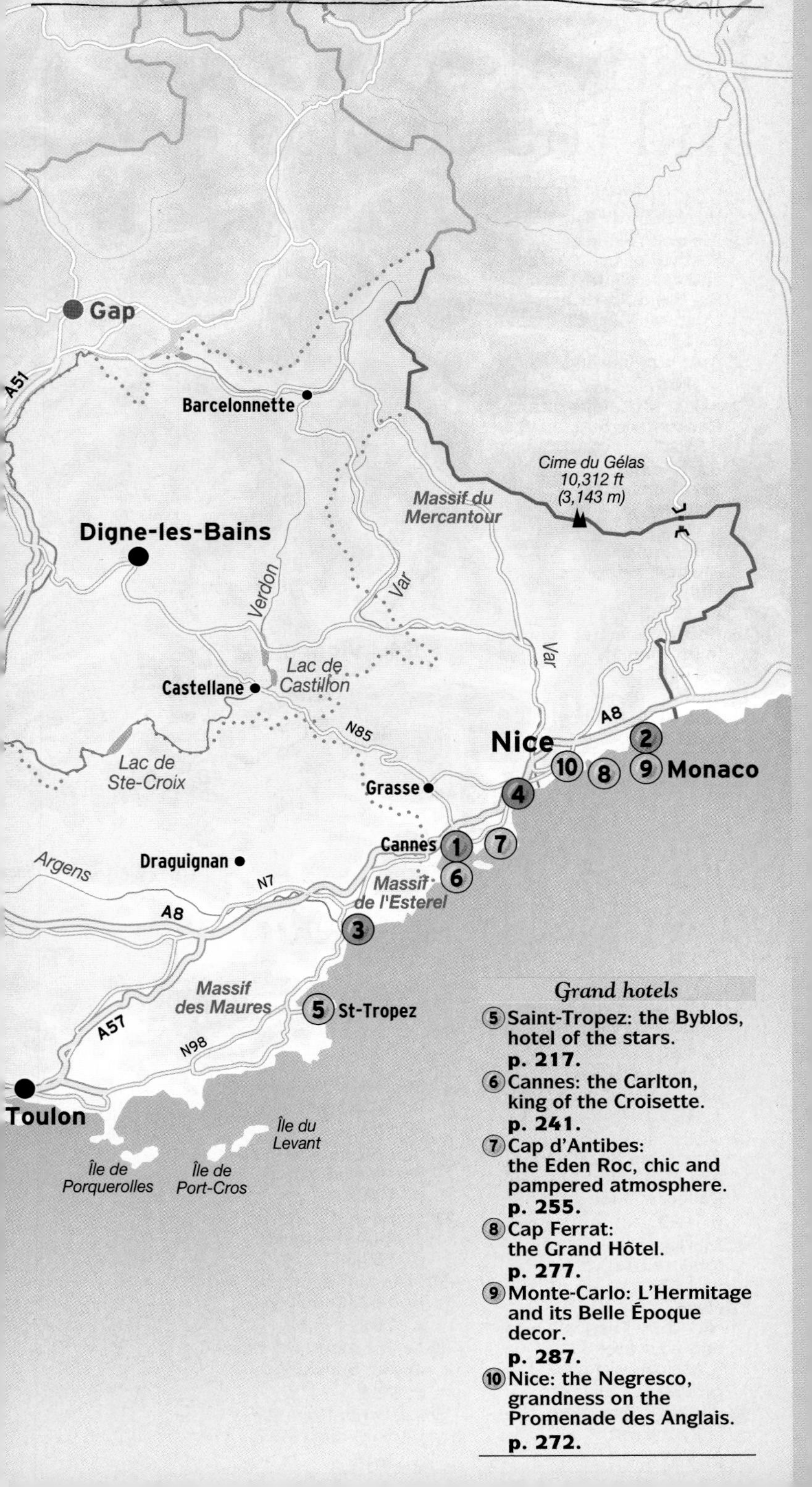

Gap

Barcelonnette

Cime du Gélas
10,312 ft
(3,143 m)

Massif du
Mercantour

Digne-les-Bains

Verdon

Var

Var

Lac de
Castillon

Castellane

Lac de
Ste-Croix

N85

A8

Nice

② Monaco

⑩ ⑧ ⑨

Grasse

④

Argens

Draguignan

Cannes ① ⑦

⑥

N7

A8

Massif
de l'Esterel

③

Massif
des Maures

A57

⑤ St-Tropez

N98

Toulon

Île du
Levant

Île de
Porquerolles

Île de
Port-Cros

Grand hotels

⑤ Saint-Tropez: the Byblos,
hotel of the stars.
p. 217.

⑥ Cannes: the Carlton,
king of the Croisette.
p. 241.

⑦ Cap d'Antibes:
the Eden Roc, chic and
pampered atmosphere.
p. 255.

⑧ Cap Ferrat:
the Grand Hôtel.
p. 277.

⑨ Monte-Carlo: L'Hermitage
and its Belle Époque
decor.
p. 287.

⑩ Nice: the Negresco,
grandness on the
Promenade des Anglais.
p. 272.

Festivals, concerts and the cinema

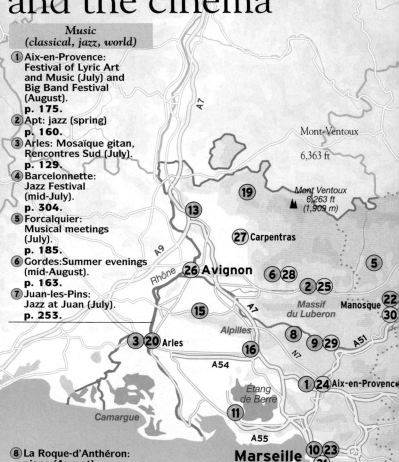

**Music
(classical, jazz, world)**

(1) **Aix-en-Provence:
Festival of Lyric Art
and Music (July) and
Big Band Festival
(August).**
p. 175.

(2) **Apt: jazz (spring)**
p. 160.

(3) **Arles: Mosaïque gitan,
Rencontres Sud (July).**
p. 129.

(4) **Barcelonnette:
Jazz Festival
(mid-July).**
p. 304.

(5) **Forcalquier:
Musical meetings
(July).**
p. 185.

(6) **Gordes:Summer evenings
(mid-August).**
p. 163.

(7) **Juan-les-Pins:
Jazz at Juan (July).**
p. 253.

Mont-Ventoux

6,363 ft

Mont Ventoux
6,263 ft
(1,909 m)

(19)

(27) Carpentras

(13)

A9

(26) Avignon   (6) (28)   (2) (25)   (5)

Rhône

Massif
du Luberon   Manosque (22)
(30)

(15)

A7

Alpilles   (8)   (9) (29)   A51

(3) (20) Arles   (16)

N7

A54

Étang
de Berre   (1) (24) Aix-en-Provence

Camargue   (11)

A55

(10) (23)
Marseille   (31)   A50

(8) **La Roque-d'Anthéron:
piano (August).**
p. 150.

(9) **La Tour-d'Aigues:
Sud Luberon (summer).**
p. 157.

(10) **Marseille:
Jazz Transfert (July)
and Festival of Marseille
(folklore, June-July).**
p. 195.

(11) **Martigues:
folklore (August).**
p. 153.

(12) **Nice:
Nice Jazz Festival (July)
and L'Escarène
(classical, summer).**
p. 272.

(13) **Orange: Chorégies
(July-August).**
p. 147.

(14) **Saint-Maximin-de-
la-Sainte-Baume: Organ.**
p. 204.

(15) **Saint-Rémy-de-Provence:
Organa (summer).**
p. 138.

(16) **Salon-de-Provence: Fiesta
Jazz (mid-August).**
p. 151.

(17) **Sisteron: festival of Fort-
Robert (mid-July).**
p. 187.

(18) **Le Thoronet: medieval
music (mid-July).**
p. 233.

(19) **Vaison-la-Romaine:
Chœurs lauréats (July).**
p. 149.

0   10   20   30 miles

0   10   20   30   40   50 km

Gap

Barcelonnette ④

17 32

Digne-les-Bains

Massif du Mercantour

Cime du Gélas

Cime du Gélas
10,312 ft
(3,143 m)   10,476 ft

Verdon

Var

Var

Lac de Castillon

Castellane

N85

A8

12

Monaco

Lac de Ste-Croix

Grasse

Nice

Argens

Draguignan

N7

Cannes **21** **7**

Massif de l'Esterel

14

18 A8

Massif des Maures

●St-Tropez

A57

N98

Toulon

Île de Porquerolles

Images (cinema, photo)

㉒ **Arles:** Photography Conference (July).
p. 128.

㉑ **Cannes:** Film Festival (May).
p. 240.

㉒ **Manosque:** Cinema and jazz meetings (January and August).
p. 183.

㉓ **Marseille:** Documentary film festival (May-June).
p. 195.

Stage arts (theatre, dance)

㉔ **Aix-en-Provence:** International Festival of Dance (spring and winter).
p. 175.

㉕ **Apt:** Jazz and Tréteaux de Nuit (spring and July).
p. 160.

㉖ **Avignon:** festival (July).
p. 141.

㉗ **Carpentras:** open-air theatre (mid-July).
p. 171.

㉘ **Gordes:** summer evenings (mid-August)
p. 163.

㉙ **La Tour-d'Aigues:** Sud Luberon (summer).
p. 157.

㉚ **Manosque:** Manosque à l'Affiche.
p. 183.

㉛ **Marseille:** festival of Marseille (June-July).
p. 195.

㉜ **Sisteron:** Nuits de la Citadelle (summer).
p. 187.

In the footsteps of Provençal writers

This sunny region has made a significant contribution to French literature through its writers, native and adopted, and through the colourful fictional characters who have become a symbol of Provençal life such as Marius, Angelo, Manon, Tartarin de Tarascon.

Jean Giono's writing case and a manuscript preserved in Manosque

Natives of Provence who praised the region almost on each page they wrote include Marcel Pagnol, Frédéric Mistral, Jean Giono, Alphonse Daudet and Henri Bosco. Other world-famous writers include Petrarch and the Marquis de Sade and more contemporary writers such as Edmonde Charles-Roux and François Nourissier.

citizen of Tarascon refused to allow Daudet to marry his daughter. Humiliated, Daudet decided to take his revenge on Mr. Barbarin through literature and settle the score. Thus Tartarin de Tarascon was born.

Alphonse Daudet

In search of Tartarin

Tartarin de Tarascon is the name of Alphonse Daudet's celebrated anti-hero. Daudet was born in Nîmes in 1840, and at the age of 20 he discovered the village of Fontvieille and the Château de Montauban which is where he created the characters for his stories. Before Daudet won fame and fortune, a prominent

The ruins of the Marquis de Sade's château at Lacoste

in Lourmarin. He also left a touching book of memoirs, *Un Oubli Moins Profond* (1961) ('A Shallow Oblivion').

Marcel Pagnol, the magician of memory

This writer, who never forgot his childhood spent in Provence, was born on 28 February 1895. Playwright, film-maker, founder of the magazine *Massilia* which became the *Cahiers du Sud* ('Journals from the South'), academician, translator from

Marcel Pagnol

Frédéric Mistral, defender of Provençal culture

In 1854, Mistral (1830-1914) created the Félibrige, a literary school which tried to perpetuate the *langue d'oc*, the ancient language of the South, and its dialects (p. 110). Mistral won the Nobel Prize for Literature in 1904. He was also the creator of the remarkable Museon Arlaten (p. 129). His works include the epic poem *Mirèio*, published in 1859.

Henri Bosco

Henri Bosco, secret of hearts

Bosco was born in Avignon in 1888. He graduated as a teacher and taught Italian in Belgrade, Naples and Morocco. His work is strongly inspired by religion and Antiquity, and celebrates the darker and the lighter Provence. His best-known books are *Âne Culotte* and *Le Mas Théotine*. Bosco died in Nice in 1976 and was buried

English and novelist, the prolific Marcel Pagnol was inspired by life in Marseille, Allauch, Aubagne and the small village of La Treille, where he was buried on 18 April 1974. His work has been translated into seven languages and many of his stories have been filmed.

Jean Giono, bard of the Haute Provence

Giono (1895-1970) spent his whole life in Manosque, the son of an Italian-born cobbler and a woman who took in ironing. His huge output is a hymn to the so-called *pays bleu* but also contains some shrewd characterisation, especially in 'the Hussard cycle'. His novel *Horseman on the Roof* was made into a film starring Juliette Binoche.

IN THE FOOTSTEPS OF THE GREAT WRITERS

Next to the Fontvieille mill, there is a small museum dedicated to Alphonse Daudet (p. 134). Marcel Pagnol, however, never succeeded in turning Aubagne into a French Hollywood (p. 117). Giono was happy to stay in Manosque and his house can be visited (p. 183). Petrarch who was in love with Laura, was also in love with the Mont Ventoux (p. 172). Why not take a stroll up there with a copy of his *Sonnets*? For those who enjoy travel books, there is a house at Digne-les-Bains which belonged to the explorer Alexandra David-Néel. It is now a foundation dedicated to the souvenirs she brought back from her trip to Tibet (p. 298).

Provençal culture

Provence is famous for its leisure activities, arts, crafts and fine food and drink, but its contribution to the national culture is mainly through its linguistic heritage. Monégasque, Mentonnais, Gavot and Rhodanien are just some of the dialects you will hear spoken. They are testimony to the vivacity and the diversity of Provençal culture. It is a region rich in tradition, with many festivities at which local peasant dress is worn.

Rooted in the past

France was once divided linguistically into the *langue d'oïl*, spoken in the north, and the *langue d'oc*, or Provençal, spoken in the south. Provençal is derived from low Latin and has a rich oral tradition, with an extensive vocabulary allowing many shades of meaning. Troubadours sang of courtly love among the hills of the Midi during the Middle Ages and all the poets of the South were influenced by the beauty of their verses, even Dante. Petrarch, who spent time in Vaison-la-Romaine (p. 148), also succumbed to the charm of the language and culture of the region.

The Golden age

Even though the troubadours gave Provençal its aristocratic credentials, the language was gradually supplanted by a mixture of French and Patois (Provençal dialect). In 1854, the Félibres (members of the Félibrige writers group), under the auspices of Frédéric Mistral, updated the language. Félibrige continues to exist and to defend the language and identity of Provence, and has branches throughout the region.

The revival

Provençal is making a comeback as a language in its own right. Certain regions insist on its use in daily life and old people still speak it. It is taught in schools and pupils can choose it as an optional subject for the Baccalauréat, the French high school graduation exam. Provençal is very much alive in common expressions often heard in the markets for example.

'Parlen provenço'

If you want to really blend in, then you will need to pick up a few words of Provençal, which is quite different from ordinary French. For example, if you spill something on yourself while eating, people will tell you that you have made a *bougnette*. A serious mistake is called a *cagade*. A simpleton is called a *fada* and *toti* is used to call someone an idiot. *Gari* is a term of endearment, but only used for *pitchouns* (kids). A dishonest

shopkeeper is a *caraque*. Too many glasses of wine and you are *empégué*. A pretty girl is referred to as a *chatto* and even if you get the giggles, you will still be able to *estrassez* yourself.

Local festivities

Each village hosts an arts event, a craft market and a folk or religious festival. From the Christmas *pastrage* to the *feux de la Saint-Jean* (bonfires lit for the summer solstice), there are plenty of special, festive occasions. The list includes the Festival of Transhumance in Saint-Rémy-de-Provence, the *Ferrades* (Camargue), *férias* (Arles), *Carreto Ramado* (Maussane-les-Alpilles), pastorals, water tournaments, cookouts (Carry-le-Rouet), *Fête de la dive bouteille* at Boulbon, or the May Tree festival in Cucuron. It is impossible to list them all, but something celebratory is always happening in Provence, especially when the weather turns warmer, and you will find it easy to get detailed information on the spot.

Traditional dress

Traditional dress is always worn at festivals. The costume worn by the women of Arles is one of the most elaborate and it can take more than 90 minutes to dress a local beauty. The basic attire consists of a long-sleeved blouse and a skirt, to which are added a lace overblouse, a muslin or embroidered *fichu*, a cap, as well as ear-rings and a crucifix pendant. The Museon Arlaten in Arles has an excellent selection of such costumes (p. 129).

Painters and light in Provence

Old masters and obscure artists, whether native to Provence or not, have flocked here since the late 19th C. to try and capture something of its mysteriously brilliant light on their canvases. Van Gogh was the forerunner when he said, in 1888: 'The entire future of the new art is in the Midi.' Provence has attracted painters ever since, slaking their thirst for colour and subject matter. Some remained faithful to the figurative tradition, others became the advocates of Impressionism, Fauvism or Cubism.

Vincent Van Gogh, *L'Arlésienne*

Félix Ziem (1821-1911)

This painter, whose father was Polish, acquired a passion for Martigues in 1839, painting the Caronte millrace and the fishermen's tartans. He was followed by other painters such as Raoul Dufy, Francis Picabia, André Derain and Nicolas de Staël who were inspired by Martigues. The museum contains a collection of Ziem's works (p. 152).

Paul Cézanne (1839-1906)

Cézanne left the Vallée de l'Oise for the Midi in 1874 and constantly praised the merits of Provence in letters to his friend Pissaro. He settled there for good in 1890. Planting his easel in the open air, he painted the Montagne

Paul Cézanne, *Still life*

Sainte-Victoire over and over again, as well as the Bibémus quarry and the Château Noir. His use of colour, in particular, remains unique in the history of painting.

Vincent Van Gogh (1853-1890)

Van Gogh went to Arles in February 1888 in a quest for more colour. The light of the Midi was a revelation to him, and he was able to forget the sadness of his native North. The paintings of this period are among his best and show

Paul Cézanne, *View of L'Estaque*

Vincent Van Gogh, *Evening in Arles*

how hard he tried to capture the intensity of the light. He painted 200 paintings in Arles and 150 in Saint-Rémy-de-Provence.

Paul Signac (1863-1935)

Signac fell in love with Saint-Tropez where he settled in 1892. He lived there for part of each year until 1911. As a precursor of pointillisme Signac was inspired in his artistic research by the light of this little port. He tried to capture

Paul Signac, *Antibes* (detail)

the changing colours of the landscape using small brush-strokes, a multitude of dots and a varied colour scheme.

Henri Matisse (1869-1954)

In 1904, Matisse spent the summer at Signac's in Saint-Tropez. As a student of impressionism, he followed the style of his master before progressively breaking away to glorify colour in all of its luminous opacity. Fauvism was born.

Georges Braque (1882-1963)

Braque was converted to Fauvism during the winter of 1905-1906, when he stayed in La Ciotat, and later in L'Estaque with Raoul Dufy. The paintings he produced during this period are exceptionally colourful. Later landscapes were progressively reduced to a few geometric patterns and compact shapes. Picasso and Braque together founded Cubism.

Raoul Dufy, *Martigues*

SEEING THE WORKS OF THE MASTERS

Cézanne's studio was in the country. Follow in his footsteps by climbing the Montagne Sainte-Victoire (p. 175), or find him in the semi-darkness of the Musée Granet, in Aix (p. 177). In Saint-Tropez, the Musée de l'Annonciade contains paintings by artists such as Signac and Bonnard (p. 216). Nice has works by Chagall and Matisse (p. 274). Those who are especially fond of Matisse should go on a pilgrimage to the Chapelle du Rosaire (p. 262). Van Gogh's luminous canvases are in the foundation of which he dreamed in Arles (p. 128). Cocteau, a Provençal by adoption, has paintings in Menton (p. 290) and in Cap Ferrat (p. 277). Fernand Léger painted in Biot (p. 265). You can visit Picasso's house in Mougins (p. 245). For lovers of Impressionism, a visit to Renoir's house in Cagnes is a must (p. 258).

Nicolas de Staël (1914-1955)

Born in Russia, de Staël settled in Nice in 1942. He met Braque, illustrated poems by René Char and gained an international reputation in 1953. This great, yet tormented, artist took the discoveries of his renowned predecessors to their limits. His abstract paintings consist of large patches of contrasting colours which portray the dynamic landscapes of the Midi.

Cinema on the Côte d'Azur

There is a museum dedicated to Raimu in Cogolin, Nice contains the famous Studios de la Victorine and, everywhere on the Côte d'Azur, you will find towns that have been used as locations by great French film directors – Pagnol, Godard, Truffaut, Vadim. Ever since the Lumière brothers filmed *Train entering La Ciotat station* in 1895 and the film festival took up residence in Cannes, the Midi has been in the cinematic limelight.

Cameras rolling

On the hills above Nice, opposite the airport, the Victorine Studios were first opened in 1919 (not open to the public). Classic French films were filmed here such as *Les Visiteurs du Soir* by Marcel

Carné, *Mon Oncle* by Jacques Tati, *Fanfan la Tulipe* and *Till l'Espiègle*, starring Gérard Philippe. The tragic story of *Lola Montes* by Max Ophuls, starring Martine Carol, was also filmed at Victorine. The studios were sold in 1992 and are now leased to a variety of production companies, so films are still being made – in a much more modern style, of course. Michael Jackson inaugurated the new studios by filming one of his videos here.

Through the eyes of Marcel Pagnol

Jean Giono's best friend, Marcel Pagnol, had always dreamed of turning his books into films. In 1935, the writer founded his own production company and set up his studios in Marseille (see also p. 117). However, location filming was always his favourite, since it was a way of paying tribute to his beloved Provence. He did so through the Provençal accent of his favourite actors – Fernand Joseph Désiré Constantin, better known in France as Fernandel, and Jules Muraire, better known under the name of Raimu.

attend the festival annually. With the Palme d'Or awards and the attendance of fledgling and famous film-makers and actors, the Cannes Festival is always highlighting new talent. Alongside the Oscars, Cannes is now the most important meeting-place for international stars of the silver screen.

Truffaut and Godard in Hyères

On one of the walls of the administrative centre, Place Théodore-Lefèvre, a fresco by Ernest Pignon-Ernest represents the last scene of *Pierrot le Fou*. Filmed in Ayguade and in Porquerolles in 1965, Godard starred Jean-Paul Belmondo and Anna Karina in a New Wave movie. In the small streets surrounding the church of Hyères, Truffaut located the estate agency of his last film, *Vivement Dimanche!* (1983), a thriller starring Fanny Ardant and Jean-Louis Trintigant.

And Vadim created Saint-Tropez...

In 1956, the divine Brigitte Bardot caught everyone's attention in this part of the Côte d'Azur with Roger Vadim's first movie *And God Created Woman*. Her sexy hip-swaying walk as she strolled around the port of Saint-Tropez made Bardot, Vadim and the port itself world-famous and has attracted crowds there ever since.

You are breaking my heart !

Born in Toulon in 1883, Raimu started by performing in cafés. He made his name in *César* (1929). His daughter and his grandchild have dedicated a museum in Cogolin to their famous relative (p. 221). The home of this (temperamental) actor in Bandol has been turned into a hotel. You can visit it or, better still, stay the night (Hôtel Ker Mocotte, 103, Rue Raimu, ☎ 04 94 29 46 53. Rooms from 290 F to 890 F).

Cannes and its festival

The idea was to make the Côte d'Azur a rival to Hollywood and the first festival was due to be held on the Croisette in September 1939. It never happened due to the outbreak of World War II. It was not until 20 September 1946 that the Cannes Film Festival got off to a flying start. The international competition is now held in May in the conference centre built in 1982, whose official name is the Palais but which was soon renamed 'the Bunker'. More than 20,000 visitors

Provençal literature

I s there anything more delightful than lazing on the beach or by the swimming pool, rediscovering the pleasure of reading? Here is a selection of books about Provence by classical and contemporary writers.

The authors of the region

Tartarin of Tarascon by Alphonse Daudet is the comic character who embodies so many Provençal qualities. Marcel Pagnol is, however, the Provençal writer best known to English speakers (with the possible exception of the Marquis de Sade!). Most of Pagnol's stories have been translated into English and have been published in the UK and the US. Guy de Maupassant, although he came from Normandy, wrote two short stories set in Provence: *Le Port*, subtitled 'the misadventures of a sailor from Normandy in Marseille', and *Le Champ d'Olivier* (The Olive Tree Field), which contains the terrible secret of the Abbé Vilbois.

Adventures in Provence

Jean Giono is the most popular Provençal author as far as the French are concerned. His greatest work is considered to be *Horseman on a Roof*, of which a film has been made. *The Man who Planted Trees*, a children's story, has also been translated. However, by no means has all of Giono's work been translated into English, and, if you are able, it is worth taking the trouble to try and read his books in French.

The English love affair

The English have always been fascinated by Provence,

and the south of France in general. Among the many travel books written about the region, there are *Aspects of Provence*, by J. Pope-Hennessy, and Lawrence Durell's *Caesar's Vast Ghost: Aspects of Provence*. English-language novels which use Provence as their setting include F. Scott Fitzgerald's *Tender is the Night* which takes place in the Hôtel L'Eden Roc, in the Cap d'Antibes, and Peter Mayle's *Hôtel Pastis*. Mayle is also the author of the very successful *A Year in Provence*.

Provence forever

The great classic written in the local language is *Mirèio*, a poem by Frédéric Mistral. Tudor Edwards wrote an excellent book about this Provençal poet entitled *The Lion of Arles – Portrait of Mistral and His Circle*. It is a vivid portrait of life in Provence in Mistral's day and the poet's attempt to revive Provençal culture. Another useful book is *Romantic Cities of Provence* by Mona Caird. For reading matter about local dishes, there is *Traditional Provençal Cuisine* by Stéphanie de Méry.

Provence on film

Many film-makers have immortalised Provence, either using original scripts or by drawing their inspiration from novels. A great number of these films are now available on video. Here is a selection which are worth seeing to put you in a Provençal mood.

Classics with a Provençal accent

The superb trilogy inspired by the work of Pagnol consists of *Marius* (Korda, 1931), *Fanny* (Allégret, 1932) and *César* (Pagnol, 1936). Pagnol also directed *The Baker's Wife* (1938). In 1986, Claude Berri adapted *Jean de Florette* and *Manon des Sources* from two books by Pagnol, and Yves

Robert directed *Le Gloire de Mon Père* (My Father's Glory) and *Le Château de ma Mère* (My Mother's Castle) in 1990.

Demons of the sun

Jeanne Moreau, her hair dyed platinum blond, played the vamp to Claude Mann in *The Bay of Angels* (Jacques Demy, 1963). *The Swimming Pool* (Jacques Deray, 1968) is another tale of passion, jealousy and murder set in the south of France, and starring Romy Schneider, Alain Delon and Maurice Roney.

The American dream

In the classic *To Catch a Thief* (1951), directed by Hitchcock, Cary Grant's elegance and Grace Kelly's angelic grace were brought together in a story about

thieves stealing from the swankiest hotels on the Riviera, in those days an exclusive playground for the rich. With *Horseman on the Roof* (1995), Jean-Claude Rappeneau turned Jean Giono's classic into an American-style adventure movie, with twists and turns in the plot, scenes of passion and magnificent settings.

Contemporary chronicles

The tortured *Un, Deux, Trois, Soleil* (One, Two, Three, Sun) by Bertrand Blier (1993) is set in a suburb of Marseille. It was the film that made Anouk Grinberg's reputation in France. *Marius et Jeannette* by Robert Guediguian (Warner) is another classic set in Provence which has already delighted thousands of French movie-goers.

THE UTOPIAN CINEMA CITY

As a scriptwriter, dialogue writer, director and producer, Marcel Pagnol created twenty or so films which are classics in their own right. In 1932, he opened his own studios in Marseille and bought 59 acres (24 ha) of land near Aubagne to use for outdoor locations. But the cinema city of which he dreamed never came to fruition. You can visit the locations where he shot his films, and spent his childhood, by following the three itineraries suggested by the Office de Tourisme in Aubagne (☎ 04 42 03 49 98). Be warned, however, that the paths are closed in summer because of the risk of fire. You can also visit the 'Little World of Marcel Pagnol', a recreation of the settings and characters in his works, produced by local *santon* makers.

Nice carnival

To forget the winter and welcome the spring Provence celebrates with festivals. There is an old tradition of lighting a bonfire to make a 'belle flambe' – a beautiful flame – which is still alive in many towns. Nice is one of them, and it cheerfully celebrates Shrove Tuesday with large numbers of floats and revellers in huge, decorative masks.

King of the Carnival

No fewer than 2,000 children in fancy dress surround a King of the Carnival who rides amid a band playing lively music. The king's float enters the city along the Avenue Jean-Médecin and stops at the Place Masséna. This is where he will sit enthroned for the eighteen days of his reign, i.e. the Nice Carnival period. The Carnival is generally held three weeks before Shrove Tuesday.

Permission to party

The carnival marks the end of the period of religious penitence – Lent – which follows Christmas. 'Escorts' with huge festive heads accompany the numerous floats and there are humorous performances which follow a different theme every year. The Promenade des Anglais is alive with the sounds of mock battles in which the participants pelt each other with flowers and confetti. Finally, on the evening of Shrove Tuesday, the King of the Carnival is ceremonially burned to great applause and the grand finale of the whole event is a gigantic firework display.

THE REAL KINGS OF THE CARNIVAL
Concept, Animations, Festivités,
Z. I. Fuon Santa, La Trinité,
☎ 04 93 54 64 74.
The Povigna family have been making carnival floats for four generations. In their busy workshop, they create at least five floats a year and their famous skills have enabled them to open a delightful shop, where you can hire out fancy dress (babies 50 F; children 75 F; adults from 150 F to 200 F), and buy stage make-up and fireworks.

His Majesty's carnival float

To create a float, you need 1.5 t. of paper, 2 t. of iron, 1 t. of electrical equipment, mechanical and hydraulic engines, 44 lb (20 kg) of paint and nails, wire netting, foam, paper, wood, 550 lb (250 kg) of flour to make the paste glue, 330 yds. (300 m) of fabric – and six months hard work! Once it is finished, a float will weigh nearly 7 tonnes.

Carnival work

For each carnival, no fewer than 1,500 people are mobilised to prepare and perform in the parade which consists of about 20 floats and 600 'big heads'. There are no fewer than 120 float makers – a skill which is passed down through the generations – who secretly labour in their workshops. Model-makers, sculptors, craftsmen in iron, metal-workers, electricians, painters, dressmakers – everyone gets involved. And although modern processes and techniques have mechanised the floats and their characters, basic manufacture remains unchanged. Pasteboard is still used, as it was in the old days.

Nice bedecked in a thousand colours

The Battle of Flowers starts with a procession of floral floats. There are flower fights and local girls hand out blooms. The flower industry of the Côte d'Azur supplies more than 10,000 t. of flowers (daffodils, gladioli, roses, chrysanthemums, mimosa, dahlias, lilies, Transvaal daisies and snapdragons) which add their brilliant colours to the town. Red and yellow banners are flown all along the procession route.

Preparing for the carnival

It is a good idea to book a seat on the procession route of the King of the Carnival. Entrance to the route costs 50 F, but you will have to pay 100 F for a seat in one of the wooden stands. You can also buy a combined ticket for the procession and the Battle of Flowers. (Information November to February, ☎ 04 92 14 48 14). You can purchase tickets from one of the four Nice Reception Offices (☎ 04 93 87 07 07 or 04 92 14 48 00) from mid-January, or order them by post from the Nice Office de Tourisme, Acropolis, BP 4079, 06302, Nice Cedex 04.

Places of commercial and scientific interest

If you want to see how the famous Marseille soap is made or how an astronomical observatory operates, how a perfume is created or how a dam is built, this is your opportunity.

Factory and site visits

① Barcelonnette: Ubaye soap factory.
p. 305.

② Castellane: Chaudanne dam.
p. 239.

③ Èze: soap factory.
p. 279.

④ Giens: mine.
p. 207.

⑤ Grasse: perfumery.
p. 248.

⑥ L'Isle-sur-la-Sorgue: paper mill.
p. 167.

⑦ Marseille: soap factory.
p. 194.

⑧ Martigues: power station.
p. 152.

⑨ Sainte-Croix-du-Verdon: hydroelectric power station.
p. 237.

⑩ Salon-de-Provence: soap factory, steelworks, refinery and autonomous port.
pp. 150-151.

Gap

① Barcelonnette

Cime du Gélas
10,312 ft
(3,143 m)

*Massif du
Mercantour*

Digne-les-Bains

⑫

Verdon

Var

*Lac de
Castillon*

Castellane ②

N85

⑨ *Lac de
Ste-Croix*

⑪

⑬

③ Monaco

⑮

Grasse ⑤

Nice

Argens

A8

Draguignan •

N7

• Cannes

*Massif
de l'Esterel*

A8

*Massif
des Maures*

• St-Tropez

A57

N98

Toulon

④

*Île du
Levant*

*Île de
Porquerolles*

*Île de
Port-Cros*

Scientific visits

⑪ **Caussols:
Calern observatory.
p. 239.**

⑫ **Digne-les-Bains:
geological site and
observatory.
p. 299.**

⑬ **Èze: Astrorama.
p. 278.**

⑭ **Forcalquier: observatory
and geological site
p. 185.**

⑮ **Nice: observatory.
p. 275.**

| 0 | 10 | 20 | 30 miles |

| 0 | 10 | 20 | 30 | 40 | 50 km |

Provence in detail

The Camargue 126

Arles... 126
The Camargue 130
Les Saintes-Maries-de-la-Mer 132

The Alpilles 134

The Alpilles.................................. 134
Les-Baux-de-Provence.................. 136
Saint-Rémy-de-Provence 138

Around Avignon 140

Avignon.. 140
Tarascon and la Montagnette 144
Orange 146
Vaison-la-Romaine
and the Haut Vaucluse.................. 148

Around Crau 150

Salon-de-Provence 150
Martigues..................................... 152

Luberon 154

The Petit Luberon 154
The Grand Luberon....................... 156
The Vallée de la Durance 158
Apt and Roussillon 160
Gordes and the Abbey
of Sénanque......... 162
Cavaillon..................... 164

Comtat venaissin 166

L'Isle-sur-la-Sorgue........................ 166
Pernes-les-Fontaines 168
Carpentras.................................... 170
The Mont Ventoux 172

Around Aix 174

Aix-en-Provence............................ 174
The Aix district............................. 180

Haute Provence 182

Manosque..................................... 182
Forcalquier 184
Sisteron 186

Around Marseille 188

Marseille 188
Cassis and Cap Canaille 196
From La Ciotat to Bandol 198

Toulon coast and the Sainte-Baume 200

From Bandol to Sanary 200
Toulon 202
The Sainte-Baume range.............. 204
The Giens peninsula.................... 206
Hyères.. 208
Porquerolles................................ 210
Port-Cros and Levant 212

The Maures 214

Bormes-les-Mimosas
and Le Lavandou...................... 214
Saint-Tropez................................ 216
Sainte-Maxime............................ 218
Grimaud, Cogolin and
Port-Grimaud............................ 220
The Maures range 222

The Esterel coast 224

Saint-Raphaël and Fréjus 224
The Esterel Coast 226

The Argens 228

Draguignan 228
Deep in the Haut-Var................... 230
The Vallée d'Argens 232

Around Verdon 234

The Verdon Gorges... 234
The route
Napoléon 238

Around the Côte d'Azur 240

Cannes.. 240
The Îles de Lérins 242
Mougins and the
Vallée de la Siagne 244
Grasse and its perfumes 248

The Fayence district...................... 250
Antibes and Juan-les-Pins............. 252
The Cap d'Antibes......................... 254
Vallauris....................................... 256

Around Vence 258

Cagnes-sur-Mer 258
Saint-Paul-de-Vence 260
Vence.. 262
Biot.. 264
The Vallée du Loup 266

Around Nice 270

Nice.. 270

Cap Ferrat 276
Èze and La Turbie 278
The Paillons Basin 280

Around Monaco 282

Monaco 282
Monte Carlo 286
Roquebrune, Cap-Martin
and Beausoleil.............................. 288
Menton... 290

The Hautes Vallées 292

The Vallée de la Vésubie............ 292
The Haute Vallée de la Roya .. 296

The Préalpes 298

Digne-les-Bains 298
The Haute Vallées of the
Var and the Verdon 300
Barcelonnette and
Vallée de l'Ubaye 304
Parc du Mercantour...................... 306

Provence in detail

On the following pages, you will find details of the most interesting places to visit in Provence and the Côte d'Azur. For your convenience, the region has been divided into zones. The colour code will enable you to easily find the area you are looking for.

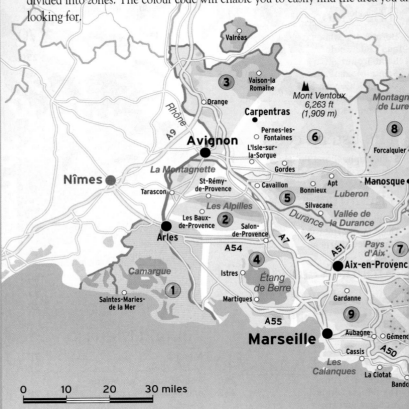

```
0        10        20        30 miles
0    10   20   30   40   50 km
```

① The Camargue
pp. 126-133.

② The Alpilles
pp. 134-139.

③ Around Avignon
pp. 140-149.

④ Around Crau
pp. 150-153.

⑤ Luberon
pp. 154-165.

⑥ Comtat venaissin
pp. 166-173.

⑦ Around Aix
pp. 174-181.

⑧ Haute Provence
pp. 182-187.

⑨ Around Marseille
pp. 188-199.

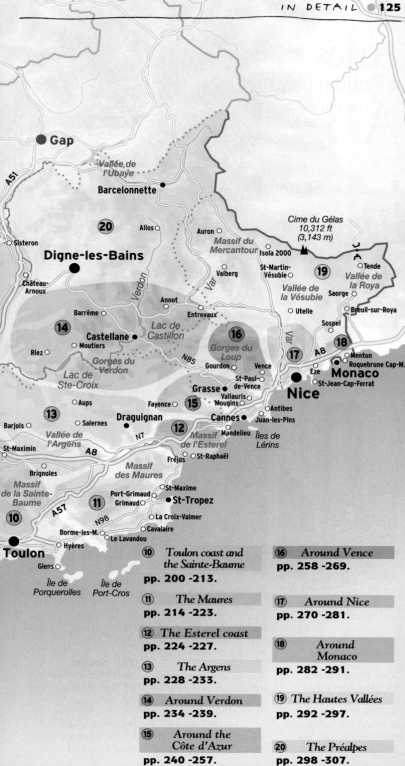

Gap

Vallée de l'Ubaye

Barcelonnette

A51

(20)

Allos○

Auron○

Cime du Gélas
10,312 ft
(3,143 m) ▲

Sisteron○

Massif du Mercantour

Isola 2000○

○Tende

Digne-les-Bains

Valberg○

St-Martin-Vésubie○

(19)

Vallée de la Roya

Château-Arnoux

Annot○

Verdon

Var

Saorge○

Barrème○

Entrevaux○

Vallée de la Vésubie

○Breuil-sur-Roya

(14)

Castellane

○Moutiers

Lac de Castillon

(16)

Utelle○

Sospel○

Riez○

Gorges du Verdon

N85

Gorges du Loup

○Gourdon

Vence○

St-Paul-de-Vence○

(17)

A8

(18)

○Menton
Roquebrune Cap-M.

Lac de Ste-Croix

Grasse○

Vallauris○

Mougins○

Eze○

Monaco

○St-Jean-Cap-Ferrat

Nice

○Aups

Fayence○

(15)

Antibes○

Draguignan

(13)

Barjols○

Salernes○

N7

(12)

Massif de l'Esterel

Mandelieu○

Juan-les-Pins○

Cannes●

Îles de Lérins

St-Maximin○

Vallée de l'Argens

A8

Fréjus○

○St-Raphaël

Brignoles○

Massif des Maures

Massif de la Sainte-Baume

(11)

St-Maxime○

A57

Port-Grimaud○
Grimaud○

St-Tropez●

(10)

Borme-les-M.○

N98

○La Croix-Valmer

Toulon

○Le Lavandou

Cavalaire○

Hyères○

Giens○

Île de Porquerolles

Île de Port-Cros

(10) *Toulon coast and the Sainte-Baume*
pp. 200 –213.

(16) *Around Vence*
pp. 258 –269.

(11) *The Maures*
pp. 214 –223.

(17) *Around Nice*
pp. 270 –281.

(12) *The Esterel coast*
pp. 224 –227.

(18) *Around Monaco*
pp. 282 –291.

(13) *The Argens*
pp. 228 –233.

(14) *Around Verdon*
pp. 234 –239.

(19) *The Hautes Vallées*
pp. 292 –297.

(15) *Around the Côte d'Azur*
pp. 240 –257.

(20) *The Préalpes*
pp. 298 –307.

Arles
a Roman city

Arles stands at the entrance to the Rhône and boasts an exceptional historical and architectural heritage. A Roman colony, it was founded by Julius Caesar in 46 BC and possesses outstanding Roman ruins. The Office de Tourisme offers tours on a particular theme including Antiquity, the Middle Ages, the Renaissance, and Van Gogh. Yet Arles is not obsessed with its past. There are plenty of modern festivities, *ferias* and cultural events to enjoy.

Constantine baths

Musée Réattu

Town hall

Arena

Museon Arlaten

Saint-Trophime

Place de la République

Ancient theatre

Espace Van Gogh

The Alyscamps

The ancient theatre of Arles, which could hold nearly 12,000 spectators, shows how important the town was at the start of the Christian era

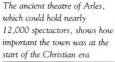

The amphitheatre of the arenas has two storeys of 60 arches

The Necropolis of the Alyscamps
Guided tours, 15 Jun.-30 Sep., open daily except Sun. and public holidays; out of season, go to Les Alyscamps at 5pm, on Sat.

The Alyscamps are the remains of a Roman necropolis at the south-east edge of the town, beside the Aurelian Way. They consist of a wide shady path, bordered by sarcophagi and Christian funerary monuments dating from the 4th to the 12th C. At the end, stands the church of Saint-Honorat. The Alyscamps inspired Rilke and Saint-John Perse. Van Gogh and Gauguin frequently painted there.

The portal and the cloister of Saint-Trophime
Arles was a great religious centre in the Middle Ages, and it is proud of its two Provençal Romanesque art treasures dating from the

12th C. The splendid portal with its carvings depicting the Last Judgment is reminiscent of the Arch of Glanum, in Saint-Rémy-de-Provence. The ancient cloister, next to the church (open daily, 9am-noon; from Oct.

to Mar., 10am-4.30pm. Paid admission) has beautiful carvings.

Place de la République: the Péru fountain (17th C.) and the very beautiful portal of Saint-Trophime

TRADITIONAL CELEBRATIONS

The arenas were dug out of the rock in the 1st C. AD. They have been constantly rebuilt ever since. After their restoration in 1846 they were again used for entertainment. Events now held there include bullfights and traditional celebrations such as the Fête des Gardians (Herdsmen's Festival) on 1 May, the Festival of Arles (end of June-end of July) and the Rice *Feria* (Sept.). Information at the Office de Tourisme. The ancient theatre also dates from the 1st C. Although only two columns remain from the original stage wall, it continues to flourish as a theatre. The tiers of seats are packed with spectactors, particularly during the epic film festival held during the last week of August (☎ 04 90 93 19 55).

The Renaissance city

Arles also has some handsome Renaissance buildings, such as the **Tour de l'Horloge**, the town hall constructed by Mansart (flat vaulting in the hall) and various mansions.

Moreover the **Musée Réattu** is situated in a 14th C. building, extended in the 16th C. (10, Rue du Grand-Prieuré, ☎ 04 90 49 37 58. Open daily, 9am-noon and 2-7pm; out of season 10am-noon and 2-5.30pm. Paid admission.) This is one of the cultural centres of the town. It contains Provençal paintings of the 17th and 18th C., almost all the works of the local painter, Jacques Réattu, and modern items such as a series of 57 drawings by Picasso. A special section is devoted to photographic art.

In the footsteps of Van Gogh

Vincent Van Gogh lived in Arles for 15 months from February 1888. During his stay, he painted more than 300 canvases including *Le Pont de Langlois* (The Bridge of Langlois), *La Maison Jaune* (The Yellow House) where he lived, the portrait of his friend the postman *Joseph Roulin*, *La Nuit Étoilée* (The Starry

Night), *L'Arlésienne* (The Woman from Arles), the cafés, and the *Jardin de l'Hôtel-Dieu*, the hospital which has been a foundation since 1989. He and his friend Gauguin, the painter, dreamed of creating a studio in the Midi. This dream came true thanks to the **Fondation Vincent Van Gogh** (Palais de Luppé, Rond-point des Arènes, ☎ 04 90 49 94 04. Open daily, 10am-7pm; out-of-season, 9.30am-noon and 2-5.30pm. Paid admission.), where many contemporary artists pay him a magnificent tribute. The Office de Tourisme also organises 2-hour guided tours called 'in the footsteps of Van Gogh' (1st July-30 Sept., Tues. and Fri. at 5pm).

FONDATION VINCENT VAN GOGH ARLES

Festivals and markets on the Boulevard des Lices

This is the focus of activity in Arles. The boulevard is lined with plane trees and edged with café terraces. A Saturday morning market is held here (the other market is held on Bd. Émile-Combes on Wednesday). Other, festive, events take place on the boulevard throughout the year, including an **abrivado** (bull-running) on the Easter Monday, a **pégoulade** (torch-light procession in traditional costumes) on the last Friday in June, and a costume festival on the first Sunday in July.

FERIAS AND BULLFIGHTS

Do not leave Arles without visiting the arenas to watch bull-fighting for the *cocarde*, or *course camarguaise* (all summer, *course à la cocarde d'or*, at the beginning of July) . The *cocarde* is a small red rosette tied between the bull horns which the *razeteurs* (the competitors), dressed in white, try to remove merely as a gesture and for a modest prize. These harmless events (the bull is not killed) are enjoyed by the spectators especially when the beast, carried along by its own impetus, leaps over the *talanquère*, the wooden fence surrounding the arena. These competitions are held throughout Provence, in the Alpilles, the Camargue and the Montagnette. Reservations for arenas (☎ 04 90 96 03 70). In September, Arles celebrates the Rice *feria*.

International Photography Conference

10, Rond-point des Arènes,
☎ 04 90 96 76 06.

The Photography Conference (Rencontres Internationales de la Photographie) was begun in Arles in 1970, and is held every July. Famous photographers from all over the world flock to Arles, and many exhibitions are held (open until the end of August), as well as special presentations followed by discussions. Since 1982, the town has also been home to the École Nationale de Photographie (National School of Photography).

The garden of Arles

The Jardin d'Été (Summer Garden), right in the centre of the town, was created by a botanist who wanted to protect Mediterranean flora. It is a quiet place with large, shady trees.

Music from around the world

In July, Arles sways to the rhythm of music from around the world. Around 15 July, 'Mosaïque gitan' presents gypsy dance and music (information at the Tourist Office) and in the third week, the Rencontres du Sud hold Latin-American and Oriental evenings, with dance and music lessons (☎ 04 90 96 06 27).

The sausage

The pork-butcher Godard created his special recipe on 6 July 1655, to mark the accession to the throne of King Louis XIII. Arles sausage is still made in the traditional way by some butchers. It consists of minced beef and pork, *herbes de Provence* and bacon macerated in the local wine; once made up, it is dry-cured for six months. The most famous of these butchers is **Pierre Milhau** (11, Rue Réattu, ☎ 04 90 96 16 05) who holds the record for making the longest sausage in the world. It used up 770 lb (350 kg) of minced meat stuffed into 266.7ft (80 m) of casing!

Trinquetaille
An original wine

Le Mas de Rey,
☎ 04 90 96 11 84.
Nearly 2 miles (3 km) from Arles, the Mas de Rey is well worth visiting. This 17th C.-estate stands among rice fields and vineyards. The Mazzoleni family will be delighted to show you their vineyard which is famous for its excellent wines. The reds are Caladoc and Marsalan from their own grapes, the white is Chasan.

Salin-de-Giraud
Salt gathering

The salt-pans of Giraud in the Camargue are the biggest in Europe and despite their imminent closure, they produce almost 700,000 t. of salt per year. The principle is simple: seawater is pumped into shallow pre-concentration ponds. The water evaporates, leaving the 'table' ready for the mechanical harvesting of salt bound for either the chemical industry or for snow removal. As you leave the Salin-de-Giraud, there is an information point near a *camelle* (salt mountain) with excellent signposts.

(For visits to the salt pans, consult the Office de Tourisme in Arles.)

Servanes
The Servanes golf course

Domaine de Servanes, at 12½ miles (20 km NE) from Arles on D17, ☎ 04 90 47 59 95.
This 18-hole golf course is 6700 yds (6,121 m) by 78 yds. (72 m). It has been created in a wonderful natural environment of cypresses, pines, olive trees and a view of the Alpilles.

MUSEON ARLATEN

**29, Rue de la République,
☎ 04 90 96 08 23.
Open daily 9.30am-noon and 2-5pm (6.30pm in summer), closed on Mon. except in Jul.-Aug.-Sep.**
Paid admission.
This ethnographic museum was founded by Frédéric Mistral in 1896 in the old palace of Laval-Castellane (16th C.) and covers all aspects of traditional Provençal life. There is a herbarium, a collection of traditional costumes, furniture and pottery, a description of the customs and legends of the region, ancient occupations, and much more.

The Camargue
flamingoes, horses, bulls…

Between the two fast-flowing branches of the Rhône River lies the Camargue, a paradise of migratory birds, bulls and horses. You'll encounter much wildlife on long, leisurely rambles, bicycle and horse rides or on boat trips. This vast alluvial plain forms a 540 sq. mile (1,400 km²) triangle. The Grande Camargue covers 289 sq. miles (750 km²) between the two branches of the Rhône, the Petite Camargue lies to the west of the Petit Rhône, and the Plan de Bourg is east of the Grand Rhône.

Camargue Museum (Musée Camarguais)

Mas du Pont-de-Rousty, 6¼ miles (10 km) from Arles on the road to Saintes-Maries-de-la-Mer,
☎ **04 90 97 10 82.**
Open daily, Apr.-Jun., 10am-6pm; Sep.-Mar. 10am-5pm (closed on Tues.).
Paid admission.
A depiction of the history of the Camargue has been created in a former sheepfold. It demonstrates daily life in the region. There is a 2 mile (3.5 km) tour of the crops, pasture and marshland of the Camargue landscape.

The Camargue Regional Park

Its 212,506 acres (86,000 ha) are dedicated to the protection of the environment and wildlife. The **Centre de Ginès** (Pont-de-Gau, ☎ 04 90 97 86 32) is open daily, 9am-6pm; out of season, 9.30am-5pm, except on Fri. It provides information for organising hikes as well as an exhibition on the protected environment of the Camargue.

VILLE DE ST REMY DE PCE

The flamingoes of the Pont-de-Gau

Parc Ornithologique du Pont-de-Gau,
☎ **04 90 97 82 62.**
Paid admission
Open daily from 9am (10am in winter) until sunset.
A paradise for birds, this living display contains more than 350 specimens of bird life, in an aviary and in the

open-air. They include egrets, herons, ducks and, most notably, pink flamingoes. Don't forget to take your binoculars!

On the beaches

The Camargue is also a paradise for sun-worshippers with its 37½ miles (60 km) of fine sandy beaches (*plages*). South of Salin-de-Giraud (see p. 129), the **Piémançon beach** (15 miles (25 km)) is the only one which is supervised in winter. You also have the choice of Beauduc (west of Piémançon), or Pertuis-de-la-Comtesse which is further away, near the Gacholle lighthouse (a naturist beach).

Boats are kings in the land of canals

How about a short cruise into the interior of the Delta? The boats leave from the port of Les Saintes and sail along the Petit Rhône. There is a commentary.

PRELUDES
TO THE RACE

The Camargue bull has inhabited the Rhône Delta since ancient times. It was domesticated as a farm animal before being reared for its delicious meat (it has its own AOC). The bull is also the hero of races and bullrings. Its black coat and long slim horns make it a beast that is more feared than admired. There are 15,000 bulls belonging to about a hundred herds, and they are mainly free to roam. It is possible for a visitor to experience a day in the life of a herd and its herdsmen. The Domaine Paul-Ricard (Méjanes, ☎ 04 90 97 10 10) recommends you attend the round-up, branding, and the race for the *cocarde*. (Sun. and bank holidays, from Palm Sunday to the end of June. Paid admission.)

'Le Camargue'
(☎ 04 90 97 84 72), and
'Les Quatre Maries'
(☎ 04 90 97 70 10).
West of Les Saintes on D38, at the mouth of the Petit Rhône, 'Le-Tiki-III'
(☎ 04 90 97 81 68) invites you to go back in time on board, thanks to its paddle

wheels. The Louisiana-style
'Barques de Camargue'
(☎ 04 90 97 55 52, March-Oct., daytime reservations 280 F with lunch) takes you to the Grand-Radeau beach, at the mouth of the Petit Rhône, which is inaccessible by road.

Horse riding

The perfect way to get to the remotest parts of this area is on horseback. The Office de Tourisme can give you the list of the regional livery stables (it should cost 230 F for half a day).

Bike rides

The road which runs along the Digue à la Mer (sea-wall between the Étang de Vaccarès and the Mediterranean Sea) from Les Saintes to Salin-de-Giraud is 12½ miles (20 km) long and was built in the 19th C. Cars are banned.
Bike hire at the Mas Saint-Bertrand, 4½ miles (7 km) from Salins-de-Giraud, ☎ 04 42 48 80 69 or at Le Vélociste (Les Saintes, ☎ 04 90 97 83 26).

The Rice Museum

La Rizerie du Petit Manusclat, Le Sambucau, S. of Arles, dir. Salins-de-Giraud on D570 then D36. ☎ 04 90 97 20 29.

Spotcheck
A3

Bouches-du Rhône

Things to do

See the flamingoes of the Pont-de-Gau
Camargue by boat
Horse rides
Bike rides
Visit a herd of bulls

Within easy reach

Les Baux-de-Provence, 25 km NE, p. 136.

Tourist Office

Saintes-Maries-de-la-Mer:
☎ 04 90 97 82 55

Guided tour with reservation. *Paid admission.* Nowadays, rice covers slightly more than half of all cultivatable land. In September, the Rice *Feria* in Arles celebrates this ancient cereal with enthusiasm. The Musée de Riz tells the story of the crop.

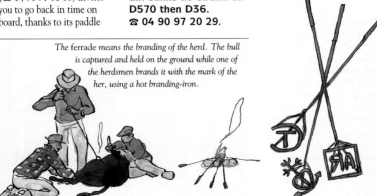

The ferrade means the branding of the herd. The bull is captured and held on the ground while one of the herdsmen brands it with the mark of the her, using a hot branding-iron.

Les Saintes-Maries-de-la-Mer
the gypsy pilgrimage

According to legend, a small boat arrived miraculously from Palestine in AD 40, and ran aground on the shore of Les Saintes. On board were Mary Jacobus, sister of the Virgin, Mary Magdalene, her brother Lazarus, her sister Martha, Mary Salome, mother of the apostles James and John, and their black servant Sarah. The saints settled here and spread the Gospel through the region. Sarah became the patron saint of the gypsies and is venerated every Spring with a long pilgrimage.

Sunday closest to 22 October celebrates the birthday of Saint Mary Salome. After the mass, *gardians* mounted on horseback and women in the traditional costume of Arles accompany the saints' boat to the sea, where it is blessed.

The church of Saintes-Maries

The church (*église*) is perched on the highest point of the Camargue and is visible for miles around. It is the birthplace of the legend of the Saintes Maries, and contains the relics of the saints and the small ceremonial boat. Relics of Sarah are located in the crypt, as is the statue of the Black Virgin which the gypsies carry during the annual pilgrimage. It is well worth climbing the 53 steps to the flat roof of the church to admire the view of the surrounding Camargue and the sea.

The gypsy pilgrimage

Twice a year, Les Saintes is visited by the Travellers. They arrive in their thousands from all over Europe, to take the route of the pilgrimage. Saint Sarah is celebrated on 24 and 25 May, and the

The Baroncelli Museum

Rue Victor-Hugo,
☎ **04 90 97 87 60.**
Open daily, 10am-noon and 3-7pm; out of season, 2-6pm. Closed Tues. and in winter.
Paid admission.

Interior of Baroncelli Museum

THE HORSE *FERIA*

Res. ☎ 04 90 97 10 60 and information at the Office de Tourisme.
For four days, around the weekend of 14 July, there is a festival in honour of the horse. Animals are branded, and other events include a mounted bull-fight, Camargue races, dressage events and gymkhanas. Most are held in the arenas of Les Saintes-Maries. There is also imported flamenco and Spanish dancing from Seville to fire up the atmosphere.

This museum, dedicated to the history of the town, the folklore and the fauna in Camargue, also houses the collection of the Marquis Folco de Baroncelli who experienced the hard life of a herdsman in Saintes at the end of the 19th C. As a poet and friend of Mistral, and equally keen to preserve traditional local life, he saved the region's particular breeds of horse and bull. The equestrian games and the actual clothes worn by the herdsmen exist thanks to him (see below).

The Virgin Celebration

Created in 1904 by Mistral, the Festo Vierginenco, on the last Sunday of July, honours the 16-year-old girls who are authorised to wear the 'ruban d'Arlésienne' (the local costume) for the first time. After mass, they all go to the arenas to attend the equestrian games and the Provençal dances, in a warm atmosphere and an array of magnificent costumes.

The Panorama du voyage

Route de Cacharel, ☎ 04 90 97 52 85.
Open daily, 10am-8pm; out of season, 10am-5pm. *Paid admission*.

6¼ miles (10 km) North of Saintes, there is an evocation of the Tzigane history, circus world and funfair. The *verdines* (seven 60-year-old caravans which are always ready to leave) help you to imagine the travelling entertainers' universe.

Kayaking (Kayak vert en Camargue)

Mas des Baumelles, ☎ 04 90 97 88 89.
Discover the Camargue via the stream which flows down the Petit Rhône, 5½ miles (9 km), duration 2 h 30 mins, 90 F per person, returning by mini-bus. You can choose between many different boat trips, from 1 hour to 2 or 3 days, where you can sleep on the shore.

Everything for the herdsman

11, Rue Victor-Hugo, ☎ 04 90 97 82 33.
Open daily, in summer, 9.30am-12.30pm and 2-7pm.
In this shop, you can buy all the herdsman's (*gardian*) equipment: black braided velvet coat with red satin (1,300 F), beige trousers ornate with borders on each side, hat with turned up brims and boots.

The Alpilles
the soul of Provence

The range of hills known as the Alpilles spreads from south of the Durance River to the outskirts of Arles. It is a geological continuation of the Luberon, and is like a look-out post, with its tortuous crests and its chalky ridges whose whiteness illuminates the scenery. The varied landscape offers magnificent views, alternating between the wild, untamed uplands and the rich soil of the valley where the vine and the olive tree fight for every inch of space.

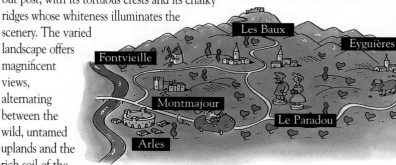

Montmajour

Romanesque Abbey

Rte de Fontvieille,
☎ 04 90 54 64 17.
Open daily except Tue. and public holidays, Oct.-Mar., 10am-1pm and 2-5pm; Apr.-Sep., daily 9am-7pm.
Paid admission.

Montmajour is just a few miles from Arles and was one of the favourite retreats of Van Gogh, who often painted here. The abbey was founded in the 10th C., but of the original building only the small chapel of Saint Pierre still stands. The main buildings were erected in the 12th C. around the cloister. Of the abbot's lodgings, only the tower remains (1369).

Mouriès

Fête de l'Olive

Since 1966, olive growers and curers have gathered in Mouriès for two days on the 3rd weekend of September to celebrate the start of the olive harvest. In December, the city annoints itself with the first oil, barely off the press. A cart carrying seven jars of oil is blessed, and a ceremony is held to induct notables into the *Ordre de l'huile nouvelle* ('Order of the new oil'). The green nectar is then tasted.

Fontvieille

Alphonse Daudet's mill

With its crumbling stone houses, this little village is extremely picturesque and is built from the same stone which was used to build the arenas of Arles and Nîmes. Fontvieille owes its fame to the writer Alphonse Daudet, who lived in a mill (*moulin*) at the southern end of the village, in which he wrote *Les Lettres de mon Moulin* (Letters from my Windmill). There is a museum dedicated to him. (☎ 04 90 54 60 78, open

Daudet's mill

Spotcheck
B3

Bouches-du Rhône

Things to do

La fête de l'olive
Visit to a wrought iron workshop
Summer festivals at Maussane
Visit an oil mill

With children

Le musée des Santons animés

Within easy reach

Arles, 25 km SW, p. 126.
Avignon, 25 km N, p. 140.
Cavaillon, 20 km NE, p. 164.

Tourist Office

Maussane-les-Alpilles:
☎ 04 90 54 52 04
Eyguières: ☎ 04 90 59 82 44

daily, 9am-noon and 2-7pm). There is a pleasant walk to the Château de Montauban, where the author also lived.

Wrought iron workshop

Ferronnerie d'art, Rue Michelet, ☎ 04 90 54 72 37. Daily 8am-noon and 1.30-6pm.

Michel Buchwalter creates and shapes wrought iron for outdoor and indoor use in typical Provençal styles. Visit him and see him smithying at the forge in his workshop and let yourself be tempted to buy some of his beautiful wares.

Maussane

Visit an oil mill

Moulin Jean-Marie Cornille, ☎ 04 90 54 32 37.

Maussane became famous for its olive oil and its production of olives from the Valley of Les Baux. Visit the lovely 17th C. mill, which belongs to the oil cooperative. It still uses the old millstones and presses to turn the olives into the beautiful, green, golden liquid. Do not leave without your 1¼ pts (1 litre) of oil. It is rather expensive (about 100 F per litre), but very precious. At the **confiserie Martin**, olives have been

cured in a tradition handed down through generations since 1920. Depending on the season, there are green olives with fennel or salted grossane olives. Tapenades, fried aubergines with tomatoes and pesto are also available. (Rue Charloun-Rieu, ☎ 04 90 54 30 04, open Mon. to Sat., 9am-noon and 2-6pm).

Eyguières

Bull-running

'Sobriété est mère de beauté' (Sobriety is the mother of beauty). This is the motto on the shield of the local aristocracy, the d'Eyguières family. Discover the pre-Romanesque chapel of Saint-Védereme, and the ruins of a medieval castle. The village comes alive when its shady **arenas**, host annual *courses à la cocarde* (p. 128). Jun.- late Aug., information at Eyguières Office de Tourisme.

SUMMER FESTIVALS AT MAUSSANE

The village, once the property of the lords of Les Baux, lies on both sides of the old Roman road. It is a delightful holiday resort in the country where summer seems to be dedicated to partying. On the second weekend of June, the Carreto Ramado parade honours St. Éloi, the patron saint of metal-workers, accompanying manual threshing of the wheat and an *aïoli* (garlic mayonnaise) competition. The 14 July and 5 August celebrations are occasions for renewing tradition: *abrivado* (bull-running in the street), the Camargue races, *pégoulade*, and heffer-racing (information at the Office de Tourisme). The penultimate Sunday in August is the day of 'Le temps retrouvé', when Maussane harks back to the 19th C. with a crafts market, traditional costumes, and reconstructions of street scenes. At the entrance to the village, visit the Musée des Santons Animés (crib figures). (☎ 04 90 54 39 00. Open daily, 10am-7.30pm in summer.)

Les Baux-de-Provence
Rock formation

The rocky outcrop of Les Baux is perched on top of the small massif of the Alpilles. Ancient ramparts and a dismantled citadel seem to compete with the cliff. The village of Les Baux-de-Provence with its Renaissance façades looks almost like a stage set.

The lower town

It is a good idea to visit the town on foot in the morning, to avoid the heat of the day. From the Mage gate, climb the narrow streets lined with carefully restored houses.

A stop in the ancient town hall will enable you to visit the **Musée des Santons**. On your way to the Place Saint-Vincent, you will pass the Chapelle des Pénitents-Blancs. The paintings on the

walls of this little church are by Yves Brayer (1907-1990), a retrospective of whose works can be seen in the museum which bears his name. The museum is housed in the 16th C. Hôtel des Porcellets.

The citadel
☎ 04 90 54 55 56.
Open daily, 9am-8.45pm; out of season, 9am-5/6pm. *Paid admission.*
The citadel tops a rocky outcrop and is a vestige of the power of the proud lords of Les Baux, who claimed to be the sons of Balthazar, one of the three Wise Men. The only remnant of this glorious past is on the walls of the

chapel, the castle and its imposing dungeon. Separate towers protect the surrounding area. The Sarrasine Tower and the Bannes Tower overlook the south, and the Paravelle Tower overlooks the north. The 16th C. houses inside the ramparts are a reminder that there were 6,000 inhabitants at that time. The Hôtel de la Tour de Brau, at the foot of the ruined castle, contains a museum recording important events in the history of the citadel and its residents, including such medieval machines of war as a catapult, a battering-ram and a pillory. The panoramic view from the crest of the

rock topped by the dungeon is ample reward for the difficult climb.

✤ THE VAL D'ENFER AND THE CATHEDRAL OF IMAGES

The road leading to the Val d'Enfer (legendary haunt of witches and goblins) winds through a jumble of rocks and offers a very fine view of Les Baux. It was here that a mineralogist named Berthier discovered bauxite in 1821. These jagged cliffs which are perforated with caves and underground quarries served as the location for Jean Cocteau's film *The Testament of Orpheus*. Some quarries have been converted for use as the backdrop to an audiovisual presentation called The Cathédrale des Images (departmental path 27; ☎ 04 90 54 38 65. Open daily 10 am-7 pm; out of season, 10-11 am. Paid admission). The audience can walk in and out as they please. More than 2,800 images, enlarged 10,000 times, are projected in spaces 67 ft (20 m) high, from 45 different sources, on to the white rock which forms a natural screen of over 43,060 ft^2 (4,000 m^2). There are also exhibitions and a theatre in 64,580 ft^2 (6,000 m^2) of galleries. The theme changes annually.

Spotcheck
B3

Bouches-du Rhône

Things to do

Musée des Santons
Scenic walk
The Cathedral of Images
Learning sports in the Alpilles

With children

The Musée des Santons
Sports in the Alpilles

Within easy reach

Arles, 16 km SW, p. 128.
Avignon, 27 km N, p. 140.
Tarascon, 18 km W, p. 144.
Cavaillon, 25 km NE, p. 164.

Tourist Office

Les Baux-de-Provence:
☎ 04 90 54 34 39

Musée de l'Olivier

Château des Baux,
☎ 04 90 54 55 56.
Entirely dedicated to the olive tree, this museum will teach you all you will ever need to know about the cultivation, production and secrets of the olive. There is also a slide-show entitled 'Van Gogh, Cézanne and Gauguin in the land of the olive tree'.

Sports in the Alpilles

Association Alpilles Passions,
Mas du Chevrier,
☎ 04 90 54 40 20 or
06 14 81 87 79.
Enrol in advance.
There are many open-air activities, including some for which courses are available. They include archery, walks and rock-climbing. Weekly multi-activity courses are held in July-August (450 F).

Saint-Rémy-de-Provence

a mix of Antiquity and Provence

In the capital of the Alpilles, history lovers and pétanque players will mix happily. The Greeks founded this site, the Romans occupied it, and today visitors wander through its sunny streets.

and with Caroline of Monaco, who enjoys peace and quiet here.

A town loved by artists

Nostradamus was born in 1503 in Saint-Rémy, Van Gogh produced more than 150 paintings here, and Frédéric Mistral and Joseph Roumanille found their inspiration here. Nowadays, Saint-Rémy is a cheerful little town, very popular with show-business personalities

Exploring the old town

The *Cours*, the main street, follows the line of the old ramparts. It is lined with ancient gateways and plane trees and is surrounded by a network of narrow lanes and squares that have hardly changed throughout the centuries. On the *Cours* stand the **Collégiale Saint-Martin** with its gothic steeple, the **Musée des Alpilles** which occupies the Hôtel Mistral de Montdragon, the **Présence-Van Gogh** contemporary art centre in the Hôtel Estrine, the **Fondation Mario Prassinos** in the Chapelle Notre-Dame-de-Pitié (information at the Office de Tourisme office). Perhaps the most fascinating museum is the **Musée des Arômes** (Museum of Fragrance) (☎ 04 90 92 48 70) where the making of essential fragrance oils is explained. (Open daily, from 9am-noon and from 2-6pm, Mon. to Fri.; 10am-noon and 3-6pm on weekends, except out of season.)

Organa

This famous organ festival is held at the Collégiale Saint-Martin whose organ is played by the most famous organists in the world, sometimes with trumpet, vocal or orchestral accompaniment. (Information at the Office de Tourisme.)

Glider Flying Club

Aérodrome de Romanin, 3 miles (5 km) E. of Saint-Rémy, take the D99 then the D140.
☎ **04 90 92 08 43.**
Daily. 8am-8pm.
The Romanin Flying Club makes best use of the strong winds by offering glider flights (250 F), initiation flights and many training courses, with the option of accommodation.

'Ruins with prospects'

Les Antiques, Route de Maussane,
Free admission.
0.6 miles (1 km) south of

The Provençal
Feria

The Bull *Feria* (4 days around the weekend of 15 August) produces great excitement in the streets. Events include the *carredo ramado* (parade), *abrivados*, *bandidos*, *encierros* (setting a bull free on the Place de la République) and Camarguaise bull-running (information at the Office de Tourisme). If you prefer tamer animals, the Fête de la Transhumance on 1 June marks the departure of the flocks to the mountains, and 3,000 sheep roam through the town!

Below the Alpilles foothills lies the ancient Roman city of Glanum, which lay hidden for centuries beneath river silt. Excavation began in 1921, and still continues. The reconstruction of the temple and the ruins that are exposed are well worth seeing. A rest-stop at the **Taverna Romana** (☎ 04 90 92 65 97) will allow you to enjoy Roman food and wines.

Saint-Paul-de-Mausole
☎ 04 90 92 77 00.
Open daily, 9am-noon and 2-6pm; out of season, 9am-noon and 1-5pm.
This ancient monastery that is now a nursing home has a beautiful Romanesque church

Saint-Rémy, two Roman monuments remain which are amazingly well preserved. The **arc de triomphe** marks the entry to the city of Glanum, built on the old Via Domitia that links Italy and Spain; the **mausoleum** is dedicated to the grandsons of the Emperor Augustus who died in battle.

Glanum (Roman city)
Rte de Maussane, at ½ mile (1 km) south of Saint-Rémy.
☎ 04 90 92 23 79.
Open daily except public holidays, 9am-7pm; out of season, 9am-noon and 2-5pm. *Paid admission.*

and cloister. Van Gogh was a patient here in 1889. His bedroom has been reconstructed. The window overlooks the wheat fields and irises that inspired his paintings.

Spotcheck
B3

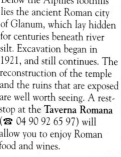

Bouches-du-Rhône

Things to do
The Musée des Arômes
The Provençal *Feria*
Glanum (Roman city)
Fly in a glider

With children
The Musée des Arômes
The Fête de la Transhumance

Within easy reach
Arles, 16 km SW, p. 128.
Avignon, 27 km N, p. 140.
Tarascon, 18 km W, p. 144.
Cavaillon, 25 km NE, p. 164.

Tourist Office
Saint-Rémy-de-Provence:
☎ 04 90 92 05 22

Le mas de la Pyramide
☎ 04 90 92 00 81.
Open daily. 9am-noon and 2-5pm (until 7pm in summer).
Paid admission.
Not far from Saint-Paul-de-Mausole this troglodyte house, built in the incredible romanesque quarries of Saint-Rémy, was turned into a country museum.

Confectionery
The **pignolat de Nostradamus** is a speciality of Saint-Rémy-de Provence, based on a recipe in Nostradamus' confectionery book written in 1555. It is a tasty mixture of pine kernels, sugar, rose water and fennel (Petit Duc, 7, Bd Victor-Hugo, ☎ 04 90 92 08 31). The **Maison d'Araxie** sells delicious crystallised fruit made by the **Confiserie Artisanale Lilamand**, a veritable institution: about 150 F for 14 oz (400 g).

Avignon

The Palace of the Popes, the bridge from the famous French nursery rhyme, and the festival, are what mainly attract thousands of visitors to Avignon. However, the memorable medieval display inside the ramparts should not overshadow the fun to be had in the town squares, the classic architecture of the mansions and the treasures to be found in the museums.

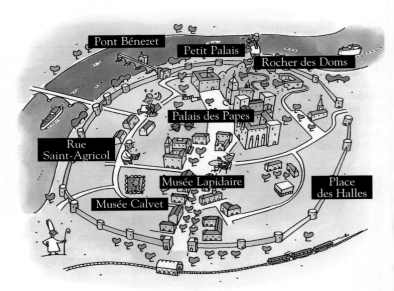

Pont Bénezet

Petit Palais

Rocher des Doms

Palais des Papes

Rue Saint-Agricol

Musée Lapidaire

Place des Halles

Musée Calvet

Holy city for a century

In 1309, Pope Clement V decided to move the pontifical court to the Comtat-Venaissin, the district in which Avignon is situated, which had been a papal state since 1274. At the time, the popes felt unable to rule from Rome since they were at the mercy of the internecine struggles between Rome's ruling families. At first Avignon saw very little of the Pope, but John XII, successor to Clement V, decided to settle there permanently. Benedict XII, to the great displeasure of the Italians, enlarged the episcopal palace, and Clement VI continued the work of his predecessor by

purchasing the town from the Comtesse de Provence. The results of this prosperous period are still very much in evidence. The town also has many mansions from the Baroque period. They cluster

around the Place de l'Horloge, the Place Pie and the Place Crillon (where the **flower market** is held on Saturday morning). They are also to be found in the back streets, the Rue des Teinturiers, the Rue Joseph-Vernet, the Rue du Roy-René and the Rue Banasterie. The Office de Tourisme conducts **tours of the town** (2 hours, 50 F), every Tuesday and Thursday at 10am, from 1 April to 30 October.

The ramparts

Pope Innocent VI had a 2½ miles (4.2 km) wall erected around Avignon in the 14th C. It was meant to protect the town from the Rhône flooding as much as from the attacks of

THE FESTIVAL

**Bureau du festival,
☎ 04 90 14 14 14.**
The courtyard of the
Palais des Papes has
been brought to life by
the festival for the past
52 years. It attracts
thousands of visitors
each year, from 10 July
to 2 August. Away from
the courtyard, there
are special shows for
children and many
cultural events,
including theatre,
ballet and puppet
shows. Information is
available from the
'Dolphin Blues' barge
(☎ 06 07 60 20 84).
Contemporary dance
displays are held next
to the theatre.
(☎ 04 90 14 14 26).

On the bridge at Avignon

The French nursery rhyme is
known around the world; but
only four arches and the
Chapelle Saint-Nicolas, dedicated to the patron saint of
bargees, remain of the original
bridge which linked the town
to the city of the cardinals
(now Villeneuve-lès-
Avignon). According to legend, Bénezet, a humble shepherd from the Vivarais, was
ordered to build a bridge over
the river by an angel. The
dances on the bridge were
actually held on the **Île de la
Barthelasse** where there were
dance halls.

Spotcheck
B2

Vaucluse

Things to do

The Festival of Avignon
See the orchid houses
(Parc Floral Tropical)
Antiques market at Roquemaure
Rambles in the Vaucluse

Within easy reach

*Saint-Rémy-de-Provence,
20 km S, p. 138.
The Vallée de la Durance,
p. 158.
Cavaillon, 25 km SE, p. 164.
L'Isle-sur-la-Sorgue,
23 km E, p. 166.
Pernes-les-Fontaines,
25 km NE, p. 168.
Carpentras, 28 km NE,
p. 170.*

Tourist Office

Avignon: ☎ 04 90 82 65 11

The Palais des Papes

☎ 04 90 27 50 74.
Open daily Apr.-Sep.,
9am-7pm (9pm in July,
8pm from Aug. to
mid-Sep.); Nov.-Mar.,
9.30am-5pm. Guided
tours. *Paid admission.*
The proportions of this handsome edifice can be admired
from the esplanade. It covers
16,100 sq. ft. (1,500 m²) and
was created mainly by Popes
Benedict XII and Clement VI
in 1334 and in 1352. Many
artists and craftsmen decorated this Gothic fortress.

marauders. No fewer than
39 towers and
7 gates
remain,
thanks to
the restora-
tion work
of Viollet-
le-Duc.

The main courtyard resonates with the sounds of the Avignon Festival.

The Doms Rocks

From the belvedere in the English-style park which adjoins the north rampart of the Palace, there is a magnificent view of the floodplain of the Rhône, looking out beyond the lake and the rocks. The Fort Saint-André and the Tour Philippe-le-Bel protect the valley at Ville-neuve-lès-Avignon. The nave of the Cathedral of Notre-Dame-des-Doms offers the coolness of stone and the great beauty of its Romanesque architecture.

The Musée du Petit Palais

Pl. du Palais-des-Papes,
☎ 04 90 86 44 58.
Open daily except Tue., Sep.-Jun., 9.30am-noon and 2-6pm; Jul.-Aug., 10.30am-6pm.
Paid admission.

The former episcopal residence of the bishops contains the **Gian Pietro Campana collection**. Campana was a director of the Mont-de-Piété in Rome, an insatiable collector who used the public purse for private gain and thereby amassed more than 15,000 objects and paintings. He was sentenced to hard labour, and his goods were bought by Napoleon III to be scattered in several provincial museums. Some of the collection was assembled in Avignon after 1945. The treasures include works by Botticelli and Carpaccio, and more than 300 other Italian paintings. The museum also catalogues the history of Provençal and Italian art from the Middle Ages to the Renaissance.

The Musée Calvet

65, Rue Joseph-Vernet,
☎ 04 90 86 33 84.
Open daily except Tue. 10am-1pm and 2-6pm.
Paid admission.
Major restoration work has been in progress here since 1986, but the museum can still be visited. The exhibits are contained in an elegant, aristocratic mansion. The character of the collection displayed here challenges all classification. The period covered ranges from prehistory to the 20th C. The new display

Botticelli, *Virgin and Child*

of ironwork is one of the highlights.

❀ The Angladon-Dubrujeaud foundation

5, Rue Laboureur,
☎ 04 90 82 29 03.
Open daily except Mon. and Tue., 1-7pm; out of season, 1-6pm.
Paid admission.
This collection is housed in the heart of old Avignon, in the intimacy of an 18th C. mansion. It displays furniture, objects and modern art collected by the designer Jacques Doucet. The treasures include works by Manet, Cézanne, Daumier, Picasso, Degas, Sisley, Van Gogh and Modigliani.

The Musée Lapidaire

27, Rue de la République,
☎ 04 90 85 75 38.
Open daily except Tue., 10am-1pm and 2-6pm.
Paid admission.
Little trace remains of the Roman occupation of Avignon, unlike in Arles. However, the Musée Calvet has set aside a special site at which local archeological excavations are preserved. Votive and

Modigliani, *The Pink Blouse*

PLACES TO GO — FOR A BIÈRE OR A BROWSE

Have a drink at La Civette, a fashionable bar on the Place de l'Horloge and a favourite haunt of actors and journalists. If you feel like reading, then go the La Roumanille bookshop, Rue Saint-Agricol. Built in 1855, this is an excellent hideout for browsers. For those who prefer shopping, the Rue Joseph-Vernet is a smart street lined with lots of chic boutiques. Not far away, antiques, art galleries and tea-rooms are to be found in the Rue de la Petite-Fusterie. You will also find some nice souvenirs of your visit at Aux Jardins de Provence (2, Rue Petite-Fusterie, ☎ 04 09 82 21 78).

funeral inscriptions and graves can be seen in the former chapel of the Jesuits' college, which is temporarily the archeological annex of the Musée Calvet.

Les *papalines*

Georges Poutet, 15, Rue des Trois-Faucons, ☎ 04 90 82 93 96.
In 1960, a competition was held to create a local Avignon sweetmeat designed to rival the *calissons* of Aix-en-Provence. Georges Poutet, a famous confectioner from Avignon, invented *papalines*, tiny pink confections flavoured with the local oregano. They cost 24 F for 3½ oz (100 g).

Rambles in the Vaucluse

Le Comité Départemental du Tourisme (CDT), 63, Rue César-Frank, ☎ 04 90 80 47 00.
The CDT can tell you anything you need to know about routes for rambles and hikes, horse rides or bike rides (with accommodation and the option of a guide). You can also obtain an information booklet with maps.

Villeneuve-lès-Avignon

The Chartreuse du Val-de-Bénédiction

Rue de la République, ☎ 04 90 15 24 24.
Open daily, 9am-6.30pm; out of season, 9.30am-5.30pm. Cafeteria open during the festival.
Paid admission.
Former home of Cardinal Étienne Aubert, who became Pope Innocent VI, the charterhouse has some handsome rooms, as well as cloisters, a church, a hospital, a prison and monastic cells. It is also used for art exhibitions and concerts.

Barbentane

Orchid houses

Parc Floral Tropical de Provence (Tropical Flower Park of Provence), Rte. de Terre-Fort, 6¼ miles (10 km) S. of Avignon by the N570 and the D 5, ☎ 04 90 95 50 72.
May-Sep., 10am-7pm; Oct.-Apr., 10am-5pm.
Paid admission.
A few miles from Avignon, under a glass roof covering more than 43,000 sq. ft (4,000 m²), grows a tropical forest in which thousands of varieties of orchids hang their roots from the trees. They germinate by joining forces with a fungus, and take 7 or 8 years to flower.

Roquemaure

Antiques market

At 9 miles (15 km) N. of Avignon, by the D980, ☎ 04 66 82 82 10.
1st Sun. of Apr., Jun. and Sep.
Antiques buyers and sellers congregate at this market. You will find many beautiful Provençal objects such as oil jars, Anduze vases and *boutis* (fabrics).

Tarascon and La Montagnette

Between Tarascon and Barbentane, the range of hills called La Montagnette offer a spectacular landscape. Tarascon, where Souleïado cloth is woven, was named after the local myth of the Tarasque monster. It is surrounded by the villages of Graveson and Boulbon and the Abbey of Saint-Michel-de-Frigolet stands on top of a hill. The area is planted with pine trees, olive trees and cypresses.

Tarascon

In the shadow of the castle

☎ 04 90 91 01 93.
Open daily, Apr.-Sep., 9am-7pm ; out of season, 9am-noon and 2-7pm, except Tue. and public holidays.
Paid admission.
The castle of the counts of Toulouse was begun in 1400 by Louis II of Anjou and completed by his son, King René. This typical medieval fortress is very well preserved, making it one of the loveliest castles in France. Its formidable ramparts conceal an elegant interior.

Saint Martha and the Tarasque

According to local legend, in the 1st C. AD, Saint Martha saved the town from a terrible monster called the Tarasque, who came each year to demand his quota of young people to devour. The local people dedicated a collegiate church to the saint, a few yards from the castle. It was founded in the 12th C. and became one of the most famous sanctuaries in Provence. The Tarasque, however, is fêted on the last weekend in June. There is a parade featuring King René and his court, women from Arles, and the famous Tartarin.

The true false home of Tartarin

55 bis, Bd Itam,
☎ 04 90 91 05 08.
Open daily except Sun., 15 Sep.-14 Dec. and 15 Mar.-14 Apr., 10am-noon and 1.30-7pm; out of season, 10am-noon and 2-7pm. Closed 15 Dec. to 15 Mar.
Paid admission.

The people of Tarascon became so fed up with being asked where the mythical Tartarin lived that they created a house for him, based on the descriptions of his creator, the writer Alphonse Daudet.

Sky-diving — an incredible feeling

Para-club de Tarascon,
1, Rue André-Perrot,
☎ 04 90 91 37 45.
Perm. Sun.-Fri.
9am-noon.

Spotcheck
A3

Bouches-du-Rhône

Things to do
The Cloth Museum
Sky-diving
The bottle procession

Within easy reach
Arles, 15 km S, p. 126.
Les Baux-de-Provence,
18 km SE, p. 136.
Saint-Rémy-de-Provence,
16 km E, p. 138.

Tourist Office
Tarascon: ☎ 04 90 91 03 52

In summer, you can obtain an official licence from the Fédération française de Parachutisme which lets you jump anywhere in France. One jump may be enough but you have the right to repeat the experience (1,000 F).

The Cloth Museum
Musée Charles-Démery,
39, Rue Proudhon,
☎ 04 90 95 50 72.
Closed Sat. and Sun.
By appointment only,
10am and 3pm.
This 14th C. mansion houses the Souleïado workshop

GRAVESON: GARDEN OF DELIGHTS
Mas La Chevèche,
Rte du Grès,
☎ 04 90 95 81 55.
Open daily, 10am-noon and 2-6pm (10am-6pm Jul.-Aug.).
Paid admission.
This 19th C. farmhouse contains a museum of perfume, offering you an enchanted voyage into the world of fragrance. It is filled with flasks, alembics and copper vats. The tour continues in the specialised area of the garden, where aromatic plants destined for distillation are cultivated. You can also enjoy refreshment at the 'fruit bar'.

and shop. Open Mon.-Fri., 8.30am-noon and 1.30-6pm. (See also p. 52.) There is a collection of 40,000 designs. The company was founded by Charles Démery in 1938 and carries on the tradition of the local cloth-makers. The museum traces the history of Indian fabric and how it was converted into something inherently Provençal.

Eating the Tarasque monster
Pâtissier Morin,
56, Rue des Halles,
☎ 04 90 91 01 17
The Tarasque inspired the pastry-cook Morin who named a cake after it, made of truffle paste and almond sponge flavoured with Cointreau. Unfortunately, the monster has to share its stardom with the town's other celebrity, Tartarin. For him, Morin created the **bézuquette de Tartarin**, a little cake filled with hazelnut praline.

Saint-Michel-de-Frigolet

The Pastrage tradition
The abbey of Saint-Michel-de Frigolet was founded in the 12th C. by the order known as the White Canons. Every Christmas Eve, they perpetuate the moving tradition of the *Pastrage*, a procession of shepherds carrying lambs, symbol of Christ's sacrifice,

followed by the inhabitants of Arles offering the 13 desserts. The abbey shop sells liqueurs and honey.

Boulbon

The bottle procession
Boulbon lies at the foot of the Montagnette, a farming village dominated by the imposing ruins of its castle. Every 1 June, a strange pilgrimage is held here. Men walk in procession with bottles of wine and attend a mass in the Chapelle Saint-Marcellin which is recited in Provençal. The wine is blessed by the priest. Only men are admitted to the chapel.

Orange
Gateway to the Midi

Orange is the second largest town in the Vaucluse. It was founded as Arausio at the foot of the hill of Saint-Eutrope, and despite the ravages of time, its Roman ruins are unique. Orange is almost a foretaste of Italy with its brilliant light and Roman remains. The district is famous for its wines.

Municipal Museum
Pl. des Frères-Mounet,
☎ **04 90 51 18 24.**
Open daily, 30 min. later than the theatre.
The museum is housed in a 17th C. mansion, and faces the theatre. It contains a remarkable array of Roman sculptures. A contemporary display traces the origin of Provençal cloth (of which attractive examples can be found at the Saturday morning **market**).

Gardens of the Municipal Museum

Arc de Triomphe
This monumental 3-arched gateway stood at the entrance to the town, on what was once the Via Agrippa which linked Arles to Lyon. It has been very well preserved and has bas-reliefs depicting the victories of Julius Caesar's famous second legion, whose veterans founded the city of Orange.

The Hill of Saint-Eutrope
The hill is a park containing the ruins of the 12th C. castle of the princes of Orange-Nassau, who ruled when Orange was the capital of a small independent principality. The castle was destroyed in the 17th C. on the orders of Louis XIV. The view over the plain of Orange and the ancient theatre is worth the effort of climbing to the top of the hill.

Châteauneuf-du-Pape
Great wines
The reputation of this wine needs no enhancement, but the charms of the little town of Châteauneuf are not so well-known. The popes of Avignon were quite aware of them when they made it their summer residence. Today only a few walls remain of the château in which they stayed.

Augustus

The gardens of the Hill of Saint-Eutrope

9am-noon and 2-6pm). A grape-ripening festival is held in early August. Why not extend your stay by visiting the vineyards of the appellation? (Information from the Office de Tourisme.)

Two other monuments deserve a visit. They are the 10th C. chapelle Saint-Théodoric (medieval frescoes in the choir), and the church of Notre-Dame-de-l'Assomption for its handsome Roman ceiling. Of course, Châteauneuf has a wine museum; it is called the

L'Origan du Comtat

There are wonderful liqueurs in Provence as well as wines. In 1870, Auguste Blachère created L'Origan du Comtat, a distillation and maceration of 60 herbs growing on Mont Ventoux which is still made at Châteauneuf (Rte de Sorgue, ☎ 04 90 83 53 81. Tour and tasting are free.). This delicious drink, a stomachic, is said to have saved Avignon from the cholera epidemic of 1884.

Sérignan-du-Comtat
L'Harmas de Fabre
5 miles (8 km) N. of Orange by the D976, ☎ 04 90 70 00 44. Open daily 9-11.30am and 2-6pm.

Musée du Père-Anselme (Rte d'Avignon, ☎ 04 90 83 70 07. Open daily

Spotcheck
B2

Vaucluse

Things to do

Chorégies in the amphitheatre
Taste the wines of
Châteauneuf-du-Pape
Taste L'Origan du Comtat
L'Harmas de Fabre garden

Within easy reach

Carpentras, 25 km SE, p. 170.

Tourist Offices

Orange: ☎ 04 90 34 70 88
Châteauneuf:
☎ 04 90 83 71 08

The magnificent Mediterranean garden of Harmas, created by the entomologist Jean-Henri Fabre, contains more than 800 varieties of trees and shrubs, including cedars from the Atlas Mountains and black pine from Corsica.

A nature walk

There are delightful walks to take between Camaret, Sainte-Cécile-les-Vignes,

Sérignan, Travaillan, Uchaux and Violès, starting from l'Harmas. The pretty path from Mont-Serein is an introduction to the typical flora and fauna of Mont Ventoux. (Information, ☎ 04 90 63 42 02.)

CHORÉGIES IN THE ANCIENT AMPHITHEATRE

☎ 04 90 51 17 60.
Open daily, 9am-6.30pm; out of season, 9am-noon and 1.30-5pm
Paid admission (ticket valid for the museum).
Used for the Chorégies Festival (☎ 04 90 34 24 24), this handsome amphitheatre dating from the Ist C. has retained its imposing stage back wall, in which a niche contains a colossal statue of the Emperor Augustus. The tiers are banked against the side of the hill of Saint-Eutrope. In summer, opera buffs attend performances here as the theatre is famous for its exceptional acoustics. The classical drama and music festival known as Les Chorégies d'Orange began in 1869 and is held in July and early August. It was mainly theatrical at first, but opened up to music in the 1970s. It has now acquired an international reputation.

Vaison-la-Romaine and the Haut Vaucluse
the wines of Provence

I n a land smelling deliciously of wine and of ancient history, you can travel from Vaison, Roman indeed but also Romanesque, to Séguret, tucked into the hillside; from the famous vineyards of Gigondas (*jocunditas* is the Latin for 'joy') to those of Vacqueyras, passing through landscapes laced with stones and rocky outcrops.

Vaison
A Roman jewel

Vaison is set in a hilly landscape and jealously guards its ruins, only discovered in the early 20th C. The first inhabitants, the Voconces, were defeated by the Romans and abandoned their hilltop village to settle in the plain. Then a city with connections to Rome was built on the banks of the River Ouvèze. It has public baths, villas, a theatre and porticos. The upper town was abandoned but was recolonised in the Middle Ages.

The ruins
Collines de Puymin and de la Villasse,
Office de Tourisme,
☎ **04 90 36 02 11.**
Open 10am-12.30pm and 2-6pm (until 7pm in summer).
Paid admission.
Most of the ruins date from the 1st and 2nd C. AD. The **Roman theatre,** beside the Colline de Puymin, held 5,000-6,000 spectators. There are the **Maison des Messii,** the **portico of Pompey,** part of the public baths and the **house of the silver bust**

(in the Villasse district). Unfortunately, the centre of the ancient city remains buried under the present city. The **Musée Théo-Desplans** (☎ 04 90 36 50 00) also exhibits objects found during the excavations.

In the lanes of the upper town

After taking a detour by the **Cathedral of Notre-Dame-de-Nazareth** (11th-12th C.) with its very beautiful Romanesque **cloister,** visit the **Roman bridge** which crosses the River Ouvèze. It leads to the medieval town, whose 14th C. surrounding wall, mainly built with stones from the ruins of the Roman city, is still intact. At the foot of the **Château** of the counts of Toulouse lie the **calades** (small, narrow cobbled streets) which were abandoned until recently, but are slowly returning to life thanks to local craftsmen.

MONTMIRAIL CLIFFS

South of Vaison, the white chalk cliffs, 2,090 ft (627 m), known as Les Dentelles de Montmirail (Montmirail Lace) have been eroded into silvery needles. They stretch from Prébayon to Montmirail and are 5 miles (8 km) long. Once used as lookouts, they are now a paradise for climbers and ramblers. The North face is shaded in summer and is climbed from June to October – over 1½ miles (2.5 km) of paths. Information ☎ 04 90 80 47 00.

At the end of July Vaison holds a **Festival des Choeurs Lauréats**, (Festival of Laureate Choirs) and in November, there are the **Journées gourmandes** (Feast days) and other events (information from the Office de Tourisme).

Gigondas
Wine cellars galore

Gigondas, topped with a castle, looms up at a bend in the road. Although its ramparts have challenged time for seven centuries it is surrounded by a contemporary sculpture garden. The wine of Gigondas is one of the best Côtes-du-Rhône, along with those of Vacqueyras and of Châteauneuf-du-Pape. You can visit a great number of vineyards and cellars if you first make an appointment. They include Jean-Pierre Cartier, at Les Gouberts (☎ 04 90 65 86 38); Franck Alexandre at the Teysonnières domain (☎ 04 90 65 86 39) and Pierre Lambert and Sons at the Mavette domain (☎ 04 90 65 85 29).

Sablet and Séguret
Villages among the vines

Sablet is a typical Provençal village with its church and its concentric streets. The surrounding vineyards produce a great wine. The next village, Séguret, resembles a Christmas crib – which is what it becomes every year when all its inhabitants dress up in Provençal costume to re-enact the Christmas story in the **pastorales**.

Vacqueyras
Wine and flora

The village lives from its ancient vineyards. The wine can be tasted at the **caveau des Dentelles**. Nearby, on a hill dominated by the chapelle Notre-Dame-de-Pitié, the **botanical garden of Coste de Coa** covers 5 acres (13 ha) and is planted with more than 100 species of local flora, all clearly identified. (Open daily. Information, ☎ 04 90 12 39 02.)

Salon-de-Provence
around Crau

Salon-de-Provence stands at the gateway to Marseille, and is famous for the Patrouille de France (French ace flying team) and the École de l'Air (flying school). It was an important commercial centre in the early 1900s, and nowadays has a certain relaxed elegance with its shady avenues of plane trees. Soap is still made here, the scholar and seer Nostradamus is still honoured here, and sweetmeats are still sold bearing his effigy, in memory of the book of confectionery and beauty treatments that he wrote in 1555. All of which makes this pleasant provincial town really worth a visit.

Salon-de-Provence
Museums

Nostradamus lies buried within the gothic walls of the **Collégiale Saint-Laurent** and you can visit his grave. The traditional arts and crafts of the region are on display at the **Musée de Salon et de la Crau** (Av. Donnadieu, ☎ 04 90 56 28 37. Open daily except Tues., 10am-noon and 2-6pm; 2-6pm weekends).

Musée Nostradamus

11, Rue Nostradamus, ☎ 04 90 56 64 31. Open daily, 9am-noon and 2-6pm; out of season, Sat. and Sun., 2-6pm. *Paid admission.*

Nostradamus was 45 when he settled in Salon and nothing, not even death, could separate him from the place. In the street that is named after him, there is a museum devoted to this scholar and astrologer, who became famous for his prophesies in verse.

Soap factories

Marseille is famous for its soap but soap is also made in Salon. The art of combining the heated natural oils with alkaline vegetable matter is still practised in the Savonneries Fabre (148, Av. Paul-Bourret, ☎ 04 90 53 24 77; factory visits Mon. and Thu. at 11am) and Rampal (71, Rue Félix-Pyat, ☎ 04 90 56 07 28; visits 10am-noon and 4-6pm, except Fri.). Did you know that for a soap to be labelled 'pure olive oil', it has to contain at least 72% virgin oil?

VISITS TO FACTORIES AND INDUSTRIES

This part of Provence claims the 'privilege' of having a major industrial complex. Even if you are not passionate about the iron and steel industry, you might like to take a quick look at the steelworks at Sollac (a subsidiary of Usinor-Sacilor conglomerate, ☎ 04 42 05 58 24), the Esso refinery and its Museum of Energy (visit the control room, ☎ 04 42 47 73 43) or the port authority of Marseille-Fos (which can also be visited by boat). It has to be said that these visits to factories and industries are fascinating (Marseille Office de Tourisme, ☎ 04 91 13 89 00).

'Fiesta du Jazz'

Every summer, in the second week of August, there is an impromptu jazz concert in the Place Morgan (free admission), an offshoot of the 'Fiesta du Jazz' held in the castle courtyard every two years, alternating with the Gospel Festival: street entertainment, open-air masses, concerts in the church of Saint-Laurent. (Information, ☎ 04 90 44 82 28 or at the Office de Tourisme.)

Istres
Water sports

The three ponds (*étangs*) in the area (Berre, Olivier and Entressen) lie close to the wooded hills and the mysterious Plaine de la Crau. There are 284 acres (115 ha) of salt marshes which produce 50 000 t. of salt annually. The **Musée Archéologique** has a magnificent medieval centre, and displays exquisite amphorae (☎ 04 42 55 50 08, daily, 2-7pm). The Club Nautique d'Entressen (☎ 04 90 50 52 39) offers sailing, canoeing and kayaking from June to October. At the Maison Nautique de l'Olivier, the Club Istres Sports offers rowing lessons (☎ 04 42 55 51 52).

Saint-Chamas
History and confectionery

This lakeside village beside the Étang de Berre is divided in two (the Delà and the Pertuis) by a hillside perforated with caves that were once inhabited. Look for the remains of the medieval walls and a 15th C. gate. The Pont Flavien (1st C.) with its two **arcs de triomphe** crosses the River Touloubre in a single 71 ft (21 m) span. The speciality of the town are *pichoulines*, olive-shaped sweets made of almond paste, pistachios and white chocolate.

Spotcheck
B3-B4

Bouches-du-Rhône

Things to do

Visit a soap factory
The 'Fiesta du Jazz'
Musée Nostradamus
Water sports
Visits to factories and industries

Within easy reach

Camargue, 30 km SW, p. 130.
Cavaillon, 30 km N, p. 164.
Aix-en-Provence, 40 km E, p. 174.

Tourist Office

Salon-de-Provence:
☎ 04 90 56 27 60

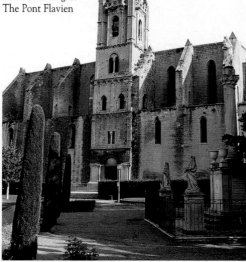

Martigues the Venice of Provence

Every August, Martigues resounds to the echoes of the World Folk Festival. Afterwards, the little port, bathed in the delicate light of the Étang de Berre, reverts once again to its habitual tranquillity. The town, crisscrossed with canals, is set on the Côte Bleue, a coastline of wild rocky coves.

Bridges and canals
Between the Chenal de Caronte and the Étang de Berre, three canals divide the town into three districts, each with its own village-like atmosphere. Each district has its own church and its own history. The **Chapelle de l'Annonciade**, with its highly decorated walls and ceilings, and the **Église de la Madeleine** ('cathedral' for the locals) with its Baroque façade, are both worth a visit.

Le Musée de Ziem
Bd du 14-Juillet,
☎ 04 42 80 66 06.
Open Sep.-Jun., 2.30-6.30pm. except Mon.-Tue. Jul.-Aug. 10am-noon. and 2.30-6.30pm. except Tues. and public holidays. *Free admission.*
In 1860, the painter Félix Ziem fell in love with Martigues and its light, and bought a property at Le Chat-Noir. This prolific artist, who produced more than 3,000 paintings, donated some of his work to the town and the museum was thus founded. In addition to fine paintings from Provence, it contains some contemporary art and a collection of local archaeological finds.

Visiting a power station
Although Martigues has successfully retained its air of being a small Provençal port, it is surrounded by industry and you can visit some high tech installations. At the Électricité de France (EDF) power station in

Martigues-Ponteau (☎ 04 42 35 56 03. Mon.-Fri. by appointment. Free tours.) you will learn how power stations work by obtaining electricity from the heat produced by fuel. The mysteries of cooling tanks, steam boilers, turbines, control rooms and high-voltage room will all be revealed.

Folk Festival

For 8 days (from end of July to end of August) Martigues becomes the stage on which more than 500 artists, dancers, choreographers, musicians and folk

groups from the five continents perform in the open air, on a floating platform erected on the Saint-Sébastien canal. The World Folk Festival, which was only instituted in 1989, has proved to be an outstanding success for performers and spectators alike. (Information from the Office de Tourisme.)

In the vicinity
The Côte Bleue

The area remains unspoilt thanks to its having been declared a regional marine park in 1983. The Côte Bleue boasts almost 15 miles (24 km) of magnificent coastline; its limestone cliffs are interspersed by the coves of Niolon, La Redonne and Gignac. Near **Carro**, which is tuna-fishing territory, the fort of Port-de-Bouc dominates the entrance to the Caronte canal. The villages of **Carry-le-Rouet** and **Sausset-les-Pins** are seaside resorts. Fernand Joseph Désiré Contandin, the famous French actor Fernandel, is buried in the Carry cemetery.

The *oursinades* festival in Carry

Just as oysters are traditionally eaten at Christmas and New Year in this part of the world, the people of Carry eat sea-urchins (*oursins*) and celebrate the **Oursinade** on the first three Sundays in February. Locals enjoy this spiny echinoderm by eating it raw on fingers of bread. The sea creature is full of protein, phosphorus and calcium, but fishing for it on the rocky sea-bed is strictly regulated.

SARDINADES AND WATER TOURNAMENTS

Even though Martigues doesn't live off fishing as much as it used to, one sardine out of four is caught here and sold by auction at Port-de-Bouc. This wonderful fish is a good excuse for a celebration. There is feasting on sardines at the *Sardinades* and water tournaments are held along the shore. Other seafood delicacies from the Blue Coast are the sea urchin and the *martiguaise,* a type of Mediterranean mussel which is smaller and more delicate than the Toulon mussel. The Étang de Berre yields the *testu,* a variety of mullet whose eggs are salted and pressed before being left to dry. This is how the delicacy called *poutargue* is made and its price can rise to more than 1,000 F for a kilogram (2¼ lb)! It is eaten on slices of bread drizzled with olive oil. You will find it being sold by fishermen's wives at the market in the Île district, which is held on Thursdays and Sunday mornings.

The Petit Luberon
villages perched high on the hills

Scattered over its north-facing slope and fully exposed to the *mistral* wind, the hilltop villages of the Petit Luberon look down from on high. They take pride in their ancient buildings, which have found a new lease of life with the arrival of artists and craftspeople. Despite their peaceful appearance today, in the 16th C. they were the scene of the massacres of the Vaudois, a prelude to the Religious Wars

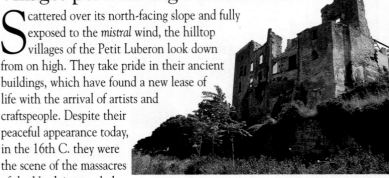

The ruins of the Château of the Marquis de Sade at Lacoste

which plagued France between 1562 and 1598, and which were the pretext for a power struggle between contenders for the French throne.

String quartets

From May to September, the Abbaye de Silvacane and many of the little churches of Luberon (at L'Isle-sur-la-Sorgue, Roussillon, Fontaine-de-Vaucluse), host the **Festival International du Quatuor à Cordes** (International String Quartet Festival). Many famous musicians come to play in these lovely surroundings. (Information, ☎ 04 90 75 89 60.)

The Eglise de Ménerbes contains two 16th C. painted panels

Ménerbes
Castelet and the Corkscrew Museum

The village looks like a stone ship on a steep rugged headland. The rock on which the village is built forms its ramparts. The *castelet* (little castle) at the tip of the promontory had a perfect strategic position. This ancient fort contains a pretty 14th C. church and the

Hôtel de Tringy (16th-17th C.), a stately home. The unusual and amusing **Musée du Tire-bouchon (Corkscrew Museum)** (☎ 04 90 72 41 58, daily, 9am-noon and 2-6pm, Sat., Sun. and public holidays, 10am-noon and 3-7pm) demonstrates 1001 different ways of opening a bottle. And, of course, there is a wine-tasting as the finale!

Lacoste
Under the watchful eye of the Marquis

Facing Bonnieux, once its bitter rival, and dominated by the ruins of the Marquis de

Sade's castle, the lanes of Lacoste are lined with ancient houses and topped by ruined ramparts. Around the castle, gigantic underground quarries of molass stone are an excellent source of material for restoring the houses. The **Abbaye Saint-Hilaire** lies about 1¼ miles (2 km), in the direction of Ménerbes. (☎ 04 90 75 88 83. Open 10am-7pm; out of season, 10am-5pm.)

Bonnieux
Climbing steps under the cedars

Bonnieux is reached by crossing the Pont Julien built in

the 3rd C. BC. The village stands at the foot of the spur topped by the walled castle. The church crowns the summit and is reached by climbing 86 steps, in the shade of 100-year-old cedars. In the village itself, a few 13th C. remains of towers and ramparts stand beside beautiful old houses, such as the Hôtel de Rouville, now used as the town hall.

THE CEDAR FOREST

If you enjoyed the shade of the Bonnieux cedars, breathe the bracing and refreshing air of the Atlas cedar forest, 3 miles (5 km) east of the village. Planted in 1861 with saplings from the Atlas Mountains of Morocco, the forest flourishes and continues to spread despite numerous forest fires. Stop at the car park (paid admission) and walk along the path, following the signs that feature information regarding the flora and fauna of the surrounding area, the Petit Luberon.

Alternative way back via the Musée de la Boulangerie (Bakery Museum) (12, Rue de la République, ☎ 04 90 75 88 34. Open daily except Tue., 10am-noon and 3-6.30pm. Paid admission.)

Spotcheck
B3

Vaucluse

Things to do

String quartet festival
Corkscrew Museum
The cedar forest

Within easy reach

Apt, p. 160.
Gordes, p. 162.

Tourist Office

Bonnieux:
☎ 04 90 75 91 90

Lourmarin

In memory of Camus

Lourmarin has the reputation of being one of **the most beautiful villages in France**. It overlooks the valley which separates the Petit Luberon from the Grand Luberon. Narrow, winding lanes lead to the rocky spur of the Renaissance castelet which has a 'salt-box' belfry. Built on the site of a medieval castle, it has welcomed such illustrious visitors as King François I, Winston Churchill and Queen Elizabeth II. (☎ 04 90 68 15 23. Guided tours daily, 10am-noon and 2.30-5.30pm; out of season, 4.30pm). One of the features is an unusual double spiral

staircase, consisting of 93 steps created from a single piece of wood. Lourmarin is also famous for the tomb of the writer Albert Camus who was buried in the village cemetery in 1960.

Le Pont-Julien

Ceramic tile making

Ets. Vernin, 3 miles (5 km) from Bonnieux on the RN100 ☎ 04 90 04 63 04. Show room open daily except Sun., 9am-noon and 1.30-6.30pm. Workshop open weekdays, 8am-noon and 1.30-5.30pm. After the tiles are cut and baked in the kiln for what may sometimes be hours, some of them are then painted, and baked again in an enamelling kiln to bring out the colours. The Vernin-Carreaux company of Apt makes some of its products in this way and has been using the traditional methods for making tiles since 1885. Floor tiles and roof tiles are a traditional feature in Provence.

The Grand Luberon
a tour of the châteaux

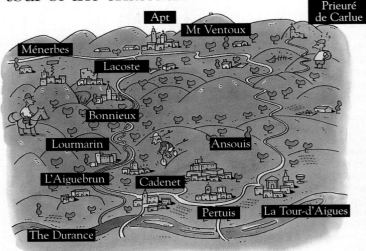

Prieuré de Carlue

Apt

Mt Ventoux

Ménerbes

Lacoste

Bonnieux

Lourmarin

Ansouis

L'Aiguebrun

Cadenet

Pertuis

La Tour-d'Aigues

The Durance

Unlike the Petit Luberon, there are no small rocky valleys or cliffs here. Although the hills are higher, they are more rounded and are planted with evergreen or white oaks and Aleppo pines. In this beautiful landscape, the villages have clock towers, ancient buildings and châteaux whose walls often lie in ruins. The views are breathtaking.

Cadenet
Musée de la Vannerie

Cadenet offers the visitor the chance to see its beautiful 17th-18th C. houses, the site of its feudal castle and its cave dwellings, not to mention its famous **statue of André Estienne**, a young drummer who, during the battle of the Pont d'Arcole in 1796, swam across the river and beat the advance on the opposite bank, making the Austrians flee as they thought they were caught in crossfire! The **Church of Saint-Étienne** has a 3rd C. marble baptismal font and Provençal bell-tower. In the **Musée de la Vannerie** (Wickerwork and Basketry Museum), the various tools and products on display trace

the history of one of the principal activities in the region from the 18th C. to 1978. (☎ 04 90 68 24 44. Open daily except Tue. and Sun. morning, Apr.-Oct., 10am-noon and 2.30-6.30pm. Paid admission.)

Ansouis
Extraordinary Museum and concerts

The **château** (☎ 04 90 09 82 70, open daily 2.30-6pm) which dominates the village has been in the same family

La Tour-d'Aigues

Spotcheck
C3

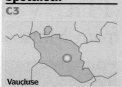

Vaucluse

Things to do
**Festival of the Sud-Luberon
Medieval village
Mountain biking and walks**

Within easy reach
Apt, 35 km NW, p. 160.

Tourist Office
Cadenet :
☎ 04 90 68 38 21

since 1178. It contains some fine examples of tapestry and Renaissance furniture. The kitchen is very popular and concerts are held in the terraced gardens, which are of typically French design, throughout the summer.
In the vaults of the 15th C. **Musée Extraordinaire** (☎ 04 90 09 86 98, open daily 2-7pm, paid admission) there are paintings, ceramics and stained-glass windows by Georges Mazoyer.

Pertuis
16th C. ruins
The Aigues valley is in the south of the Luberon and contains 11 villages, of which Pertuis is the 'capital'. Built along the Vallée de la Durance valley, this little village is aptly named (*pertuis* means 'passage') as it once stood at a busy crossroads. It has retained some handsome old buildings which include the home of Queen Jeanne (1585), an old shop, the house owned by King François, the Church of St. Nicolas (1520s triptych) and the castle keep, which was destroyed in 1596.

Vineyards and a festival
The village was built in a region of plains and low hills in which a famous wine is produced. It owes its name to an 11th C. fortification which was replaced by the existing Renaissance château. Destroyed by fire in 1792, this château is now in ruins but the imposing entrance, inspired by ancient triumphal arches, still stands. The cellars contain the **Musée de l'Histoire du Pays d'Aigues** and the **Musée des Faïences** (☎ 04 90 07 50 29). Every year in the main courtyard there is the **festival of the Sud-Luberon** (mid July to mid August) with music, dance and theatre, with a strong Latin-American influence.

Céreste
Medieval village
This is an ancient Roman site, but the remains of the **village médiéval** surrounding the château are the main

attraction. The village also contains important geological sites which are part of the Luberon Nature Reserve. Here you will find remarkable **fossils** (fish and plants) formed in the limestone schist.

MOUNTAIN BIKING AND WALKS
For keep-fit enthusiasts, there is always the man-made lake at Cadenet (July-Sept.) or exhausting mountain bike rides (mountain bikes available for hire) or hikes (there are three signposted walks). At Lauris, several miles from Cadenet in the direction of Cavaillon, the Mas de Recaute (☎ 04 90 08 29 58) offers pony-treks lasting from 1 to 7 days (reservations necessary). Six different routes are offered.
At the Parc du Luberon Centre, in Apt (1, Pl. Jean-Jaurès, ☎ 04 90 04 42 00), there is plenty of information about the local flora and fauna, as well as about the best hikes and rambles, bicycle rides and other excursions.

The Vallée de la Durance
from Manosque to Avignon

Everyone forgets that the Durance was once a river in its own right, not a mere tributary of the Rhône. Admittedly that was several hundred years ago. Then, suddenly, the River Durance changed its course, deserting the Crau plain. Previously considered one of the three plagues of Provence for its floods and violence, its waters have been calmed by dams and hydro-electric plants. Nowadays, the Durance occupies a river bed which is too big for it.

The course of the River Durance

Whereas downstream from Sisteron, the river still rushes like a torrent (fed by numerous tributaries from the Alps), its course becomes calmer just after Manosque. The waters of the Durance and the Verdon meet at the Cadarache dam 6 miles (10 km) south of Manosque. Further downstream, in the Mirabeau Gorges, the river flows westward leaving the Haute Provence. It can be crossed by a suspension bridge, at which point you can take a **walk along the river bank beside the Luberon** which will lead you to the gates of Avignon.

The canals of Basse Provence

These irrigation canals connect the Durance to the Mediterranean. They are also used to supply water to towns and factories and to produce electricity. The waterworks have put an end to the water shortages in the coastal towns between Toulon and Marseille, as well as those experienced by numerous summer holiday makers! The canals of Marseille and Verdon, downstream from Manosque, have fallen into

disuse but still have beautiful features, such as the Saint-Christophe basin, S. of Cadenet on the D973, the Roquefavour aqueduct 7 miles (12 km)W. of Aix-en-Provence on the D9 then the D65, or the Réaltor reservoir, 6 miles (10 km) SW. of Aix on the D9.

Mérindol
Bird watching
Maison du Parc,
☎ **04 90 04 42 00.**
Open Mon.-Sat., 8.30am-noon, 1.30-7pm out of season, closed Sat. pm. The Mallemort dam (S. of Mérindol) is an outstanding lake for **bird watching.** Winter and spring are the best seasons for seeing the

finest species nesting on the Durance. There are non-migratory birds (coots, herons, shellducks, terns and so on) and migratory birds (flamingos, bee-eaters, cormorants). The many noticeboards inside the hide will help you to identify them.

Birds of Luberon

In the Aix district, the riverbank north of the Durance runs through the Luberon. At the Pertuis bridge, take the south bank. A wide cement pathway on top of the dyke runs alongside the river. It is not very attractive in itself but is easily forgotten when you contemplate the **view over the Luberon**. This route will enable you to watch the birds migrating in spring (allow 3 to 6 hours, depending on how often you stop).

Régalon Gorges

From Mérindol, follow the signs on GR6.
Although not as impressive as the Verdon Gorges, those at

Régalon are nevertheless impressive. The deep cleft is long and no wider than 40 in. (1m) in places. Blocks of stone have become wedged in the cracks. Make sure you don't get stuck there yourself in wet weather because the trickling stream could suddenly become a torrent.

La Roque-d'Anthéron

Silvacane Abbey

☎ 04 42 50 41 69.
Open daily. Apr.-Sep., 9am-7pm; Oct.-Mar., 10am-1pm and 2-5pm. Closed Tue. in winter. *Paid admission.*

Like the Cistercian abbeys of Thoronet in the Argens valley, and Sénanque near Gordes, the Abbaye de Silvacane lies hidden in a remote spot, nestling on the left bank of the River Durance. Built between 1175 and 1300, it is a subtle combination of Romanesque and Gothic styles. Its massive walls and clean lines reflect the austerity of the Cistercian order. The monks who founded and built the abbey wanted to emphasise its plainness and strip it of all superfluous decoration. It is such a wonderful stone monument that you cannot fail to be moved by it.

Spotcheck
C3

Bouches-du-Rhône

Things to do

Bird watching
Trip down the Régalon gorges
Piano Festival

Within easy reach

Avignon, p. 140.
Cavaillon, p. 164.
Manosque, p. 182.

Tourist Office

Avignon: ☎ 04 90 82 65 11

Apt and Roussillon

a colourful district

Between the Luberon and the steep hills of the Vaucluse, Apt wears the brilliant colours of the ochre-bearing region with pride. The ancient Roman colony of Apt is a good starting point for excursions into the Luberon, or for discovering the Provençal Colorado. Gourmets can stock up on crystallised fruit and linger in some of the best produce markets of the Midi.

Apt

Country market

Between the Place de la Bouquerie (market on Sat. morning) and the Porte Saignon, you will find 16th-17th C. mansions, the tower of the ramparts and the old town. The **Cathédrale Sainte-Anne** (open daily, 10am-noon and 4-6pm) has a chapel royal which contains actual relics of St. Anne. On Tuesday mornings (May-Sep.), there is a **marché paysan** (farmers' market) on the Cours Laure-Perret (the square).

La Maison du Parc du Luberon

1, Pl. Jean-Jaurès, ☎ 04 90 04 42 00. Open daily except Sun., 8.30am-noon and 1.30-6pm (7pm in summer); closed Sat. afternoon in winter. *Paid admission.* Those who enjoy walking or mountain biking, nature-lovers, or even casual strollers, should head for the Maison du Parc du Luberon. There is plenty of information about the various routes, the fauna and flora in this protected site. Lavender lovers are particularly well provided for (see p. 81).

Apt china

This is made using a particular technique called *terres mêlées* (mixed earths), which creates a marbling effect. The tradition carries on today and you will find examples by Jean Faucon (**Atelier Bernard**, 12, Av. de la Libération, ☎ 04 90 74 15 31. Open 8am-noon and 2-6pm).

The kingdom of crystallised fruit

Madame de Sévigné used to compare Apt to a huge jam-making pan. Trust the judgement of this great woman of letters and indulge yourself in Apt's gourmet delights. You will find a large selection of crystallised fruit in the **Confiserie Saint-Denis** (Gargas, ☎ 04 90 74 07 35) or at **Jean Ceccon** (24, Quai Liberté, ☎ 04 90 74 21 90).

Jazz and 'Tréteaux de Nuit' festivals

This jazz festival lasts from the end of April to the beginning of May and introduces new talent, both from France and other countries. (☎ 04 90 74 00 34 or ☎ 04 90 75 54 27). In the second half of July, 'Les Tréteaux de Nuit' (Night Stage) festival offers an

OCHRE COUNTRY

You can see the ochre both in its natural state or when it has been processed. Those who simply wish to gaze at the natural ochre can follow the very beautiful track of the old quarries on the Giants' Causeway (la Chaussée des Géants), signposted by the Maison du parc du Luberon (Easter-Aug. Paid admission). The colours and the light of the Cirque des Aiguilles are unforgettable. The 'Conservatoire de l'Ocre', on the site of the old Mathieu factory offers you the chance to see how the mineral is transformed into pigment (on D104 ; ☎ 04 90 05 66 69. Open daily, Mar.-Nov. 9am-7pm; out of season daily, except Sat and Sun.,10am-noon and 2-6pm. Paid admission. 2¼ lb (1 kg) of ochre : 30 F). 'Ochre tours' departing from Rustrel are also available (p. 58). Once you have seen the ochre country, there is still the pretty lavender route to explore, starting from Apt (p. 81).

Spotcheck
C3

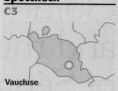

Vaucluse

Things to do

The country market in Apt
See Apt china
Sample crystallised fruit
See the Ochre country
Jazz festival
Walks in the Luberon

Within easy reach

Petit Luberon, p. 154.
Grand Luberon, p. 156.

Tourist Office

Apt: ☎ 04 90 74 03 18

Goult
Terraced pathways

Chemin de la Roche-Redonne,
Info. at the town hall (*mairie*),
☎ 04 90 72 20 16.
Free admission.
High above the village, near the mill, this delightfully fragrant path of the Roche-Redonne is the highlight of a trip to the 'Conservatoire des Terrasses'. In ochre country, olive trees, vines, almond trees, ferns and Venus fly-traps grow on the *restanques* terraces, which are supported by low, dry stone walls.

unusual mixture of entertainment with plays, classical music, blues and pop (information and bookings at the Office de Tourisme).

Roussillon
Shades of ochre

Roussillon, which is about 6 miles (10 km) from Apt, is aptly named 'the Red Delphi'. The history of this village which crowns the summit of Mont Rouge, is closely linked with the exploitation of ochre,

responsible for both its colour and its fame (p. 58). The golden and red hues that adorn the walls of the houses are an enticement to walk in the shady lanes. Don't miss the Tour du Beffroi (tower of the belfry), which straddles a narrow street. From the fort, you will have **splendid panoramic views** over the Val des Fées, the Luberon and the steep hills of Vaucluse.

Gordes and the Abbey of Sénanque
monumental stones

Standing opposite the Luberon, perched on the foothills of the Vaucluse plateau, the dry stone buildings of Gordes seem to reach for the blue sky. At the foot of the town olive and almond trees spread their green foliage, iridescent in the light. Above, the fortified château and the church dominate the buildings, which seem to melt into the rock. This beautiful place is no stranger to hordes of visitors and each summer the walls resound to the noise of the festival.

A LITTLE DIALECT DICTIONARY

Aiguier: free-standing cistern for storing rain water.
Clapas: heap of stones used for building the *restanques*.
Jas: sheepfold separated from the farm, where the flock sleep.
Restanque (or bancau): name given to the low walls used to shore up hillside terraces.

Artists and craftsmen

The 11th C. **château** was rebuilt around 1500 in the Renaissance style (magnificent fireplace in the large room on the first floor). It is used annually for exhibitions of modern art (open daily, except Tue., 10am-noon and 2-6pm). The art overflows into the nearby streets lined with **artists' studios** and **craft shops**. Visitors can wander around the paved, vaulted alleyways, dry stone steps and ancient stones, in splendid shades of sun-drenched golden-beige.

The surrounding area

Le Moulin des Bouillons

3 miles (5 km) South of Gordes, D148 towards Saint-Pantaléon,
☎ 04 90 72 22 11.

Open daily except Tue., 10am-noon and 2-6pm. Closed 15 Nov.-1 Feb. *Paid admission.*

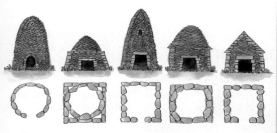

Spotcheck
B2

Vaucluse

Things to do

The Moulin des Bouillons
The village of the 'bories'

Within easy reach

Petit Luberon, p. 154.

Tourist Office

Gordes : ☎ 04 90 72 02 75

In the middle of a park stands a 16th-17th C. *mas* (farmhouse) which contains an ancient oil press. The **Musée du Vitrail**, which is within easy reach, tells the story of stained and painted glass and celebrates the work of Frédérique Duran, who is both a painter and a stained glass artist.

The village of the 'bories'

☎ 04 90 72 03 48.
Daily, 9am-8pm. Out of season, 9am-5pm.
Paid admission.
Just outside the village, there is a fascinating group of twenty or so dry stone buildings, covering about 2½ acres (1 ha). They include dwellings, sheepfolds, bread ovens, curtain walls – all built with impressive skill. These flat-stone constructions use no cement or mortar and the vaulted roofs have no frame.

A museum of stone

A visit to the village of the 'bories' is also an opportunity to discover what life was like in the district. A small country museum displays objects and farm tools that were in everyday use in the area until the 19th C.

An abbey amidst lavender fields

1.8 miles (3 km) North of Gordes by the D177,
☎ 04 90 72 05 72.
Open daily, March-Oct., 10am-noon and 2-6pm (closed in the mornings, Sun. and Catholic holidays); Nov.-Feb., 2-5pm (until 6pm Sat., Sun. and school holidays.).

The excellent Roman art bookshop is open from 10am to 7pm.
Paid admission.
The Abbey of Sénanque is situated in a peaceful valley, surrounded by fields of lavender. It is a classic example of the utter simplicity sought by the monastic order which built it. It is also an extraordinary example of early Cistercian architecture (12th C.). The austerity of the stonework and great simplicity of shapes are all reminders of the first principle of the Cistercian order, that of the renunciation of the pleasures of this world. The interior of the church is a wonderful resonance chamber, designed for monastic chant.

SUMMER EVENINGS IN GORDES

Since the first two weeks of August, 1993, the Gordes Soirées d'Eté have become an opportunity of hearing music, drama and song performed in the open air. The Theatre of the Terraces, which overlooks the valley, presents performances of classical music, songs and plays. The choice is eclectic and ambitious. (Information and booking from 15 July, ☎ 04 90 72 05 35.)

Cavaillon
melon-growing country

Between the River Durance, the Alpilles and the Luberon, at the foot of the hill of Saint-Jacques, lies Cavaillon, whose history and heritage are not well-known. This old town, which was part of the wealthy Comtat des Papes, was an important centre of Jewish life in Luberon. Cavaillon has become an important agricultural centre which hosts the largest wholesale fruit and vegetable market in France. In addition Cavaillon considers itself to be the melon capital of the world.

Jewish Museum is situated in the old bakery. It documents Jewish life in this former papal state. (☎ 04 90 76 00 34, Mon. to Thu., 9.30am-noon and 2.30-6.30pm).

Climbing the hill of Saint-Jacques
This lump of sheer rock in the heart of Cavaillon seems to have detached itself from the Luberon during a past seismic upheaval. It is used for rock-climbing for which there are 300 routes, separated into 3 sectors: the east face (above the town), the beginners' sector (above the Théâtre Georges-Brassens) and the west face. (Information at Luberon Escalade, ☎ 04 90 71 05 23. The association publishes a guide available at the Office de Tourisme.) There are also ruins of a 2nd C. BC Roman fort. Saint-Jacques offers easy hikes with a **panoramic view** over the Luberon, the Durance and the Alpilles.

The Old Town
Take time to stroll through the streets of the old town centre and discover its lovely buildings. The Romanesque Cathedral of **Saint-Véran** contains beautiful wood carvings and an elegant cloister (open daily 3-6pm; out of season, 2-4pm). The **Chapelle du Grand Couvent** (1684) has beautifully carved doors; it is

occasionally used for exhibitions. (Information at the Town Hall (*mairie*), ☎ 04 90 71 24 18.)

The synagogue
The synagogue, built between 1772 and 1774 on the Place Castil-Blaze, is one of the most beautiful in Europe, with its original decoration and its ironwork. A

Hiking through the garrigue
Between town and the hill, a hiking trail has been laid out through the garrigue. It leads to a **little hermitage** and to the 12th C. Chapelle Saint-Jacques. The trail starts at the Place François-Tourel, near a Roman arch dating from the 1st C. which was moved here stone by stone in 1880. The

OPPÈDE-LE-VIEUX HILLTOP GARDENS AND PUBLIC WASH-HOUSES

From Cavaillon, a road runs through the pretty hillside villages of Robion and Maubec and leads to Oppède-le-Vieux, which stands on a rocky spur. Its steep little streets lead to the Church of Notre-Dame-d'Alidon (12th C.). If you follow the path past the Chapelle des Pénitents-Blancs, you will reach the ruins of the medieval castle which has a wonderful view over the valley. On your return, do not miss the four restored public wash-houses and the landscaped terraces of Sainte-Cécile, a 7½ acre (3 ha) garden full of local plants and shrubs, including ancient species of fruit from the region.

Spotcheck
B3

Vaucluse

Things to do

Visit the melon fields
Celebration of the melon
Hilltop gardens at Oppède-le-Vieux

Within easy reach

*Saint-Rémy-de-Provence, 18 km SW, p. 138.
Avignon, 24 km NW, p. 140.
Salon-de-Provence, 30 km SE, p. 150.
The Durance Valley, p. 158.*

Tourist Office

Cavaillon: ☎ 04 90 71 32 01

Office de Tourisme runs a 'discovery tour' every Wednesday at 4.30pm in the summer. Don't forget to wear shoes suitable for long walks.

Visiting the melon fields

The melon originated from Africa or Asia, but is mentioned in the town archives as early as 1495. If you want to learn all there is to know about the Cavaillon melon, the Office de Tourisme organises **visits to the melon fields** (mid-May to end of August. Paid admission).

Market of national importance

Registration at the Office de Tourisme. *Free admission.* This is where the melons are first put on sale, from grower to shipper. The important time of day is 5am, when traders gather for coffee in the brasserie and deals are made. From 6-7am, there is trading 'on the square' where growers sell their wares on the basis of the samples they display.

❀ Celebration of the melon

Alexandre Dumas loved melons so much that he offered his entire

published work (between 300 to 400 volumes) to the local library in exchange for an annuity of 12 melons a year! Of course, melon is permanently on the menu of Cavaillon's restaurants (p. 41) and features in specialities such as liqueur, jam or the *melonette, a* (melon-flavoured chocolate, costing 300 F for 2¼ lb (1 kg) (available at the **Confiserie L'Étoile du Délice,** 57, Pl. Castil-Blaze, ☎ 04 90 78 07 51). The melon is celebrated over the weekend of 14 July, and the *Confrérie des chevaliers de l'ordre du melon* (Brotherhood of Knights of the melon order) contributes to enhancing the reputation of the melon.

L'Isle-sur-la-Sorgue
antiques capital of Provence

I n this green and slightly undulating landscape, you will discover a new side to Provence. The area surrounded by the waters of the River Sorgue is the birthplace of the poet René Char. L'Isle-sur-la-Sorgue was renamed the Comtadine Venice because of its numerous canals. Upstream, the source of the River Sorgue lies deep in a chasm at the foot of a cliff in Fontaine-de-Vaucluse.

L'Isle-sur-la-Sorgue
Along the streets
The old town is full of Renaissance houses which are reflected in the green waters of the five branches of the Sorgue. About fifteen moss-covered **paddle wheels** remain out of the 70 which once turned the flour and oil mills, and ran the paper-making, dyeing works and textile mills. The Church of Notre-Dame-des-Anges is famous for its baroque interior dating from the late 17th C. The pharmacy in the Hôtel-Dieu contains a beautiful collection of **Moustiers china** and an enormous 17th C. bronze mortar.

Market on water
Original events take place on the River Sorgue such as the water *corso* (end of July), a nocturnal parade of flower floats on the water. At the beginning of August there is a floating market at which stall-holders sell their produce from small boats moored to the quays of the river. In the summer, you will also be able to watch the **water tournaments**.

Mysterious sources
Although the chasm remains mysterious, something is known of it thanks to a dive performed in 1985. The sandy bed lies 1,030 ft (308 m) deep. As for the origin of the water, the mystery has been cleared up by an experiment. Dyes put in the water show that it emerges from a huge underground network, created by rainwater penetration, and melted snow from the Ventoux, the mountains of Vaucluse and the Montagne de Lure.

ANTIQUE HUNTING ON THE ISLAND
There are a lot of antiques and second-hand goods traders in this town. At the Sunday flea market and three times a year (Easter, 14 July and 15 Aug.), there is much wheeling and dealing by the quayside. Two 'emporia' should be visited in the hunt for valuables: the antique shops at the railway station and those along the Cour de François.

The total average flow is 2,224,845,000 cu. ft (630 million m³) a year. The flow has never reduced to less than 160 cu. ft (4.5 m³) even during droughts. One question remains to be answered: where is the reserve which permanently feeds the spring with water?

Fontaine-de-Vaucluse
Petrarch's songs
The name of the town and the *département* derive from *Vallis Clausa*, Latin for closed valley. The River Sorgue has its source in a narrow valley, where it emerges from a mysterious chasm. This landscape of green valleys and caves inspired the poet Petrarch (14th C.) when he lived there, and his sonnets resonate in the museum which bears his name, (☎ 04 90 20 37 20. Open daily except Tues., 24 Mar.-30 Sep., 10-noon and 2-6pm; out of season, weekend only. Paid admission).

Museums galore
On your way to the chasm, you can visit the Vallis Clausa **paper mill** (☎ 04 90 20 34 14, daily, 9am-7pm. Out of season, 9am-12.20pm and 2-6pm) and discover how to make paper, using a perforated frame or a vat. The **Musée de la Résistance**, (Museum of the Resistance) (☎ 04 90 20 24 00, daily, except Tues., 10am-7pm. Out of season, 10am-noon and 2-6pm) evokes life in the Vaucluse during the Nazi Occupation and exhibits the works of resistance writers and artists.

Stalagmites and Stalactites
Le Monde souterrain de Norbert Casteret ☎ 04 90 20 34 13. Open daily 10am-noon and 2-6pm. Out of season, last dep. at 5pm. Before you visit the source of the river, this museum has a reconstruction of a cave showing the equipment used by speleologists, as well as the collection of 400 limestone formations gathered by Casteret during his underground explorations. At 7½ miles (12 km) from the Fontaine-de-Vaucluse, the village of Thor contains the **Grotte de Thouzon** (☎ 04 0 33 93 65. Open Apr.-Oct., 10am-noon and 2-6pm; Jul.-Aug., 10am-7pm; on Sun. in Mar. and Nov., 2-6pm. Paid admission). Discovered in

Things to do
The market on water
Antique hunting
Kayaking on the River Sorgue
With children
Water tournaments
Within easy reach
Avignon, 23 km W, p. 140.
Le Petit Luberon, 25 km SE, p. 154.
Tourist Office
L'Isle-sur-la-Sorgue:
☎ 04 90 38 04 78

1902, this natural cave has stalactites and stalagmites.

Kayaking in the River Sorgue
When you leave the Fontaine-de-Vaucluse why not follow the river in a kayak? (**Kayak vert**, ☎ 04 90 20 35 44. Open Apr.-Nov.). Relaxation, pleasure and excitement in magnificent scenery. Those who prefer trout-fishing can also do so here.

Pernes-les-Fontaines
pearl of the Comtat Venaissin

This beautifully preserved small town stands at the western extremity of the Plateau du Vaucluse against the backdrop of the Mont Ventoux in the distance. This ancient capital of the Comtat Venaissin and former papal state, has magnificent architecture and resounds to the sound of the cascading waters of the 36 fountains which gave it its name.

A town full of fountains

Pernes-les-Fontaines is a delightful town with three 14th and 16th C. fortified gates opening onto pleasant lanes and

squares. Enter through the **porte de Villeneuve** (1550), which has 2 crenellated towers and a covered walkway, and head towards the 13th C. tower known as the **tour Ferrande**, to see the murals on the third floor. On your way, you will notice the 16th C. **Hôtel de Vichet**, with a wrought iron gate and balcony. Communion wafers for church services have been made here for the past 150 years. The **fontaine Guilhaumin** (1760) stands in the adjoining square. Further away, the 12th C. **tour de l'Horloge** offers you a magnificent view. It is topped by a campanile, and is the last vestige of the wall which protected the castle of the counts of Toulouse. The **Notre-Dame**

gate faces the River Nesque. The **fontaine du Cormoran** (1761) on the square is close to an indoor market. The **Notre-Dame-des-Grâces** Chapel acts as a support for the bridge over the River Nesque, which leads to the 11th C. **Notre-Dame-de-Nazareth** Church. You have a wonderful view of the town from the square. Return to the old city and visit the **Saint-Gilles** gate, passing by the **fontaine Reboul** which is carved with fish scales. Then

return to your starting point, seeing three magnificent fountains on the way: the **fontaine des Dauphins**, the **Porte-Neuve** and the **fontaine de l'Asne**.

The Comtat Venaissin Costume Museum

Rue de la République, Information at the Office de Tourisme, ☎ 04 90 61 31 04. Open daily except Sun. and Mon. morning, 15 June-15 Sept., 10am-noon and 4-7pm; out-of-season, Sat.,10am-noon and 2-5pm. *Free admission.* The museum is situated inside a 19th C. draper's shop and exhibits regional and traditional costumes. There are displays which show old ironing, sewing and embroidery techniques. Perfect for those who long to return to old-fashioned domestic bliss…

Sweets and candies

Pernes-les-Fontaines is well served by pâtisseries and confectioners. Try Pâtisserie Battu (72, Rue Gambetta, ☎ 04 90 61 61 16) which makes delicious local sweets. The **soleil pernois** is a gorgeous crystallised melon-based cake topped with raspberries and almonds costing 120 F per 2¼ lb (1kg). The **esprit blanchard**, was named after Louis XV's court musician who was born in Pernes and contains soft praline and cinnamon-flavoured chocolate, 320 F per 2¼ lb (1kg).

Mountain biking

Pernes has created signposted paths for mountain-bike tours – a 5½ mile (9 km) trip for all the family and a 12½ mile (20 km) tour which is more strenuous. Departure from the fontaine de Couchadou. Information at the Pernes Mairie (☎ 04 90 61 31 04) or at the Point Infos Jeunes (☎ 04 90 66 52 44). Bike rental at VTT Loisirs Vaucluse (Rte. d'Avignon, in Althen, ☎ 04 90 62 18 14).

Visit an ostrich farm

Provence Autruche, Ch. du Tilleul, Rte de Saint-Saturnin, ☎ 04 90 62 09 69. Open Sat. and Sun. 10am-7pm. Mr Mazon's *autrucherie* (ostrich farm) houses about fifty birds. You can also have something to eat and drink here. Did you know that ostrich meat is low in fat and cholesterol, and ostrich leather is highly prized by leather workers for its softness and suppleness? The huge eggs are also edible (1 ostrich egg is equivalent to 24 hen eggs). Owing to their size the empty shells make eye-catching decorative objects.

Carpentras
capital of the 'berlingot'

Carpentras, one of the most historic towns in the Midi, lies in the heart of a natural amphitheatre, between the Ventoux plain and the Monts du Vaucluse in the east, and the Dentelles de Montmirail in the west. It stands on a promontory overlooking River Auzon and was once the capital of the Comtat Venaissin. Its former status is evident from its many historic buildings and monuments.

The Porte Juive and the apothecary

The city walls were destroyed in the 19th C., but there is still a good number of monuments to see within the town, including a splendid Roman triumphal arch dating from the year 16 AD. Saint-Siffrein Cathedral (12-17th C.) has been thoroughly restored. It is especially famous for its Porte juive (15th C.), a beautiful example of flamboyant Gothic decorated with mysterious 'boule aux rats' carvings; converted Jews had to enter the cathedral by this door on the day of their baptism. The 18th C. Hôtel-Dieu (hospital), has a noble Italianate façade and its own apothecary and happily appears to have resisted the effects of age.

The synagogue
Pl. de la Mairie,
☎ 04 90 63 39 97.
Open. 10am-noon and 3-5pm (4pm on Fri.) except on Sat., Sun., public holidays and Jewish festivals.
In 1229, the Comtat Venaissin was annexed by the Pope, and was no longer under the authority of the French king.

The 'prophet Élie throne' in the synagogue

It is during this period that the Jews, banished from France by Philippe le Bel, took refuge in Carpentras (and in Cavaillon). The town

offered them protection, but forced them to live in ghettos called *carrières* (from the Provençal word for 'street'). When the Comtat returned to France in 1791 they became French citizens again. This synagogue, built in 1741, is one of the oldest in France.

park full of flowers has been created. There are a number of things to see near here, including the **Notre-Dame-de-Santé Chapelle**, and a dam and a sluice-gate supplying water to the tanneries that once stood here. The canal bridge dates from the

Spotcheck
B2

Vaucluse

Things to do

Carpentras market
The *Estivales*

Within easy reach

Avignon, 28 km SW, p. 140.
Orange, 18 km NW, p. 146.
Vaison-la-Romaine, 27 km N, p. 148.

Tourist Office

Carpentras:
☎ 04 90 63 00 78

On the banks of the River Auzon

The **porte d'Orange**, the last vestige of the 14th C. city wall, has a 90 ft (27 m) tower. The view from the top is fabulous, you can see down to the banks of the River Auzon below where a shady

THE BONO FAMILY'S CRYSTALLISED FRUITS

280, Av. Jean-Jaurès,
☎ **04 90 63 04 99.**
Open daily except Sun. 8.30-noon and 2.15-6.30pm, Sat., 10-noon.
The Bono family's crystallised fruits are famous. The home-made candied plums, apricots, pears, melons, figs or pineapples are sold in sachets or in baskets (240 F per 2¼ lb (1 kg)).

19th C. Start your walk in the Chemin de la Roseraie (rosary path).

Carpentras markets

If you are in Carpentras on a Friday don't miss the morning market. Thanks to the irrigation provided by the Carpentras canal, since 1857 the Comtat Venaissin has become the garden of France and the agricultural produce and the vineyards of the Côtes-du-Ventoux have made the town rich. The market was voted an 'exceptional market' in 1996 for the quality of its goods and its atmosphere. A **truffle market** is held in the Place Aristide-Briand from the end of November to the beginning of March. The Apt region is the centre of black truffle-growing, so do take advantage of this market if you visit in winter.

Open-air *'Estavales'*

From 15 to 31 July, in the open-air theatre (1,140 seats) and a 3,300 sq. ft (300 m²) stage backing on to the Saint-Siffrein Cathedral), the *Estivales* of Carpentras offer a programme of dance, music, comedy and theatre. (Information and bookings from 15 May, ☎ 04 90 60 46 00, from July 04 90 67 03 12).

Confectionery

288, Av. Notre-Dame-de-Santé,
☎ **04 90 63 05 25.**
The speciality of Carpentras is the humbug, called *berlingot* in French. Once they were only mint-flavoured, but now they are produced in many other flavours – aniseed, lemon, orange and coffee. They are sold in 8¾ oz (250 g) boxes or loose by weight. You can also visit the factory (all year round, by arrangement).

Mont Ventoux
the roof of Provence

E xposed to the winds, from which its name
probably derives, (*vent* means wind) the
Ventoux proudly looks down on the region
from its height of 6,363 ft (1,909 m). Its limestone
dome, as bare as a lunar landscape, contrasts with
the different scenery on its slopes. The mountain
covers a huge area, 15 miles (24 km) from east to
west and 9.3 miles (15 km) from north to south.

Climbing the Ventoux

Mont Ventoux stands out
against the surrounding
Provençal landscape and looks
down over the nearby wild
Nesque Gorges, **Vallée du
Toulourenc**, plateau de Sault
and the hilltop villages of
Aurel and Entrechaux. The
village of Barroux is dominated by its feudal castle, and at
Malaucène there is the
Groseau spring. All are perfect
places for rambling and hiking.
As for the Mont Ventoux
itself, the view from which
left Petrarch 'stunned', why
not try to climb it? (Office de
Tourisme of Malaucène,
☎ 04 90 65 22 59. Night
climbing on Fri. in Jul.-Aug.,
paid access. From 10 July, start
from the Office de Tourisme at

9.30pm, return the next day
at 11am. Climbers must be at
least 12 years old and in good
physical condition.

A mountain resort

sault

Situated on a rocky spur at a
height of 2,553 ft (766 m),
the town overlooks a valley
where golden wheat grows
beside fields filled with the
soft blue of fragrant lavender.
The temperate and bracing
mountain air makes this a
delightful resort. Its very
pleasant strolling through the
picturesque lanes of its old
centre. Unfortunately the
only remains of the old castle
are the ramparts.

Sault market

There has been a market in
Sault on Wednesday morn-
ings since 1515. It presents a
good opportunity to see and
buy the local specialities, such
as lavender honey, goat's
cheese, local lamb and spelt –
a kind of wheat. This 'Gallic
wheat' has a good flavour and
is added to soups, ground into
flour and used for bread-mak-
ing or for pancakes. At **André
Boyer**'s (☎ 04 90 64 00 23)
you can taste delicious macaroons and the best honey-
and-almond nougat in

Provence. It has either a black or white base.

Lavender fair

Each year, on 15 August, people pour into Sault for the two day *Fête de la Lavande*. There are displays of cutting the lavender by hand and parades of carriages and other old vehicles covered with flowers, as well as an exhibition.

Lavender garden

Route de la Lavande,
☎ **04 90 64 14 97.**
Open daily, Jul.-Aug., 10am-1pm and 2-7pm; out of season, by reservation:
☎ **04 90 64 10 74.**
Free admission.
If you're not in Sault on 15 August, make up for it by visiting the beautiful collections of the **Jardin des lavandes.** You can buy lavender seedlings (a large range of plants and horticultural products are on sale).
To find out all about lavender essence, visit the **Distillerie du Vallon** (☎ 04 90 64 02 16 or 04 90 64 14 83.
Open from mid-July to the end of August).

The Gorges of the river Nesque

Fantastic views

The D942 road to Sault, between Monieux and Villes-sur-Auzon, hugs the steep precipice over the Gorges of the River Nesque. The views are magnificent, especially from the lookout point at the Cire rock. If you feel like walking along the gorges from the Monieux lake (swimming is forbidden but there is a rest area), a signposted path will take you to the Saint-Michel Chapel (1½ hours there and back).

Le Barroux

Llama farm

☎ **04 90 65 25 46.**
Guided visit in the morning, advance reservation required, duration 1½ hours.
Paid admission.
Not far from the village of Le Barroux, you can visit the llama stud, an experimental farm

Spotcheck
B2

Vaucluse

Things to do
Climb Mont Ventoux
Sault market
Lavender fair

Things to do with children
Llama farm

Within easy reach
Vaison-la-Romaine about 25 km NW, p. 148.

Tourist Office
Malaucène:
☎ **04 90 65 22 59**

owned by M. Sherrer with more than 40 llamas. You will discover how useful these strong animals can be (the French army hires them to clear land). You can visit the workshop where woven fabrics and tapestries are made from their wool.

Aix-en-Provence
chic and charming

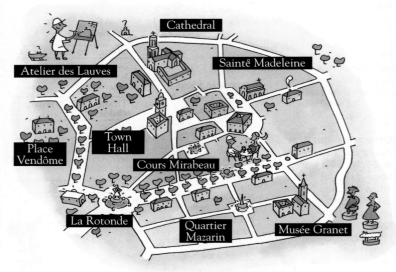

Is it because Aix was the first town to be settled by the Romans in Gaul in 122 BC that it has a distinctly Italian air about it? It certainly cultivates an art of living which reflects its magnificent architecture and illustrious past. Aix is a town of fountains, art and history, and has become world famous thanks to its Festival of Lyrical Art and Music, the sounds of which echo throughout the town every July.

Out and about in Aix
A good deal of the buildings in Aix Old Town have retained their 17th and 18th C. features making it an interesting and rewarding place for a stroll. The town is divided in two by a wide avenue called the **Cours Mirabeau**. The Old Town, with its pretty pink-tiled roofs, nestles around the Saint-Sauveur Cathedral on one side. Its Roman remains, winding lanes, elegant squares and many attractive small boutiques and shops, all contrast with the Quartier Mazarin on the other side of 'le Cours'. Here, the streets are long and straight and lined with town houses hidden behind high walls. Aix is reputed to have **101 fountains**. Don't forget to visit the fountain on the Place Albertas, nor the Quatre-Dauphins fountain in the Quartier Mazarin. Take a guided tour of Aix from the Office de Tourisme (2, Pl. du Général-de-Gaulle, ☎ 04 42 16 11 61. Open July-August, until 10pm).

The fountain on the Place Albertas, restored in 1912

Spotcheck
C3

Bouches-du-Rhône

Things to do

Search for Cézanne
The International Festival of Lyrical Art and Music
The markets of Aix
The gardens of Albertas (Jardins d'Albertas)
Visit the Château Simone cellars
A Provençal cookery lesson

With children

Visit to a *santon* factory

Within easy reach

*Salon-de-Provence, 30 km NW, p. 150.
The Durance Valley, 30 km NW, p. 158.
Marseille, 30 km S, p. 192.
La Sainte-Baume, 30 km SE, p. 204.*

Tourist Office

Aix-en-Provence:
☎ 04 42 16 11 61

In search of Cézanne

**Atelier des Lauves,
9, Av. Paul-Cézanne,
☎ 04 42 21 06 53.
Open daily from 1 Apr.
to 30 Sep., except Tues.
and public holidays,
10am-noon and 2.30-
6pm; Out of season,
2-5pm. *Paid admission.***

Interior of the Atelier des Lauves

Another way to discover Aix is by following in the footsteps of the painter Paul Cézanne, a local boy whose talent was long ignored by his home town. Aix is now determined to make amends by offering a 2 mile (3 km) tour marked out with a 'C' for Cézanne. The route takes you from his birthplace to the cemetery where he is buried, via his studio on the Chemin des Lauves, in the northern part of the town. It is here that Cézanne admired the view of Sainte-Victoire, which he painted tirelessly. Some memorabilia, watercolours and original drawings have been assembled here. There is also a 25 mile (40 km) tour of Cézanne's favourite local landscapes.

The festivals of Aix

Every July, the International Festival of Lyric Art and Music attracts crowds of faithful music lovers. (Information and booking, ☎ 04 42 17 34 34.) In August, the International Big Band Festival plays Glenn Miller hits, and there is also a gospel evening and a 'cine-jazz' night (☎ 04 42 63 06 75). The International Festival of Contemporary Dance is held in spring and winter and is a showcase for the work of leading choreographers (☎ 04 42 23 41 24).

Cours Mirabeau: cafés and mansions

In Aix, this avenue is simply called 'le Cours'. Plans for a splendid avenue lined with plane trees to replace the city walls were drawn up in 1649. It is now the place where all the action is, especially the famous **Café des Deux Garçons** ('les 2 G'), a favourite haunt of Cézanne, and later of the writer Blaise Cendrars and the painter Gabriel Lorrain, who used to

spend time there. The locals prefer to enjoy a quiet drink on the terrace of the **Grillon**. The Cours is lined with grand mansions built in the reign of Louis XIV with classical and baroque façades. The most interesting are the Hôtel de Villars at no. 4, the Hôtel d'Isoard-de-Vauvenargues at no. 10 and at no. 38 the unforgettable Hôtel Maurel-de-Pontevès.

The Old Town

On leaving the **Moussue** (moss-covered) fountain (Cours Mirabeau, at the top of the Rue Clemenceau) whose waters spurt out at 93°F

(34°C), you should visit the 17th C. Hôtel Boyer-d'Éguilles housing the fascinating **Muséum d'Histoire naturelle** (National History Museum) 6, Rue Espariat. (Open daily except Sun. morning, 10am-noon and 2-6pm, ☎ 04 42 26 23 67.) Deeper into the old town you will find the Place Albertas and the Place Richelme, famous for its **markets,** and finally the beautiful Italian-style baroque town hall, with a clock tower. ❀ The **Musée du Vieil-Aix** whose exhibits illustrate the history of the Old Town is not far away (17, Rue Gaston-de-

Saporta. Open daily except Mon. 12.30-6pm; out of season, 10am-noon and 2-5pm. Paid admission).

Saint-Sauveur Cathedral

Work began on this church in the 5th C. but was not finished until the 17th C. Only the Merovingian baptistry remains from the original structure. See the magnificently carved

double doors (early 16th C.),
hidden beneath heavy false
doors. They can be visited on
request (apply at the sacristy)
when no service is being held.
Other features are the 15th C.
Burning Bush triptych and the
remarkable tapestries created
in 1511. The late 12th C.
romanesque cloister south of
the church is a forest of
little columns which

have unfortunately suffered
much damage.

Calissons and other sweets

The *calisson* makers of the
town revived the *Bénédiction
des Calissons*, held on the first
Sunday of September to commemorate the Mass of 1630
which ended the plague in
Provence. For a taste of these
delightful almond-and-citrus
sweets, visit **Léonard Parli**
(35, Av. Victor-Hugo,
☎ 04 42 26 05 71) or **Au
Roy René** (Rue Papassaudi,
☎ 04 42 26 67 86). They
cost around 180 F for 2¼ lb
(1 kg) and you can also buy
them in gift boxes shaped
like the calisson itself. Aix
offers more sweet treats in
the form of the **biscotin**,
toasted hazelnuts coated with
a sponge mixture, 240 F for
2¼ lb (1 kg), and the **clou de
Cézanne**, a chocolate-coated
fig dipped in Vieux Marc de
Provence liqueur.

Quartier Mazarin

Created on the initiative of
Archbishop Mazarin, brother
of the famous cardinal, this
district was built from 1646 to
1651 around the first Gothic
sanctuary in the town.
Peaceful gardens are hidden
behind 17th-18th C. façades,
often separated from the road
by vast courtyards. The mansions are built of golden limestone topped by tiles and
have classical façades decorated with statues. The Hôtel de
Marignane, associated
with the statesman
Mirabeau, the
Hôtel de
Caumont, which
now houses the
Conservatoire de Musique
et de Danse, the
Musée Paul-
Arbaud and
its beautiful
collection of

ceramics, and the Hôtel de
Villeneuve-d'Ansouis are all
worth seeing.

Cézanne,
Portrait of Madame Cézanne

Musée Granet

**13, Rue Cardinale,
☎ 04 42 38 14 70.
Open daily except Tues.,
10am-noon and 2-6pm.**
In the former priory of the
church of St. John of Malta,
in the heart of the Quartier
Mazarin, the Musée Granet

bears the name of one of its main donors, the painter François Granet of Aix. The museums exhibits are very varied, ranging from Egyptian, Roman and Gallo-Roman antiquities, as well as paintings from all the European schools from the 16th to the 19th C. These incude eight paintings by Cézanne and statues by Pierre Puget, a Baroque sculptor and prolific architect whose work can be found throughout the Midi.

Painted furniture
**Mélodie Mauve,
14, Rue Matheron,
☎ 04 42 96 45 54**
Open from Tues. to Sat., 10am-noon and 3-7pm. Chests, Provençal wedding wardrobes and dressers are all hand-made. The workshop offers authentic copies of antique furniture and you can have your own furniture decorated. It will cost you between 3,000 and 5,000 F, depending on the size of the piece.

The 'santonniers'
**Santons Fouque,
65, Cours Gambetta,
☎ 04 42 26 33 38.**
Open daily except Sun., 8am-noon and 2-6.30pm. *Free admission (20 min.).* Aix has many 'santonniers', makers of *santon* figures. Paul Fouque is the most famous of them. His figures are very lifelike. The oldest is a shepherd crouching against the wind; Fouque called it 'coup de mistral' (the *mistral* gust). Since then, he has continually created new figures and his entire collection contains nearly 1,800 models made in the traditional way, baked for 15 hours, dried for 48 hours and then hand-painted. Around 80 F for a 4-in (10-cm) figure. There is an annual *santon* fair in December, on the Avenue Victor-Hugo.

Bouc-Bel-Air

The Albertas Gardens
**7 miles (11 km) S. of Aix, towards Marseille,
☎ 04 42 22 29 77.**
Open daily, Jul.-Aug., 3-7pm; May, Sep.and Oct., plus weekends and public holidays, 2-6pm; by appointment at other times.

A Provençal cookery lesson

**Les Cuisines du Sud
Château d'Arnajon, 13610 Le Puy-Sainte-Réparade,
☎ 04 42 61 87 47.**
Marc Héracle, a craft potter by trade, settled in a magnificent old country house and decided to offer courses explaining the secrets of Provençal cuisine to those who love Provence. His recipes for jams, sweet and savoury pies and tarts are delicious, as you will discover if you are lucky enough to taste any of them fresh from the oven. Marc's cookery courses last an entire day and everything is provided. Groups of 4 to 25 people, 850 F for a private lesson, 650 F in a group (550 F off-season).

The Albertas Gardens at Bouc-Bel-Air

This wonderland of greenery was planned by the Marquis d'Albertas in 1751, in the French and Italian styles. While strolling between the upper garden (designed to surround a château which was never built) and the lower garden, you will discover terraces, ponds, monumental statues, flower beds, and a waterway with a fountain at the end. A haven of peace for the casual stroller.

Tennis, squash and swimming

Those who like racket sports can work on their backhand in the many tennis and squash clubs, all of which also have swimming pools: the **Country Club Aixois** (Bastide de Solliers, Ch. des Cruyès, in Célony, ☎ 04 42 92 10 41) ; the **Set Club** (Le Pey blanc, Ch. des Granettes, ☎ 04 42 59 52 05). Best for tennis are the **Complexe sportif du Val de l'Arc** (Ch. des Infirmeries, ☎ 04 42 16 02 50) and the **Tennis Part** (Ch. d'Eguilles, ☎ 04 42 92 34 70).

Meyreuil

Visiting cellars

Château Simone,
☎ **04 42 66 92 58.**
Open daily except Sun., 8am-noon and 2-7pm. No tasting.
This little vineyard beside the villages of Meyreuil and Tholonet, 2 miles (3 km) on the D 5, produces fine white wines of the 'appellation palette'. A visit to the famous domain of Mr Rougier will confirm Cézanne's claim: 'He who has never drunk Château-Simone cannot understand the soul of Provence'.

La Gaude

Jardin de Buis

Rte des Pinchinats, 3 miles (5 km) from Aix by RN96 and D63,
☎ **04 42 21 64 19.**
Open daily 9am-7pm. Visits by appointment.
This country house is set behind Italianate terraces, a vineyard and a park. It nestles at the end of a small valley. Stroll between the box-wood hedges whose geometric designs are inspired by the mazes of the 16th C. The groves of trees are reflected in pools surrounded by Judas trees, thornbushes and acacia. Delightful surroundings for a quiet walk. There is also a 'tèse', a magnificent avenue of tall trees and shrubs, laid out in the traditional style favoured by the nobility of Provence. This tèse is one if the last of its kind.

The ruins of the Oppidum

Puyricard and the Plateau d'Entremont

Chocolate factory and local ruins

Chocolaterie Puyricard, 420, Route du Puy-Sainte-Réparade,
☎ **04 42 96 11 21.**
Open daily, except Sun., 9am-7pm.
Paid admission (1 h).
When in Puyricard itself you can visit the ruined **Château de Grimaldi**, ½ mile (1 km) NW on the D 14, which was never finished because its founder cared more for his gardens. Stop afterwards at the

chocolaterie,
320 F for a 2¼ lb (1 kg) box. The **Oppidum** of the Plateau d'Entremont, 2 miles (3 km) N towards Puyricard (open daily except Tues., 9am-noon and 2-6pm), was the economic and religious capital in the 3rd and 2nd C. BC. It stands at an altitude of 1,216 ft (365 m). There are also old oil-presses and an exceptional view.

The Aix district
and the Sainte-Victoire

The Montagne Sainte-Victoire was originally called Mont Venture until the time of the Revolution at the end of the 18th C. However, since it was renamed Sainte Victoire, it seems to have found more peaceful times. The painter Cézanne spent many happy days here, painting the surrounding landscape until he finally collapsed one sunny day in October 1906 whilst painting a mountain hut. In August 1989 a forest fire devastated the area, though fortunately the vegetation has since recovered.

Precious eggs

Due to the find of enormous dinosaur eggs 65 million years old, the Sainte-Victoire is one of the most important archaeological sites in France and is known throughout the world. The Roques-Hautes area, where the most important finds have been made, has been declared a geological nature reserve from which nothing must be removed. The area is also closed to visitors, but you can see these gigantic dinosaur eggs for yourself in the natural history Museum in Aix-en-Provence (p. 176). The museum also contains life-size models of dinosaurs.

A walk through Le Tholonet

To understand Cézanne's obsession with the Montagne Sainte-Victoire, take the Le Tholonet road, also called the Route de Cézanne (p. 175). You will see the same crystal-clear light that so inspired him. The **Château de Tholonet** is the starting point for a 3½ hour circular hike called the *circuit des deux barrages* (around the two dams) a distance of 7½ miles (12 km). You can also visit the Croix de Provence by taking the Imoucha path from the Bimont dam (about 2 hours). The easy way to see Sainte-Victoire is by taking the D17 which will lead you to Tholonet castle, in the Cause valley, a favourite walk for the local people; then on to Saint-Antonin-sur-Bayon (wonderful walk in the Plateau de Cengle). The D10 will take you to Vauvenargues, a village perched above the Infernet, whose **château** was once Picasso's home and where he is buried.

The Château du Tholonet, built in 1613 and rebuilt in the 17th C.

THE MOUNTAIN ITSELF

Take the GR9 from the hamlet of Les Cabassols, 7½ miles (12 km) from Aix via the D10. This is the only path open in summer. The Sainte-Victoire is 11¼ miles long and 3¼ miles wide (18 km and 5 km), and is 3,370 ft (1,011 m) high at the Pic des Mouches. The Croix de Provence stands on the west summit at 3,153 ft (946 m), and has resisted the *mistral* since 1875. However, the wind has managed to knock down three other crosses erected here since the 15th C. Behind it, there is a small monastery built in 1661 and restored in 1955. From the terrace there is a wonderful view of the slopes, though not as good as from the one in Croix de Provence.

Saint-Antonin-sur-Bayon

La maison Sainte-Victoire

6¼ miles (10 km) E of Aix.☎ 04 42 66 84 40. Open daily, 10am-7pm, (6pm out of season). Overlooked by the mountain, the new **Sainte-Victoire centre** contains an information office dedicated to the area. The centre organises hikes and walks, leisure and sports activities (from 12 Sept. to 30 June), including. climbing, paragliding, mountain biking, and more; 3 paths are open to the visitors during the summer. There are also guided, themed visits and temporary exhibitions. You can learn about the mountain flowers and wildlife by following the **botanical path.** There's a shop selling books about the area and local craftwork, as well as the **wines** of Sainte-Victoire at cellar prices.

Spotcheck
C3

Bouches-du-Rhône

Things to do

Walking or mountain biking
Picasso's château

Within easy reach

*Vallée de la Durance,
30 km N, p. 158.
Marseille, 30 km S,
p. 192.
The Sainte-Baume range,
30 km SE, p. 204.*

Tourist Office

Saint-Antonin-sur-Bayon:
☎ 04 42 66 84 40

Watch out!

To minimise the danger of forest fires, visits to the Sainte-Victoire range from 1 July to the second Saturday in September, and when the wind is high are totally banned. This ban applies to all walkers (only the *Chemin des Venturiers* remains open), climbers and mountain bikers. Information is available at the Association des Excursionnistes Provençaux (Provençal Hikers Association) (☎ 04 42 21 03 53). This regulation seems rather strict, but clearly it is the only way to ensure that the disastrous forest fire of August 1989, when all the trees and vegetation on the mountain were burned down, never happens again.

Manosque

Situated with hills to either side, at an altitude of 1,300 ft (380 m), the modern town of Manosque is next to the Old Town. Marcel Pagnol, the renowned author who was born in Aubagne further south, recreated the atmosphere of the Old Town in his writing with great success. Today many of the houses have been restored beautifully and retain much of their former charm.

The gates of the Old Town

Although the medieval ramparts and their turrets have almost completely disappeared, the town is still laid out in the medieval pattern, with a maze of narrow streets lined with tightly-packed tall houses. The outstanding features of the Old Town are its gates: the Porte de la Saunerie (or Porte du Sel), which has kept its ribbed ceilings and crenellations, the Porte Soubeyran which is crowned by a bell-tower, the remains of the Porte d'Aubette in the east, and the Porte Guilhempierre which was restored in 1986.

A stroll through old Manosque

Take a walk through the streets of old Manosque, and see where they lead you. You may well come across the elegant presbytery or the Maison Voland, the building housing the Town Hall, which has an elegant 18th C. façade, or the Hôtel d'Herbes which has one of the richest medieval collections in France. **The Saint-Sauveur Church**, in typical Provençal Romanesque style, has a fine wrought-iron bell-tower dating from 1725. Further on, the church of Notre-Dame-de-Romigier

The Porte de la Saunerie

Entrance to the Chuch Saint-Sauveur

has a beautifully carved portal. Inside there is a 5th C. sarcophagus and a 12th C. statue of the Virgin Mary.

Giono

Jean Giono was a local author who wrote *Le Hussard sur le Toit*, or, *The Horseman on the Roof*, an historical novel set in the region. He spent his childhood at 14 Rue Grande near the clothing factory where his mother did the ironing. From the ruined tower of the château on the Mont d'Or you can see over the rooftops with their round tiles which provided the inspiration for Giono's famous novel. Down below, a footpath leads to the villa in which Giono lived from 1929 until his death in 1970. Everything remains just as it was in his lifetime (villa Le Paraïs ☎ 04 92 87 73 03. Free admission by appointment Fri., 3-5.30pm).

The Centre Jean-Giono

1, Bd. Élémir-Bourges,
☎ 04 92 70 54 54.
Open Tues.-Sat., 9am-noon and 2-6pm, except public holidays.
Paid admission.
At the entrance to the town, in a beautiful 17th C. Provençal house, there is a permanent exhibition of photographs, drawings and sketches by Giono's painter friends. There is also a library, a small bookshop, a video library which contains films about the writer and film adaptations of his books.

The festivals of Manosque

Every two years, in June, Manosque holds its 'medieval days' when the town returns to the Middle Ages for a few days. There are performances, concerts, street entertainers

Spotcheck
C3

Alpes-de-Haute-Provence

Things to do
Festivals of Manosque
Pony-trekking

Within easy reach
*Le Grand Luberon,
25 km W, p. 156.
Vallée de la Durance,
5 km SE, p. 158.*

Tourist Office
Manosque:
☎ 04 92 76 16 00

and equestrian tournaments, all helping you to travel back in time. There is a film festival in January (les Rencontres cinématographiques), a jazz festival in July (Festival de jazz) and a festival dedicated to Jean Giono (Journées Jean Giono). In August, there is a Festival International Folklorique du Luberon which is dedicated to the regions folklore and traditions. Information available at the Office de Tourisme.

❀ The Fondation Carzou

9, Bd. Élémir-Bourges,
☎ 04 92 87 40 49.
Open Fri., Sat. and Sun., 10am-noon and 2.30-6.30pm; Oct.-Apr., 10am-noon and 2.30-6.30pm.
Paid admission.
Jean Carzou is the second most famous native of Manosque. His gigantic fresco, *The Apocalypse*, painted between 1985 and 1991 covering no less than 7,200 sq ft (670 m²) of wall, can be seen in the ancient Couvent de la Présentation.

PONY-TREKKING ON THE VALENSOLE PLATEAU

Numerous riding-schools offer treks through the Valensole plateau. The gîtes on the way can also accommodate your horses. Make sure you take with you a hat, flask for water, sleeping bag, detailed IGN map, topographic map and waterproof clothes (storms in the summer). More information available from the Comité Départemental du Tourisme Équestre (☎ 04 92 31 27 50) or from the Comité Départemental d'Équitation (☎04 92 78 84 14).

Forcalquier
between Lure and Luberon

The town is named after the spring which still feeds its fountains and old wash-houses (*font calquier* means 'spring flowing from the rock' in the Oc language). In the Middle Ages, Forcalquier was the capital of an independent state and still possesses some beautiful old houses.

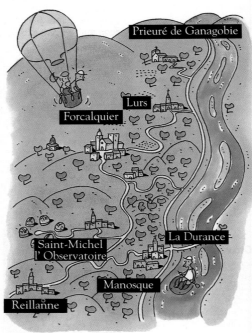

Forcalquier
Markets by the cathedral
Near the square where food and antiques markets are held every Monday morning (it is one of the most famous in the region) stands the Cathedral of Notre-Dame-du-Bourguet. It is topped by a huge fortified medieval bell-tower.

Pilgrimage to the Citadel
Every year, on 8 September, there is a pilgrimage to the Virgin Mary, when the faithful gather at the ruins of the citadel which was destroyed in 1601. The neo-Byzantine Chapel of Notre-Dame-de-Provence was built here in 1875. Bell ringers have been playing here since 1920. Their medieval melodies can be heard throughout the town on Sunday mornings, at noon and on feast days.

Hot-air ballooning
As a last reminder of the late lamented hot-air ballooning contests which were once held in September when the sky was filled with colourful balloons, the Mongolfière de Forcalquier offers daily hot-air balloon trips. You can enjoy the experience at any time throughout the year, provided that you have booked at the Office de Tourisme. Daily flights at 6am. Cost is 1200 F per person for the morning.

Lurs
Graphic arts
This fortress north-east of Forcalquier became the residence of the bishops of Sisteron in the 12th C. It is

now a picturesque village. It became famous in 1952 due to the Dominici case, when an English family camping at the foot of the village were murdered by a local farmer. The village is more welcoming nowadays. In the last week of August, commercial artists and copywriters meet here for the Rencontres Internationales de Lurs, first launched by the typographer, Maximilien Vox (Information, ☎ 01 45 74 38 38).

Ganagobie
The Benedictine priory
Open Tues.-Sun., 3-5pm.
☎ **04 92 68 00 04.**
Cloister not open to the public.
To get to the priory, take the winding road which has a beautiful view over the Vallée de la Durance. Built in the

mid-10th C. and handed over to the Abbey of Cluny soon after, the priory remained prosperous until the end of the 14th C. It was destroyed during the Wars of Religion, then sold as national property in 1791. It was subsequently left to fall into ruins. A small community of Benedictine monks now occupy new buildings here. Of the original Romanesque priory, only the cloister and part of the church remain, but they constitute one of the most beautiful

Romanesque buildings in Haute Provence. The church contains a 12th C. mosaic floor.

OBSERVATORY OF HAUTE PROVENCE

☎ **04 92 70 64 00**
Open on Wed., Oct.-Mar., 3-4pm; Apr.-Sep., 2-4pm. Closed on public holidays.
Paid admission.
The observatory stands in 242 acres (100 ha), and looks like a futuristic city. The site was chosen in 1936 because of the good light and clear skies. Each year, French and foreign researchers come here to study the solar system and the galaxy. During your visit you can see two telescopes, 6 ft (1.93 m) and 5 ft (1.52 m) in diameter. You can also walk in the park and watch a video about the Observatory.

Saint-Michel-l'Observatoire

Thirteen domes for one archangel

The old village of Saint-Michel is situated between Reillanne and Forcalquier, in the heart of a region called the Alpes-de-Lumière. Cypress trees, hilltop houses and ancient streets are overlooked by the church, dedicated to the archangel Michael. At the foot of the small village, the 13 domes of the Haute-Provence Observatory offer a complete contrast.

A small pastis distillery

Distillerie et domaines de Provence,
☎ **04 92 75 00 58.**
Tour, sampling and sales from Easter to late Sep. (except Tue. and Sun.; daily Jul.-Aug.).

Spotcheck
C2

Alpes-de-Haute-Provence

Things to do
The Forcalquier market
Hot air ballooning
Observatory (Observatoire)
Visit to a pastis distillery

Within easy reach
Le Grand Luberon, 25 km SE, p. 156.

Tourist Office
Forcalquier:
☎ **04 92 75 10 02**

Paid admission.
A natural pastis has been made here for a century, which is greatly appreciated by connoisseurs. Henri Bardouin pastis is the only one to be made on a 'site remarkable for taste' (there are 100 such sites in France). This sun-drenched area is famous for the diversity and quality of its aromatic herbs.

Mane

The priory of Salagon

2 miles (3 km) S of Forcalquier, on RN100.
☎ **04 92 75 70 50.**
Open daily 10am-noon and 2-7pm.
There are three wonderful botanical gardens here, containing more than 300 different varieties of shrubs, flowering plants and vegetables. The Rencontres Musicales de Haute Provence, a classical music festival, is held here in the last two weeks of July. Some of the concerts take place in the lovely cathedral at Forcalquier.

Sisteron the key to Provence

S isteron has a breathtaking location on the banks of the River Durance. Ancient houses climb up a steep slope topped by an imposing citadel, whilst the rock of la Baume stands solidly on the opposite bank. Sisteron is a delightful town at the gateway to Provence.

The Lure mountain

The mountain is a favourite with hikers and mountain bikers, but you can also drive along the scenic route which crosses the Massif du Sud in the north and shows the gradual change in vegetation.

Sisteron
The Old Town
Narrow lanes turn into flights of steps spanned by houses known as *les andrônes*. Covered passageways providing shade from the hot sun link houses with decorated façades to tiny squares in this charming medieval town. Its most important buildings, such as the **Romanesque cathedral** of Notre-Dame-des-Pommiers, the **Citadel**, the towers of the ramparts with picturesque names Porte Sauve (Safe Gate), Porte de la Médisance (Slander Gate) are all well worth a visit.

Gliding or hang-gliding?
If you are feeling brave you could take to the air for a birds-eye view. The Aéro-Club de Sisteron (aérodrome de Vaumeilh, open daily, ☎ 04 92 62 17 45) offers glider flights or hang-gliding at the Club Altitude which organises paired flights for novices (☎ 04 92 61 24 10). Before taking off, consult the local weather forecast (special glider and freeflight forecast ☎ 08 36 68 10 14).

Farmhouse lamb
Sisteron is also famous for its delicious Sisteron lamb, a dish of very young lamb no older than four months and fed on milk. *Pieds et paquets* is another local speciality which ensures that nothing of the sheep is wasted. It consists of stuffed tripe with bacon, herbs and pepper served with flambéd lamb's feet. The French are not squeamish or sentimental about animals and vegetarianism has yet to make its mark in the provinces.

Montagne de Lure
Hiking and biking
The Montagne de Lure is 6086 ft (1826 m) high and covers an area of about 30 sq. miles (50 sq. km) between the Albion Plateau and Sisteron.

Banon
Goat's cheese
Banon is a medieval village at the foot of the Lure. Its attractions include ruined fortifications and a 14th C. gateway. The village gave its name to a delicious goat's

Spotcheck
C2

Alpes-de-Haute-Provence

Things to do

Nights of the Citadel festival
Gliding and hang-gliding
Trips through the
Montagne de Lure
The Château-Arnoux festival

Within easy reach

*Dignes-les-Bains,
30 km E, p. 298.*

Tourist Office

Sisteron: ☎ 04 92 61 12 03

'NIGHTS OF THE CITADEL' FESTIVAL

☎ 04 92 61 06 00.
Open daily ,15 Mar.-
11 Nov., 9am-5.30pm;
Jul.-Aug., 9am-8.30pm.
Cashdesk closes an
hour earlier.
Paid admission.
**Every summer, from
mid-July to mid-August,
this fortress serves as
the magical venue for
the Nights of the
Citadel festival.
The quality of the
performances matches
the magnificent
surroundings. The
programme includes
theatre, recitals, ballet
and orchestral concerts.
The citadel itself is an
imposing military build-
ing whose construction,
begun in the 13th C.,
was completed by Jean
Erard, Henri IV's
military engineer. From
the highest point, one
can see for over 93
miles (150 km).**

cheese (fromage de chèvre)
matured with brandy and
wrapped in chestnut leaves.
This is the place to taste it.
Banon celebrates its cheese
with a festival in May.

Château-Arnoux
Lake and festival

Château-Arnoux stands on
the right bank of the Lac de
l'Escale and has a Renaissance
château, built by Pierre de
Glandevès between 1510 and
1515, which serves as the
backdrop for the **Festival de
Font-Robert** (evenings of
blues, jazz, French songs) in
the second half of July. The
château contains a huge **spiral
staircase,** decorated with statuary busts. The Chapelle
Saint-Jean outside the village
affords a lovely view over the
Durance and the Bléone.

A walk around the **Lac de
l'Escale**, at the foot of the cliff
is very pleasant.

Les Mées
Penitents in stone

The village of Mées is best
known for its Pénitents,
outcrops of pale stone (a
strange mixture of pebbles
and a natural cement), rising
to almost 333 ft (100 m) and
covering an area of about 1½
miles (2.5 km). According to
legend, the stones are a
procession of monks who
were turned to stone for
falling in love with beautiful
Moorish women, brought
home by a local lord from
one of his campaigns against
the infidels.

The stone Pénitents of Mées

Marseille

Marseille is really a collection of several villages, so its plethora of 'town centres' makes you almost forget that it is the biggest port in France and its second-largest city. Founded by the Greeks twenty-six centuries ago, this cosmopolitan city has always been a melting pot of disparate cultures. Marseille is an unruly, sunny and lively town which fits its inhabitants like a glove. You will love it too!

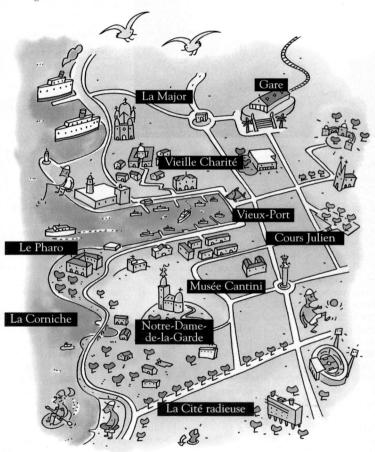

La Major

Gare

Vieille Charité

Vieux-Port

Cours Julien

Le Pharo

Musée Cantini

La Corniche

Notre-Dame-
de-la-Garde

La Cité radieuse

Le Vieux-Port

In Marseille, all roads lead to the Vieux-Port, or old port. Tall ships, luxury yachts and fishing-boats jostle alongside each other in the harbour which lies at the end of the Canebière, the city's most famous street. The restaurants in the old port offer a deli-cious range of fish dishes including the finest, most authentic *bouillabaisse* (fish soup) in France. You will

see the fresh fish being sold every morning on the Quai des Belges by the fishermen's wives. Their cry is 'Du vivantau prix du mort!' – 'Live fish at a dead price!' There is a lovely view of the old port with all its hustle and bustle from the Fort Saint-Jean.

Spotcheck
C4

Bouches-du-Rhône

Things to do

Festivals
A hydrocycle trip
Auctions and markets
Marseille soapworks
Clothing and antiques on
the Cours Julien

With children

Le Balaboum Théâtre (p. 192)
El Dorado City (p. 195)

Within easy reach

Martigues,
30 km W, p.152.
Aix-en-Provence,
30 km N, p.174.
La Sainte-Baume,
30 km NE, p. 204,

Tourist Office

Marseille: ☎ 04 91 13 89 00

Walking in the Panier

The Quartier du Panier, on the north shore overlooking the quay from a hilltop, resembles southern Italy, with its colourful houses and washing hanging out to dry from windows. This is where the *pescadous* (fishermen) used to live. Today, the houses are being renovated and gentrified, but the neighbourhood is getting a new lease of life. From the harbour, take the (steep) Montée des Accoules to reach this old district, crisscrossed with narrow lanes.

Les Arcenaulx

25, Cours Estienne-d'Orves.
☎ 04 91 59 80 30 (tea-room) and
☎ 04 91 59 80 37 (bookshop).

AUCTIONS AND MARKETS

The markets are the places to go to if you want to sample the best food the town has to offer. In addition to the fish auction and market every morning on the Quai des Belges, there is the Prado market (Castellane tube station, every morning except Sun.) in the heart of Marseille. You can buy fruit, vegetables, herbs, bunches of flowers, a fly-swatter or Provençal fabric.

Bookshop opens 10am-midnight (except art and old books); tea-room opens at noon (last service 2.30pm) and 8pm (last service 11.30pm).

This complex contains a bookshop, a tea-room and a publishing house, all run by Jeanne Laffitte, descended from several generations of Marseille publishers. The publishing house specialises in reprints of old books. The bookshop has a large section devoted to general literature, and sections on fine art and

the building contrasts beautifully with the golden sun and blue sky of the Midi, especially during a summer sunset. Walk under the arcades and visit the **Musée d'Archéologie Méditerranéenne** or the **Musée des Arts Africain, Amérindien et Océanien,** an ethnographic museum.

The southern quay and Saint-Victor Abbey

Opposite the modern buildings of the north shore, stand the façades of 18th C. buildings, former warehouses, on the south shore. Disused for a long time, they have been converted into artist's studios and luxury flats. Further up the hill, overlooking the former dry dock, the abbey-fortress of Saint-Victor (open daily, 8.30am-6pm, paid admission to the crypts) is the oldest church in Marseille. It was founded in the 5th C., rebuilt in the 11th C., and fortified in the 14th C. It has extensive crypts and beautiful tombstones.

Carré Thiars and Cours d'Estienne-d'Orves

This is one of the most lively districts in Marseille. The square stands on the site of the naval arsenal for the galley-ships. It is full of restaurants and cafés with terraces where you can sit and relax. Higher up, the Cours d'Estienne-d'Orves is a wide Italian-style square in which city festivals are often held.

on Provence and its dialect. The shop stocks new and second-hand books.

Le Miramar *bouill-abaisse*

12, Quai du Port,
☎ 04 91 91 10 40
Fishermen used to make *bouillabaisse* from the fish they had left over and could not sell. It is now a very famous dish and the preparation is a real art. Each fish must be added at the right time, since they do not all take the same amount of time to cook, and if they are all added together, some will disintegrate. At the Miramar, an institution in Marseille, you will pay approximately 255 F for this world-famous delicacy, which must contain the local fish known as *rascasse*.

La Vieille Charité

2, Rue de la Charité,
☎ 04 91 14 58 80.
Open daily except Mon., 11am-6pm; out of season, 10am-5pm.
Paid admission.
This complex of almshouses was built in 1670 by Pierre Puget, a famous name in Baroque sculpture. This is the only public building he ever designed. The pink stone of

Saint-Victor Abbey

The Corniche and beaches

Accessible by bus (no. 83) from the Vieux-Port.
Supervised beaches.

From the Avenue du Président-Kennedy (known to the Marseillais as the Corniche) to the Promenade de la Plage, the town has a variety of sandy, pebble and rocky beaches. Visit the tiny, picturesque port of the Vallon des Auffes and have a drink at

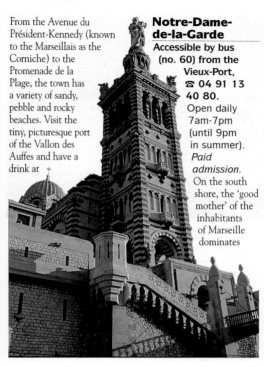

one of its bars, or go for a swim at the **plage du Prado** (beach), 2 miles (3 km) from the centre of Marseille. The 100 acres (45 ha) of land reclaimed from the sea thanks to the embankments created when the Marseille underground rail was built, are a good place to enjoy beach activities. You can also take a walk in the gardens.

Notre-Dame-de-la-Garde

Accessible by bus (no. 60) from the Vieux-Port, ☎ 04 91 13 40 80.

Open daily 7am-7pm (until 9pm in summer). *Paid admission.* On the south shore, the 'good mother' of the inhabitants of Marseille dominates

the city from a height of 500 ft (154 m). The basilica, a mixture of Romanesque and Byzantine styles, was built in the late 19th C., in the reign of Napoleon III. It has a large collection of votive offerings, a living chronicle of the woes and concerns of the people of Marseille. There is a lovely view from the esplanade.

THE *NAVETTES* OF SAINT-VICTOR

Le four des navettes, 136, Rue Sainte, ☎ 04 91 33 32 12. Open daily 7am-8pm. At Candlemas (2nd Feb.) each year the procession of the Black Virgin ends at the former bakery of Saint-Victor Abbey. The inhabitants of Marseille stock up on *navettes*, long and orange-flavoured biscuits whose shape is supposed to be reminiscent of the little boat (*navette*) which miraculously brought the Saintes Maries from Palestine to the coast of Provence. These biscuits are very 'moreish' and delicious but if you are superstitious, you must keep at least one for a whole year as it is supposed to bring luck. *Navettes* are best eaten slightly warm (and can be stored for up to 8 months). They cost about 40 F a dozen.

The little port of La Madrague, at the foot of the Corniche

The Château d'If

Le Balaboum Théâtre

16, Quai de Rive-Neuve, 7e, ☎ 04 91 54 40 71.
Show at 40 F, children's party and workshop 40 F.
This theatre and circus school for children of between 3 and 10 years of age organises readings of fairy tales every Saturday afternoon. A good opportunity for children to practice their French, followed by a party and a theatre workshop run by actors. Meanwhile, parents can brush up on their French and watch a play at the TNM de la Criée as the two theatres have synchronised their performances (32, Quai de Rive-Neuve, ☎ 04 91 54 70 54).

Musée du terroir marseillais

5, Pl. des Héros à Château-Gombert, ☎ 04 91 68 14 38.
Open daily except Tue. and public holidays, 2.30pm-6.30pm.
At the gateway to Marseille, there is a magnificent collection of folk arts and crafts. This is where you can find out if the little basket you bought in the antiques market is genuine. There are wooden utensils and carved furniture in typically Provençal patterns: intertwined hearts, bouquets of flowers, ears of wheat and baskets of fruit, symbols of love and fertility.

Swimming at the Îles du Frioul

Navettes GACM, Quai des Belges, ☎ 04 91 55 50 09.
Crossing time: approx. 30 min.
From the Vieux-Port, take a boat trip to the Îles du Frioul. They once comprised the largest quarantine area and hospital complex for the French Mediterranean coast. The Caroline Hospital (1822) on the Île de Ratonneau, was built facing windwards, to chase away the germs brought in by those with contagious diseases. Pomègues was the quarantine port. There are delightful little inlets and creeks to explore.

The Château d'If

The Château d'If is an island in the harbour of Marseille, offering the protection of its 16th C. fortress. Built on orders from King François I, it was soon converted into a prison. At the start of the novel *Count of Monte-Cristo*, Alexandre Dumas paints a terrifying picture of the place. Its famous 'guests' included the Marquis de Sade, the statesman Mirabeau – who was imprisoned at the request of his father – and, according to legend, the Man in the Iron Mask .

Le Jardin des Vestiges

Centre Bourse, Square Belsunce, ☎ 04 91 90 42 22.
Open daily except Sun. and public holidays, noon-7pm.
Paid admission.

The Jardin des Vestiges and its ancient ruins.

When the stock exchange centre was built in 1967, the excavations revealed the fortifications of the ancient Greek city and the old port of Marseille (quays, berths, docks, etc.). Some of these ruins are displayed in the lovely Vestiges garden, surrounded by pine trees and fig trees. Afterwards, visit the **Musée d'Histoire de Marseille**, which displays smaller objects discovered on the site and the wreck of a 3rd C. ship.

Santon makers

Santons were created in Marseille, so your visit could be an opportunity to start your own Provençal crèche. You will find *santons* at **Carbonel** (47, Rue Neuve-Sainte-Catherine, ☎ 04 91 54 26 58, from 52 F) and **Jacques Flore** (48, Rue du Lacydon, ☎ 04 91 90 67 56, between 41 and 57 F for one *santon*, 3 in (7 cm) high.

The Palais Longchamps

Accessible by métro (line 1, Longchamps-Cinq-Avenues station).
The Palais Longchamps is really just a water-tower, but it is worth a visit. It is the terminal building of the Marseille canal, which brings the waters of the Durance right into the heart of the city. It was built in the late 19th C., when the water supply was one of the city's main preoccupations. The completion of the works was then commem-

orated with this monument. The **Muséum d'Histoire Naturelle** (☎ 04 91 14 59 50. Open daily except Mon.) has a collection of stuffed animals, a prehistory room and a huge aquarium. The **Musée des Beaux-Arts de Marseille** (☎ 04 91 14 59 30. Open daily except Mon., 10am-5pm and 11am-6pm in summer) has paintings and sculptures from the 16th to the 19th C. (Rubens, Corot, Rodin). Both museums are housed in the Palais.

Modern art at the Musée Cantini

**19, Rue Grignan,
☎ 04 91 54 77 75.
Open daily except Mon., 10am-5pm (11am-6pm in summer).**
Paid admission. Guided tours Sat. and Sun.
The museum was built in a smart residential area of Marseille, inside a mansion. Behind the elegant, classic façade, there is a wonderful collection of modern art from early to avant-garde movements.

César

A HYDROCYCLE TRIP
☎ 04 90 59 49 39.
Reservations required. May-Oct., minimum of 3 people.
(Marseille and its islands, 330 F a day.)
The *Evasia* 16 is part sailing craft, part amphibious cycle. An instructor will accompany you. The vessel is propelled by pedalling or by sail, but don't be daunted, neither require that much effort or knowledge. Take a break at the Îles de Pomègues, Ratonneau and go for a walk to admire the view.

The Musée d'Art Contemporain

**69, Av. Haïfa, 8e,
☎ 04 91 25 01 07.
Open daily except Mon., 11am-6pm; out of season, 10am-5pm.**
The locals have nicknamed it the MAC because of its initials. A massive metal thumb, created by the sculptor César, is installed in the entrance which makes it easy to find. The museum has held exhibitions since 1960. It hit the headlines when an artist exhibited a work compiled from items he had stolen from all over the place. One of his victims came to claim his possessions, which pleased neither the artist nor the museum!

'La Maison du fada'

Bd Michelet (accessible by bus, nos. 21 or 22, Le Corbusier stop).
Reservations required through the Tourist Office or with the manager, ☎ 04 91 77 14 07.
Open daily.
Paid admission.
This was the nickname given to the famous *Cité Radieuse* of the architect Le Corbusier (*fada* means mad in Provençal). It is a concrete building perched on stilts which was supposed to symbolise the urban habitat. It was not without ambition: nine storeys with internal streets, services and shops, 337 maisonettes with loggias, and a terraced roof with a racing track, theatre, gym, fountain, crèche and solariu. It is highly sought after by Marseillais looking for a flat to buy.

The Marseille tarot pack

The city has given its name to a French version of tarot cards. The firm of Camoin, which made the cards, closed in 1974, but the Musée du Vieux Marseille took over its collection (☎ 04 91 55 10 19, daily 10am-5pm). There are some excellent examples on display. The Marseillais publisher, Vigno, asked a local illustrator to invent a new variation of tarot portraying local life, so the Queen of Hearts

became a Fishwife; her King, the Prince of Pétanque; the Knave is a supporter of the O.M., the local football team. This set is sold for 120 F at the Tourist Office and at the Arcenaulx (p.189).

Marseille soap

The shop:
La savonnerie artisanale du Sérail, 50, Bd Anatole-de-La-Forge, 14e,
☎ 04 91 98 28 25.
Open daily 8am-noon and 2-6pm.
The soapworks:
La Compagnie du savon de Marseille, 66, Ch. de Sainte-Marthe, 14e,
☎ 04 91 10 30 90.
Marseille soap owes its reputation to its high fatty acid content (72%). It also contains no artificial colouring and keeps very well. To visit a soap factory, ask at the Tourist Office. (☎ 04 91 13 89 00).

Clothing and antiques on the Cours Julien

The market in the Cours Julien, which is held every second Sunday in the month, is an antique-hunter's paradise. There are also a lot of antique dealers and second-hand shops in the area, as well as fashion boutiques and designers, such as Mademoiselle Zaza of Marseille. A good place for window-shopping or to relax in a café with a drink.

A football match at the Vélodrome stadium

Stade Vélodrome, 3, Bd Michelet, 8e,
☎ 04 91 29 14 00.
Football is almost a religion in Marseille. Support reaches fanatical proportions and fans debate players' merits long into the night. On match nights, the only club to support is O.M., the local team. Olympique Marseille was founded in 1898, and has an

Le Corbusier, la Cité Radieuse

impressive record. It has won the French championship and the Coupe de France many times. Despite the various scandals surrounding its former chairman, Bernard Tapie, O.M. was allowed to take part in the 1998 World Cup. In order for it to be worthy of the event, the grounds, the Stade Vélodrome, were completely renovated.

Les Calanques on foot or by boat

From the Callelongue, the GR 98 links all the coves known as the Calanques right up to Cassis. If you intend to walk it take plenty of water because this is a 17½ mile (28 km) hike. Camping and lighting fires are not allowed and there is nowhere to stay overnight. In summer, walks are organised by the **Société des excursionnistes marseillais** (☎ 04 91 84 75 52). From the Quai des Belges, in the Vieux-Port, there is a 4-hour boat trip to the Calanques (☎ 04 91 55 50 09. Sailings at weekends in fine weather throughout the year).

Rococo mirrors and frames

Galerie d'art La Poutre, 206, Rue Paradis, ☎ 04 91 37 10 93. Open daily except Sun. and Mon., 9am-noon and 3-8.30pm. The Sajous family owns a gallery of Baroque and rococo furniture, crazed glass, mirrors and other Italian items.

Olympic Marseille supporters' shop

203, Rue Paradis or Centre commercial Grand V-La Valentine, ☎ 04 91 81 54 54. Open daily except Sun. and Mon. morning, 9am-noon and 2.30-7.30pm. **The other shop is at 3, Bd Michelet,** ☎ 04 91 71 47 00. The supporters club constitutes what the Marseillais call 'the twelfth man'. Their support is so valuable they are almost an integral part of the team. Football fans can buy all kinds of wonderful souvenirs from the shop next to the stadium. The shop stocks more than 2000 items in the club's blue-and-white colours, from a scarf to a football, and including the strip (tee-shirt and shorts), bag, cap and pennant, from between 5 F and 700 F.

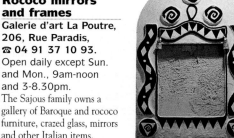

The shop even sells a stone from the old stadium stamped O.M. for 120 F.

Châteauneuf-les-Martigues

✦ El Dorado City

5 miles (8 km) S. de Marignane, ☎ 04 42 79 86 90 Open daily, 10am-7pm (11am-6pm during the school holidays). Out of season, Wed., Sat. and Sun.,10am-6pm. *55 F (45 F for children under 12) including the show.* Out in the *garrigue*, the Provençal scrubland, this authentic Wild West town rings to the sounds of realistic bank robberies and passing steam trains. More than 40 actors and stuntmen inhabit the streets and saloons. The gold mine is open to prospectors and there is a daily rodeo.

FESTIVALS

Marseille is a bustling city all year round. Among the various events it holds, three are perhaps the most exciting for visitors. 'Jazz Transfert' (12 June-18 July) the best of international jazz, is held at the Town Hall (☎ 04 91 33 33 79). 'Vues sur les Docs' is a documentary film festival which has been going since 1989 and is a showcase for the brightest talents. (May-June, at the Palais du Pharo, 58, Bd Livon, ☎ 04 95 04 44 90.), whilst the 'Festival de Marseille' presents a brilliant combination of modern dance and the best of modern music. It is held in June and July (☎ 04 91 99 00 20).

Cassis and Cap Canaille
Marseille's playground

Cassis is pronounced 'Cassi', the final 's' being silent. This little fishing port sheltered by the sheer cliffs of Cap Canaille is a favourite destination for a day trip from Marseille, for both the locals and the tourists who invade the place in the summer. But it is also popular with artists (Pagnol filmed there and Matisse and Derain painted it).

Cassis

Walk to Pointe des Lombards
Approx. 30 min.
The walk offers a lovely view of the bay from the foot of Cap Canaille. Start from the Plage de la Grande-Mer (next to the harbour) and aim for Corton cove, passing the Pointe des Lombards. At the end you can climb up to the ruins of a 13th C. castle from the Plage de l'Arène. There are flights of steps and a covered passage leading to the clifftop.

Bar de la Marine
5, Quai des Baux,
☎ 04 42 01 76 09.
Open daily except Feb., from 7am to 2am.
This was the actor Raimu's favourite hideout. It is also where Marcel Pagnol shot many scenes from his films and one can almost picture his characters in this atmos-

pheric setting. Try a glass of pastis or, if you dare, play a hand of cards with the regulars, who bear a striking resemblance to their screen counterparts.

Le Musée des Arts et Traditions Populaires
Rue Xavier-D'Authier (1st floor of Office de Tourisme),
☎ 04 42 01 88 66.
Open Wed., Thu. and Sat., Apr.-Sep. 3.30-6.30pm; Oct.-Mar. 2.30-5.30pm. *Paid admission.*
This small but pleasant folk museum traces the history of Cassis, much of which has

been brought to life through archeological excavations at the foot of Cap Canaille. Roman remains, mosaics and amphora are arranged side by side with modern art, including paintings by Kundera, Henri Crémieux, Ponçon, Ziem and others.

Cosquer's cave
The wonders of Cassis are not all on the surface. This cave, 120 ft (36 m) beneath the sea, was only discovered in 1991 by a scuba-diver named Cosquer. Deep inside, where it is completely dry, there is an amazing collection of rock paintings made by Cro-Magnon man 27,000 years ago. Entry is strictly forbidden.

Around Cassis

La Route des Crêtes
45 min. by car to La Ciotat, 3½ hours on foot.

This mountainous road runs up to Cap Canaille and hugs the highest sea-cliff in Europe 3328 ft (416 m). By car,

take the D14. There are extraordinary views all the way, and you can stop to admire them at each bend. To enjoy them to the full, however, leave your vehicle at the crossroads leading to the Relais de la Saoupe and the Route des Crêtes (not the la Colle road). About 50 yards (50 m) from the second bend,

at the end of the Avenue des Calanques and aim for Port-Miou, Port-Pin and En-Vau (the most famous of the calanques) following the GR98. They can also be visited by ship, there are frequent sailings from the harbour (☎ 04 42 01 02 89).

Aubagne

Two *santons* workshops

Two *santon*-makers share the honours in the town of Aubagne. **Santons Chave** (37, Rue Frédéric-Mistral, ☎ 04 42 70 12 86. Daily 9am-noon and 2-7pm, except weekends) make more than a thousand different models of all sizes. The workshop can also be visited at these times.

Spotcheck
C4

Bouches-du Rhône

Things to do

Walk to Pointe des Lombards
La route des Crêtes (highest sea-cliff in Europe)
Excursions to the *Calanques*

With children

Visit a *santon* workshop

Within easy reach

La Sainte-Baume, 25 km NE, p. 204.

Tourist Office

Cassis: ☎ 04 42 01 11 91

follow the signposted path on your right. You will feel quite dizzy looking down.

Excursions to the *calanques*

Calanques are former river beds which were invaded by the sea and are now sea inlets. They are situated west of Cassis. Their white-weathered rocks topped by Aleppo pines have some of the **loveliest scenery of the Provençal coast**. To take a stroll, park

Scaturro Daniel (20, Av. de Verdun, ☎ 04 42 84 33 29. From Mon. afternoon to Sat., 10 am-noon and 2.30-6pm) tastefully models the characters popularised by the books and films of Marcel Pagnol.

Craft pottery

**Av. des Goums,
☎ 04 42 03 05 59.**
Daily except Sun. 8am-noon and 2-6pm.
The **Maison Ravel** has specialised in garden pottery for 150 years. The pottery is made from unpainted terracotta, the most popular item being the Provençal jar (1800 F for a large one, 32 in. (80 cm) high). Tableware, *tians*, and different varieties of cooking pots are also on sale.

THE WHITE WINE OF CASSIS

**Clos Sainte-Magdeleine, Av. du Revestel,
☎ 04 42 01 70 28.**
Open Mon.-Fri., 10am-noon and 3-7pm; weekends: visits by appointment.
The Zafiropulo family has been making the white and rosé wines for which Cassis is famous for over 50 years. Visit their vineyard, above the village, to taste this pale yellow wine in lovely surroundings. There are 216 acres (9 ha) of vines overlooking the sea. This AOC appellation wine has hints of rosemary, heather and myrtle. It goes especially well with fish and *bouillabaisse* (57 F a bottle).

From La Ciotat to Bandol
beside the Gulf d'Amour

Between La Ciotat and Bandol, the villages perch on the clifftop, surrounded by terraced vineyards which produce the grapes to make Bandol wine. The cliffs of the Gulf d'Amour have some spectacular coastal walks.

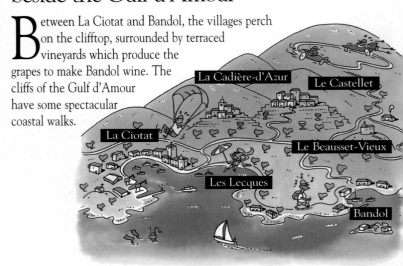

La Cadière-d'Azur • Le Castellet • La Ciotat • Le Beausset-Vieux • Les Lecques • Bandol

---

La Ciotat
Parc du Mugel
1¼ miles (2 km) SW of La Ciotat via the Avenue des Calanques,
☎ 04 42 08 09 62.
Open daily, 8am-8pm; Oct.-Mar., 9am-6pm.
The Cap de l'Aigle stands out against the sky, its ochre-coloured rocks dominating the massive gates and lifting gear of the naval dockyard. At the foot of the rocks, the Parc du Mugel offers peace and quiet and shade from the sun under its oak, carob and chestnut trees. There is an ingenious irrigation system which makes it possible to collect rainwater and channel it to the plants.

Bathing, diving and hiking
The beach at Saint-Cyr-sur-Mer/Les Lecques is a fine sandy one, and its waters are a favourite with scuba-divers (Info. ☎ 04 94 26 42 18). For hikers and walkers, follow the coastal path, a historic customs officer's route between the port of La Madrague and the Renecros cove at Bandol, which will take 3½ hours. It is a 7 mile (11 km) round trip along steep headlands which overlook the site of the port of Alon and the *calanques*.

La Cadière-d'Azur
Night-time walk
5 miles (8 km) N. of Bandol.
The charm of this village lies in its flower-lined streets. You can also visit the remains of the **medieval city walls, the clock tower** and the flamboyant portal of the

La Cadière-d'Azur

16th C. Saint-André Church. If you are in the mood for an evening stroll (though take care as it's easy to get lost), walk northwards. From this side of the hill, there is a magnificent view over the Sainte-Baume range with Le Castellet in the foreground.

Deltaplaning and para-gliding
If you are a fan of the kind of sport that requires nerves of steel, you'll find the climatic and aerological conditions of the Provençal coast ideal for paragliding. Detailed information from the club called **Les Rapaces d'Azur** (☎ 04 94 90 05 29).

The Ott family lives in an 18th C. château and for more than a century has dedicated itself to winemaking. Visit the estate and taste the wines of Bandol which have had an AOC since 1941. The great wines of Provence are exported to 51 countries. A bottle of 1996 rosé will cost around 90 F and 100 F for a 1993 red or white.

Bouches-du Rhône

Things to do

**Bathing, diving and hiking
Deltaplaning and para-
gliding
Visit to the Ott estate
The Paul-Ricard Racetrack**

Within easy reach

Bandol, 18 km E, p. 200,

Tourist Office

**La Ciotat:
☎ 04 42 08 61 32**

Le Castellet

Craftsmen and wine-makers

6 miles (10 km) N. of Bandol.

This is where Marcel Pagnol filmed *The Baker's Wife*. The feudal village is surrounded by terraced vineyards, and the narrow streets are lined with 17th and 18th C. houses occupied by local craftspeople including potters, leather-workers, weavers and *santon-*makers. There is a wonderful view of the Sainte-Baume range from the esplanade of the 15th C. château.

The Ott estate

**Château Romassan, by the D66,
☎ 04 94 98 71 91.**
Open every day except Sun. and bank holidays, 9am-noon and 2-6pm. Guided tour by appointment. *Free admission.*

Le Beausset-Vieux

Votive offerings

(4 km) S. of Beausset.
The chapel on the summit of Beausset-Vieux contains a collection of 80 votive offerings. There is a magnificent view of Toulon harbour, the Sainte-Baume, La Ciotat, the gorges of Ollioules and medieval villages. Le Beausset has a **Museum** of antique dolls (46, Rue de la République, ☎ 04 94 98 63 37).

Around Beausset

The Paul-Ricard Racetrack

**5 miles (8 km) N. of Beausset via RN8.
☎ 04 94 98 45 00.**
Tours (non-race days) daily by appointment.

Free admission.
Drive around the famous Castellet racetrack in a single-seater or Formula 3 car, and pretend you're Alain Prost. The Winfield driving school is

open for inspection and the Renault workshops will display their latest racing models. However, the pits are only open for visits on days when there is no racing. If you want to be a spectator at a race such as the Bol d'Or, come in the second or third week of September. If you want to attend the Grand Prix for lorries, come between the end of May and beginning of June.

From Bandol to Sanary

rosé wine and hilltop villages

P icturesque little roads lead into the hills or down towards the ports to which the fishermen return to in the early hours of the morning. These coastal waters are rich in a variety of fish which find their way onto the tables of the local people, all washed down with the smooth wine of Bandol.

There are some pretty strange buildings around today as a result. You can obtain a brochure about them which is available from the Sanary Office de Tourisme.

Nearby
Notre-Dame-de-Pépiole
2½ miles (4 km) NE of Sanary via the D 63.
This extraordinary little chapel dates from the 6th C. and looks like a fortress, with a massive porch and crooked roofs.

Sanary-sur-Mer
Festivals and sea-urchins
Between 1933 and 1942, this pretty seaside resort was home to more than 500 people objecting to the Nazi regime, including many German writers and dissidents. Today, the town's visitors are summer tourists watching the morning catch of sea-urchins brought into the port. The quayside is lined with palm trees and is most picturesque. During the first weekend in October, the town plays host to one of the loveliest traditional festivals in France with folk costumes and a Provençal feast at which all are welcome.

Eastern promise
A certain Mr. Michel (1819-1907), a former mayor of Sanary, was appointed Director of Lighthouses to the Ottoman Empire. He was made a *pasha* by the Sultan, and came home with a large fortune and a new name – Michel Pasha. He devoted himself to encouraging tourism in his native town and to this end built hotels, shops, a casino and villas on the Tamaris corniche.

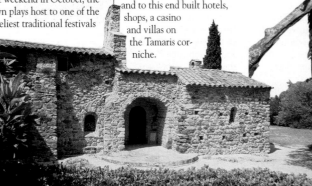

This pre-Romanesque construction makes an interesting stop on the road to Six-Fours-les-Plages. The cradle-shaped naves are interconnected and some of the stones of the interior have strange blue tints.

Île des Embiez
Aquarium on an island
**Embarcadère du Brusc,
☎ 04 94 74 99 00.
Sailings daily, Oct.-Jun.,
7am-8pm; Jul.-Sep.,
7am-8.45pm.**
Paid admission.
A delightful trip to a pretty little island planted with vines and owned by the Ricard Foundation, which was begun

Sanary-sur-Mer: the port

by the Ricard pastis company. The harbour, with its brightly-coloured houses and classical statuary, is rather kitsch. At the **Musée de la Fondation Océanographique Paul-Ricard**, an oceanographic museum (☎ 04 94 34 02 49, open daily, 10am-noon and 1.30-5.30 pm except Wed. and Sat. morning, daily in summer), sea creatures are displayed side-by- side with fossils and shells. The sea-water aquariums contain beautiful examples of Mediterranean underwater flora and fauna.

BANDOL WINES
**Maison des vins de Bandol,
22, Allée Vivien, Bandol,
☎ 04 94 29 45 03.
Open daily except Sun., 10am-noon and 3-4.30pm.Closed in Jan.**
Bandol was one of the first wines to be awarded an AOC as long ago as 1941. The wines have an intense colour, a fragrant bouquet and powerful flavour. They are primarily red wines and age extremely well and they can be kept for up to 20 years.

Île de Bendor
Leisure Ricard-style
This most civilised of the islands of Provence was acquired by Paul Ricard in 1950. He opened a scuba-diving centre, (the **Centre international de plongée,** ☎ 04 94 29 55 12) and a leisure centre. The island also has a lovely little wine museum (**Musée du Vin** p. 47), a craft glassworks, a zoo and an art centre, where you can learn to draw and paint.

❀ SANARY-BANDOL EXOTIC GARDEN AND ZOO

**Quartier Pont-d'Aran,
1 mile (3 km) from Bandol
☎ 04 94 29 40 38.
Open daily, 8am-noon and 2-6pm. Sun.,
10am-noon and 2-7pm**
Paid admission.
This miniature paradise contains a huge collection of cacti and succulents from North, Central and South America, as well as other tropical plants from across the world. The zoo contains marmosets, coatis, makis, monkeys and gibbons, as well as llamas, parrots of all kinds, pink flamingos and parakeets.

Spotcheck
C4

Var

Things to do
Bandol wines
Oceanographic museum
Scuba-diving

With children
Sanary-Bandol exotic garden and zoo.

Within easy reach
La Ciotat, 18 km E, p. 198.

Tourist Offices
Bandol: ☎ 04 42 08 61 32
Sanary: ☎ 04 94 74 01 04

Toulon

Toulon has expanded behind a stretch of coast which ranks with the most beautiful in Europe, and at first glance the city seems to have been disfigured by concrete and modern architecture, but its ancient centre has some pleasant surprises for visitors. The port, overlooked by Mont Faron has retained its warmth and liveliness.

Old Toulon market

The market is held every day in the **Cours Lafayette** and the **Rue Paul-Landrin**, which the people of Toulon call 'the little Cours Lafayette'. This market, which is at its best in the morning, is one of the most famous in Provence, and is always great fun. It is a good opportunity to discover the narrow lanes of the old part of town early in the morning, and to taste one of the local delicacies, *la cade chaude*, a cake of chick-peas sold in the Place du Mûrier and the Rue Paul-Landrin.

Mont Faron: lookout and zoo

The view is spectacular from the top of the mount, with the shore and port laid out before you with the ships, the quays and the dockyards. From here, the countless blocks and towers of concrete look less ugly. You can get to the top of Mont Faron by **téléphérique** (cable-car) (daily except Mon., 9.30am-7.30pm; out of season, 9.30am-noon and 2-5pm. ☎ 04 94 92 68 25) or by climbing a very picturesque route with many viewpoints. The walks start in the Sainte-Anne district. The zoo (open daily, 10am-6.30pm, ☎ 04 94 88 07 89) is also worth visiting.

Atlases and boatmen

If you take the busy Rue d'Alger, you will reach the **Square Léon-Vérane** which contains a statue of the spirit of the sea. Higher up, the **Place Puget** offers shade under its plane trees. From here, you can return to the **port**, where the former town hall is decorated with Atlas figures sculpted by Pierre Puget – stevedores, backs bent under heavy sacks of grain as they unload the ships. In the port, boatmen vie with each other for trade, accosting tourists and offering them trips around the harbour, exclaiming about the wonders to be seen from their boat (about 40 F).

Along the Corniche

Halfway up Mont Faron, the **Corniche Marius-Escartefigue** which links Toulon to La Valette has beautiful views of the sea,

Spotcheck
C4

Var

Things to do
Old Toulon market
Tasting *chichi-frégis*

With children
Aqualand

Within easy reach
*La Ciota, 35 km W,
p. 198.
Le massif des Maures,
30 km NW, p. 222.*

Tourist Office
Toulon : ☎ 04 94 18 53 00

the pinewoods and gardens. The elegant palm-lined **Corniche Frédéric-Mistral** overlooks the **Plage du Mourillon**. It makes a very pleasant walk very early in the morning or at sunset. The 16th C. royal tower, the **Fort Saint-Louis,** between les Mourillons and the Pointe de la Mitre, overlooks a delightful little port full of rowing boats and tiny yachts.

Municipal Museum

from the Age of Enlightenment, figureheads, paintings and models of ships' cannons which show how important the navy was to Toulon, a town whose entire working life focuses on the sea.

Municipal Museum
113, Bd du Maréchal-Leclerc,
☎04 94 93 15 54.
Open daily except public holidays, 1-7pm.
Free admission.
The municipal museum contains an important collection of paintings, including 17th C. to 20th C. Provençal art. There are also some important modern works. In fact, Toulon has a good deal of modern art, covering the years 1960-1986, by Arman, César, Niki de Saint-Phalle, Klein and Fontana.

Tasting *chichi-frégis*
This is what the Toulonnais consider a treat. *Chichi-frégis* is a long strip of sweet, deep-fried dough

Home of the French Navy
Pl. Monsenergue,
☎04 94 02 02 01.
Open daily except Tues. and public holidays, in summer 9am-noon and 3-7pm, in winter 9.30am-noon and 2-6pm. The **Musée de la Marine** tells the story of Toulon from the late 15th C. There are models of sailing ships and frigates

AQUALAND SAINT-CYR-SUR-MER
ZAC des Pradeaux,
15 miles (25 km) W of Toulon,
☎04 94 32 08 09.
Open Jun.-Sep., 10am-6pm.
Don't miss the 'cobra', a water toboggan ride more than 330 ft (100 m) long.
For breakneck speed there is 'rapid rafting'. Entry is free for children less than 3 ft 4 ins (1 m) tall, and for grandparents over 60 accompanied by a paying child.

rolled into a crispy ring. The 'in' place to eat one is still the **kiosk in the Place Paul-Conte**, at the top of the Cours Lafayette.

The Sainte-Baume mountain range

St. Mary Magdelene retired to a *baoumo* (grotto in Provençal), which gave its name to this mountain range whose peaks average 1000 ft (300 m). It is 7½ miles (12 km) across and the highest peak, which is 3823 ft (1147 m), is a favourite with rock-climbers, hikers and even pilgrims.

Saint-Maximin
Gothic basilica

Basilica open daily, 8.30am-6pm (until 7pm in summer).
Couvent Royal open daily, 9.30am-6pm (until 7pm in summer).
Paid admission.

The vast 13th C. basilica is a masterpiece of Provençal Gothic, and is indicative of the number of pilgrims who made their way to Sainte-Baume – until the French Revolution. There is a skull in the crypt which is venerated as being that of Mary Magdalene, and the gallery contains one of the most beautiful organs in the world, dating from the 18th C. It is played in July and August for 'L'été de l'orgue historique' (historic organ summer festival). The basilica is flanked by the 15th C.

cloister of the royal convent of the Jacobin monks, which has a large garden.

In the district
A walk to Saint-Pilon

Access on foot from the place called L'Hôtellerie, 5¼ miles (9 km) S of Nans-les-Pins. Follow the GR9.
Round trip lasts 2 hours.
The best view over green Provence is on the rocky peak

of the Sainte-Baume. Follow in the footsteps of Mary Magdalene and walk through the forest, after about an hour's walk you will come across a fabulous view.

Pilgrimage to the Grotto

Access on foot from the Trois-Chênes crossroad where the D80 and D95 meet, 5 miles (8 km) S of Nans-les-Pins. Follow the Chemin des Rois.
Round trip lasts 1½ hours.

OK CORRAL
CUGES-LES-PINS

☎ 04 42 73 80 05.
Open daily in summer
10am-6pm. Out of
season, Wed. and week-
ends. Closed mid-Nov.
to mid-Mar.
*Admission: 75 F
(children: 65 F; free for
those less than 3 ft 4 in
(1 m) tall.*
**Huge roundabouts and
attractions in a Wild
West atmosphere.
Waggon trains, the
Grand Canyon, the
Colorado River rapids.
See if you can keep
your seat on a mechani-
cal bucking bronco or
try the 'lassoo loop'.**

St. Mary Magdalene retired
here 2000 years ago to do
penance. Behind the altar, a
statue of her in a prostrate
position marks the presumed
spot where she lay. After the
Carrefour de l'Oratoire
(oratory crossroads) a
staircase of 150
steps cut into
the rock leads
to the terrace,
which is at
an altitude
of 2953 ft
(886 m).
Hundreds of
pilgrims gather
here every Whit
Monday.

Parc de Saint-Pons

**2 miles (3 km) E of
Gémenos on the D2.**
A haven of coolness at the
foot of the heights of Sainte-
Baume. The beech-trees, ash
trees and the waters of the
Frauge are the main elements
in a park which managed to
escape the forest fires that
ravaged the nearby hills.
Wander through the ruins of
a 13th C. Cistercian abbey.

If you have the strength for a
climb, l'Espigoulier, 2426 ft
(728 m), has a superb view
over Marseille.

Saint-Zacharie
Parc du Moulin-Blanc

**Av. Gaston-de-Saporta,
17 km SW of Saint-
Maximin,**
☎ 04 42 62 71 30.
Open daily, Jun.-Sep.,
10am-7pm; out of
season, weekends and
festivals by appointment.
Paid admission.
In 1851, a French Marquis
created an English-style park
here, thanks to the cool
microclimate.

Signes
Confiserie Fouque (nougat factory)

**2, Rue Louis-Lumière,
21 miles (37 km) S of
Saint-Maximin,**
☎ 04 94 90 89 96.
Free guided tour.

Spotcheck
C4

Var

Things to do

Walk to Saint-Pilon
Parc du Moulin-Blanc
(English-style park)

With children

OK Corral

Within easy reach

*Aix-en-Provence,
30 km NW, p. 174.
Marseille, 30 km SW,
p. 192.
Cassis, 25 km SW, p. 196.
La Ciotat, 25 km SW,
p. 198.
Vallée de l'Argens,
25 km NW, p. 232.*

Tourist Office

Saint-Maximin:
☎ 04 94 59 84 59

If the bishop of Marseille
had only known that his
summer residence would be
turned into a **nougat**
factory! Roland Fouque
and his wife make a
unique Provençal
nougat using
mountain honey
which they gather
themselves. The
recipe dates from
1701, and must
have improved with
age – a gourmet's delight.

The Giens peninsula

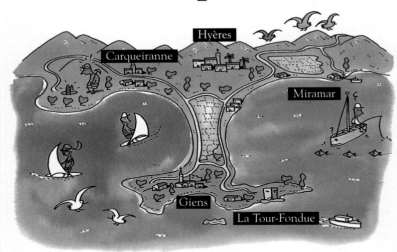

Hyères

Carqueiranne

Miramar

Giens

La Tour-Fondue

The Giens peninsula, facing Hyères, is in danger of turning into an island. At least that is the prediction of the geologists who are watching the gradually shrinking vulnerable strip of land which attaches it to the mainland. At the moment, however, it is still all dry land.

The peninsula
Access is across the 'double tombolo', two sand bars which gradually filled up the space separating the original island from the mainland. This is the most southerly seaside resort of the Côte d'Azur, covered with pine trees, and surrounded by sandy beaches which rival those of the Greek islands.

Beaches and windsurfing
The Almanarre (access via D559), on the western side of the 'double tombolo', is a paradise for sand-yachting fans. This 4 miles (6 km) of its coastline is also the venue for the annual World Windsurfing Championship. The beaches of **La Capte** and **La Bergerie**

(access via D97) are extremely safe. The water is so shallow you will not be out of your depth until you are more than 66 yards (60 m) from the shore. Ideal for children.

The coastal footpath
From La Madrague to Tour-Fondue and back 10¾ miles (17.2 km). Takes 5 hours on foot. Sling a camera over your shoulder and tour the penin-

sula from the south. It is an extraordinary experience and very photogenic. You can walk or cycle out to visit the picturesque fishing ports of La Madrague and Le Niel, and look across to

the Porquerolles and Port-Cros Islands across the water. Do not miss La **Tour-Fondue**, an ancient fort built by Cardinal Richelieu, nor the wild and windy **Pointe des Chevaliers**. The view is magnificent, but beware of the sheer drop.

The Decugis nursery (Pépinières)

1211, Chemin de Nartettes, 1¼ miles (2 km) W of Hyères, ☎ 04 94 57 67 78. Open daily 8am-noon and 2-7pm; Sun. by appointment. Closed 25 Dec.-15 Jan.
Since 1904, this nursery has been supplying exotic vegetation for the whole region. Violette Decugis has thousands of cold-resistant

SEA-FISHING

Port de Miramar, La Londe-les-Maures, ☎ 04 94 66 91 19. You won't need to bring rods or bait, everything is supplied. Just set your alarm clock: the morning trip starts at 7.30 am precisely. The Lou Gabian Club will take you out to sea to track bream, rainbow wrasse, and pandora fish. Night fishing departure is at 8pm and the catch (depending on the season) will be squid or gilthead bream. Groups and family outings catered for (13 people max.).

palm-trees, such as sambal palms, Canary palms and Chilean jubeas. See if you can spot *Trachycarpus Fortunei*, which can even grow in Paris and London. Taste her delicious palm jam (21 F a pot).

Scuba-diving

The waters off the Giens Peninsula and the Îles d'Or are littered with the finest wrecks in the Mediterranean (the *Donator*, the *Michel C.*, the *Grec*). The Ulysse Club (Port de la Madrague, Giens, ☎ 04 94 58 25 07 or 10 76) organises scuba-diving expeditions daily in summer (out of season at the week-end) for level 1, 2 or 3 divers. At Tour-Fondue, the TVM company operates glass-bottomed boats, which means you can see it all without getting wet. Departures from the sea terminal (☎ 04 94 58 95 14).

Le Pradet

Cap-Garonne mine

Ch. du Bau-Rouge, 3 miles (5 km) W de Carqueiranne, ☎ 04 94 21 71 69. Open daily, 15 Jun.-15 Sep., 2-5.30pm; out of season, Wed., Sat., Sun., 2-5pm. *Paid admission.*
These 17th C. copper mines were discovered by accident, when a young goat fell into a hole, its rescue sparking off the discovery of a rich seam of copper, making the region's fortune. The miners, both women and men, worked in semi-darkness.

Spotcheck
D4

Var

Things to do

**Beaches and windsurfing
Sea-fishing
Scuba-diving
Decugis nursery
Cap-Garonne mine**

With children

**The beaches
Tropical bird garden (Jardin d'Oiseaux Tropicaux)**

Within easy reach

Maures range, 25 km NW, p. 222.

Tourist Office

Hyères : ☎ 04 94 65 18 55

La Londe-les-Maures

❀ Tropical bird garden

Route de Valcros, 6 miles (10 km) E of Hyères via N98, ☎ 04 94 35 02 15. Open daily, Jun.-Sep., 9.30am-7.30pm; Oct.-May, 2-6pm. *Paid admission.*
The birds kept here are all very exotic and colourful. Some of them can talk and all of them sing. This 14 acre (6 ha) natural park is inhabited by 80 species of bird, exhibiting their colourful plumage.

Hyères
sedate and charming

Almost 3 miles (5 km) from the beaches and smart resorts of the Côte d'Azur, the ancient Phocean city of Olbia, today known as Hyères, overlooks the Palyvestre plain and the Giens Peninsula. It has many examples of Moorish-style architecture and handsome turn-of-the-century public buildings, as well as exotic trees and flowers lining its broad avenues. Hyères has the charm of an old-fashioned seaside resort, simple and classic.

Exhibitions at the Templars' Tower

Open daily, 9am-noon and 2.30-6pm.
Paid admission.
The Sainte-Blaise Tower in the Place Massillon, dubbed The Templars' Tower, is now an exhibition hall. The 12th C. chapel was part of the fortress of a command post of the Order of the Knights Templar. From the terrace, there is a panoramic view of the plain.

Votive offerings of the collegiate church of Saint-Paul

☎ 04 94 65 83 30.
Guided tours on Wed., meet at 9am at the Office de Tourisme.
(☎ 04 94 65 18 55).
Paid admission.
The building is partly 12th C. and contains reredos, reliquaries and gilded statues, but the most interesting exhibits are the 400 paintings donated by grateful sailors rescued from the sea. The oldest dates from 1613. On the left upon entering, there is a huge crèche of Provençal *santons*.

OLBIUS-RIQUIER GARDENS AND ZOO

Av. Amboise-Thomas, 650 yds (600 m) from the centre,
☎ **04 94 35 90 65.**
Open daily, 7.30am-6pm; until 8pm in summer.
Paid admission.
The 144 acre (6.5 ha) park contains rare and exotic plants which can survive outdoors in this mild climate. Greenhouses shelter tropical plants and birds from all corners of the world. The children will enjoy the animal enclosure and pets' zoo where the animals include emus, goats and monkeys. There is also a special play area. The gardens are a haven of peace and tranquillity for the accompanying adults.

The Old Town
The picturesque Old Town is spread out before the ruins of the 11th-13th C. castle. The Rue Sainte-Claire has some beautiful examples of medieval façades, and Renaissance buildings bearing armorial crests. There is a restored Romanesque house at no. 6 Rue Paradis. The Place Massillon market (daily, from 7am to 5pm) is colourful and charming.

Country market
Find your way through the maze of narrow streets and take the picturesque Rue Barbacane, whose houses have mullioned windows, to the Place de la République. Every Saturday and the 3rd Thursday of the month, this regional market attracts people in search of local produce.
The produce on sale includes honey and jams as well as well as a wide variety of flowers.

Castel Sainte-Claire and Saint-Bernard gardens
Open daily
Free admission.
The 'city of palms' began growing its favourite tree during the last century, the palm still flourishes in the Parc du Castel Sainte-Claire. Colonel Voutier, who discovered the Venus de Milo, built a magnificent villa here in 1850. Only about 50 yards (50 m) away, the gardens and terraces of the Parc Saint-Bernard extend to the castle ruins. The park is like a maze of plants filled with wonderful fragrances.

La villa de Noailles
☎ 04 94 65 18 55.
Open Jun.-Aug., guided tours.
Paid admission.
The villa is right next to the Saint-Bernard park. This Art Deco house, owned by the de Noailles family, was designed by the architect Robert Mallet-Stevens. In the 1930s the great celebrities of the age stayed here, including Cocteau, Man Ray and Giacometti. Its shape is that of a ship, with additions of concrete cubes and terraces. This 'cubist château' remains one of the few examples of avant-garde architecture to be considered successful. The interior can be visited out of season during exhibitions.

Oriental houses
Hyères, the veteran Côte d'Azur seaside resort, is very representative of the fashion for all things eastern which swept France in the 18th and 19th C. Two houses, La Mauresque (Av. Jean-Natte) and La Tunisienne (Av. Beauregard) are fine examples of this craze, with oriental minarets, cupolas and brightly coloured, tiled façades. The effect is enhanced by the fact that they are surrounded by palm trees.

Porquerolles
the place for pleasure

This, the largest of the Hyères islands is a stranger to traffic jams and campsites. It can only be reached by boat from the Giens Peninsula or Le Lavandou, and the only transport available to tourists is the bicycle. This was a pirate hideout in the Middle Ages, when the booty stolen in the Mediterranean was hoarded here. However, today the island's real treasures are natural – fine sand, paths lined with pines and heather, and charming little sheltered inlets.

The marina

Fishermen still remember the little stone jetty, which welcomed Jean-Luc Godard and his camera crew in 1965, when they made *Pierrot le Fou* here. Anna Karina and Jean-Paul Belmondo strolled hand-in-hand on this very spot. The port has since been completely rebuilt, and unfortunately as a result it has lost much of its former charm.

The pueblo

In the Place d'Armes, shaded by eucalyptus and nettle-trees, pétanque players exhibit their considerable skills. The square has the atmosphere of a Mexican pueblo, with the little Church of Sainte-Anne and its steeple dominating the square and the terraces of the cafés. Simenon set one of his Maigret adventures here, during which the detective

sampled the local wine and tasted the wonderful cuisine. The Domaine de l'Île

rosé was the first to get the AOC Côtes-de-Provence, and the perfect place to enjoy it is in the shade of the nettle-trees.

Fort Sainte-Agathe

☎ 04 94 12 30 40.
Open May-Sep., 10am-12.30pm and 2-5.30pm.
Paid admission.
François I built this fortress and Napoleon restored and enlarged it. Perched on a rocky outcrop, its massive round tower dominates the village. It was the perfect place for the artillery to defend the approaches to the harbour. Nowadays the fort is used for more peaceful purposes. There is a permanent exhibition

dedicated to discoveries on the sea bed and the history of the Islands of Hyères.

The view from the top of the tower is spectacular.

Botanical Conservation Centre

Southern exit from the village,
☎ 04 94 12 30 40.
Open May-Sep., 9.30am-noon and 1.30-5pm.
Paid admission.

WALKING TO THE LIGHTHOUSE AND THE SEMAPHORE

You can't possibly get lost. There are two main footpaths around the heights of Porquerolles. One leads to the highest point of the island, where the semaphore perches at 473 ft (142 m), from which you will have a lovely view over the island of Giens. The second, more southerly, path brings you directly to the lighthouse built in the early 19th C. On this side of the island there are cliffs 664 ft (83 m) high.

It is here that scientists work at preserving endangered species of regional plants. The centre is surrounded by a 432 acre (180 ha) orchard where you can see, but not eat, traditional varieties of fig and apricot. One of the most interesting sights is the plantation of ancient olive trees. There are also rare plants from Corsica and mainland France. The best time to visit is in May and June when most of them are in flower.

The best beaches

Apparently, Porquerolles gets more sunshine than anywhere else in France, which makes it the ideal place for sunbathing and swimming. There are two beaches at the western tip of the island, on either side of the isthmus of the Grand-Langoustier: the **Plage Noire** (black beach) coloured by deposits from a former soda factory, and the **Plage Blanche** (white beach) where the sand is particularly fine. For those who prefer not to make the trip, there is a beach just a few yards from the village, the **Plage de la Courtade**, which is large but much more crowded.

Other beaches are the **Plage de l'Argent** and the **Plage de l'Ayguade**, but these are less attractive than the **Plage Notre-Dame**, situated beside a pine wood.

Spotcheck
D4

Var

Things to do

Botanical Conservation Centre
Mountain biking
Walking to the lighthouse

Tourist Office

Porquerolles:
☎ **04 94 58 33 76**

MOUNTAIN BIKING

The scrubland (*maquis*) on Porquerolles covers an area 4 miles (7 km) long and 2 miles (3 km) wide, thick with eucalyptus, pines and shrubs. It makes Porquerolles one of the nicest places to stay on the Côte d'Azur. About 300 islanders share some 3000 acres (1250 ha) of luxurious vegetation. In the summer, however, the population increases tenfold.

The island can be explored by bicycle, preferably a mountain-bike. Three shops rent bikes on the Esplanade, in the village centre (60-75 F per day). Go there straight from the boat. Information from the Office de Tourisme.

Port-Cros and Levant

the golden isles

The easiest way to reach the islands is from Le lavandou. The trip is fairly short and the sailings quite frequent. The bay of Port-Cros looks like a picture postcard with a palm-fringed shore and deep blue waters. The island has been a national park since 1963, and is an ecological haven and the perfect place for scuba-diving, whilst the Île du Levant is a famous as a mecca for naturists.

L'île de Port-Cros

Discovering nature

Bureau du Parc National de l'Île, ☎04 94 05 90 17.

The information centre in the port has lots of brochures and booklets about the island. Top prize goes to a plasticised brochure that can be read underwater! It is a guide to the **underwater path** created in the Baie du Palud, to enable divers to explore these carefully protected waters without harming the marine life, which includes posidonia, algae, starfish, sea anemones, *rascasse* and rainbow wrasse.

Underwater path and swimming

The **Plage du Palud** is the only one on the island from which swimmers are allowed to share the sea with fish. All you need to go diving off this beach are flippers, goggles and a snorkle, although you will find it more rewarding to go scuba-diving so that you can follow the

underwater path between the coast and the Rascas rock. Diving is perfectly safe here. There are also guided tours of the underwater path (from 15 Jun. to 15 Sep., daily, 10am-5pm, free participation, ☎ 04 94 05 90 17). Fish and plantlife are easily accessible to swimmers, while those who prefer to remain above the surface have the option of glass-bottomed boats. (Jun. to Sep., daily, ☎ 04 94 05 92 22.)

Tour of the forts

Port-Cros is covered in forts and defences. A signposted route marked with yellow arrows points them all out. It also links the two forts, the Fort de l'Estissac (magnificent view from the terrace) and the Fort de l'Éminence, which dominate Port-Cros. A botanical footpath (signposted in green) from the port leads to the old castle and the Fort du Moulin.

THE PORT-CROS NATIONAL PARK

Castel Sainte-Claire, Hyères, ☎ 04 94 12 82 30. The Port-Cros National Park, created in 1963, covers the Île de Bagaud and the islets of La Gabinière in the south and those of Rascas in the north. It includes 4320 acres (1800 ha) of sea and is thus the only national park in Europe to include both underwater and terrestrial wildlife. More than 100 species of bird, thousands of fish and countless species of sea and land plants make it a paradise for nature-lovers. Very strict rules protect the wildlife. Camping, lighting fires, smoking outside the village, picking wild flowers, hunting and underwater fishing are forbidden.

The bay of Port-Man

There is a footpath to the Col des Quatre-Chemins, a lookout post from which the Île du Levant can be admired. The sweep of the bay is like a vast green amphitheatre with the village of Port-Cros nestling at its centre. On the right, the Port-Man headland extends right up to the fort. On the way back, skirt round the north shore of the island via the Pointe de la Galère and the Plage du Palud.

The Vale of Solitude

About 2 hours.
The Vallon de la Solitude crosses the island at its widest point. The path winds among the groves of holm-oaks and taller scrub before reaching the Sémaphore and the Napoleonic fort of La Vigie. Further on, the Chemin des Crêtes (peak pathway) overlooks the sea by Mont Vinaigre, the highest point of the island, at an altitude of

Spotcheck
D4

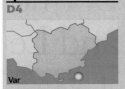

Var

Things to do

Underwater path
Tour of the forts
The Vale of Solitude

Tourist Office

Port-Cros:
☎ 04 94 05 90 17
Levant: ☎ 04 94 05 93 52

656 ft (197 m). The walk ends in the Vallon de la Fausse-Monnaie.

L'île du Levant
Getting a tan

When the monks of Lérins lived on this narrow, rocky island it was the most fertile of the archipelago. A penal colony for delinquent boys was established here in the mid-19th C., but today the island is occupied by the French army, with the

exception of the area which was turned into a naturist centre in 1931. Access is via the little port of L'Ayguade, next to the **Plage des Grottes**. You can laze around, sunbathe and swim or visit the village of Héliopolis, though to do the latter you do have to be a naturist.

Bormes-les-Mimosas and Le Lavandou

These two towns are situated very close together at the foot of the Maures range. Bormes-les-Mimosas' glorious gardens and Le Lavandou's twelve beaches compliment each other well. Bormes-les-Mimosas has always been popular with high society and the President of the French Republic sometimes holidays here.

You can visit the nursery all year round but in February, the mimosa will be in bloom.

Bormes-les-Mimosas

Walking and bathing

This flowery paradise hugs the side of a steep slope. The 12th century village overlooks the sea and its narrow lanes and sunny weather are ideal for walks. Don't miss the view right opposite the chapel of Saint-François, and the **Provençal market** held on Wednesday mornings. At the bottom of the hill, 10½ miles (17 km) of bathing beaches surround the Cap Bénat. The **Fort de Brégançon**, a little way off, is where the President often stays (visits not allowed).

Hiking and rambling

Bormes-les-Mimosas has many hiking and walking paths, including GR 90, GR 51 and a 6 mile (10 km) stretch of coastal footpath. There are also six different walks around the village, lasting 2 to 6 hours, and a signposted tourist route of 1½ hours through the lanes of medieval Bormes. Information at the Office de Tourisme.

Mimosa nursery

Le mas du Ginget, 488, Ch. de Bénat, ☎ 04 94 71 22 68. Open Mon.-Fri., 8am-noon and 1.30-5.30pm ; Jun.-Sep., mornings only. This Australian flower, a symbol of security, has become thoroughly acclimatised here. Gérard Cavatore cultivates 120 species of mimosa which come from all over the world.

Le Lavandou

Twelve beaches

Le Lavandou has always been a favourite with 'the beautiful people'. Its 12 sandy beaches stretch for more than 7½ miles (12 km). Some are wide and flat and others curve into small coves, so there is something for everyone, from the large, central family beach at Le Lavandou to the Plage du Layet, which is reserved for naturists. If you want to check them out, board the **Petit Train des plages** which tours them every summer (daily departures, Jun.-Sep., from the port or Pramousquier, ☎ 04 94 12 55 12).

Sailing on a tall ship

Port du Lavandou, ☎ 04 94 71 69 89 or ☎ 06 09 37 30 62.

Spotcheck
D4

Var

Things to do

Hiking and rambling
Mimosa nursery
The beaches at Le Lavandou
Sailing
Explore beneath the waves
The gardens of Rayol

Within easy reach

Hyères, 16 km SW, p. 208.

Tourist Office

Bormes: ☎ 04 94 71 15 17

Daily departures at 10am in summer (book the previous day). *Paid admission.*
Spend the day on board the *Hoëdic*, a traditional sailing ship. Embarkation is by the harbour master's office in the new port. You'll have a great day at sea, under full sail until you reach Port-Cros where you'll have a trip round the bay, a swim and a scuba-diving lesson, after which you return home at about 6pm.

Beneath the waves

15, Quai Gabriel-Péri and Gare maritime (Seascope),
☎ 04 94 71 01 02.
Daily, 9am-6pm, every 40 min, if the water is clear (book in advance). During the 35 minutes spent on this trimaran you are taken on a magical tour of underwater sea life in the

Mediterranean, encountering gilthead bream, sea-bass, mullet, two-banded bream and rainbow wrasse. The central hull of the vessel cuts through the waves and its transparent bottom enables you to watch the sea creatures to your heart's content.

Around Le Lavandou

Domaine de l'Angueiroun

1077, Chemin de l'Angueiroun, 2 miles (5 km) W of Le Lavandou via the D559,
☎ 04 94 71 11 39.
Open daily except Sun. and public holidays, 8am-noon and 2-6pm. From Apr. to Oct., until 7pm. This traditional farmhouse is in the centre of the Côtes-de-Provence wine-growing country. It faces the sea in a beautiful setting of pines, cork-oaks, olive trees and heather. Visit the cellars and taste the house specialities – the white which has won several prizes, and the rosé – and drink a toast to the tortoises which still roam freely in the adjoining hills. The wines cost around 35 F a bottle.

Rayol-Canadel

Glorious gardens

Av. des Belges, 7½ miles (12 km) E of Le Lavandou,
☎ 04 94 05 32 50.
Open daily, 9.30am-noon and 4.30-8pm; out of season, 9.30am-noon and 2.30-6.30pm.
Paid admission.
This estate is evidence of the high life lived on the Corniche des Maures at the turn of the 19th and 20th C. – the Belle Époque. Each of these gardens reflects a region of the world which has a Mediterranean climate (Australia, South Africa, Chile, California, and so on). In summer, you can also dive in the bay. (Advance booking, diving equipment provided).

Saint-Tropez
a Provençal legend

Its reputation today is as dazzling as ever. This former fishing village lies in the beautiful sweep of a bay, bathed in brilliant light. The artists who loved it at the start of the 20th C. have been supplanted by show-biz and movie stars and the harbour front is thronged with people in the summer.

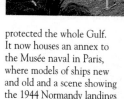

Pétanque and antiques in the Place des Lices

The port, which is packed in summer, is the pride of the town. Luxury yachts and their passengers are on view and their slightest movements scrutinised. The Old Town has quaint medieval streets: the Ruelle de la Miséricorde, Rue du Clocher and especially the **Place aux Herbes**, where a fish market is held in the morning. The Place des Lices is always busy in the evening when people play pétanque, as is the antiques market on Tuesday and Saturday morning. As you pass the Rue Clemenceau, try the **tarte tropézienne** at No. 38.

Model ships at the Citadel

☎ 04 94 97 06 53.
Open daily except Tue. 10am-6pm; out of season, until 5pm. Closed in Nov.
Paid admission.
The 16th C. castle keep in the east of the town once protected the whole Gulf. It now houses an annex to the Musée naval in Paris, where models of ships new and old and a scene showing the 1944 Normandy landings can be seen. The view from the castle keep is superb.

Impressionists at the Annonciade

Pl. Grammont.
☎ 04 94 97 04 01.
Open daily except Tue., Jun.-Sep., 10am-noon and 3-7pm; Oct.-May 10am-noon and 2-6pm. Closed in Nov.

THE COAST ROAD AND THE BEACHES

Leave from the Tour du Portalet, at the end of the Quai Mistral. The 12 mile (20 km) route is marked in yellow and lasts a total of 6 hours. Walk out to the Cap Camarat and its lighthouse, following the contours of the Saint-Tropez peninsula. Make sure you have sturdy shoes because espadrilles are unsuitable for some of the rocky patches. The Maures range and the outline of the Esterel are visible in the distance. The fine sand at your feet and the surrounding coastline has featured in many a French film.

Paid admission.

The magnificent canvases in this museum were painted at the beginning of the century by the first artistic visitors to Saint-Tropez – Braque, Bonnard, Dufy, Matisse, Rouault and Utrillo. Don't miss this exceptional museum, situated in the port, which bears witness to the importance of Saint-Tropez in post-impressionist painting.

Sénéquier
Quai Jean-Jaurès,
☎ 04 94 97 00 90.
Closed 11 Nov.-15 Dec.
Pâtisserie open daily,
8am-12.30pm and
2.30-7pm.
Order an iced coffee (46 F) or a nougat (excellent) in this hangout for the smart set of 'Saint-Trop'. A lovely place to come and sit and watch the world go by.

Le Byblos hotel
Av. Paul-Signac,
☎ 04 94 56 68 00.
Closed from mid-Oct. to mid-Apr.
One of the best hotels on the Côte d'Azur, a favourite with the stars (rooms cost between 1,100 F and 3,800 F a night).

Butterfly House
La Maison des Papillons
9, Rue Étienne-Berny,
☎ 04 94 97 63 45.
Open daily, except Tue.,
10am-noon and 3-7pm.
This old family home, typical of Saint-Tropez, contains a fabulous collection of all the species of butterflies in Europe. It was created by the painter Dany Lartigue and contains more than 20,000 specimens, including numerous rare species which are now protected.

Saint-Tropez sandals
Rondini, 16, Rue Georges-Clemenceau,
☎ 04 94 97 19 55.
Open daily, (except Sun.

and Mon.) 9.30am-noon and 2.30-8pm,
7pm out of season.
Closed in Nov.
These existed long before the place became fashionable.
The Rondini family has been making these leather sandals which are

Spotcheck
E4

Var

Things to do
Pétanque and antiques
Vineyards at Ramatuelle

With children
Butterfly house (La Maison des Papillons)

Within easy reach
Fréjus, 30km NE, p. 224.

Tourist Office
Saint-Tropez :
☎ 04 94 97 45 21

specially designed for Saint-Tropez summers since 1927.

Ramatuelle
Vineyards
About 6¼ miles (10 km) via the D93.
The Saint-Tropez peninsula has retained all the charm of the Provençal countryside set beside the sea. Stroll among the vineyards of Ramatuelle, and climb the steep flights of steps which Gérard Philipe loved so dearly.

Gassin
A charming village
NE via the D93.
This village teeters on a steep hill. Its sloping streets, old houses bedecked with flowers, and magnificent views are yours for the taking, and don't forget to try the delicious jam made by M. Schwieck (Route du Bourrian, ☎ 04 94 43 41 58. Open daily, 9am-8pm).

Sainte-Maxime
and coast of the Gulf of Saint-Tropez

Sainte-Maxime is less glittery than Saint-Tropez, which lies on the opposite side of the Gulf. It is more of a family resort, yet still remains very fashionable. There is a marina, fishing port, sandy beach, old town and Provençal market.

Musée du Phonographe

Col de Bougnon

Route de Muy

Aquascope

Sainte-Maxime

Le Musée des Traditions Locales

Tour Carrée,
☎ 04 94 96 70 30.
Open daily except Tue., Nov.-Apr., 9.30am-noon and 2.30-6pm (until 7pm in summer).
Paid admission.
The Tour Carrée was built in 1520 to protect the region from constant invasions by pirates. It is now a folk museum displaying local occupations and costumes.

Craft Market

This Provençal market is a living tradition. It is held in the pedestrian precinct, all day every day, from 15 June to 15 Sept. and attracts the best craftsmen in the district.

The Aquascope

Port de Sainte-Maxime,
☎ 04 94 49 01 45.
Daily departures every 35 min., Mar.-Sep., 10am-noon and 2-7pm.
Paid admission.

If you look out to sea and notice a strange yellow object bobbing up and down on the waves, don't be alarmed. It actually contains about 20 people who are underwater looking at the sea bed. A trip inside this strange machine will leave you feeling like Jacques Cousteau. Not advisable in bad weather.

Nearby

Le Musée du Phonographe et de la Musique Mécanique

Route de Muy, 6¼ miles (10 km) N of Sainte-Maxime, D25
☎ 04 94 96 50 52.
Open Easter-late Sept., 10am-noon and 3-6pm.
Paid admission.
In the middle of the Saint-Donat Forest Park, on the hilltops of the Maures, there is a unique museum containing 350 musical instruments and numerous types of reproduction equipment, from the earliest inventions to the latest techniques. You can also see the ancestor of the accordian, which was the melophone, invented in France just before the Revolution.

Olive wood and olive oil

Rte de Muy.
(☎ 04 94 96 53 18. Open Mon., Wed. and all day on Thu.; 3-8pm Tue. and Thu.)
The craftsman, Marcel Bietti, makes wonderful objects out of olive wood in his workshop, which he'll show to people who visit him.
A salad bowl costs between 250 and 1500 F. Nearby in the covered market, the aptly named Olivier (La Pierre-Plantée ☎ 04 94 96 23 36)

sells extra-virgin, cold-pressed olive oil made in the traditional way. It costs 65 F for a 12 fl oz (75 cl) bottle.

Themed walks

Departure from the Col de Bougnon 6¼ miles (12 km) from Saint-Aygulf via D 8, or from La Gaillarde cemetery (between Les Issambres and Saint-Aygulf via N 98).

The vale of la Gaillarde, at the eastern end of the Maures range has a wonderful view of the gulfs of Saint-Tropez and Fréjus. Use the signposted routes above Saint-Aygulf and Les Issambres. There is a **farming route** (3 hours) marked in green, a **prehistoric treasures** route (3½ hours) marked in red, a **tree discovery** route (3 hours) in orange and a **streams route** in blue (1½ hours, the easiest). (Information ☎ 04 94 68 97 66).

Les Issambres

Santons

Imp. des Driades,
☎ 04 94 96 94 62.
Open daily, except Sun., 9am-noon and 3pm-6pm.
The *santons* on sale in this particular workshop are splendidly dressed in clothes worthy of an haute couture house.

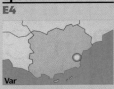

TUNA FISHING

Port de Sainte-Maxime, The *Geronimo*
☎ 04 94 43 82 05 or 04 94 49 25 45.
Jun.-Oct.
A skipper will take you out into the open sea to fish for blue-fin or yellow-fin tuna which live in the Mediterranean depths. You can go as a group (maximum of 5) in a large fishing boat that will take you straight to the deep-water fishing grounds. You can also take guided trips or excursions to the Îles d'Or (p. 100 and p. 212). Reservations required.

Grimaud, Cogolin and Port-Grimaud

At the seaward end of the Maures range, the D14 descends to the Gulf of Saint-Tropez. The little village of Grimaud is old and typically Provençal, in stark contrast to Port Grimaud, a resort, but one which was astonishingly created out of a swamp in the early 1960s. The village of Cogolin lies close by and, despite its main claim to fame for pipe manufacturing, is quite lively.

Cogolin
Pipe-making

The village is largely known as a centre for the manufacture of pipes and carpets, making it a hive of activity at all times, even out of the tourist season. The upper village is rather attractive with its old houses framed by serpentine stone carvings, and the pretty 11th C. church of Saint-Sauveur whose Renaissance portal comes from the charterhouse of the Verne. The pleasant lanes are perfect for a stroll.

Grimaud
At the foot of the château

Grimaud is topped by the ruins of its **château féodal**. It is a village filled with flowers and sudden glimpses of the sea. Facing the Renaissance house of the Knights Templar, a pretty 11th C. **Romanesque church** contains a magnificent 12th C. marble font.

❧ Cogolin pipes

Maison Courrieu, 58, Av. Georges-Clemenceau,
☎ **04 94 54 63 82.**
Open daily, 9am-noon and 2-7pm.
Pipe-smokers will be interested to see the manufacture of various kinds of pipes. At Cogolin, the pipes are made from the roots of briar collected from the Maures forest. This tradition carried on by the Maison Courrieu is more than 200 years old and the firm is famous throughout the world.

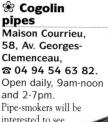

Carpet-weaving
**Ets Louis-Blanc,
Bd Louis-Blanc,
☎ 04 94 55 70 65.**
Open Mon.-Fri., 9am-
noon and 2-7pm. Closed
public holidays.
Louis-Blanc carpets are all
hand-woven, whether they are
made of wool, cotton, jute or
rafia. Examples can be seen in
the factory showroom. Cogolin
carpets have a style of their
own, their geometric patterns
being designed for contemporary interiors. You can take a
carpet away with you or order
designs in the size and colours
of your choice; 8,400 F for a
carpet measuring 4ft 8in by 6ft
8 in (1.4 m by 2m).

❀ The Musée Raimu
**18, Av. Georges-
Clemenceau,**

☎ 04 94 54 18 00.
Open daily except Sun.
morning, 10am-noon and
4-7pm; out of season,
10am-noon and 3-6pm.
Paid admission.
Raimu was an actor whose
interpretations of characters
in the Marcel Pagnol films,
such as *Fanny, César, The
Baker's Wife* and others, was
perfect. He was the greatest
French character actor of his
generation and yet it was his
own family who created this
museum devoted to him. It is
housed in a former cinema
and through posters, pho-
tographs, letters and personal
items, tells the story of Jules
Muraire, aka Raimu, born in
Toulon (1883-1946).

Port-Grimaud
Little Venice
Each region of France has a
'Little Venice'; on the Côte
d'Azur, it's Port-Grimaud. This
village built on the sea is best
visited by passenger-barge.
(☎ 04 94 56 21 13. Daily
departures, Place du Marché.
8am-10.30pm, every 15 min.
in summer. Closed 11 Nov.
to mid-Dec.). Cruise the
4 miles (7 km) of navigable
waterways, passing under
Venetian bridges, around
islets and along fortified
gateways – and you will realise
that Port Grimaud is really
just a (superior) housing
development scheme.

From pedalos to paragliding
**École de Voile
Les Alizés,
Ch. de la Plage
de Port-Grimaud,
☎ 04 94 56 46 51.**
Open daily, May-Sep.,
9am-7pm.
Windsurfing, dinghy sailing,
pedalos, water-skiing and
paragliding are all available
here. Whether you are a beginner or more advanced, you can
take lessons or follow a course
with qualified instructors. For
those who prefer the joys of
fresh water, the Niagra Water
Park (**Parc Nautique du
Niagara**) (Route du col du
Canadel, ☎ 04 94 49 58 87,
open 15 Jun.-15 Sep., 10.30am-
7pm) has a Californian
swimming pool with six giant
chutes, games and a Jacuzzi.
It is a paradise for children.

Spotcheck
D4

Var

Things to do
**Port-Grimaud by barge
Water-sports**

With children
Niagara Water Park

Within easy reach
Fréjus, 20 km NE, p. 224.

Tourist Office
Grimaud:
☎ 04 94 43 26 98

THE BIRTH OF PORT GRIMAUD
**In 1962 François Spoerry, an architect from
Alsace, discovered a swamp in the area which
was too shallow to navigate. This gave him the
idea of constructing Port-Grimaud. In 1966, iron
piles were embedded in the earth, bridges built
and canals dug and the sea rushed in to surround the settlement which had been constructed. Quite a feet of engineering, some 24,000 t.
of granite was required to create the embankments on which more than 2000 privately owned
houses now stand.**

The Maures range
pines, cork-oaks and chestnut trees

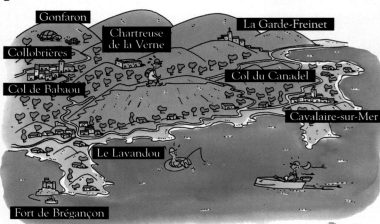

Gonfaron

Chartreuse
de la Verne

La Garde-Freinet

Collobrières

Col du Canadel

Col de Babaou

Cavalaire-sur-Mer

Le Lavandou

Fort de Brégançon

B etween the sea and the valleys of the Gapeau and the
Argens Rivers lies a range of hills called the Maures, which
extends from Hyères to Saint-Raphaël. The rounded hills
are covered with 'dark woods' (*mauro* in Provençal) which
gave them their name. The forests of pines, cork-oaks and
chestnut trees have been seriously reduced by forest fires, but
most have managed to survive.

Collobrières

Maures chestnuts

This village at the edge of the
forest owes its name to the
Réal-Collobrier, the stream
that runs through it. The
riverbank is lined with
impressive houses and there is
a square, shaded with plane

trees, in which the villagers
play pétanque. This delightful
spot is famous for its *marrons
glacés* and its chestnut jam.
The Confiserie azuréenne
(☎ 04 94 48 08 00) stocks
local produce.

The charterhouse
of the Verne
☎ 04 94 43 45 41.
Open daily, 10am-6pm,
except Tue. and religious
festivals.

In the
commune of
Collobrières,
4 miles (6 km)
away at the end of a small
track, the ruined charterhouse
stands on the edge of a
precipice, surrounded by
forests, with the sea in the
distance. The monks settled
here in 1170, at the initiative
of the bishops of Fréjus and
Toulon. Today the building is
still a holy site housing

The charterhouse of the Verne

a monastic community of the Order of Bethlehem. Little remains of the Romanesque period, but the charterhouse is remarkable for its carvings in dark green serpentine stone highlighting the brown shale of the buildings.

Beaches and the crest road

The coastal chain of the Pradels descends straight to the lovely **beaches of Cavalière, Pramousquier** and **Canadel-sur-Mer**. At Bormes-les-Mimosas (p. 214), a road runs right through the hills, overlooking the vineyards.

FROM HILLTOP TO HILLTOP

South of Collobrières (via D14 then D41), before the road descends to the valley of Réal-Collobrier, the Babaou pass rises to 1,400 ft (415 m), dominating the Islands of Hyères, Giens peninsula and the salt marshes. Beyond this pass are the highest summits of the Maures, including the Col de Canadel, 890 ft (267 m), midway along the crest road. From here, the magnificent view stretches 3 miles (5 km) as far as the stone of Avenon.

Gonfaron
Tortoise village
Village de Tortues,
☎ 04 94 78 26 41.
Open daily, 9am-7pm in season. Closed Dec.-Mar.
Hermann's tortoise is the oldest species of French

vertebrate, and freely admits to being 35 million years old. Once common throughout the Midi, it is now confined to the *département* of Var and is threatened by pollution. Out of 1,000 eggs laid, only one tortoise will survive. At Gonfaron, however, they have an astonishing 2500 tortoises, left to their own devices. Don't miss seeing them having their breakfast (daily at 10am, Apr.-mid-Oct.). Every year, between 300 and 500 tortoises are released into the Maures hills.

Cork Museum
L'Écomusée de Liège,
5, Rue de la République,
☎ 04 91 68 14 38.
Open daily except Mon., Oct.-Mar., 10am-noon and 2-6pm. *Paid admission.*

Spotcheck
D4

Var

Things to do
From hilltop to hilltop
Beaches and the crest road
Cork Museum

With children
Tortoise village

Within easy reach
Hyères, 30 km SW, p. 208.

Tourist Office
Collobrières:
☎ 04 94 48 08 00

This museum is devoted to the cork industry. It gives a fascinating insight into a traditional craft that employed nearly 900 workers in the early 20th C. (guided tour with film, see also p. 53).

La Garde-Freinet
Rezvani and *Le Feu*
Pâtisserie Grimaud, Rue du Château,
☎ 04 94 43 60 83.
Approx. 50 F for 2¼ lb (1 kg) of biscuits.
The village of La Garde-Freinet is built on the ruins of a medieval fortress and is a compulsory stop in an excursion to the Maures.

The French writer Rezvani lives close to the centre and his experience of witnessing a huge fire that ravaged the region led him to write the novel, *Le Feu.* ('Fire'). This is the place to stock up on biscuits flavoured with orange flower water called *'patience'*.

Saint-Raphaël and Fréjus
twins of the Côte d'Azur

These two towns merge together and have the drawback of any popular seaside resort – shores covered with hawkers, big city traffic jams, candy floss sellers… But there are also Roman remains, walks under shady palms and the magnificent Esterel hills.

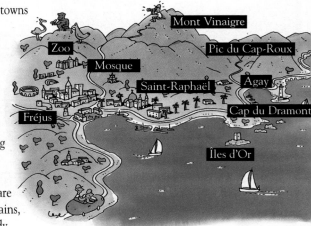

Mont Vinaigre · Zoo · Pic du Cap-Roux · Mosque · Saint-Raphaël · Agay · Fréjus · Cap du Dramont · Îles d'Or

Fréjus and Saint-Raphaël still have a lot to recommend them.

Paths through the scrub

Successive forest fires have denuded the hills which have gradually become covered with scrubland. In places, the original forest has all but disappeared. For this reason, the Esterel is carefully protected. A 28 mile (45 km) ring encircles an area that is barred to cars, but has well signposted footpaths.

Fréjus

Discovering the old town

This archbishopric was founded on the remains of a Roman forum. The **Porte des Gaules**, the aqueduct and the **amphitheatre** are all Roman. Old Fréjus contains a remarkable group of religious buildings, including the **cathedral** and the early Christian **baptistry** which is one of the oldest in France (all open daily 9am-7pm; Oct.-Mar., daily except Mon., 9am-noon and 2-5pm. Paid admission to the episcopal buildings). The cathedral cloister contains an **Archaeological Museum** (☎ 04 94 51 26 30) which has an interesting collection of Gallo-Roman antiquities, including the so-called 'leopard mosaic' and a beautiful white marble head of Jupiter.

The purple hills of Esterel

These hills have been ravaged by forest fires. Starting from Fréjus, follow the N7 to the north-east. After walking for half an hour, you reach the highest point, Mont Vinaigre, by leaving the highroad at the Maison Forestière du Malpey. This beauty spot is 2060 ft (618 m) above sea level and offers an amazing **view** of the Alps as far as the Montagne Sainte-Victoire. The Tourist Office organises trips to the Esterel on three Tuesdays a month.

✸ Aquatica
RN98,
☎ 04 94 51 82 51.
Open daily, Jun.-Sep.,
10am-6pm. *110 F;
children: 90 F; free for
those less than 3 ft 4in
(1 m) tall.*
20 acres (8 ha) devoted to every kind of watersport, including the 'pentaglisse', the 'kamikaze' – huge chutes

and flumes – and the biggest wave pool in Europe. This adventure lagoon is like a tropical paradise.

Le Capitou
Fréjus open zoo
4 miles (6 km) NW by N7 and D4,
☎ 04 94 40 70 65.
Open daily, 10am-5.30pm; May-Sep., 9.30am-6pm.
Paid admission.

The 50 acres (20 ha) of the Fréjus open zoo should be visited by car. Tigers, bisons, buffalos, hippopotamuses, flamingoes and ostriches all roam around freely. Children will adore the gibbon colony (performances every day at 3pm during school holidays).

The Missiri mosque
Rue des Combattants-d'Afrique-du-Nord, 2½ miles (4 km) NW via N7 and D4.
This is a small scale replica of the Djenné mosque in Mali. Its red ochre silhouette is surrounded by pine trees. The marabou storks and artificial termite hills in front of the mosque were designed to make

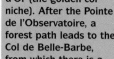

WALKING WITH A VIEW OF THE SEA
You can also walk the Estérel via the Corniche d'Or (the golden corniche). After the Pointe de l'Observatoire, a forest path leads to the Col de Belle-Barbe, from which there is a magnificent descent into the Mal-Infernet ravine. Seasoned hikers can continue on to the Col Notre-Dame and then to the Pic de l'Ours, 1,650 ft (496 m). The Cap Roux (p. 226), is the final viewpoint.

the Senegalese regiment of sharpshooters in the French army, for whom the mosque was built, feel as if they were back in Africa.

Saint-Raphaël
Pleasant walks
The town was a winter resort for the well-heeled in the 19th C. The harbour, shaded by enormous plane trees, and the pleasant

Spotcheck
E3-E4

Var

Things to do
Purple hills of Esterel
Esterel golf course

With children
Aquatica (water park)
Fréjus open zoo

Within easy reach
*Sainte-Maxime,
19 km SW, p. 218.
Cannes, 30 km NE, p. 240.*

Tourist Office
Saint-Raphaël:
☎ 04 94 19 52 52
Fréjus:
☎ 04 94 51 83 83

Plage du Veillat date from that time. St. Raphaël is dominated by the huge purple rocks of the *Lion de mer* (sea lion) and the *Lion de terre* (land lion). There are some pleasant walks to the **casino**, the strange Byzantine-style **church** and elegant districts such as Notre-Dame or Valescure. The Office de Tourisme offers guided tours on Wednesdays, 10am-noon.

Esterel golf course
Av. du Golf, at the Saint-Raphaël exit via A8, ☎ 04 94 82 47 88.
Open daily 8am-6.30pm.
Two miles (3 km) from the beaches of Saint-Raphaël, this superb 18-hole golf course covers 100 acres (40 ha) and is set among pine forests by the sea. Facilities include a putting green, tennis court and swimming pool.

The Esterel coast
wild coastline and red rocks

The Corniche d'Or runs through a wild and rocky landscape of red shale. The Esterel coast, between Saint-Raphaël and Cannes, has superb views, lovely walks and sheltered beaches.

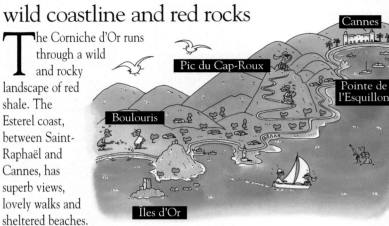

Cannes

Pic du Cap-Roux

Pointe de l'Esquillon

Boulouris

Îles d'Or

Coves, inlets and islets are dotted along the shore-line, interspersed with patches of trees and shrub which cling tenaciously to the rocky slopes.

Boulouris

Bowling competitions

Eastern exit from Saint-Raphaël.
The name Boulouris comes from *boules* (bowls). The competitions held on the bowling ground (Bd de la Paix) are open to all comers (☎ 04 94 95 23 70). For bathing, there are nine beaches nestling in inlets, which are linked by a coastal path along the clifftop. Take the path from the ports of Saint-Raphaël or Agay. The walk lasts 2½ hours from start to finish.

Le Dramont

A hike through the forest

3 miles (5 km) E of Saint-Raphaël via N98.
This was the beach on which American soldiers landed on 15 August 1944. To the right of the road, a monument commemorates the event. Park a little further, in the Camp-Long car park, and climb the path signposted in blue (a two-hour round trip) to the lookout point via the Dramont forest park. At your feet lie the *calanques* and out in the bay, the Île d'Or.

Agay

✿ Sea trips

Guy de Maupassant described the coast as 'one of the most beautiful shorelines of the Côte d'Azur'. The red rocks of Rastel which overlook the bays are a good starting point for trips out to sea. Start from the Agay harbour and sail to Saint-Tropez or the Îles de Lérins (in summer), to the *calanques* and golden corniche (Apr.-Sep.). Or look down into the depths to discover the underwater world in specially designed boats (**Les Bateaux bleus**, ☎ 04 94 95 17 46; **Aquavision**, ☎ 04 94 82 75 40; departures every hour, 10am-6pm).

Cap-Roux

Climbing the peak

7 miles (11 km) NE of Saint-Raphaël by N98.
Take the N98, and at the Pointe de l'Observatoire, park the car and climb on foot to the **Pic du Cap-Roux**, 1,500 ft (452 m) above sea

level. A forest road will take you – in two hours at most – to the most magnificent view of the Corniche d'Or. On the way, the Saint-Barthélemy rock (steps cut into the stone) and the Grotto of the Sainte-Baume offer a foretaste of the summit.

La pointe de l'Esquillon
Superb views
Exit N from Miramar, 6 miles (10 km) S of Cannes.
The road offers views of the Îles de Lérins, where the Man in the Iron Mask was imprisoned, and the bay of Cannes. Don't miss the view around the headland. Drive north out of Miramar, then walk up the path which leaves the main N98 at the bend by the Hôtel La Tour de l'Esquillon.

Théoule-sur-Mer
Stained glass window workshop
Pointe de l'Esquillon,
☎ 04 93 75 40 26.
Free admission.

DIVING FOR BEGINNERS

Off the Cap de l'Estérel, the depths shelve from 0 to 160 ft (from 0 to 48 m), attracting the most experienced divers, so, take advantage of this fantastic site and learn how to scuba-dive. The underwater landscape is extremely diverse (rocks, flora and fauna). Michel Ayot (Port Miramar à Théoule-sur-Mer, ☎ 04 93 75 48 51) will be happy to arrange a dive for you, children included. All year round, reservations required (250 F for a beginner's dive).

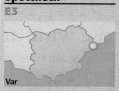

Spotcheck
E3

Var

Things to do
Bowling competition
Hike through the forest
Sea trips
Diving for beginners
Visiting a stained glass workshop

Within easy reach
Cannes, 25 km NE, p. 240.

Tourist Office
Boulouris: ☎ 04 94 19 52 52

Craftsmen work on their intricate glass creations while you watch, in this small stained glass window workshop. Watch how they measure and cut the coloured glass, enamel it, steam it and ask them how they produced the example displayed at the entrance. The glass has to be fired for 2 hours and you have to wait 18 hours before it can be worked. It is a fascinating craft well-suited to this colourful region. From 500 F for 10 sq. in (25 sq. cm).

Draguignan
rosé wine and olive oil

Draguignan was made the capital of the *département* of Var in 1797, but lost its prefecture to Toulon in 1974. However, in exchange, it was chosen as the site of a military academy. It is now the largest garrison town in France. Draguignan has long straight boulevards designed by Baron Haussmann, who redesigned much of Paris during the 19th C., and some interesting museums, but also has the reputation of being a rather serious, solid town.

Draguignan
Municipal Museum
9, Rue de la République,
☎ 04 94 47 28 80.
Open daily except Sun. and public holidays, 9am-noon and 2-6pm.
Free admission.
This museum, housed in a 17th C. former Ursuline convent, contains works by the leading old masters – Rembrandt, Rubens, Mignard, Renoir, Camille Claudel. Six rooms are furnished with a handsome collection of pottery, porcelain, Etruscan vases, Gallo-Roman

artefacts and ancient weapons. The library stocks valuable books including a 15th C. copy of the Roman de la rose.

❀ Le Musée des Arts et Traditions Populaires
15, Rue Roumanille,
☎ 04 94 47 05 72.
Open daily except Sun. morning and Mon., 9am-noon and 2-6pm.
Paid admission.
This folk museum reflects the traditions of Middle Provence, at home and at work. There are displays featuring farm and farmhouse where you can see various country crafts, e.g. grapevine growing, olive oil production and

ROSÉ WINES
Château de Selle, Taradeau, D73, 9 miles (15 km) S of Draguignan, ☎ 04 94 47 57 57.
Open daily except Sun., 9am-noon and 2-5.30pm; Sat., 10am-noon and 2-6pm. Visits by appointment. In this handsome 18th C. country house, wine-makers from the Upper Var still make wines in the great tradition. The cellars contain the massive oak tuns in which Provence wines mature. The Château Sainte-Roseline (Les Arcs, ☎ 04 94 99 50 30, tasting room, daily, 9am-noon and 2-6pm) which is nearby also welcomes visitors to its cellars in a beautiful French garden. The Château has a chapel (open daily, except Mon., 2pm-6pm) decorated with mosaics by Chagall and bronzes by Giacometti.

bee-keeping. Be sure to see the cork-maker's workshop before ending your visit in the kitchen, the epicentre of Provençal family life, in town and country.

It is protected by high cliffs which are dotted with prehistoric caves. Follow the straight road (D955) which turns into a *corniche*, and ends at the medieval village of

Nearby
Le musée du Canon et des Artilleurs
**École d'application de l'artillerie, 2¹/₂ miles (4 km) SE of Draguignan via D59, ☎ 04 94 60 23 85 or ☎04 94 60 23 86.
Open daily except w.-e., 8.30-11am and 2-5pm (until 4pm on Fri.).
Closed between 15 Dec.-15 Jan.**
Free admission.
Inside the military academy, there is a museum detailing the history of artillery, from the invention of gunpowder to the end of World War II. It highlights the invention of the cannon and its key role in all major conflicts, particularly the Napoleonic wars. Hundreds of weapons are on display, and in the mezzanine, there is a full replica of an army camp.

Nartuby Gorges
The Nartuby river, north of Draguignan, has gouged a deep bed through the rock.

Châteaudouble, a dizzying 430 ft (130 m) above the torrent through this splendid landscape.

Flayosquet oil mill
Rte d'Ampus, 5 miles (8 km) W of Draguignan, ☎ 04 94 70 41 45.

Open daily, 9.30am-noon and 2-7.30pm.
Paid admission.
This 13th C. mill is still operational and boasts a huge paddle-wheel. The Doleatto family have been making olive oil for several generations. Follow the traditional stages of cold oil-pressing. When you reach the local produce shop you'll see that even the residue of the

pressing is used in the manufacture of Marseilles soap.

The Fairy Stone
0.6 miles (1 km) NW of Draguignan by D955.
The Celtic and Ligurian civilisations which flourished here before the Romans arrived left spectacular evidence of their passing in the form of a huge dolmen. Dressed stones more than 7 ft (2 m) high support a colossal tabletop 20 ft (6 m) wide, 16 ft (4,70 m) long and 20 in. (50 cm) thick. It is known as the Pierre de la Fée (the Fairy Stone) and is the subject of many legends.

Deep in the Haut Var

Aups, Salernes, Tourtour et Lorgues

A stop to sample the food and drink in this part of the country is an absolute must. The vineyards produce delightful wines whose bouquet mingles with the herbs of the scrubland. Salernes is famous for olive oil and Aups black truffles, so any excuse will do for enjoying the culinary delights these pretty villages have to offer.

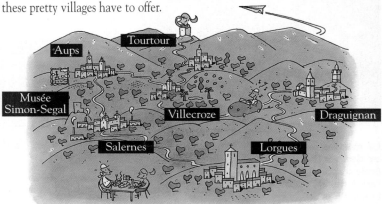

Paid admission.
This delightful little modern art museum is housed in a former Ursuline convent. The paintings are mainly early 20th C. and mostly by artists from the Paris school.

Aups
Truffle market

The winding medieval lanes are surrounded by the ruined ramparts. The Tour de l'Horloge, which has a bell-tower with a sundial, the wash-house and fountains resemble a scene from an old picture postcard. Between November and March, the village becomes a hive of activity every Thursday morning at the truffle market, which always attracts a host of sellers and eager buyers. Other local produce is also sold in the market.

The Simon-Segal Museum
Rue Albert-Ier,
☎ 04 94 70 01 95.
Open daily, 15 Jun.-15 Sep., 10am-noon and 4-7pm.

The caves of Villecroze

Villecroze means 'hollow town' and the village does indeed nestle in a hollow at the foot of a cliff which is honeycombed with caves. Wander through its pretty streets and laze about in the lush vegetation of its public park. A local landowner built a cave-dwelling residence here and added several fountains. The caves and the house are open to the public. (Daily in summer, 10am-noon and 2.30-7pm out of season,
☎ 04 94 70 63 06.
Paid admission.)

Spotcheck
D3

Var

Things to do

Truffle market
Caves of Villecroze
Floor-tile factory
Pony-trekking

Within easy reach

Verdon Gorges, 30 km N, p. 234.

Tourist Office

Salernes: ☎ 04 94 70 69 02

salernes
Pretty houses

Salernes is a large village by the River Bresque. It has a very unusual Romanesque church with a tower at each corner and many 17th C. houses line its streets. Salernes is best known for the coloured floor-tiles, known as **tomettes provençales**, which have been manufactured here since the early 18th C. Nowadays, the factories tend to produce these square tiles in contemporary patterns.

EDIBLE SOUVENIRS

If you were unable to benefit from the truffle season in Aups, you can at least buy the local olive oil (which is delicious and never out of season) at the old village oil-press (Montée des Moulins, ☎ 04 94 70 04 66. About 77 F a 1¾ pt (1 l) bottle. The Tourtour farm (☎ 04 94 70 56 18), on the way to Villecroze, sells its savoury preserves and potted meats, including wild boar, rabbit or venison terrines, 26 to 28 F for 6½ oz (180 g); tapenades and anchoïades, 22 F for a 4 oz (125 g) pot.

Floor-tile factory

Despite what has been said, there are still a few factories making **tomettes** in the traditional way. The **carrelages Boutal** (Rte de Draguignan, ☎ 04 94 70 62 12).

Showroom open daily except Sun., 8am-noon and 2-6pm), the **Terres cuites de Launes** (Quartier des Launes, ☎ 04 94 70 62 72), the **Atelier Pierre Basset** (Rte de Draguignan, Quartier des Arnauds, ☎ 04 94 70 76 72) and the **Atelier Alain Vagh** (Rte d'Entrecasteaux, ☎ 04 94 70 61 85) are the most notable ones.

Tourtour
Medieval village

Tourtour stands on a rocky outcrop in wooded countryside, and still retains a medieval air, with its

COULIS DE TOMATES AU BASILIC

fortifications, old houses and vaulted passageways. About ½ mile (1 km) away, the 12th C. **Tour Grimaldi** offers a magnificent view of the Montagne Sainte-Victoire, the Maures hills and the Luberon.

Lorgues
Among the olive groves

Lorgues is surrounded by olive groves and vineyards and extends down the side of a hill. Its main street is planted with handsome plane trees. The village is worth a stop because of its pretty fountains, elegant houses with fine wrought-iron balconies and above all, the imposing Collegiate Church of Saint-Martin.

Pony-trekking

Appaloosa Ranch, at the entrance to Lorgues ☎ 04 94 45 58 55. Open daily, all year round. The ranch organises half-day and full-day pony treks into the hinterland, during which you will be able to swim in streams and visit a potter in Salernes. You can also have riding lessons.

The Vallée d'Argens
springs and caves

The valley is also called Green Provence due to its many springs, streams and caves. Many abbeys and monasteries were built here and the counts of Provence also set up home in this lush region.

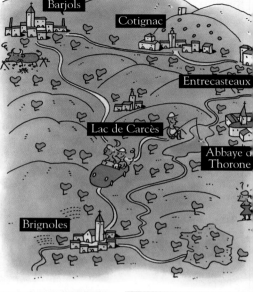

Barjols

Cotignac

Entrecasteaux

Lac de Carcès

Abbaye de Thorone

Brignoles

Barjols
The Tripe Festival

Barjols, which is built around a handsome collegiate church, has 25 fountains and 16 wash-houses. It was very prosperous in the 19th C. thanks to its leather tanneries. Every second weekend in January, the village celebrates St. Marcel, who arrived miraculously in the Middle Ages in the midst of a famine, with an ox. Every four years an ox is roasted in celebration, while the inhabitants dance the *Danse des Tripettes* to the sound of tambourines and pipes.

Fishing and potholing

The **Vallon du Sourn** near Barjols has 3 miles (5 km) of gorges surrounded by rocks and caves suitable for potholing. (Information from the Association Spéléologique

Valoise, ☎ 04 94 86 31 12). A few miles to the east (via D45 then D562), the Lac de Carcès is a favourite with fiishermen. Bathing is fobidden but you will fiind crayfiish, tro and huge freshwater mussels.

Brignoles
✿ Medieval city

Brignoles was in the territory of the counts of Provence in the Middle Ages and extends along the banks of the Caramy River. The palace is now the home of the **Musée du Pays Brignolais** folk museum (☎ 04 94 69 45 18. Open daily, except Mon. and Tues., 10am-noon and 2.30-5pm; in summer 9am-noon and 2.30-6pm. Paid admission.) It also contains the famous 2nd C. **La Gaylole Sarcophagus**, paintings, regional crafts and artefacts.

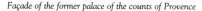

Façade of the former palace of the counts of Provence

Mini-France

Mini-France, 4 miles
(6 km) E of Brignoles by
N7,
☎ 04 94 69 26 00.
Open daily, 9.30am-
nightfall; out of season,
10am-6pm.
Paid admission.
Visit France in miniature in a
5 acre (2 ha) park. Lakes,
rivers, mountains, seas, all are
there as well as the Eiffel
Tower, the Château de
Chambord, the Mont Saint-

Michel, and Carcassonne.
The reduced-scale models of
famous buildings are very
popular with children.

Le Thoronet Cistercian abbey

12½ miles (20 km) NE
of Brignoles by D79,
☎ 04 94 60 43 90.
Open daily from 1 Apr.
to 30 Sep., 9am-7pm.
Closed between noon
and 2pm on Sun. and
public holidays; out of
season, 10am-1pm and
2-5pm. Guided tours.
**The Cistercian monks
who built the abbey
between 1160 and
1190, made it a model
of serenity in
a wilderness. The only
concession to luxury is
the beautiful stone
from which the building
is built, hewed to
perfection and laid
without mortar. The
light plays beautifully
across it. The abbey
holds a Rencontres
de Musique Mediévale
(medieval music
festival) in July.**

Entrecasteaux

Castle and gardens

12½ miles (20 km) NE
of Brignoles by D562,
☎ 04 94 04 43 95.
Open daily except Wed.,
11am-noon and 2.30-
6pm; guided tour on Sun.
3.30pm.
Paid admission.

The 11th C. fortress has been
replaced by a Renaissance
château whose gardens were
designed by Le Nôtre. It is the
former residence of the
Marquis de Grignan, son-in-
law of the writer, Mme de
Sévigné. It subsequently
belonged to Bruny
d'Entrecasteaux, a sea-farer
and explorer.

Cotignac

The quince

This little town is built at the
foot of a tufa cliff 270 ft
(80 m) high which is honeycombed with caves. Cotignac
is famous for its quince preserve, the colour of which is
very reminiscent of the

stonework of the houses. The
tree-lined **Cours Gambetta** is
a lovely place to linger (market on Tuesdays). While here,
taste the local *pâte de coing*
(quince paste) at Georges
Dalmasso's pâtisserie.

Valley des Carmes

Signposted walks

This valley is a lovely place for
a walk. The sights include the
17th C. **Chapel of Notre-
Dame-du-Bon-Refuge,** built
into a cave, as well as caverns
and waterfalls, especially the
Le Fauvery falls. The walks
last 1½ hours and are signposted. (Information at the
Maison Régionale de l'eau de
Barjols ☎ 04 94 77 15 83).

Spotcheck

D3-D4

Var

Things to do

The Tripe Festival
Fishing and potholing
Signposted walks through
the Vallée des Carmes

With children

Mini-France

Within easy reach

*The Maures range, 30 km
S, p. 222.*
*The Verdon Gorges,
40 km NE, p. 234.*

Tourist Offices

Barjols: ☎ 04 94 77 20 01
Brignoles: ☎ 04 94 69 27 51

The Verdon Gorges
from Sainte-Croix Lake to Point Sublime

Jean Giono loved the countryside around Moustiers, with its lavender-bordered paths and wonderful climate with three hundred days a year of 'pure light'. The huge Sainte-Croix lake and the Verdon Gorges make this part of Haute Provence a magical region with hilltop villages and shimmering lakes.

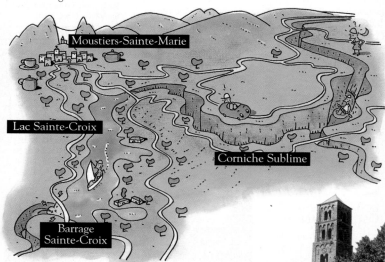

Moustiers-Sainte-Marie

Lac Sainte-Croix

Corniche Sublime

Barrage Sainte-Croix

Romanesque church at Moustiers-Sainte-Marie

Moustiers-Sainte-Marie
Village by a ravine

This village lives dangerously, being built among ochre rock, on the edge of a crevasse, and containing a torrent which descends in a series of waterfalls. Climb up through a maze of narrow streets and covered passageways to visit the 12th C. church which has lovely sculptured choir-stalls. A huge (760 ft (227 m)) golden chain links the two sides of the ravine, above an ancient monastery.

Faïence Museum

Inside the town hall, ☎ 04 92 74 61 64. Open except Tues., 9am-noon and 2-6pm (until 7pm in summer). Closed Nov.-Mar. (except school holidays, 2-5pm).
Paid admission.

This building is another former monastery, now dedicated to local industry. The history of Moustiers faïence (tin-glazed earthen-ware) is traced from the earliest pieces to modern examples (see also the box on p. 237). The industry had a stroke of luck when Louis XIV forced the nobility to melt down their gold table-ware thus creating a market for replacements made out of earthenware.

Moustiers-Sainte-Marie

Nearby
The Ségriès workshop

Rte de Riez, 6 miles (10 km) before Moustiers,
☎ **04 92 74 66 69.**
Shop open daily in summer, 9.30am-noon and 1.30-7.30pm; out of season, 10am-noon and 1.30-6pm from Mon. to Fri. *Free visit on appointment, except weekends.*
The Ségriès workshop uses an old-fashioned kiln and produces masterpieces of the potter's art which are modelled, then retouched and fired. The decoration is done freehand on the fired clay and each design is totally original. Good faïence should be durable, light and ring pleasantly when struck. From 150 F a plate.

Lake Sainte-Croix

This magnificent stretch of water was created when the Verdon was dammed in 1972. The villages which once stood on hilltops overlooking the river now stand by the water's edge. The old village of Salle-sur-Verdon lies at the bottom of the lake, so a new village was built beside it. Although the site is new it is a good place to stay, especially as a base for touring the surrounding countryside.

Water sports on the Verdon

People long avoided sailing down the gorges because they were too difficult to negotiate, but today the lower reaches of the canyon are no longer

Spotcheck
D3

Alpes-de-Haute-Provence

Things to do
Water sports on the Verdon river
Hiking through the gorges
The crest road
The Grand Canyon of the Verdon
Kayaking down the Verdon

Within easy reach
Haut Var, 30 km S, p. 230.
Vallée d'Argens, 40 km SW, p. 232.

Tourist Office
Moustiers:
☎ **04 92 74 67 84**

In the Verdon Gorges

deserted. The Verdon has been tamed by a series of five dams and now boasts several water-sports centres along its course which offer an impressive range of activities for you to try. (Information available from the Castellane Office de Tourisme, ☎ 04 92 83 61 14).

The shores of Lake Sainte-Croix

The Grand Canyon of the Verdon

The Verdon canyon is the largest in Europe. Jean Giono described it as a 'prodigious mixture of rocks and chasms'. To see it at its best, go to the north bank, below the village of Rougon, then hike up to Point Sublime using the path from the chalet-restaurant (D952). There is an extraordinary view of the course of the Verdon over a sheer drop of 610 ft (183 m). Then climb to the village (D17) for another unforgettable view.

Hiking through the gorges
GR 4 signposted, north shore. Depart from the Chalet de La Maline (D23).

An 8 hour hike to Point Sublime, 9 miles (14 km).
Follow the Martel footpath, along the bottom of the ravine. It is a dramatic route, including a flight of 240 iron steps over a cleft in the rock (not for those who have no head for heights!). Another highlight is the Couloir de Samson, a natural corridor created by the huge block of stone obstructing the entrance to the canyon (bring a torch, it's dark inside). Above all, do not go alone and take all the equipment you need.

The ridge road
Access via D23, turn left before La Palud, coming from Rougon.
This offers dizzying sights of bottomless gorges. Follow the D23 to La Palud-sur-Verdon and stop at all the beauty spots. The first one displays 1,000 ft (300 m) of polished cliffs, the third twists and turns, and the

IN THE SWIM
Water-sports fanatics have made the Verdon canyon their private preserve. The various rapids, with their evocative names (the Niagara, the Tourniquet, the Cyclops, the Styx, the Mousetrap, the Saturation Point, the Pit-bulls, the Pole-axes), offer the opportunity of indulging in the pleasures of white-water rafting, canyoning, swimming in white water or kayaking. But be warned: you need to be very proficient to go down the canyon. And never leave without finding out the depth of the water and the weather conditions. (EDF recorded message: ☎ 04 92 83 62 68; weather report: ☎ 08 36 68 12 34).

last faces the Sublime Corniche. Do not use this road in winter.

⚜ Kayaking down the Verdon
**Aqua-Viva Est,
☎ 04 92 83 75 74.
Loisirs Aventure Kayak,
☎ 04 92 74 09 05 or
04 92 74 01 36.**

You must be accompanied by an instructor. Departure is from Castellane in classes graded according to proficiency, down towards Point Sublime. It is a distance of about 12 miles (19 km). From Point Sublime to the Sainte-Croix Lake for 22 miles (35 km), the canyon is only navigable by very experienced kayakers. The less fraught descent of the lower gorges of the Verdon (departure from Quinson, 6 miles (10 km) below the Sainte-Croix Lake) is open to any kayakers (4 hour round trip).

The hydroelectric power station
Sainte-Croix-du-Verdon, dam (D111).
Information at the nearest Office de Tourisme.

Guided tour by appointment, Jul.-Aug. only, except Sat.-Sun. and public holidays.
Free admission.
In power-station country, the tension mounts all along the course of the river. After visiting the huge Électricité de France (EDF) power station at

Sainte-Croix at the foot of the dam, and watching the turbo-alternators and piezometers (pressure meter) in action, go to the top of the building for a superb view of the Verdon Gorges and the lake which covers some 6,200 acres (2,500 ha), and is so vast it stretches out of sight.

DECORATING MOUSTIERS FAÏENCE

Each piece is shaped and then fired at 1,920°F (1,050°C). This produces a matt, whitish 'biscuit'. It is then dipped in a bath of enamel, and dried, before a pattern is traced on it from a template. Decoration is then added by hand and the piece is returned to the kiln where it is fired at 1,740°F (950°C).

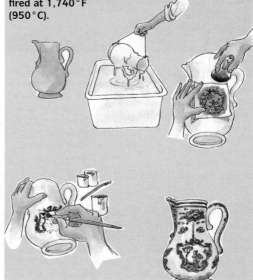

Napoleon's route

from Grasse to Digne in the foot-steps of the Emperor

This was the road used by Napoleon to return to Paris in 1815, before the Hundred Days. On his journey from the island of Elba, he chose to cross the mountains between Grasse and Digne in order to avoid his royalist enemies in Provence. It was a wise decision. The route has since become historic and filled with imperial and post-imperial places of interest.

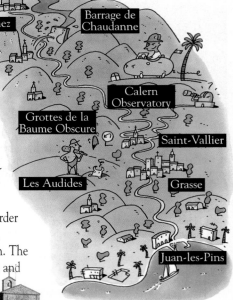

Senez

Barrage de Chaudanne

Calern Observatory

Grottes de la Baume Obscure

Saint-Vallier

Les Audides

Grasse

Juan-les-Pins

the single nave which is 110 ft (32 m) long and 50 ft (15 m) high, hung with Aubusson and Flanders tapestries and large canvases. Other features include carved wooden choir stalls. It is bizarre to find this huge church in such a tiny village.

Imperial pilgrimage

To follow in the exact foot-steps of the Emperor, begin on the promenade at Golfe-Juan at 3pm on 1 March. A stone tablet marks the exact spot where the imperial party landed. Then on to Cannes (bivouacking on the beach in front of Notre-Dame-du-Bon-Voyage), and take the N85 to Saint-Vallier-de-Thiey. Stop in the Place de l'Apié and spend the second night at Séranon. After breakfasting at Castellane, in the Rue Nation-ale, spend the following night at Barrême (in a house near

the little square) and enter Digne on 4 March by the Rue Mère-de-Dieu, where you will lunch in the Rue du Jeu-de-Paume (perhaps a picnic in front of the commemorative plaque?). Your imperial pil-grimage should end on 20 March in Paris.

Senez

A cathedral in the mountains

On 3 March, 1815, Napoleon passed right by this 12th C. Romanesque building in this tiny hamlet which until 1790 had been a bishopric. Admire

Saint-Vallier-de-Thiey

❀ Grottes de la Baume Obscure

Ch. de Sainte-Anne, ☎ 04 93 42 61 63.
Open daily, Apr.-Sep., 10am-5pm (until 7pm week-ends and public holidays); Jul.-Aug., daily 10am-7pm; Oct.-Mar., 10am-4pm Wed., Thu. and Fri., 10am-5pm weekends and public holidays. Closed Jan.
Paid admission.
These stalagmite caves have been enhanced with a *son et*

Spotcheck
D2-D3-E3

Things to do

Grottes de la Baume
Obscure
Prehistoric Audides caves
Calern observatory
Barrage de Chaudanne
(Dam)

lumière performance, combining their age-old wonders with those of modern technology. There are more than 600 yards (600 m) of galleries, at a depth of 200 ft (60 m), enhanced with music, lights and images. On the nature path you'll find species of cave-dwelling plants. Be warned, the temperature is a constant 55°F (13 °C).

❦ The prehistoric Audides caves

1606, Rte de Cabris,
☎ **04 93 42 64 15.**
Open daily, Jul.-Aug.
10am-6pm; out of season, 2-5pm, except Mon.-Tues. or on booking.
Paid admission.
Prehistoric man has returned to the area he once inhabited. You'll see him outside the caves in lifesize representations of scenes from prehistoric daily life. Then enter any of the six caves where stalactites and stalagmites surround a cristalline stream (279 steps take you 200 ft (60 m) underground). Take a sweater and wear comfortable shoes.

Castellane

Barrage de Chaudanne (Dam)
☎ **04 92 83 61 14**
(Office de Tourisme).
Guided visits Jul.-Aug., Mon. and Thu. afternoon at 2pm, 3pm, 4pm and 5pm, meeting in front of the factory;
out of season, Mon.-Fri. by appointment (groups).
Free admission.
Discover how to perform a healthcheck on a dam, using a pendulum. In the control room, you can see the vast amount of electricity

produced by the massive turbines registering. On the top of the dam, you'll be impressed by the view. This very considerable feat of engineering has the additional functions of irrigating the region, regulating the flow of the Verdon and putting out forest fires whenever they occur.

THE CALERN OBSERVATORY
☎ **04 93 85 85 58.**

Guided tour on Sun. at 3.30pm, May-Sep.
Paid admission.
The laser beam of the Cerga research centre is positioned at a height of 4,000 ft (1,200 m) and constantly checks the fluctuating distance between the Earth and the Moon. Its telescope measures anything larger than a human being in the universe. Tides on earth are also monitored. They take us 23½ in (60 cm) further from the centre of our planet twice a day! Visitors can see firsthand how our entire universe is constantly changing.

Cannes city of stars

This elegant town that attracts the stars is situated gracefully overlooking a magnificent bay. Luxury hotels, Rolls Royces and casinos line the Croisette. But behind this glittering display the old town of Cannes, indifferent to the film world, clings to the Suquet hill, immediately above the old harbour.

The Croisette

You can do a quick tour of the luxury hotels (Majestic, Hilton, Carlton, Martinez) which link the Palais des Festivals (in the far west) with the Pointe de la Croisette (in the extreme east). On your left as you walk along, you can see 2 miles (3 km) of flowery gardens and palm trees and on your right, the private beaches. Just before Palm Beach, stop in front of Pierre-Canto port (lovely rose-garden) where the luxury yachts anchor.

Palais des Festivals

Guided tours (Wed. out of season): information at the Office de Tourisme, to the right of the grand staircase.
☎ 04 93 39 24 53.
Get yourself photographed in film star mode on the 24 steps

of the grand staircase. Its red carpet remains in place all year round. At the foot are handprints from the stars who have visited the film festival. Inside, the large Lumière auditorium, the Debussy theatre and the numerous reception rooms can only be visited in winter.

Ciné-Folies

14, Rue des Frères-Pradignac,
☎ 04 93 39 22 99.
Open daily except Sun., 10.30am-noon and 2.30-7.30pm.

Film fans will find their mecca only 5 minutes from the Palais des Festivals. You can stock up on videos, photos, books, postcards and posters from all over the world, including those of the Cannes Film Festival (p. 114) – the genuine articles – which are only sold here. For instance, ask for the 50th anniversary posters (1997), a future collectible.

Musée de la Castre

Château,
☎ 04 93 38 55 26.
Open daily except Tues., Jul.-Aug. 10am-noon and 3-7pm; Apr.-Jun., 10am-noon and 2-6pm; Oct.-Mar., 10am-noon and 2-5pm. Closed in Jan.
Paid admission.

High up in the Suquet quarter, the outbuildings of the 12th C. former château of the monks of Lérins (XIIe s.) house collections donated to the museum by wealthy patrons. The 70 ft (22 m) high square tower offers a lovely view of the Croisette.

Canolive

16 and 20, Rue Venizelos,
☎ 04 93 39 08 19.
Open daily, except Sun., 10.30am-noon and 2.30-7.30pm.
This is a real Ali Baba's cave. The whole of Provence is contained in these two shops which are next door to each other. The left-hand shop sells local craft items – clothing, *santons*, potteries, pewter and Moustiers faïences. The other sells local produce – olive oil, honey, herbs, wines, sardines, soaps and fragrances.

Visiting the islands

Embarcadère des Îles, Vieux-Port,
☎ **04 93 39 11 82.**
Round trip: 60 F.
Do as the locals do and take a trip to 'the isles'. The islands of Lérins (p. 242) lie side-by-side 2¹/₂ miles (4 km) out to sea, a 20 minute boat trip away. Enjoy your visit.

Carlton Casino

The Carlton,
58, Bd de la Croisette,
☎ **04 93 06 40 06.**
With 338 rooms, restaurants, caviar club and gigantic marble lobby, the Carlton is the ultimate luxury hotel on the Riviera. The casino is on the 7th floor. In high

DIVING TO LOOK AT WRECKS

Nature et Plongée, 70, Bd Eugène-Gazagnaire,
☎ **04 93 94 29 00.**
Departure from the port of Moré-Rouge at 9am and 2pm all year round.
This could be the chance for your first scuba-dive (from 8 years upwards, 180 F); you can dive solo (190 F with equipment) or in a group and explore the sea-bed which is littered with wrecks.

season, the imperial suite costs 45,000 F a night. A single room costs between 1,290 F and 3,900 F.

Shopping and markets

At the **Forville Market** in the Rue Louis-Blanc, the fishermen sell their own catch every morning (except Mon.) from 7am to 1pm. The same applies to the flower-sellers in the **Allée de la Liberté**. The **Rue Meynadier**, a pedestrian precinct, is a good shopping street where the local vendors sell to the hordes of tourists. Further on, the elegant **Rue d'Antibes**, parallel to the Croisette, is full of antique dealers, jewellers, haute couture boutiques and art galleries.

The Îles de Lérins
the prison of the Man in the Iron Mask

T ake a boat from Cannes and head for the islands. On the first island (Sainte-Marguerite), the mysterious Man in the Iron Mask was imprisoned by Louis XIV. On the other (Saint-Honorat), peaceful monks still live in a magnificent abbey, far from the hustle and bustle of the world. No cars are allowed on the islands which are natural and unspoilt. There are delightful walks and lovely coves for bathing.

The fort on the Île Sainte-Marguerite
☎ 04 93 43 18 17.
Open daily except Tue., Jul.-Sep.,10.30am-noon and 2.15-6.30pm (until 4.30pm out of season). *Paid admission.*
The grim fortress on the northern cliff was a prison from which no one was ever released. Visit the cells of the famous prisoners associated with it: the Man in the Iron Mask, the Seven Huguenots and Maréchal Bazaine. Find the crag from which the Maréchal escaped, in 1874, by simply dropping a rope down into the pounding surf. At the entrance, the **Musée de la Mer** contains wrecks discovered around the island.

Tour of the Île Saint-Honorat
Departure from the *embarcadère.*
Follow the coast along a pine-shaded path which will take you to all 7 chapels on this Cistercian island, including La Trinité at the eastern tip and the Saint-Sauveur in the north-west, which have retained their 5th C. appearance. At the Pointe Saint-

Férréol, there is an oven built by Napoleon to heat cannon balls. In the centre of the island, the monks have planted vines, orange groves and lavender fields.

The monastery-fortress
On the Île Saint-Honorat,
☎ 04 92 99 54 00.
Open daily 9am-4.30pm (until 5.30pm in summer).

*Paid admission in Jul.-
Aug. (guided tours).*
This is where the Cistercian
monks lived for more than
seven centuries, safe from
attacks by pirates. The fortified monastery is at the
water's edge on a headland.
Entrance is via a door 13 ft
(4 m) above ground, which
once had a simple ladder. A
visit to the upper floors gives
an idea of the cloistered life
the monks led until the
Revolution.

A living monastery
☎ 04 92 99 54 00.
Only the chapel can be
visited (daily except during mass, 11am-2pm).
Cistercian monks still live
here so only the church and
museum can be visited. The
latter contains items dated to
the Roman era and the
island's first inhabitants. The
church was built in the late
19th C. (the public may
attend services) on the site of
an old collegiate church,
of which the
only relic is
an 11th C.
funerary
chapel.

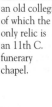

The monks' liqueur
**For sale in the modern
monastery.**
The monks called the
liqueur Lérina after the original name of the island,
which changed to St.
Honorat after the saint
came here on retreat in the
5th C. The Cistercian
brothers produced this
liqueur in homage to their
founder, using aromatic
herbs picked on the island.
It has been made for over
1,000 years. Lérina is available in two colours: green,
165 F for a 11 fl oz (70 cl)
bottle, and yellow, 155 F a 7
fl oz (20 cl) bottle.

The latest theory about the Man in the Iron Mask
If the most recent theories
prove to be based on fact,
French history will be
shaken to its founda-
tions.

Spotcheck
E3
Alpes Maritimes

Things to do
Ecological footpaths
Tour of the island

Tourist Office
Cannes: ☎ 04 93 39 24 53

Louis XIII did not like women
and his presumed heir, Louis
XIV, did not incarcerate his
own twin brother on the Île
Sainte-Marguerite, but his real
father, the Duke of Beaufort.
On discovering that the duke
was a 'gallant companion' of
his mother, Anne of Austria,
the Sun King protected his
throne – which he was in fact
usurping – by locking up his
real father, the Duke; whom
he did not dare execute.

ECOLOGICAL FOOTPATHS
**Departure from the
*embarcadère***
☎ 04 93 43 49 24.

Ramble through the
350 acres (140 ha)
of lovely Mediterranean
forest which covers
Sainte-Marguerite.
In summer there are
ecological guided
tours (daily, Jul.-Sep.,
10.20am, 2.20pm
and 4.20pm. Free
admission). A botanical
path will take you
from the fort of
Vauban along an
avenue of eucalyptus
trees planted in 1865,
and close by the
Batéguier salt lake
which is populated
by sea-birds.

Mougins and the Vallée de la Siagne

Saint-Cézaire

Mougins

Auribeau

Montauroux

Notre-Dame-de-Vie

Musée de l'Automobile

Mougins winds upwards like the shell of a giant snail. Overlooking the bay of Cannes it is where Picasso painted his last pictures and Winston Churchill also tried his hand at the easel. Mougins has inspired countless artists and is a retreat for the stars who try to avoid the crowds at the Cannes Film Festival, held every year in May.

Mougins

The old village
Lose yourself in the winding streets of this charming village, the list of whose famous residents is pretty impressive. Jacques Brel lived at 71, Rue des Lombards, not far from Édith Piaf, Christian Dior, Jeanne Moreau, Catherine Deneuve, Picasso and Jean Cocteau. The Porte Sarrasine, all that remains of the 14th C. fortifications, stands by the Church of Saint-Jacques. There is a wonderful view from the belfry (open daily, 2-8pm; out of season, 2-5pm; the keys are kept at the Photography Museum).

Notre-Dame-de-Vie
1¼ miles (2 km) SE of Mougins via D3.
Churchill frequently painted this 12th C. chapel which is built in typical Provençal style. It is set slightly apart from the village. There is a three-arched porch, and a neighbouring sanctuary where sickly new-born babies were 'resuscitated'. The interior also contains a handsome 16th C. reredos.

Musée de l'Automobile
Between Antibes and Cannes, via A8, coming from Nice, Aire des Bréguières,
☎ **04 93 69 27 80.**
Open daily 10am-6pm; until 7pm in summer. Closed Nov. to mid-Dec. *Paid admission.*
This famous museum contains one of the finest collections of vintage and classic cars in Europe. More than 100 vehicles in working order trace the history of the car from 1894 to today. See the first horseless carriages, examples

of the great marques and the latest racing car designs. Car auctions and Concours

THE GREAT CHEFS

Mougins has always had the knack of producing great chefs who in turn attracted celebrities to the town. In the 1930s, the chef Célestin Véran made *bouillabaisse* for the rich and famous, including the Duke of Windsor. Then, in 1969, Roger Vergé converted an old oil-mill into a restaurant, where he now teaches his world-famous 'cuisine of the sun'. You can sit at a little bistrot table and taste, question and take notes – then try and create the same thing at home. The menu changes daily, depending on what is fresh in the market. For information call ☎ 04 93 75 35 70 (5 half-days per month).

d'Elégance parades are sometimes held at the museum.

Picasso's House

La Maison de Picasso
Av. de l'Orangeraie,
beside the chapel of
Notre-Dame-de-Vie.
The house can be glimpsed on the outside, but is not open to the public. Approach it from the lower end. This is where the great master was inspired by the wonderful light for the last 12 years of his life (he nicknamed it 'the Minotaur's lair'). In 1936, before taking over the house, he took up residence in what is now the Hôtel Les Muscadins, where one evening he repainted all the walls of his bedroom. The proprietor was furious and insisted that he restore them to their original condition.

Musée de la Photographie

Porte Sarrasine,
☎ 04 93 75 85 67
Open daily except Tues., Jul.-Aug., 2-11pm; out of season, 1-6pm. Closed Nov. to mid-Dec. *Paid admission.*
When Picasso was in his Mougins period, he was immortalised posing at his easel by the greatest photographers of the 20th century including Robert Doisneau, Jacques-Henri Lartigue, André Villers and Raph Gatti, (second floor). The first floor houses a collection of

Spotcheck
E3

Alpes Maritimes

Things to do

The car museum (Musée de l'Automobile)
The Saint-Cézaire caves
The Hubac bamboo grove
May antiques fair

Within easy reach

Biot, 10 km E, p. 264.
Vallée du Loup, 20 km N,
p. 266.

Tourist Office

Mougins: ☎ 04 93 75 87 67

old cameras. Photographic plates are on show on the ground floor.

Saint-Cézaire-
sur-Siagne

Caves and pool

9 miles (15 km) W of
Grasse by D613,
☎ 04 93 60 22 35.
Open daily, Jun.-Sep, 10.30am-noon and 2.30-6pm; Jul.-Aug., 10.30am-6.30pm; out of season, 2.30-5pm. Closed 1 Nov.-15 Feb., except Sun. afternoon. *Paid admission.*

VALMASQUE PARK

Access via D35, towards Antibes

This huge park covers 1,055 acres (427 ha) next to the Fontmerle pond, east of Mougins. The water attracts many migrating birds and is covered with huge pink lotus flowers in August. Take the green signposted paths along the D 35, over the three hills which are covered with pines and evergreen oaks. In the forest clearings there are adventure playgrounds for the children.

Descend 170 ft (50 m), into a red underground world full of stalactites and stalagmites. The caves were discovered in the late 19th C. Follow the path through the Drapery Room and the Organ Room, before stopping on the edge of an impressive abyss, beside the Alcove des Fées (Fairy Alcove). Bring a sweater, the temperature is around 57°F (14°C).

Siagne Gorges

Saint-Cézaire exit towards Saint-Vallier via D105.

These deep, lush gorges can be seen from the feudal village of Saint-Cézaire which overlooks them. There is a lookout at the end of the signposted path leading from the church. After you have enjoyed this view, drive 3 miles (5 km) along the narrow road which climbs steeply above the gorges. At the point where the bridge crosses the river,

turn around and look back down the canyon. The view is really quite magnificent.

Auribeau-sur-Siagne

Hilltop village

7½ miles (12 km) S of Grasse.

Auribeau is one of the most picturesque hilltop villages of the Côte d'Azur, perched precariously on a cliff edge overlooking a deep gorge. In the 12th C. the protection needed against invaders was very much uppermost in the minds of the villagers. Enter this well-preserved village by the 16th C. Soubran gate, and follow the narrow lanes that climb to the church or descend to the river.

Auribeau's Candlemaker

Moulin du Sault
☎ **04 93 40 76 20.**
Open daily 10am-noon and 3-6.30pm.

Wax candles and other items are made in a medieval mill. You can watch the craftsman

RIDING CENTRE

Ch. de Font-de-Currault, Mougins,
☎ 04 93 45 75 81.
Open daily all year round, except Sun. in summer and Thu. in winter, 9.30-10.30am and 4.30-8pm. 65 F per person
The centre organises 1 hour guided rides through the Valmasque park. They are suitable for all levels of horse-manship and all ages.

colour candles and decorate them with dried flowers from the local fields.

La-Roquette-sur-Siagne

Caillenco sculpture park

1411, Bd du 8-Mai,
☎ 04 92 19 13 84.
Open all year round except rainy days. Guided visit by appointment.
Paid admission.
In this large Provençal park, famous sculptors have created 'plantations' of contemporary art. Standing in the grounds of an 18th C. *bastide* (country mansion), the sculptures share the space with the local wildlife. This delightful spot is also the venue for other cultural events, such as poetry readings, recitals and performances of all kinds.

Pont-de-Siagne

The Hubac bamboo grove

Rte de Draguignan,
☎ 04 93 66 12 94.
Open Sat., Mar.-Nov., 8am-6pm and by appointment.
Benoît Béraud is a bamboo-lover and expert and grows this elegant oriental plant on the banks of the Siagne. About 30 varieties are grown here, originating from many countries. Choose a plant for house or garden but above all, ask Monsieur Béraud how to cook bamboo shoots.

Montauroux

May antiques fair

From Fréjus, take the A8 (Les Adrets exit), then the D37,
☎ 04 94 47 75 90 (Office de Tourisme).
1st or 2nd Sun. in May.

Nearly 200 exhibitors set up their stalls either in the Place du Clos in the upper medieval village, or at the lower end of the village. There are also many antique and second-hand shops along the D562.

Grasse and its perfumes

Grasse is the perfume capital of France, responsible for two-thirds of the national output. The flower market is held daily in the place aux Aires, against a picturesque background of old houses with terraced gardens. The climate is so mild that Napoleon's sister used to spend the winter here for her health, as did Queen Victoria.

The perfumery industries

Fragonard, 20, Bd Fragonard,
☎ **04 93 36 44 65.**
Galimard, 73, Rte de Cannes,
☎ **04 93 09 20 00.**
Molinard, 60, Bd Victor-Hugo,
☎ **04 93 36 01 62.**
Free daily guided tours.

Find out how the delicate fragrances which are sold throughout the world are created, by visiting the workshops of the three greatest perfumers in the world: Fragonard, Galimard and Molinard. From petal to perfume, all the stages of production of the great perfumes start in the 'nose' laboratory of the perfumer, who can recognise up to 500 different smells. You will have plenty of opportunity to test the various fragrances in the factory shop.

Musée International de la Parfumerie

8, Pl. du Cours,
☎ **04 93 36 80 20.**
Open daily except public holidays, Jun.-Oct., 10am-7pm; Nov.-May, daily except Mon., Tue. and public holidays, 10am-noon and 2-5pm. Closed Nov.
Paid admission.
Here is a museum that doesn't smell musty! The perfumery museum traces the history of the industry, different techniques for extracting essences and the development of the perfumer's art. Test your skill at perfume composition (guided tour and presentation if booked in advance).

Musée d'Art et d'Histoire de Provence

2, Rue Mirabeau,
☎ **04 93 36 01 61.**
Same opening hours as the perfumery museum.
Paid admission.

The best of Provence, in a magnificent 18th C. mansion. Delve into the history of the region from prehistoric times (items found in local excavations) to the latest technology, not forgetting arts and crafts (painting, pottery, ceramics), as well

as furniture (furnished rooms) and folk traditions.

Villa Fragonard

23, Bd Fragonard,
☎ 04 93 36 01 61.
Same opening hours as the Musée de la Parfumerie. *Paid admission.* The painter Fragonard was a native of Grasse, and took refuge here during the Revolution. On the ground floor there is a copy of the panels, now in New York, which he painted for Madame du Barry. On the staircase, there are works by his son who at the age of 14 discovered the effect of trompe-l'œil. Upstairs, paintings by his grandson and sister-in-law are on display.

❀ Domaine de Manon

36, Ch. du Servan-Plascassier,
☎ 04 93 60 12 76.
Roses: May to mid-Jun., preferably early afternoon, when they are picked. Jasmine: 20 Jul.-end Oct, early morning (8-10am). *Paid admission.*

Roses and jasmine have been grown here for 3 generations. To witness the beginning of the perfume process Hubert Biancalana welcomes you into his brightly-coloured, fragrant fields at harvesting time (the rose season comes first, followed by the white jasmine). It is like being inside a huge bowl of sun-drenched pot pourri.
Did you know

that it takes between 450 and 2,200 lb (200 and 1,000 kg) of petals (about 1 million flowers!) to obtain 1¾ pints (1 l) of essence?

For sports enthusiasts

Assoc. Acti-Loisirs,
☎ 04 92 47 75 00.
Open daily, all year round. Potholing, mountain biking, hiking, canyoning and rafting. This association covers all the water-sports and land sports in which you can indulge in the Alpes-Maritimes. Explore the lesser known hinterland of Provence and keep fit at the same time.

Spotcheck
E3

Alpes Maritimes

Things to do

Visiting the perfumeries
Create your own perfume
Domaine de Manon
Water sports and land sports

Within easy reach

Cagnes-sur-Mer, 25 km E, p. 258.
Vence, 25 km NE, p. 260.
Biot, 20km E, p. 264.
Vallée du Loup, 10 km NE, p. 266.

Tourist Office

Grasse: ☎ 04 93 36 66 66

❀ CREATE YOUR OWN PERFUME

Galimard (Studio des Fragrances), Rte de Pégomas,
☎ 04 93 09 20 00.
Daily, except Sun., by appointment (2 hours). **This is a two-hour session designing your own perfume. The house 'nose' will evaluate your sense of smell, and explain the architecture of a good perfume. It is then up to you to create your own fragrance, respecting the head notes, the heart notes, and the background notes. When you leave, they keep the formula and you can take away a 3½ fl oz (100 ml) vial of your work (cost: 200 F).**

The Fayence district
the place for a birds-eye view

This little corner of the *département* of Var is a riot of colour. The flaming red rocks of the Esterel mingle with the silver-grey olive trees and brilliant yellow mimosa. Fayence is also a good place for gliding and hang-gliding.

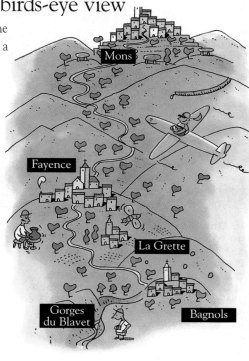

Fayence

Craftsmen in every street

Numerous craftsmen have decided to settle in this little town situated in the heart of the Camandre valley, attracted by its peacefulness and charm. They work in wood, stone or metal, weave cloth or throw pots. Climb the steep, narrow lanes to the hilltop, where there was once a château. The 17th C. **Church of Saint-Jean-Baptiste** contains beautiful 19th C. frescoes.

Olive wood crafts

Au Bois d'olivier, 14, Av. Saint-Christophe, at the foot of the village, ☎ 04 94 76 00 62.

Open daily except Mon., 9am-noon and 3-6.30pm (Sun. by appointment). Éliane and René Ragot work in olive wood which they sometimes combine with pottery from Moustiers. Their wares include salad bowls, cheese platters and plate-stands. They sometimes allow visitors into their work-shops.

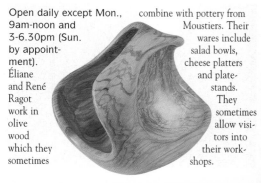

La Grotte
Beehives
Near Notre-Dame-des-Cyprès,
☎ 04 94 76 29 14.
Open daily, telephone first. Armelle Barbiéri is a beekeeper. She also sells her products to the public, honey usually costs around 50 F for 2¼ lb (1 kg). She also sells nougat (between 25 F and 27 F each), nougatine, *pain d'épices* (25 F each) and small snacks made from dried-fruit. You can also visit the hives (in autumn).

Mons
Living dangerously
Mons is perched between heaven and earth at an altitude of 2,700 ft (800 m), dominating a landscape of terraced olive groves. Its lovely **Romanesque church**

GLIDER FLYING

Centre de Vol à Voile, Aérodrome, Quartier Malvoisin,
☎ 04 94 76 00 68.
Book a few days in advance.
The sky is a great vantage point from which to admire the intricate pattern of the coastline. The Fayence-les-Tourrettes aerodrome is a former military airfield which has become the foremost gliding and hang-gliding centre in Europe. With patient instructors and good guides, you can take an initiation flight in a glider for 400 F.

has a beautiful interior. Thanks to the large map on the noticeboard in the Place Saint-Sébastien, you can identify all the good view points in the region, in clear weather. If it starts raining, take refuge in the **Musée Marine et Montagne** (Rue Pierre-Porre, ☎ 04 94 76 35 66, telephone before coming) and take a look at the models of ships made out of matchsticks by R. Audibert.

Tour of the dolmens
From the village of Mons, take the footpath to the **Chapel of Saint-Pierre**. You will find dolmens scattered over several miles. The **Riens dolmen** is only 430 yards (400 m) from the chapel, the **Colle dolmen** is 2 miles (3.5 km) from the village (beside the farm of the same name), and the **Brainée dolmen** is about 5 miles (7.5 km) from Mons.

The Roche-Taillée aqueduct
S of Mons by D56.
This impressive Roman feat of engineering was designed to provide the cities of the coast with constant drinking water. The workers opened a trench 170 ft (50 m) long,

Spotcheck
E3

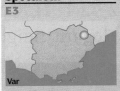

Var

Things to do
Glider flying
Visit a bee-hive
Tour of the dolmens

Within easy reach
Fréjus, 28 km S, p. 224.
Draguignan, 30 km E, p. 228.

Tourist Office
Fayence: ☎ 04 94 76 20 08

12 ft (3.6m) wide and more than 33 ft (10 m) deep which was carved out of the rock.

Bagnols-en-forêt
Stonecutters of the Blavet Gorges
Approx. 7½ miles (12 km) S of Fayence. Boulders were cut into grindstones at the bottom of these gorges. It was an industry that lasted from Roman times until the 18th C. The trip to the site will take you at least 2 hours on foot. Information at the Bagnols Office de Tourisme: ☎ 04 94 40 64 68.

Seillans
Hilltop village
This village, situated at an altitude of 1,220 ft (366 m), has ochre-coloured houses huddled around its feudal castle. The painters Stan Appenzeller and Max Ernst loved it so much that they spent the last years of their lives there. (Office de Tourisme: ☎ 04 94 76 85 91).

Antibes & Juan-les-Pins
elegant neighbours

A ntibes first became a fashionable seaside resort in the twenties. It is wonderfully situated between two coves, and has a famous yachting harbour. Founded by the Greeks as Antipolis, the old town with winding streets inspired the genius of Picasso. Its next door neighbour, Juan-les-Pins, hosts a jazz festival and has a thriving nightlife.

Antibes

The yachts of Port Vauban

Anyone interested in luxury yachts should not miss Port Vauban, one of the largest marinas in Europe. The finest yachts in the world anchor here. In the background can be seen the square fort, its 16th C. bastions laid out in a star shape around the Saint-Laurent tower.

The Church of the Immaculate Conception

This church is the cathedral of Antibes. Its square tower is also a belltower. The carved wooden doors to the sanctuary date from 1710. On the right, there is a little chapel containing a reredos of the Madonna of the Rosary, attributed to Louis Bréa.

Picasso and the Grimaldis

Pl. Mariéjol, ☎ 04 92 90 54 20. Open daily except Mon. and public holidays, 10am-6pm; out of season, 10am-noon and 2-6pm. *Paid admission.*

On the site of the ancient acropolis stands the Château Grimaldi, where Picasso worked in 1946. On holiday in Juan-les-Pins, he had been looking for a large studio and was offered this beautiful space facing the sea. He donated most of the work he did here to the city, including the very beautiful *Antipolis* series. Picasso's paintings, drawings and ceramics now hang alongside the paintings of Nicolas de Staël and the sculptures of Miró, Arman and César.

Market in the Place Masséna

Open daily except Mon. from 6am to noon.

One of the most attractive markets in the region, where fresh local produce can be found: vegetables, fruit, flowers and a delicious speciality – goat's cheese with olives. There is an antiques market on Thursdays.

le musée
Peynet

antibes

✿ Peynet Museum

**Musée Peynet,
Pl. Nationale,
☎ 04 92 90 54 30.**
Open daily except Mon. and public holidays, 10am-noon and 2-6pm. *Paid admission.*
You may well recognise the work of the artist Raymond Peynet. His pleasant, somewhat whimsical paintings, have been reproduced all over the world. He bequeathed some 300 illustrations to Antibes, which you can see here along with a few of his dolls.

Juan-les-Pins
Marineland

At the entrance to Antibes, 5 miles (8 km) from Nice by the RN7, ☎ 04 93 33 49 49.
Open daily, 10am-10pm in summer (7pm out of season).
This is the largest theme park in Provence. There are five centres to visit containing dolphins, killer whales and sea-lions (at night in July and August), water-sports, and tunnels beneath a huge shark-infested aquarium. There are many other attractions, not all of them marine, such as the butterfly jungle (a tropical greenhouse which also contains iguanas and crocodiles), a little Provençal farm and a fun miniature golf course.

JAZZ FESTIVAL

Juan-les-Pins saw the swing era of the interwar years overtaken by post-war bebop. In 1960, it became the jazz capital of Europe. Since then, its jazz festival, held every 15 August, has welcomed the great names in contemporary music, including Louis Armstrong, Miles Davis, John Coltrane, and a host of new stars who have brought new rhythms to the Pinède de Gould such as Al Jarrau, George Benson and Stan Getz (Office de Tourisme, ☎ 04 92 90 53 05. Tickets from 160 F).

NIGHTLIFE

Juan-les-Pins is good for night life. The Pam Pam (Bd Wilson, ☎ 04 93 61 11 05, open Apr. to mid-Nov.), stays open very late and presents live shows performed by Brazilian singers and musicians. There's a choice of exotic cocktails (the caipirinia is a speciality of the house and costs 67 F a glass). The place is often full to bursting, however, so you may not get in. Voom-Voom (Bd de la Pinède, ☎ 04 92 93 90 80) is also a favourite haunt of insomniacs. The crowd is well-heeled but not pretentious and there is always plenty to do and see (entrance 50 F or 100 F, depending on the night of the week).

The Cap d'Antibes
a very exclusive resort

This narrow cape which is an extension of Antibes and Juan-les-Pins, is a playground for the rich. Smart hotels and elegant villas jostle for position facing the beach among the Aleppo pines. To get a good look at them, you need to approach from the sea, but a tour of the peninsula on foot makes a very pleasant outing.

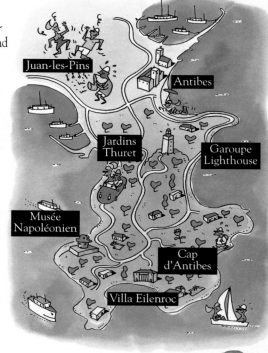

Port Vauban

Juan-les-Pins

Antibes

Jardins Thuret

Garoupe Lighthouse

Musée Napoléonien

Cap d'Antibes

Villa Eilenroc

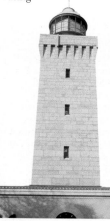

The Garoupe Lighthouse

The lighthouse takes its name from the hill on which it stands. It covers two-thirds of the Côte d'Azur, from Saint-Tropez as far as Italy. The neighbouring Chapel of Notre-Dame-du-Bon-Port (13th-16th C.) has a remarkable collection of religious offerings.

Jardins Thuret
62, Bd du Cap,
☎ 04 93 67 88 66.

Open daily except Sat., Sun. and public holidays, 8.30am-6pm. *Free admission.*
This is an important research centre, at which French botanists can study more than 3,000 species of sub-tropical trees and plants, and test their adaptability to the Mediterranean climate. Its 9½ acres (4 ha) are open to the public.

Naval and Napoleonic Museum
Bd Kennedy (beside the Eden Roc), ☎ 04 93 61 45 32.
Open daily except Sat. afternoon and Sun., 9.30am-noon and 2.15-6pm. Closed in Oct. *Paid admission.*

This museum is housed in a tower with a superb view and stands in lovely gardens. It contains many models of ships, naval paintings and other items connected with the sea and sailing. There are also some personal souvenirs belonging to Napoleon Bonaparte, a reminder of his escape from the island of Elba in 1815 before the Hundred Days. There is a good art collection, including a famous bust of the Emperor sculpted by Antonio Canova.

GARDEN OF THE VILLA EILENROC

Av. de Beaumont, ☎ 04 93 67 74 33.
Visit on Wed., Oct.- end of Jun., 9am-5pm.
This garden is the property of the city of Antibes and is open to the public. The estate was owned by a wealthy Dutchman who named it Eilenroc, as an anagram of his wife's name Cornelie. Its 27 acres (11 ha) are planted with a huge variety of fragrant plants, and the sea glistens in the back-

ground. The neo-classical villa was built by Garnier in 1867.

Spotcheck
E3

Alpes-Maritimes

Things to do

Thuret Garden (Jardins Thuret)
The coastal path
Garden of the Villa Eilenroc

Within easy reach

Cagnes-sur-Mer, 8 km N, p. 258.
Saint-Paul-de-Vence, 20 km N, p. 260.
Biot, 7 km N, p. 264.
Nice, 20 km N, p. 266.

Tourist Office

Antibes: ☎ 04 92 90 53 00

The coastal path

This walk passes close by the homes of the wealthy, though they are hidden behind trees. The Tire-Poil footpath at the end of the Garoupe beaches hugs the coastline and takes you along the water's edge to the Chemin des Douaniers (customs officers' path). Wear suitable hiking footwear, especially in winter, and avoid days when the sea is rough.

Millionaires' Bay

**Up to 6 sailings a day in summer from the Ponton Courbet in Juan-les-Pins. Advance booking required,
☎ 04 93 67 02 11.
Information in Antibes,
☎ 04 93 34 09 96.**
Duration: 1 hour.
Paid admission.
From the submerged compartment of the Visiobulle, you can study the sea bed, brightly-

coloured fish and beds of posidonia. Up on deck, you will get a good view of some fabulous seaside villas among the pinewoods. On the left is the Hôtel du Cap, where stars such as Marlene Dietrich, Douglas Fairbanks and Madonna have stayed.

Eden Roc

**Bd Kennedy,
☎ 04 93 61 39 01.**
This former villa of the founder of the newspaper, *Le Figaro*, was converted into a hotel in 1870. Guests have included Chagall, Hemingway, Chaplin and De Niro. This is where Scott Fitzgerald set his novel *Tender is the Night*. Double room in season from 2,500 F to 3,000 F.

Rose capital of the world

**Roses Astoux,
Av. de la Tour-Gandolphe,
☎ 04 93 61 41 87.**
Guided visits Apr.-Dec., 8am-noon.
Free admission.
The locals called the botanist Thuret a 'crazy Parisian' when he chose to settle here in 1865 and plant a 'lot of useless, bizarre species'. It is now the rose capital of the world, so don't leave without a bouquet of roses grown in the Astoux nurseries, only a few yards from the Thuret garden. There are 16 varieties in the widest possible range of colours. A bouquet of 10 small roses costs around 20 F.

Vallauris
art pottery

S moke rising from the kilns of Vallauris among hills dotted with olive groves, indicates the presence of potteries. This ancient art was revived here in the 1950s. Picasso had a considerable influence and his genius opened the way to a new approach, concentrating entirely on art ceramics. Jean Marais, a famous French potter, who died in November, 1998, also lived here.

Exploring the town

Vallauris was devastated by the Plague and razed to the ground in the 14th C. The current town plan dates from the 16th C. and is in a chequerboard pattern, which leaves little room for surprise. The **Place Paul-Isnard** is the heart of the city and is where the daily morning **market** is held. In the centre, there is a bronze statue of Picasso's *Man with Sheep* which the artist offered to the town in which he was made an honorary citizen.

The château de Vallauris is a former priory belonging to the Lérins monks, rebuilt in the 16th C. It is one of the few Renaissance buildings in the region and houses the town's three major museums. The **Musée national Picasso**, contains his gigantic painting *War and Peace*, 1,350 sq. ft (125 m²). Picasso's work also features in the **Musée de la Céramique**, among other 20th C. examples. The third museum is dedicated to the painter **Alberto Magnelli** (1888-1971).

Paintings and ceramics

Pl. de la Libération,
☎ 04 93 64 16 05.
Open daily except Tue., 10am-noon and 2-6.30pm.
Paid admission.

Spotcheck
E3

Alpes-Maritimes

Things to do
Pottery courses
Fête des Potiers

Within easy reach
Biot, 5 km N, p. 264.

Tourist Office
Vallauris: ☎ 04 93 63 82 58

Madoura Gallery
Rue Suzanne-et-Georges Ramier,
☎ 04 93 64 66 39.

Open daily except weekends., 10am-noon and 2.30-6pm (until 7pm in summer).

The gallery not only contains some beautiful ceramics, it is also the place where Picasso began to work in this medium, with the sculptor Prinnier, and the potters Suzanne and Georges who were running the Ramier workshop at the time. Today, the workshop makes its own wares and produces Picasso ceramics.

ORANGE BLOSSOM
Coopérative agricole du Nérolium,
12, Av. Georges-Clemenceau,
☎ 04 93 64 27 54.
Open daily except Sun., 8am-noon and 2-6pm; Mon. open 9am, Sat. 3pm.

Vallauris is a major centre for the cultivation of flowers for the perfume industry. Orange blossom, roses and jasmine are all distilled here. Distilled orange blossom produces neroli essence which is used to make the best eaux de Cologne. Visit this agricultural cooperative that has been going since 1904 and buy eau de toilette and orange flower water, around 23 F for 1¾ pints (1 l).

Pottery Museum
Rue Sicard,
☎ 04 93 64 66 51.
Open daily, 11am-7pm; Sun. by appointment. Closed Dec.

This museum explains all the production processes and shows a reconstruction of an early 20th C. pottery.

Pignatines
Pâtisserie La Griotte,
7, Bd Maurice-Rouvier,
☎ 04 93 64 52 65.

Pignatines are another speciality of Vallauris. They are chocolate pralines, stuffed with pine nuts, and flavoured with orange peel and the local orange-flower water. They come in a lovely ceramic container designed by the French master Jean Marais. 330 F or 440 F each; 300 F per 2¼ lb (1 kg) loose, by weight.

Pottery courses
École des Beaux-Arts, espace Grandjean,
Bd des Deux-Vallons,
☎ 04 93 63 07 61.
Courses in Jul. and Sep. Closed in Aug.

The art school offers a basic course for learning the techniques of potting in 5 days. The more advanced can study decoration, moulding and throwing.

Fête des Potiers
The town holds a potters' festival on the 2nd Sunday in August when potters open their workshops and give demonstrations. Visitors are given a *taraillette*, a little piece of clay shaped in front of you as a souvenir. (Information at the Office de Tourisme).

Cagnes-sur-Mer
and the Var estuary

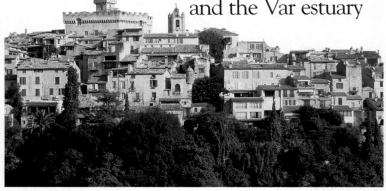

This former fishing village was popularised by Renoir and other artists and has since become a favourite seaside resort. From its medieval quarter (Hauts-de-Cagnes) to the huge – and overcrowded – Marina, its coast road overlooks one of the most beautiful bays on the Côte d'Azur.

Cagnes-sur-Mer
Château Museum
Hauts-de-Cagnes,
☎ **04 93 20 85 57.**
Open daily except Tue.,
1st May-30 Sep.,
10am-noon and 2-6pm;
out of season
10am-noon and 2-5pm.
Paid admission.

The royal family of Monaco may have lived here, because the château was owned by a former Rainier who was banished during the French Revolution. This feudal château has a lovely Renaissance patio and eight medieval rooms. The 17th C. reception rooms on the first floor were used by the Marquis de Grimaldi. From the top of the tower there is a lovely view of Nice, the Baie des Anges and the Alps.

Les Hauts-de-Cagnes
Access via the Montée de la Bourgade.
At the foot of the ramparts and the château lies a maze of picturesque arcaded streets, steps and passageways dating

MUSÉE RENOIR
Ch. des Collettes
☎ **04 93 20 61 07.**
Open daily May-Sep. except Tues., 10.30am-noon and 1.30-6pm; Oct.-Apr., 10am-noon and 2-5pm.
Paid admission.
The Impressionist painter, Auguste Renoir, loved the quality of light here. His home has now been converted into a museum. The garden contains ancient olive groves which surround a bank of orange trees and a rose-covered terrace. So like the master himself, you can indulge in enjoying fragrance and colour. There is an exceptionally good view of the old town of Cagnes from here.

from the 15th to the 17th C. The church of Saint-Pierre has an unusual double nave, which is Gothic on one side and Baroque on the other.

The 15th C. Chapel of Notre-Dame-de-Protection inspired Renoir (there are frescoes in the apse).

Water sports

Ski-Nautique Club, port Abri-du-Cros, ☎ 04 93 14 38 11 or 06 60 20 27 80. Open Apr.-Oct.
This club offers courses and private lessons in water-skiing, mono-skiing and bare-foot skiing, as well as other American-style water-sports. Sailing and yachting fans should seek out the École de Voile de Cros-de-Cagnes (port Abri-du-Cros, ☎ 04 93 31 45 65, open daily, all year round). Sailboards and water-skis are available for hire.

A day at the races

Cagnes-sur-Mer boasts one of the best race courses in France. Confirmed racegoer or not, an evening at the races makes a good family outing. (The course lies south of Cagnes on the N7.) Evening racing is a summer tradition which combines spectacle and excitement. Open Jul.-Aug. from 8.30pm on Mon., Tue. and Fri. (30 F). (Information, ☎ 04 92 02 44 44.)

Vaugrenier Park

Av. du Logis-de-Bonneau, access via N7 from Cagnes, south of the station.

The park covers 52 acres (21 ha) of meadows and 178 acres (72 ha) of woodland, a lake and protected flora. You may also see ducks, egrets, herons and foxes. The Romans chose to settle

in this haven, 2,700 years ago (visit the ruins). There are 7 miles (11 km) of signposted footpaths.

The Marina-Baie des Anges

Just before the southern entrance to the town, on the sea front.
The idea was to create a residential building by the beach with undulating forms integrating into the mountainous background. But it doesn't quite work. What do you think? The Marina-Baie des Anges is a subject of major local debate. Ought it to have been built? This huge block of flats like a massive breakwater does, however, make an impression.

Spotcheck
E3

Alpes-Maritimes

Things to do
Water sports
Musée de l'Art Culinaire (Museum of Culinary Art)

Within easy reach
Grasse, 25 km E, p. 248.
Antibes, 8 km S, p. 252.
Nice, 5 km E, p. 270.

Tourist Office
Cagnes: ☎ 04 93 20 61 64

Villeneuve-Loubet

Musée de l'Art Culinaire

Fondation Auguste-Escoffier, ☎ 04 93 20 80 51. Open daily except Mon. and public holidays., 2-6pm; until 7pm in summer. Closed in Nov. *Paid admission.*
This was the home of the great chef Auguste Escoffier, creator of the Peach Melba. A native of Cagnes, he won fame and fortune and spread the renown of French cuisine throughout the world in the early 20th C. You can thumb through his cookery books, visit his cellar and Provençal kitchen garden, and admire a collection of 1,500 menus alongside his elaborate spun-sugar creations.

Saint-Paul-de-Vence
the Montmartre of the Midi

The medieval village of Saint-Paul dominates the surrounding countryside. François I declared it to be a royal city in the 16th C. Since then scores of poets, artists and painters, inspired by the surroundings, have made Saint-Paul their home. Come and see what so entranced Jacques Prévert, Marcel Pagnol, Simone Signoret and Yves Montand.

The ramparts

The ramparts are almost in the same state as when François I had them built in the 16th C. Walk around the citadel, following the circular path from the north or south gates. There is a superb view of the Alps, the cap d'Antibes and the Esterel coast. The 16th and 17th C. houses of the old town now contain galleries and arts and craft workshops, especially in the Rue Grande, the lively main street which is a pedestrian precinct.

The collegiate church

The church has many treasures, including 15 small paintings on the theme of the mysteries in the Rosary chapel (1588). The Saint-Clément Chapel (1685) has baroque stucco mouldings and the Saint-Mathieu Chapel, wonderful stained glass windows. The treasury contains a parchment signed by King Henri III in 1588, as well as medieval gold ornaments, as well as the shoulder blade of St. George.

Waxworks

Musée d'Histoire, Pl. de la Mairie, ☎ **04 93 32 93 32.** Open daily, 10am-6pm (until 5.30pm out of season). *Paid admission.* These waxworks are lifesize and dressed in period costume. They represent those who succumbed to the charm of Saint-Paul-de-Vence over the centuries, including the Count of Provence, François I, Queen Jeanne, Vauban and Queen Victoria. The rest of the museum contains photos of celebrities, alive and dead, playing the ritual rounds of pétanque in the village square (including Yves Montand).

THE MAEGHT FOUNDATION

Rte de Cagnes (just before the village), ☎ 04 93 32 81 63.
Open daily Jul.-Sep., 10am-7pm; Oct.-Jun., 10am-noon and 2.30-6pm. *Paid admission.*

This world-famous foundation is dedicated entirely to contemporary art. Artists and art-lovers can meet and enthuse over the unique collection created by Marguerite et Aimē Maeght. There are paintings, sculptures, ceramics and drawings by the great names in modern art, including Braque, Calder, Kandinsky, Léger, Matisse and Soulages. The interior has been decorated by Miró, Chagall and Giacometti, improving on its beauty. There is also a lovely garden. Interesting temporary exhibitions are organised every three months in the Saint-Paul Museum (above the Office de Tourisme, open daily 10am-7pm, out of season 10am-6pm).

Artists and their studios

Some of the local artists will allow you to watch them working in their studios. On the west rampart, the painter Bertaux Marais will let you watch if you are quiet (☎ 04 93 32 00 31). Fred Witte and Nicole Gernez (70, Rue Grande, ☎ 04 93 32 98 36), will show you how the magic of Saint-Paul comes to life in the hands of contemporary artists. The Warneck and Orsoni studios (3, Rue de la Boucherie, ☎ 04 93 32 62 45), Christian Choisy's studio (west rampart, ☎ 04 93 32 01 80) and the Darling studio (east rampart, ☎ 04 93 32 86 93) can all be visited.

Along the canal

Information at the Office de Tourisme.
There are two delightful organised walks along the old canal path. You pass the picturesque Oratory of Sainte-Madeleine, the ruins of Saint-Pierre, and return to Vence via the woods. Departure No. 1 is from the upper village (1¼ hours) and No. 2 is from the Fondation Maeght (1½ hours).

Spotcheck
E3

Alpes-Maritimes

Things to do

Artists and their studios
Waxworks museum
Along the canal path

Within easy reach

Grasse, 25 km E, p. 248.
Antibes, 8 km S, p. 252.
Nice, 5 km E, p. 270.

Tourist Office

Saint-Paul:-de-Vence:
☎ 04 93 32 86 95

L'Auberge de la Colombe-d'Or

Pl. du Gal.-de-Gaulle, ☎ 04 93 32 80 02.
Closed from 5 Nov. to 5 Dec.
This restaurant is a highlight of any visit to Saint-Paul. Its name means 'inn of the golden dove', and it is the favourite haunt of the town's smart set. Masterpieces by Lurçat, Braque and Bonnard hang on the walls, while local celebrities sit at the neighbouring tables. This is the restaurant where Simone Signoret and Yves Montand first met.

Vence
artists' haunt

The town is encircled by two ravines. This is a region of roses, mimosa and lemon-trees, where the climate is mild and peace reigns, far from the hustle and bustle of the coast. In the interwar years and the 1950s, many writers and artists took up residence here. Vence, like Saint-Paul, is one of the most important birthplaces of 19th and 20th C. art.

Vence

Contemporary art in the château

The 13th C. château of the Barons de Villeneuve, famous rivals of the bishops of Vence throughout the Middle Ages, now contains the **Fondation Émile-Hugues,** which holds temporary exhibitions dedicated to the work produced in Vence by the great masters, including Matisse, Dubuffet, Dufy and Chagall. There are also some more recent paintings.

Rosary chapel

Av. Henri-Matisse,
☎ 04 93 58 03 26.
Open Dec.-Oct., Tue. and Thu., 10-11.30am and 2.30-5.30pm; school holidays 2.30-5.30pm except Sun. and Mon.
Paid admission.
Nothing draws your attention to this building from the outside. But this ordinary-looking structure contains extraordinary interior decoration by Henri Matisse. To thank the Dominican friars who looked after him during World

War II, the painter had the chapel rebuilt. Stained glass windows with floral designs illuminate the two converging naves. Large murals drawn on contribute brilliance and colou and colour to this rather dark area. Matisse claimed that this was his greatest masterpiece and one can only agree with him.

Nearby

A view from the hill

4 miles (7 km) from Vence by D2.
The col de Vence is 3200 ft (970 m) high and offers extensive views over the region. Not for the faint-hearted. A plaque indicates the landmarks from the left bank of the Var to Mont Agel, and in good weather you can see the coastline, including cap Ferrat, the Baie des Anges, the cap d'Antibes, the Île Sainte-Marguerite and the Esterel coast. Try and get there in the early morning or at sunset, when the view is most spectacular.

Notre-Dame-des-Fleurs

1¹⁄₂ miles (2.5 km) NW from Vence by D2210,
☎ 04 93 24 52 00.
Open daily except Sun., 11am-7pm.
This château was rebuilt in the 19th C. on the ruins of an abbey. It used to contain a Museum of Fragrances. Now, the former owners of the Galerie Beaubourg in Paris hold modern art exhibitions here. If you do not like modern art, you can take refuge in the magnificent garden (with statuary) and admire the view from the terrace which extends from cap Ferrat to the Esterel coast.

Arman: Turbeau Fountain

Spotcheck
E3

Alpes-Maritimes

Things to do

Visit a cheese-making factory
Botanical excursions
Trips down the river
Excursion to Coursegoules

Within easy reach

Grasse, 25 km W, p. 248.
Antibes, 20 km S, p. 252.
Nice, 15 km S, p. 270.

Tourist Office

Vence: ☎ **04 93 58 06 38**

Botanical excursions
Book first at the Office de Tourisme.

César: Victory of Villetanneuse (bronze)

All year round.
Paid excursion.
A passionate botanist organises half-day walks through the Vence countryside – an opportunity to study the rich local flora of Baou (orchids, lavender, aromatic herbs) and to glimpse inside a few magnificent private gardens (which are opened specially on request).

Visit a cheese-making factory
Book first at the Office de Tourisme.
Visit all year round by appointment, except Dec., Jan. and Feb.
Paid admission.
At the Domaine des Courmettes, 2,000 ft (600 m) above sea level, you can see how farmhouse goat's cheese is made, from milking through to the finished product including fermentation.

TRIPS DOWN THE RIVER
Book at the Office de Tourisme.
In summer; from the age of 9.
Water-sports fans will adore this trip down the river, a half-day divided between swimming and rock-climbing (no backtracking and a route that is accessible to all). A national guide gives assistance and supplies all of the equipment.

Of course, the highlight is the tasting and the cheese is for sale.

Coursegoules
Where only eagles dare
9 miles (15 km) of Vence by D2.
Coursegoules clings to the slopes at the foot of the Cheiron, and is a very remote spot. Its ramparts are apparently suspended in thin air, out over the River Foussa, where blackbirds and eagles dip and dive. In a little church opposite the bowling ground, there is a reredos which is attributed to the Nice painter Louis Bréa.

Biot art, glass and ceramics

The name of this little hilltop village in the Alpes-Maritimes is pronounced 'Biotte'. It hides behind the fashionable Baie des Anges and dominates the whole of the Brague valley from its rocky peak. Biot is famous for its ceramics and glass which the painter Fernand Léger greatly admired.

A walk round old Biot

The Tines gate and the Minagriers gate are all that remains of the 16th C. wall. The Place des Arcades contains a Romanesque parish church. It once had frescoes on its walls but a very prudish bishop had them removed, in 1699, since he considered them to be too explicit. Don't miss the Rosary reredos, which has been attributed to the local artist, Louis Bréa.

Bonsai Museum and nursery

Musée Bonsaï Arboretum,
299, Ch. du Val-de-Pôme,
☎ 04 93 65 63 99.
Open daily except Tue., 10am-noon and 2-5.30pm; Apr.-Sep. 3-6.30pm.
On 3,500 sq. yards (3,000 m²) of land, the Okonek family nurture nearly 5,000 bonsai trees. These nurserymen have been living in Biot for 20 years and have miniaturised local trees such as the

olive, pomegranate, apricot, lime, willows and eucalyptus. Only 20% of these dwarf trees are from Japan. A Chinese elm costs about 230 F.

Musée d'Histoire et de Céramiques Biotoises

9, Rue Saint-Sébastien,
☎ 04 93 65 54 54.
Open daily except Mon. and Tue., 10am-noon and 2-6pm; out of season, 2-6pm.
Paid admission.

The museum is housed in the former chapel of the Pénitents. It tells the story of this ancient Gallo-Roman settlement which later became the headquarters of the Knights Templar. The pottery has a place of honour, thanks to its collection of jars and indoor fountains in lacquered terra cotta. There is a reconstruction of a 19th C. kitchen, and traditional costumes. Most of the exhibits were donated by old local families.

The Biot glassworks

Ch. des Combes,
☎ 04 93 65 03 00.
Open Mon.-Sat., 9am-8pm (6.30pm out of season); Sun. and public holidays, 10.30am-1pm and 3-7pm. Guided tour by appointment.
Free admission.

The painter owned a pretty villa near the town and visited Biot to work with the ceramicist Roland Brice. When he died in 1955, his widow, Nadia Léger, commissioned the Nice architect, Svetchine, to build a museum which contains about 400 of the artist's works. The austere architecture does much to enhance the display. The museum was actually designed around two massive pieces, the large ceramic mosaic, 5,300 sq. ft (500 m²), which decorates the façade and the magnificent stained glass window in the hall, 530 sq. ft (50 m²).

A good place to get to know Léger's paintings and their development, from his break with impressionism to his *Builders*, painted in 1950. Part of the museum is devoted to less well-known aspects of his work: tapestries, ceramics, sculptures, and even architecture.

Although the little streets of the village are full of glass workshops and showrooms, the Verrerie de Biot (founded in 1956) is the only one entitled to use the name because the trademark was registered in 1956. The pieces created by the other Biot glassworks do not have the right to the label 'verre de Biot' (Biot glass).

Jean Colozzino's fougasse

Pl. de la Chapelle.
This baker makes the largest olive *fougasse* (bread) in the world.

Prepared in the traditional way, the bread is 8 ft (2.50 m) long and 2 in. (60 cm) wide. To make it requires 110 lb (50 kg) of flour, 44 pt (25 l) water, 8 oz (250 g) salt and 17½ lb (8 kg) olives! This got him into the Guinness Book of Records. Don't worry, other delicious breads he sells in his shop are of normal proportions.

Earthenware jars

Biot was an important pottery town in the Middle Ages, but lost out to Vallauris in the 19th C. Even though glass has largely taken over, there are still a dozen or so potters who make jars, vases and ornamental flower-pots for the garden and who have earned good reputations. Visit the **Poterie Provençale Auge-Laribe** (1689, Route de la Mer, ☎ 04 93 65 63 30. Open daily except Sun. morning, 8.30am-noon and 2-6.30pm). A terracotta Biot jar 28 in. (70 cm) high costs 1,345 F.

The Vallée du Loup
Tourrettes, Le Bar, La Colle and Gourdon

Gréolières

Caussols

Gourdon

Gorges du Loup

Tourrettes-sur-Loup

Le Bars-sur-Loup

The Loup is a raging torrent that has carved a path through the limestone hills over a distance of more than 25 miles (40 km), until it reaches the Mediterranean at Cagnes, having descended ¾ of a mile (1,200 m) to sea level. Picturesque hilltop villages look down onto the river and its banks where orange trees thrive and violets cover the surrounding fields from spring to autumn.

Tourrettes-sur-Loup

A carpet of violets
Altitude: 1,500 ft (400 m).
Violets cover the surrounding fields, flowering between October and March. This fortified medieval village, perched on a rocky outcrop, has hardly changed since the 15th C. Walk up the main street, the Grand-Rue – starting from the belfry south of the main square – and visit the craft workshops. Craftspeople who have chosen this quiet spot to work include ceramicists, painters, engravers, potters, sculptors and weavers.

Violets on the menu
La Tanière du Loup,
Pl. de la Libération,
☎ 04 93 24 12 26.
Open daily, 10am-8pm in summer; 2-6pm out of season.

This shop specialises in violets, and has every type of violet product on offer. Crystallised natural violets, violet petal preserve – made from violets picked during the main flowering at the beginning of the year – and violet syrup. And of course, there is violet perfume, which is actually made from the leaves of the plant, not the flower.

Le Pont-du-Loup

La Confiserie des Gorges du Loup

**5 miles (8 km) W of Tourrettes-sur-Loup,
☎ 04 93 59 32 91.**
Guided visit (samples of sweets) daily, 9.30am-6.30pm; out of season, 9.30am-noon and 2-6.30pm.
Free admission.

LA FÊTE DES VIOLETTES
The festival has been held at Tourrettes-sur-Loup since 1950, on the second Sunday in March. The village is carpeted with fresh flowers and there is a parade of flowered floats, celebrating the flower from which many families earn their living. They are picked from mid-October to mid-March and are used to make bouquets, each containing 25 flowers, and confectionery. In late April and early May, the leaves are cut to sell to the factories in Grasse, which extract the fragrance used in the perfumery industry. Annual production is 150 tonnes.

Spotcheck
E3

Alpes-Maritimes

Things to do
Hiking in the Loup Gorges
Karting and hang-gliding
Canyoning in the white water
The fête des violettes (Festival of violets)
Visit to La Source Parfumée

Within easy reach
Grasse, 10 km SW, p. 248.

Tourist Office
Tourrettes-sur-Loup:
☎ 04 93 24 18 93
Le Bar-sur-Loup:
☎ 04 93 42 72 21

This confectionery factory inside an old mill looks like an Ali Baba's cave of sweets. They will explain to you how the crystallised flowers are made; 110 F for 9 oz (250 g). There are also candied clementines, 82 F for 17 oz (500 g), candied lemon peel and other Provençal sweetmeats.

Hiking in the Loup Gorges
D3 from the Pont-du-Loup.
4 hours minimum.
This deep gully was created by the river Loup cutting deep into the limestone. There are plenty of places to stop and admire the view. The **Cascade de Courmes** is a 230 ft (70 m) high waterfall, and the river at the **Saut-du-Loup** (privately owned site, paid entry) is worth seeing. At Bramafan, turn left towards Gourdon: at an altitude of 2,300 ft (700 m) there are dizzying views into the bottom of the gorge.

Le Bar-sur-Loup
A 15th-C. church and the *Danse macabre*
Altitude: 1,170 ft (350 m).

This hilltop village has long been the guardian of the Loup Gorges due to its strategic position. Pause and admire the beauty of the site from the Place de la Tour, at the foot of the castle keep. Then visit the 15th-C. Church of Saint-Jacques, which has an interesting screen and a very rare *Danse macabre* (15th-C. painting on wood), where the devil is depicted committing a host of misdeeds in the house of God. Tour the old village inside the ramparts built between the 9th and 15th C.

Karting
Funhart,
☎ **04 93 42 48 08.**
Open daily all year round.
The circuits are outdoors: 500 ft (150 m) for children; 1,166 ft (350 m) and 2,170 ft (650 m). See how fast you can go and how good a racing driver you are (50 F for 5 minutes).

Orange wine
Le Terroir Provençal shopping centre Les Jasmins, 350, Av. Amiral-de-Grasse, ☎ **04 93 42 47 93.**

Open daily, except Sun. and Mon., 9am-noon and 3-7pm.
Orange wine is a speciality of Le Bar-sur-Loup, famous for its orange trees. It is still made according to an age-old recipe, which takes a month and a half to mature. You crush and soak 5 Seville oranges, 1 sweet orange, 1 lemon, 1 mandarin, 1 vanilla bean or cinnamon stick, 2¼ lb (1 kg) sugar in 8¾ pints (5 l) of good wine and 1¾ pts of alcohol. Filter the mixture

when ready, but only on the night of a full moon! 79 F for 24 fl oz (75 cl).

La Colle-sur-Loup
Canyoning in the cascades
Séquence évasion, parc Saint-Donat-Centre UMO. Access: via D6 towards Le Bar-sur-Loup, turn off at the stadium, ☎ **04 93 32 06 93.**
Open daily, Apr.-15 Nov. Advance bookings for all levels.
Equipment supplied.

This is where you can learn about the new sport of canyoning . You will negotiate small waterfalls of not more than 17 ft (5 m) (10 years and upwards) and discover the delight of descending the steps (with ropes) down to the Cascade de Courmes (a 230 ft (70 m) drop). State instructors will remain by your side. All you need is a taste for adventure (and to like getting wet!).

Gourdon
Arts and crafts
9 miles (14 km) NE of Grasse by D3.
Gourdon is at an altitude of 2,500 ft (760 m), and there is a magnificent view from the Place de l'Église over the whole coastline, from Nice to Théoule! Perched on the edge of the cliff, 16th C. houses huddle around the château. They contain a number of crafts shops in which you can find *santons*, nougat, objects made from olive wood.

The Château
☎ 04 93 09 68 02.
Open daily, Jun.-Sep.,
11am-1pm and 2-7pm;
out of season, 2-6pm,
except Tue.
Paid admission.
The Château looks down on
the gorges from a great
height. It was built in the
9th C. by the Saracen
invaders to help them dominate the land they had won.
A protégé of Henri IV turned
it into a residence. It houses
many furnishings, weapons,
documents and paintings
from the 17th and 18th C.
Next door there is an art
museum.

The Château grounds
☎ 04 93 09 68 02.
Same opening hours as
the Château. Guided
tour by appointment.
Paid admission.
These terraced gardens are
balanced at the very edge of
a precipice with a 1,000 ft
(300 m) drop. They were
designed by Le Nôtre in the
17th C. Cross the grand
entrance and knot garden,
and you'll find a **medieval**

garden, and an Italian
garden which has recently
been renovated.

La source parfumée
Rue Principale,
☎ 04 93 09 68 23.
Open daily.
*Paid guided tour of the
flower fields, 2½ miles
(4 km) below on D3.*
This fragrant institution
dates from 1946. The
lavender, thyme, sage and
broom are gathered by hand,
as in the past, from fields
scattered through the Vallée
du Loup. There are huge
flowerbeds, and a hand-
operated distillery with
patinated copper vessels
for the various stages of
manufacture of alpine
perfumes, soaps and fragrant
candles.

GRÉOLIÈRES
**Para-gliding:
19 miles (30 km) N
of Grasse. To book,
☎ 04 93 38 25 92.
(Cumulus para-gliding
school, Cannes).**
Launch yourself into the air
at 4,300 ft (1,300 m). You
will practise on a gradual
slope, then learn how to
handle the parachute. Then
make your first flight, taking
off from six successive
points, at higher and higher
altitudes, over the Loup
Gorges. Gréolières offers
these progressive taking off
points from 1,000 ft to
4,000 ft (300 to 1,000 m).
You will feel a real sense of
achievement. There is a
one-day taster (380 F)
and up to a 6-day course
(2 400 F).

Plateau de Caussols

Watching the stars
From Gourdon
on D12.
Drive to the Plateau of
Caussols, then continue
on foot (using GR4, which
leads northwards from the
D12). This lunar landscape is
more than 4,000 ft (1,000 m)
above sea level. It has
frequently been used as a
location for filming movie
scenes that need an unusual
landscape. Above this strange
place, honeycombed with
grottoes and crevasses, the sky
is particularly clear and very
suitable for star-gazing.

Nice capital of the Côte d'Azur

The seventh-largest town in France belonged to Italy until 1860 and many of its villas have a distinctly Italian air. Down by the sea you'll notice that the promenade is English, or at least it is called the Promenade des Anglais. It was built on the initiative of early English tourists who discovered the benefits of the delightfully mild climate. Nice remained a sedate winter resort until the 1920s, but these days is very much part of the Riviera scene, whilst still retaining much of its former appeal.

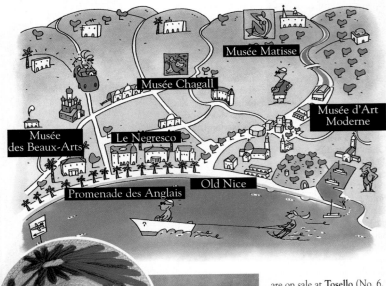

Musée Matisse

Musée Chagall

Musée d'Art Moderne

Musée des Beaux-Arts

Le Negresco

Old Nice

Promenade des Anglais

are on sale at **Tosello** (No. 6, Rue Sainte-Réparate, ☎ 04 93 85 61 95).

The markets

The most famous, the market in the Cours Saleya, is held daily and sells local flowers, vegetables and fruit. This traditional market in the heart of old Nice has a great

Shopping in old Nice

Between the Boulevard Jean-Jaurès and the port lies the old town, its narrow lanes filled with little shops and workshops. Around the Cathedral of Sainte-Réparate, craftsmen make traditional fabrics and *santons* (Rue Paradis and Rue Pont-Vieux). At No. 10, Rue Saint-Gaétan, **la maison Poilpot**

(☎ 04 93 85 60 77) still sells Eau de Nice, a mimosa-perfumed fragrance, and in the Rue de la Préfecture, the wine merchants offer you the local Bellet wine to taste. For gourmets, Nice pasta and ravioli made the old-fashioned way

Cours Saleya, in old Nice

Spotcheck
F3

Alpes-Maritimes

Things to do

The markets
Sea trips
The Phœnix park (Parc Phoenix)
The forest park of Mont-Boron
Hiking and pony-trekking
Mountain-biking, tennis and bungee-jumping
Canyoning and water-sports
The Côte d'Azur Observatory
Nice Jazz Festival
The Carnival

Within easy reach

Cagnes-sur-Mer, 5 km W, p. 258.
Monaco, 15 km NE, p. 282.
Vallée de la Vésubie, 25 km N, p. 292.

Tourist Office

Nice: ☎ 04 92 214 48 00

atmosphere filled with wonderful fragrances. (On Mondays, the food is replaced by antiques.) The fish market is also held every morning in the Place Saint-François, with fishermen auctioning off their catch of bogue, red mullet and forkbeard, all straight from the Mediterranean.

The Cathedral of Sainte-Réparate
Pl. Rossetti.
This brightly-coloured, 17th C. cathedral is dedicated to the patron saint and martyr of the city. It is topped with a dome covered in multi-coloured tiles. The brightly coloured façade was repainted in 1980. Inside, the baroque chapels are embellished with marble and stucco. The sacristy contains 18th C. panelling and carvings. The relics of St. Alexander are here, and the faithful pray to him to ask for rain during a drought.

Saint-Martin-Saint-Augustin Church
Rue Sincaire.
Luther celebrated a mass here in 1510 before he became a Protestant. Later Garibaldi, a native of Nice and founder of the Italian Republic, was baptised here in this church in 1807. The baroque decor, which includes multicoloured marble, is pretty spectacular. The choir contains a splendid 16th C. *pietà* by Louis Bréa, who has been called the 'Fra Angelico of Nice'.

Huileries des Caracoles
5, Rue Saint-François-de-Paule,
☎ 04 93 62 65 30.
Open daily except Sun., 9.30am-1pm and 2.30-6.30pm.
Free admission.
Right opposite this shop, at No. 2, Rue Saint-François-de-Paule, Napoleon set up his

headquarters in 1796. As for the shop itself, Jean-Pierre and Ginette Lopez who run it stock a wide range of typical local products, including fragrances, herbs, honey, olives, oils, 65 F for 1¾ pt (1 l). There are also bars of real Marseille soap at 16 F for 1lb 4 oz (600 g), which are available in olive or palm oil varieties.

Sea trips

**Trans Côte d'Azur,
Quai Lunel,
☎ 04 92 00 42 30.**
Open daily from Oct. to
May. Departure 3pm.
Take a sea trip eastwards at
any time of year. In one hour,
you can see the magnificent
sweep of the Baie des Anges,
Cap Ferrat and the Bay of
Villefranche. If you want to
go further afield, hop on a
boat to **Monaco** and you will
be there in 45 minutes
(departures at 10am on Mon.
and Wed., and at 9am on
Sat.; changing of the guard in
Monte Carlo is at 11.55am
daily). You can be in **San
Remo, in Italy,** in 1¾ hours
(there is a street market on
Saturdays), at the **Îles de
Lérins** in 1¼ hours (mass at
the Abbey of Saint-Honorat
is celebrated at 9am on Sun.)
or in **Saint-Tropez** in 2½
hours. Or instead, try exploring the sea-bed in the glass-
bottomed **Aquascope** boat
(☎ 04 92 00 42 30, Trans
Côte d'Azur, Quai Lunel.
From Apr. to Sep., daily,
9am-11am and 2-6pm).

Promenade des Anglais

Some might be disappointed
to find that the beach is pebbly,
but (on the other hand) it is
lined by the loveliest buildings

The Promenade des Anglais

in Nice. This palm-fringed
boulevard follows the sweep of
the Baie des Anges. Construction was financed by an
English cleric in 1820. The
grandest hotels in the town
sprang up here. They include
the **Palais de la Méditerranée**
at No. 17, the **Royal** at No. 23,
the **Westminster** at No. 27,
the **West-End** at No. 31 and
the world-renowned **Hôtel
Negresco** at No. 35, classified
as a historic monument.

Hôtel Negresco

**37, Promenade
des Anglais,
☎ 04 93 88 39 51.**
This grand hotel with its
impressive façade owes its
name to its first owner, a
Romanian. The royal reception room contains stained-
glass by Gustave Eiffel, and
the huge Baccarat crystal
chandelier was ordered by
Tsar Nicholas II. A room with
a sea view will cost from
1,300 F to 2,450 F. Try a glass
of champagne in Le Relais, to
the strains of piano music.

NICE JAZZ FESTIVAL
**The Nice Jazz Festival
is held at the Arènes
de Cimiez between
12 and 19 July
(information at the
Tourist Office,
☎ 04 92 14 48 00).
The setting is lovely
and the programme
carefully chosen.
Stars such as Joe
Cocker, Paolo Conte
or Claude Nougaro
perform alongside
up and coming
musicians. L'Escarène,
20 minutes north of
the town, holds a
baroque music festival
featuring 12th C.
organ music. From
11 July to 8 August
(information,
☎ 04 93 51 20 65).**

Musée Masséna
65, Rue de France and 35, Promenade des Anglais,
☎ **04 93 88 11 34.**
Open daily except Mon., May-Sep., 10am-noon and 3-6pm; out of season, 2-5pm.
Paid admission.
The Empire-style reception rooms are reminders of the soirées held here by the great-grandson of Maréchal Masséna, in the early 20th C. At the top of the building, Napoleon's first death mask is on display, with the Empress Josephine's fabulous tiara and her coronation robes. On the

Fragonard: *The Bathers*

The Musée Masséna

first floor, there are excellent collections of works by regional artists, and primitive art.

The Musée des Beaux-Arts
33, Av. des Baumettes,
☎ **04 92 15 28 28.**
Same opening hours as the Musée Masséna.
Paid admission.
This museum is inside a grandiose 19th C. villa, a mixture of Genoese and

Renaissance styles, which deserves to be visited as much for its architecture as for its contents. The history of French painting is traced from room to room, from Fragonard to Bonnard and includes the inventor of the modern poster hoarding, a local man, Jules Chéret. On the top floor there are beautiful sculptures by Carpeaux and Rodin.

Phœnix park
405, Promenade des Anglais,
☎ **04 93 18 03 33.**
Open daily, 9am-7pm; from mid-Oct. to mid-Mar., 9am-5pm.
Paid admission.
Take a journey through the astronomical garden, the Wadi Oasis, Mediterranean landscapes... Visit the butterfly

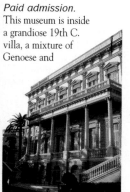

The Musée des Beaux-Arts

and insect enclosures. Then enter le Diamant Vert, a gigantic hothouse in which seven different tropical climates are reconstituted simultaneously. An unforgettable experience.

In celebration of olive oil

Mill : 334, Bd de la Madeleine,
☎ 04 93 44 45 12.
Open daily from Nov. to Feb., except Sat.
Shop: 14, Rue Saint-François-de-Paule,
☎ 04 93 85 76 92.
Closed Sun. and Mon.
Nicolas Alziari treasures his olive oil as if it were a great wine. It is pressed in the last working mill in the town, (open to the public), and is

Interior of Musée Marc-Chagall

sold in distinctive blue and gold aluminium cans. Taste the succulent olives.

The forest park of Mont-Boron

East, in the direction of Villefranche.
The park consists of 140 acres (57 ha) which were planted with Aleppo pines in 1866. There are 6¾ miles (11 km) of signposted paths, and rare species (wild orchids, lentisks, dwarf carnations, etc.) which make this lovely park a favourite with botanists and ramblers. There is a wonderful view of Saint-Jean-Cap-Ferrat in the east and the Baie des Anges in the west.

Sporting holidays

Virtually every holiday sport is catered for by the various associations – mountain-biking, horse-riding, water-sports, whitewater rafting, bungee-jumping, etc. Here are some useful addresses: Locaventure (13, Rue Fontaine-de-la-Ville, ☎ 04 9356 14 67) and Autres Terres et Espaces Sauvages (80, Rte de Grenoble, ☎ 04 93 08 15 18). The CRIJ (☎ 04 93 80 93 93) also offers many activities including sailing and wind surfing courses, tennis and canyoning throughout the Côte d'Azur. Not forgetting simple walks along the beaches.

Musée Marc-Chagall

Av. du Dr-Ménard, Bd de Cimiez,
☎ 04 93 53 87 20.
Open daily except Tue., 10am-6pm; out of season, 10am-5pm.
Paid admission.
This whole museum is dedicated to a single work of art. *The Biblical Message* by Chagall occupies the whole building, which was designed to house the series of 17 monumental paintings which compromise it. You will appreciate the power of his work in this building created especially for the purpose. The lighting is excellent. The museum also has a lovely garden.

Villa des Arènes, home of the musée Matisse

Musée Matisse

164, Av. des Arènes-de-Cimiez,
☎ 04 93 81 08 08.
Open daily except Tue., Apr.-Sep., 10am-6pm; out of season, 10am-5pm.
Paid admission.
Matisse claimed that he had found 'the necessary clarity' of light in Nice, where he lived from 1917 to 1954 in a magnificent villa, the Villa des Arènes. The museum traces Matisse's artistic development from his earliest days in 1890 to his last works. Study his *Still Life with Pomegranates* (1947) or *Nude IV*, a famous gouache découpage.

The monastery and gardens of Cimiez

Pl. du Monastère,
☎ 04 93 81 00 04.
Church open daily, 8.30am-12.30pm and 2-6.30pm.
Gardens open daily, 8am-7pm in summer; Franciscan museum open daily except Sun. and public holidays, 10am-noon and 3-6pm.
Free admission.
The Franciscan monks came here in the 16th C. and settled in the upper town. The 15th C. church of Notre-Dame-de-l'Assomption has

two cloisters, and three works of art by Louis Bréa. The Franciscan museum evokes the splendours and mysteries of the monastic life. The magnificent French-style gardens offer an exceptional view of Nice. The rose-garden flowers in May.

The Observatory of the Côte d'Azur
La Grande Corniche (dir. Menton),
☎ 04 92 00 30 11.

Guided tour (1½ hrs) Sat. at 3pm.
Paid admission.
From the top of the Grande Corniche at 1,240 ft (372 m) above sea level, the view of the city and the Baie des Anges is magical and 'the clearest sky in France' is cloudless. The observatory was inaugurated in 1881, and has three historic mirror telescopes, one of which held a world record for its 60 ft (18 m) diameter.

Thanks to this telescope, more than 2000 binary stars have so far been discovered.

Musée d'Art Moderne
Promenade des Arts,
☎ 04 93 62 61 62.
Open daily except Tue., 10am-6pm.
Paid admission (except 1st Sun. of the month).
Four glass towers linked by footbridges plunge you into the world of Yves Klein and his blue monochromes, or Christo who wraps vast swathes of the countryside or buildings in paper, or cloth. American artists are also represented, such as Andy Warhol, the 1960s icon, and Roy Lichtenstein, the pop-art guru. The terraces offer a superb view of Nice.

Maison Auer
7, Rue Saint-François-de-Paule,
☎ 04 93 85 77 98.
Open daily except Mon., 8am-12.30pm, 2.30pm-7pm. Guided tours Jan.-Feb. and Jul.-Aug. by arrangement.
Free admission.
The shop has been selling Provençal candied fruit since 1850. You can now see how they are made. The tour ends in a gift shop. A 10 oz (350 g) pot of delicious jam costs 35 F.

THE CARNIVAL

The ritual is unchanged since 1873. Every February, His Majesty King Carnival (on a float that is grander than all the others) makes his first official appearance in the streets of Nice. The celebrations begin, and carry on lasting for nearly 3 weeks. Parades of floats, large carnival heads and bands march along, interrupted by the occasional flower fight. On the last evening, the King is finally burned beside the sea shore. Each year the festival is centred around a different theme – which can vary from art, the cinema and music to sport or the circus. (See also pp. 118-119.)

Cap Ferrat
a rich man's paradise

Cap Ferrat's neighbours are the similarly wealthy Nice and Monte-Carlo. The extraordinary mildness of the winter climate, the beauty of the coast at Villefranche-sur-Mer, and the tranquillity of this peninsula has attracted the well-heeled of the world since the early 20th C.

This magnificent villa is in a superb location and it is furnished with an Ali Baba's cave of treasures. Everything is beautiful: the proportions, the decor, the furniture, the precious objects, old master paintings, tapestries, carpets. It is almost too much, but the 5,000 works of art in the museum founded in memory of Baroness Béatrice Éphrussi de Rothschild are a homage to money well spent. The Baroness wanted to commemorate her various journeys through plants and flowers. The seven gardens, from the Spanish eden to the Florentine paradise are wonderful. There is also a rose garden, a rock garden and a garden of the Muses.

Île-de-France villa and gardens
Av. Éphrussi-de-Rothschild,
☎ 04 93 01 33 09.
Open daily, Jul.-Aug., 10am-7pm; other opening hours out of season. Daily guided tours at 11.30am, 3.30pm, 4.30pm and 7.30pm. Restaurant-tea-room open from 11am.
Paid admission.

The Kérylos Greek villa
Rue Eiffel,
Beaulieu-sur-Mer,
☎ 04 93 01 01 44.
Open daily Jul.-Sept., 10.30am-7pm; 15 Feb.-11 Nov., 10.30am-12.30pm and 2-6pm; 15 Dec.-14 Feb., Mon.-Fri., 2-6pm (w.e. 10.30am-12.30pm and 2-6pm).
Paid admission.
Alexander would feel perfectly at home here. The villa is an exact replica of an ancient Greek palace, created by a

man who was a fanatical Hellenist. It contains all the elements of a Greek villa – peristyle, large reception room, marbles, frescoes, mosaics. The library contains treasures from the 6th to the 1st C. BC, and from the garden there is a wonderful view of the sea.

Grand Hôtel du Cap-Ferrat

71, Bd du Général-de-Gaulle,
☎ 04 93 76 50 50.
Closed Jan.-Feb.
This turn-of-the-century luxury hotel is surrounded by an exotic garden. Yet you can spend the day in the olympic swimming-pool, filled with sea water and kept at 86 °F (30° C) all year round, for 280 F including matresss, parasol, changing rooms and two bath towels.

Sailing lessons

École française de voile,
☎ 04 93 76 10 08.
The Cros dou Pin water-sports centre rents out all types of craft, from dinghies to catamarans, laser 420-470 yachts, craft for children, windsurfing, yachts. State-approved qualified instructors give private lessons (200 F per hour) and run courses for beginners and advanced yachtsmen (653 F, Mon.-Fri., 9am-noon).

Villefranche-sur-Mer
Saint-Pierre chapel

Quai Courbet,
☎ 04 93 76 90 70.
Open daily except Mon., 10am-noon and 4-8.30pm; other opening hours out of season.
Paid admission.
Jean Cocteau, the writer and film director who came from this region, devoted part of the year 1957 to decorating the interior of this Romanesque chapel, helped by the

ceramicists and stone-masons of Villefranche. The fishing nets covering the walls and vaulted ceiling are a reminder, according to Cocteau, that 'God also fishes for souls'.

The citadel of Saint-Elme

☎ 04 93 76 33 44.
Open daily except Tue., Sun. morning and Nov., 10am-noon and 3-6pm (until 7pm in Jul.-Aug., until 5pm in Oct.-May). Built in 1557, it was used by the army until 1965 when several museums took over. These were the **Musée d'Art et d'Histoire**, the **Goetz-Boumeester Collection** (works by Picabia, Picasso), the **24th B.C.A. Collection** (a batallion of the Chasseurs Alpins) and in the block-house, the **Fondation-Musée Volti,** a collection of the contemporary sculptor's works. (☎ 04 93 76 33 27. Open daily, except Tue. and Sun., 10am-noon and 3-7pm; out of season 10am-noon and 2-5pm).

Spotcheck
F3

Alpes_Maritimes

Things to do

Visiting the villas
Sailing lessons
Swimming at the Grand Hôtel du Cap-Ferrat

With children

Zoo and botanical garden

Within easy reach

Cagnes-sur-Mer, p. 258.
Monaco, p. 282.
Vallée de la Vésubie, p. 292.

ZOO AND BOTANICAL GARDEN

Villa des Cèdres, Ch. du Roy, ☎ 04 93 76 04 98.
Open daily 9.30am-7pm, until 5.30pm out of season. *Paid admission.*
This botanical garden is the perfect place to enjoy a walk and discover the beautiful surroundings of the peninsula. It is surrounded by magnificent villas and is planted in the former garden of King Leopold of the Belgians. It contains 12,000 species of exotic plants. The zoo next door contains 300 animals including parrots, lions, crocodiles and, most recently, bears, who live in semi-freedom amid the pines and eucalyptus.

Èze and La Turbie

reaching for the stars

These two medieval hilltop villages dominate the coast between Nice and Menton. The three coastal roads, named *Corniche* which hug the contours of the coast at varying levels with the sea down below, are glorious to drive.

Col d'Èze

Astrorama, discovering the stars

Route de la Revère, 1 mile (2 km) from the junction with the Grande Corniche, ☎ 04 93 41 23 04. Open daily, Jul.-Aug. 6.30-11pm; out of season, Tue. and Fri., 5.30-10pm (until 11pm Apr.-Sep.). *Paid admission.*
You can almost touch the stars here, 2,166 ft (650 m) above sea level. You'll experience an incredible sensation of infinity with the sea glittering far below you, you gaze up into the night sky from the terrace of the Astrorama to study the stars with the aid of the powerful binoculars and telescopes supplied. Star-gazing on a clear night in such a beautiful setting will be an unforgettable experience for everyone.

Trip to La Revère fort

Access from the Col d'Èze.
The fort is not open to the public but it offers a spectacular view of the sea 2,666 ft (800 m) below, and the landscape of the Corniche. Head towards the Astrorama: the fort is ½ mile (1 km) further on, a natural beauty spot and lookout post. The area was swept by a forest fire in 1986, as is explained at the **Maison de la Nature** (Open Wed. 1pm-5pm or by appointment, ☎ 04 93 18 51 42).

Èze-Village

The Friedrich-Nietzsche path

At the end of the Av. du Jardin-Exotique.
Friedrich Nietzsche conceived the second part of his work, *Thus spoke Zarathustra* here beneath the pines and olive trees. Take the path which will lead you down to the lower Corniche (1hr) and the resort of Èze-Bord-de-Mer. After taking a swim, return the way you came, i.e. upwards, since Nietzsche was struck with inspiration while climbing up this little path.

Galimard soap works

Pl. de Gaulle,
☎ 04 93 41 10 70.
Open daily 8.30am-
6.30pm; Nov.-Mar.,
9am-12.30pm and
2-6pm.
Free admission.
The famous Grasse perfumery,
Galimard, has its soap works
here. You can watch soaps of
every colour, every scent and
every shape being made at
this small factory which uses
some of the most delicate fragrances. The soap is moulded
while warm,
then baked
like a
cake.

La Turbie

Le Trophée des Alpes

11¼ miles (18 km) NE
of Nice. Av. Albert-ler,
☎ 04 93 41 20 84.
Daily, except public
holidays, Apr.-Jun.
9.30am-6pm; Jul.-Sep.
9.30am-7pm; Oct.-
March 9.30am-5pm.
Paid admission.

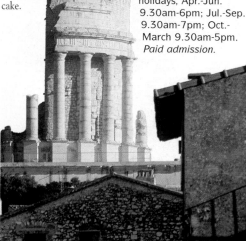

Spotcheck
F3

Alpes_Maritimes

Things to do

The Exotic Garden
Nietzsche's path
The Galimard Soap works

With children

Astrorama

Within easy reach

Monaco, 7 km E, p. 282.
Roquebrune, 12 km NE,
p. 288.

Tourist Office

Èze: ☎ 04 93 41 26 00

The Trophy of the Alps (Le
Trophée des Alpes) marks the
frontier which separated Gaul
from Italy 2,000 years ago.
This gigantic monument was
originally topped with a statue of the Roman emperor,
and was built in the year
6 BC to mark the victory of
Augustus over the Ligurians.
It gives the impression that
the might of Rome was
indeed invincible. In 21 centuries it has only lost a quarter of its original height and is
still 126 ft (38 m) high.

EXOTIC GARDENS

4 miles (6 km) E Nice via N7 ☎ 04 93 41 10 30.
Open daily in summer and school holidays,
9am-8pm; out of season,
9am-noon and 2-6pm.
**Do you know what
'Mother-in-law's
Cushions' are? They are
just one species out of
the hundreds of cacti
and succulents that pop-
ulate this hilltop garden.
At an altitude of 1,333
ft (400 m), rare plants
are cultivated around
the ruins of an old
château on the clifftop.**

A glimpse of Monaco

This is a countryside rich in
panoramas, but you shouldn't
miss the view of Monaco,
which you'll find on the road
from La Turbie. You'll see the
whole of this tiny but world-
famous principality. As you
leave La Turbie in the direction of Monaco, take the
Tête-de-Chien road on your
left. There is a small parking
area at the end, and behind
the rocks (go round them on
the right-hand side), you suddenly have a ringside view of
the whole coastline.

The Paillons Basin
the back of beyond

Nnorth of Nice, the three branches of the River Paillon converge before they enter the city. These rivers run through the valleys and mountains of the hinterland, passing by delightful medieval villages clinging to the mountainside. Explore their narrow lanes and baroque churches and you might be lucky enough to hear a few words of Nissard, the Nice *patois* which is still spoken in these more rural parts of the region.

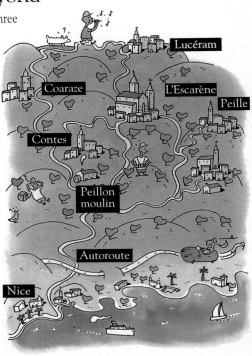

Coaraze
Sundials
16 miles (25 km) N of Nice by D15. Altitude: 2,100 ft (640 m).
Coaraze is reputed to be the sunniest village in France and as proof six huge ceramic sundials indicate the time. The most famous of these is on the front of the town hall, and was created by Jean Cocteau who particularly loved this 14th C. village, set in a landscape of olive and chestnut trees.

Lucéram
The Shepherds' Christmas
16 miles (26 km) NE of Nice by D2566. Altitude: 2,270 ft (680 m).
A tower and a few crenellated walls are all that remain of the ramparts which surrounded this 13th C. village, built on a limestone outcrop.

Gothic houses huddle around the church and vaulted passageways. The Church of **Sainte-Marguerite** contains an exceptional set of five 15th C. altar screens and a treasury containing 40 exhibits. The Shepherds' Christmas is celebrated here every year.

L'Escarène
Baroque church
12½ miles (20 km) NE of Nice by D2566.
This village lies on the ancient salt road that once linked Nice to Turin. It has a huge 17th C. baroque church, surrounded by 2 chapels. The façade resembles that of Nice cathedral. The church also holds its own festival.

The village of Peillon

Peille
Altar screen and museum
9 miles (15 km) S of L'Escarène by D53. Altitude: 2,000 ft (600 m).

The nearby ruins of the 14th C. château of the Counts of Provence is evidence of how important this village once was. The church has a well-preserved 16th C. screen. Most streets lead to the arcaded **Place de la Colle**. Visit the little **Musée du Terroir** (☎ 04 93 91 90 54. Open Jun.-Sep., Wed., Sat. and Sun., 2.30-6.30pm; out of season, 2-6pm at weekends).

Peillon
Frescoes of the Penitents
9 miles (14 km) S of Peille by D21. Altitude: 1,200 ft (370 m).

Nothing has changed since the Middle Ages in this little village on a narrow rocky spur. It is a maze of flights of steps and covered passages. The **Chapel of the Pénitents-Blancs**, at the entrance to the village, is decorated with 15th C. frescoes, and the baroque Church of **Saint-Sauveur** contains works of art.

Contes
A forge and a mill
Contes, Quartier Le Martinet, on the D15. Town hall, ☎ 04 93 79 00 01.

Open Sat., 9.30am-noon and 2.30-5pm.

The old hydraulic forge at the foot of the hilltop village of Contes is still intact and is now classified as a historic monument. It is driven by the waters of the River Paillon. Next to this delightful museum there is an old olive oil mill which has also been thoughtfully restored.

Mont Agel
Golf course
3 miles (5 km) N of La Turbie, Rte de Peille, via D153, ☎ 04 93 41 09 11. Open daily all year round. This 18-hole golf course is over 5,000 yards long (4,575 m) and covers 200 acres (84 ha) at an altitude of 2,700 ft (800 m).

Spotcheck
F3

Alpes_Maritimes

Things to do
Baguette and Snail festivals
Golf course

With children
Shepherds' Christmas

Within easy reach
Monaco, 25km S, p. 282.
Vallée de la Vésubie, 25 km N, p. 292.

Tourist Office
Contes: ☎ 04 93 79 13 99
Coaraze: ☎ 04 93 79 37 47

If you play on it you'll find yourself on the top of Mont Agel, the highest point on the coast.

BAGUETTES AND SNAIL FESTIVALS

On the first Sunday in September, the Fête des Baguettes is held in Peille. On that day, young girls offer their sweethearts a little beribboned baguette, in memory of a sorcerer who was given such a baguette by the daughter of the local lord, with a promise of marriage if he could find water for the drought-ridden village. In June, the Snail Procession lights up Coaraze, Lucéram and Levens. At nightfall, the villagers fill snail shells with oil, set fire to them and thus mark out the route of the ritual procession of the Fête-Dieu.

Monaco home of the Grimaldis

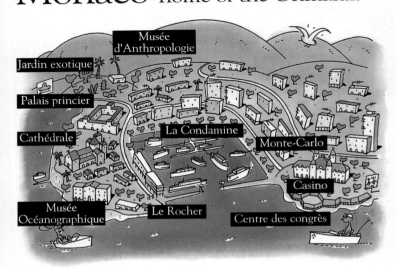

Jardin exotique

Musée d'Anthropologie

Palais princier

Cathédrale

La Condamine

Monte-Carlo

Casino

Musée Océanographique

Le Rocher

Centre des congrès

This tiny sovereign state is completely surrounded by French territory and covers just over 12 square miles (19 km²) of a rocky outcrop known as Le Rocher (the rock). The setting is magnificent and the climate particularly mild. It also has the advantage of a having a ruling prince whose family regularly supplies the gossip columns of the prurient French press with details of their sensational private lives, another reason for the attention which is paid to this small principality, out of all proportion to its size. There is always plenty to see and do in Monaco.

The geography of Monaco

The principality of Monaco consists of Monaco-Ville (that is, the rock) and Monte-Carlo. These towns stand side by side and are linked by the Quartier de la Condamine, where luxury yachts are moor-ed. Monaco, capital of the Principality, is built on a rocky ledge at a height of 200 ft (60 m) above the sea. It covers an area of just 1,200 ft (300 m) by 2,700 ft (800 m) and contains the tightly packed houses of the old town, as well as the famous princely palace, home of the Grimaldi family, Prince Rainier, and his children whose mother was the late Princess Grace.

Wandering through the old town

Wander through the narrow lanes of the medieval city and its many covered passageways. During your walk, stop to look at the Chapelle de la Paix (chapel of peace), in the gardens beside the Place de la

The princely palace

Visitation, then go on to the little Place Bosio, dedicated to a Monegasque sculptor. The Place Saint-Nicolas contains a fountain topped by a statue. The Rampe Major (1714), paved in red brick and protected by two gates, links the Condamine to the Place du Palais. If you are in search of a quiet spot, try the Saint-Martin gardens, overlooking the sea.

THE PRACTICAL SIDE

You have to buy Principality of Monaco stamps for your postcards and the local currency is accepted throughout the neighbouring French *département* of the Alpes-Maritimes, but French francs and the euro are also legal tender here. It is a good idea to leave your car in one of the Principality's paid parking lots and take the bus. In any case, access to Le Rocher is only permitted for vehicles with Monaco or Alpes-Maritimes numberplates. The town has many lifts, however, for those who are daunted by the climb to the top of the rock.

The princely Palace
☎ 00 377 93 25 18 31. Open daily, Jun.-Sep., 9.30am-6.10pm, Oct. 10am-5pm. Closed Nov.-May. Guided tours in 4 languages (French, English, Italian, German), leave every 5 minutes. *Paid admission.*

Join the large crowd to watch the daily changing of the guard which protects the princely palace (daily, 11.55am at the palace). The ceremony is full of local colour. You can also visit the interior of the palace during which you'll see a series of magnificent reception rooms, a beautiful throne room, the Italian gallery, and a courtyard in front of the entrance paved with coloured cobble-

stones. The palace also contains a collection of more than 1,000 items which belonged to Napoleon, including his distinctive hats, as well as gloves, flags, autographs and souvenirs of his exile on Saint-Helena.

Mass at the cathedral
Av. Saint-Martin, ☎ 00 377 93 30 87 70. Open daily, 7.30am-6pm (6.45pm in summer). Mass is sung by the Petits Chanteurs de Monaco every Sun. at 10.30am, all year round except Jul.-Aug. *Free admission.*

The cathedral was built in the late 19th C. in a rather clumsy neo-Romanesque style. It contains the tomb of Grace Kelly, the former American

Spotcheck
F3

Alpes-Maritimes

Things to do

Oceanographic museum (Musée Océanographique) Exotic garden of Monaco (Jardin exotique de Monaco)

Within easy reach

Nice, 15 km SW, p. 270.
Cap Ferrat, 11 km SW, p. 276.
Èze, 7 km SW, p. 278.

Tourist Office

Monaco:
☎ 00 377 92 16 61 16

The cathedral, built of white La Turbie limestone

film star and wife of Prince Rainier, which helps to explain the popularity of the building. However, beside the left-hand entrance to the ambulatory there is a beautiful 16th C. altar screen portraying St. Nicolas, by the painter Louis Bréa.

Oceanographic Museum

Av. Saint-Martin,
☎ **00 377 93 15 36 00.**
Open daily, Jul.-Aug., 9am-8pm; Apr.-Jun. and Sept., 9am-7pm; Nov.-Feb., 10am-6pm; Oct.-Mar. 9.30am-7pm. Guided tours for children by appointment. *Paid admission.*

This world-famous museum is worth a trip to Monaco in itself. The museum was founded in the early 20th C. by Prince Albert I. It has 90 tanks containing 6000 fish of 370 species from all over the world. A living coral reef, imported from the Red Sea, consists of 70 species of coral. The highlight of the museum is the Whale Room, where the skeletons of these ocean giants are exhibited. Jacques Cousteau, the famous French marine explorer, ran the museum from 1957 to 1988 and made important contributions to it.

Museum of Prehistory and Anthropology

Entrance through the Exotic Garden,
☎ **00 377 93 15 80 06.**

Open daily, 9am-6pm; until 5pm in winter; 7pm in summer. *Paid admission (ticket combined with the Exotic Garden).* Founded by Prince Albert I and inaugurated in 1902, it contains collections of prehistoric artefacts discovered in the Grimaldi caves on the Franco-Italian border.

Jardin exotique de Monaco

Exotic Garden of Monaco, 62, Bd du Jardin-Exotique,
☎ **00 377 93 30 33 65.**

Open daily, 15 May-15 Sep., 9am-7pm; out of season, until 5.30pm or 6pm. *Paid admission.* This cliffside garden contains an impressive array of cacti and succulents from Africa and North, Central and South America, including aloes from the Cape and giant century plants from the Aztec plateaux. The influence of the Mediterranean sea, the angle of the cliff and the

The monumental façade of the Oceanographic Museum

FESTIVALS OF SAINT-JEAN

On 23 June, on the eve of the midsummer festival of Saint-Jean, the Monégasques gather in front of the Palace. There are performances by ensembles of singers, dancers and musicians in traditional costume. The royal family attends mass in the Palace chapel. After the ceremony, two footmen from the royal house, in full livery, light a bonfire prepared in the middle of the Palace courtyard. The next day the festival moves to Monte-Carlo.

orientation of the site offer ideal conditions for desert flora, which are represented here in their thousands.

The history of a dynasty

Monte-Carlo Story,
☎ 00 377 93 25 32 33.
Daily, multivision show at 2pm, 3pm, 4pm and 6pm. *Paid admission.*
Right by the Oceanographic Museum, a *son et lumière* performance traces the history of the previous princes of Monaco.
The **Musée de Cire** (waxworks)
(27, Rue Basse,
☎ 00 377 93 30 39 05,
open daily, 9am-6pm in summer; 10am-5pm out

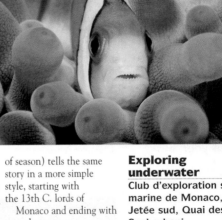

Statue of St. Nicholas in the Place Saint-Nicolas

of season) tells the same story in a more simple style, starting with the 13th C. lords of Monaco and ending with the present day ruler of the principality.

Exploring underwater

Club d'exploration sous-marine de Monaco,
Jetée sud, Quai des Sanbarbani,
☎ 00 377 92 05 91 78.
Open all year round, daily in summer, at w.e. out of season.
The sea around Monaco is an invitation to underwater exploration – you will see conger eels, squid, crabs and crayfish. Try a scuba-dive (150 F inclusive) or take lessons. All levels catered for.

Monte-Carlo luxurious showcase

Monte-Carlo is run by the powerful Société des Bains de Mer which manages its hotels and its casino. It is a mixture of ancient and ultramodern architectural styles, and its flower-decked terraces, skyscrapers, villas and boutiques represent the ultimate in glamour and style. It also provides the backdrop for many world-famous sporting events.

The Garnier Room

Situated next door to the gaming rooms of the casino, this hall was designed by Charles Garnier, the architect of the Paris Opéra. The design was ahead of its time (there is no balcony and the floor is rectangular) and some of the world's greatest singers have performed here. It is hard to obtain tickets for a performance because there are only 600 seats.

The gilded Garnier Room

Place your bets

Casino,
☎ 00 377 92 16 21 21.
Paid and controlled admission.
The world-famous casino, built between 1878 and 1910, has seen many fortunes come and go. The interior decoration is worth a look but you will have to pay to visit the gaming-rooms. You may just want to see the hall or enjoy the gardens and the splendid view from the terrace of the casino. In the Café de Paris, however, entry to the very modern gaming-rooms is free.

They offer American gambling (from 5pm), American roulette, blackjack and video-poker (from 10pm).

Prince Rainier's cars

Les terrasses de Fontvieille,
☎ 00 377 92 05 28 56.
Open daily, 10am-6pm.
Paid admission.
Prince Rainier assembled a collection of 100 cars in a 30-year period. They include a 1903 De Dion Bouton, a 1986 Lamborghini Countach, a 1929 Bugatti, a Citroën Torpedo de la Croisière and a 1952 Rolls Royce.

Sporting events

The Monte-Carlo Rally, held in January, is the main event of the World Championships. In April, the Monte-Carlo Tennis Open is the first hard court tournament of the season. In May, the **Grand Prix** is held on a circuit right in the town centre opened by Anthony Noghès. In July, the football season starts with the French football championship. Information at the Office de Tourisme.

Spotcheck
F3

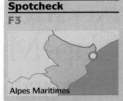

Alpes Maritimes

Things to do
Water-skiing and jet-skiing
Parascending
Monte Carlo Country Club
The Japanese garden

Within easy reach
Nice, 15 km SW, p. 270.
Èze, 7 km W, p. 278.

Tourist Office
Monaco:
☎ 00 377 92 16 61 16

Japanese garden

Av. Princesse-Grace,
Open 9am till dusk.
Paid admission.
Designed by the landscape architect Yasuo Beppu, this garden laid out on 75,348 sq. ft (7,000 m^2) alongside the Mediterranean has been blessed by a leading shinto priest. Pines and olive trees are shaped and pruned according to the tradition of the Land of the Rising Sun, and waterfalls and ornamental lakes are embellished with specially-shaped islets.

L'Hermitage

Sq. Beaumarchais,
☎ 00 377 92 16 40 00.
In contrast with the impressive Hôtel de Paris, L'Hermitage has a more homely style. This tiny, ancient inn is situated amid olive and orange groves. The decor of the winter garden is still Belle Époque. Since the turn of the last century the hotel has been a favourite with people of standing and remains a favourite with royals and the wealthy.

PARASCENDING
Monte Carlo Beach (SBM), Av. Princesse-Grace, Saint-Roman,
☎ 04 93 28 66 66.
Open Apr.-Oct., daily, 8am-8pm.
Parascending will give you a soaring sensation as you silently fly – at a height of 167 to 1,000 ft (50 to 300 m) – over the calm sea, in complete safety. From 250 F to 350 F for a 10 min flight (from 6 years old).

Water-skiing and jet-skiing

Ski Vol, Plage du Larvotto,
☎ 00 377 93 50 86 45.
Open May-Sep., daily, 9am-8pm.
Water-skiing (170 F/10 min) or a jet-ski trip (250 F/20 min, driving licence compulsory) will give you the opportunity to travel past the beaches of the Larvotto, far away from the crowds.

Saint-Roman

Country club

Monte-Carlo Country Club, Av. Princesse-Grace,
☎ 04 93 41 30 15.
Open all year round, daily, 8am-8pm.
This meeting-place of the Monte Carlo smart set has 21 hard courts and an 83 ft (25 m) swimming pool (open May-Oct.): 250 F per person per day. Jacuzzi and sauna.

Roquebrune, Cap-Martin and Beausoleil the upper classes

Roquebrune lies between Monaco and Menton, at an altitude of 1200 ft (300 m) above sea level. This old village clinging to the cliff once belonged to the Principality of Monaco. Cap-Martin lies at its foot beside the sea and is reserved for the homes and gardens of Monaco high society. Mont Agel protects them from the north wind, creating a unique microclimate. There is never any mist or fog and the average annual temperature is 62.6 °F (17 °C).

Roquebrune

Church of Sainte-Marguerite
Open 3-6pm.
The church was restored in the 17th C. and its baroque interior includes three gilded wooden altars, two paintings and a statue of Our Lady of the Snows, who saved Roquebrune from a plague epidemic in the 15th C. There is also a very faithful copy of Michaelangelo's *The Last Judgement*, of which the original is in the Sistine Chapel in Rome.

Ancient olive tree and procession
Ch. de Menton.
This amazing tree is said to be 4000 years old and is a world-famous phenomenon. If the Provençal calculations are correct, its trunk, whose diameter is 40 ft (10 m), would have been seen by Bronze Age man. The little chapel of la Pausa close by is the starting point for a big annual procession, held on 5 August, during which the whole village mimes scenes from the Passion of Christ. The tradition dates from 1467.

Carolingian fortress
Pl. William-Ingram,
☎ 04 93 35 07 22.
Open daily, except Fri. in winter, 10am-12.30pm and 3pm-5.30pm (until 7pm in summer). Closed 12 Nov.-20 Dec.
Paid admission.

This austere fortress at the top of the village merges into the shape of the rock on which it stands. See the 12th C. keep, and admire the simple decoration of the rooms on the upper floors, most of which were added in the 15th C. The main room is open to the sky and there is a prison, an armoury, and kitchen. Some spectacular views.

Cap Martin

Walking round Cap Martin

Departure Av. Winston-Churchill (parking beneath the Grand Hôtel). Time: 4 hours round trip.

The walk is also called the **promenade Le Corbusier**, because the famous architect built a little 150 sq. ft (14 m²) prototype of what he considered to be the ideal holiday home (interesting guided tour on Tues. at 9.30am, book at the Office de Tourisme,

☎ 04 93 35 62 87). Follow the steep, wild contours of Cap Martin which lead to Monte Carlo, passing some beautiful estates on the way. Magnificent Mediterranean flora.

Mont Gros on foot or by mountain bike

Detailed routes from the Office de Tourisme.

This 2,290 ft (686 m) peak dominates Cap Martin. By mountain bike the trip will take around one hour, by foot it will be nearer two. Follow the GR52 signposted in white and red, called Balcons de la Côte d'Azur, then the Chemin

de la Coupière and the track on the left through the arboretum. Mountain-bikers should depart from the place de Gorbio, about 6 miles (10 km) N of Roquebrune, and continue following the red-and-white markers. You are advised to consult a map before you go.

Beausoleil

Prehistoric camp on the Mont des Mules

Access from the La Turbie road (D53).

The temperature never drops below 50 °F (10 °C), thanks to the shelter afforded by Mont Agel. The first humans to benefit from this little paradise were prehistoric. Climb to the camp on the Mont des Mules where the Ligurians also spent happy days 2,000 years ago, among the migrating birds and tropical vegetation.

Windsurfing

Base nautique (Promenade Robert-Schuman),
☎ **04 93 57 33 59.**
Daily.

This water-sports centre offers training courses (2 hours per day, 650 F), as well as lessons

on weekdays (beginners and advanced, 120 F per hour). The equipment can also be hired (250 F for 5 hours). Reservations are required.

PARAGLIDING

Aérial, Roquebrune-Cap-Martin,
☎ **06 07 93 77 77.**
400 F per flight.
At an altitude of 2,290 ft (686 m), the takeoff platform at Mont Gros dominates the whole coast. Take to the air for the first time with an instructor, or fly alone if you are experienced. But don't forget to keep an eye on the Pointe de Cabbé, the landing spot, down below. The indescribable feeling of being a birdman is enhanced by the crystal-clear air, which is the purest in Europe.

Menton

This lovely town earned itself the nickname 'the pearl of France' back in the 19th C., and indeed it was once a favourite resort of royal families throughout Europe. Nowadays, it offers pleasant strolls through its port and pedestrianised streets and with its terraced gardens, orange and lemon groves, you can tell that Italy is close by.

Church of Saint-Michel

Saint-Michel dominates the town, surrounded by sun-drenched roofs, ancient terraced walls, and massive doors and gateways. It has a pastel-coloured façade and overlooks the sea. This typically baroque church, whose bell-tower is covered in varnished roof-tiles, contains a handsome 17th C. organ.

Its side-chapels contain the tombs of the great families of the town. As you leave, follow the Quai Bonaparte. It runs beside the beach on one side and on the other it clings to the old town, extending into the aptly-named Promenade du Soleil. On the way, stop briefly at the port, which is enclosed between the Impératrice-Eugénie and Napoleon III piers. At the end of the latter, there is a wonderful view over the whole town of Menton.

Jean Cocteau: Fawn playing the flute

In the footsteps of Jean Cocteau

The marriage room of the **town hall** has furniture and paintings signed by the 'prince of poets' (open daily, 8.30am-noon and 1.30pm-5pm. Closed Sat. and Sun. ☎ 04 92 10 50 00. Paid admission). Further along above the pier is the **Musée Cocteau** (☎ 04 93 57 72 30. Open daily except Tue., 10am-noon and 2pm-6pm. Paid admission). As an

PALAIS CARNOLÈS

☎ 04 93 35 49 71.
Same opening hours as the Musée Cocteau.
Free admission.
This museum is just outside old Menton, in the middle of the Colombières garden, one of the loveliest gardens in the town. The house, built in 1717, contains a handsome series of rooms. But the key to the Palais Carnolès is its beautiful garden, created by Ferdinand Bac, designer of the most beautiful parks on the Côte d'Azur.

honorary citizen of Menton, Cocteau insisted that the building be converted into a museum to house his work.

Lemon festival in the Biovès gardens

Daily visit to the gardens.
Free admission.
Behind the seafront casino, the Biovès gardens are strung together in a row. They offer a lovely walk among palm trees, flowerbeds and orange trees. Every February since 1934, Menton celebrates its lemons here. Decorated floats covered with citrus fruit parade along the Corso, each Sunday in the month, and

innovative decorators create monuments in which lemons are used instead of stones.

Garavan

The Beverly Hills of Menton lies between the old town and the Italian frontier. Wander around and dream of what it must be like to own one of these luxury villas. Typical of seaside resorts in the South of France, they were built for the privileged few who chose Menton as their country retreat.

Exotic garden of Val-Rameh

Av. Saint-Jacques,
☎ 04 93 35 86 72.
Open daily, except Tue., 10am-noon and 3pm-6pm in summer.
Paid admission.

Spotcheck
F3

Alpes-Maritimes

Things to do

Lemon festival
Exotic garden
Menton market

Within easy reach

Cap Ferrat, 20 km SW, p. 276.
Èze, 16 km SW, p. 278.
Haute Vallée de la Roya, 20 km N, p. 296.

Tourist Office

Menton: ☎ 04 92 41 76 76

This garden, nestling in the Bay of Garavan, and created in the 19th C., benefits from a particularly mild microclimate. Its terraces groan under the weight of citrus fruits, banana trees, Japanese bamboos, hibiscus and passion flowers.

At the market

Every morning, the market is held in a hall decorated with ceramic tiles and grimacing masks, built in 1896. The local stallholders offer local specialities, such as la *pichade* (a sort of pizza), la *socca*, la *panisse* (a chick-pea flour fritter) and sweet *fougasse* (hearthbread), as well as fruit and vegetables. Nearby in the Place aux Herbes, an **antiques** market is held on Fridays.

A villa at Garavan

The Vallée de la Vésubie

gorges and waterfalls

The upper valley of the Vésubie is one of the prettiest in the Nice hinterland. From Saint-Martin-Vésubie to Saint-Jean-la-Rivière, streams cascade from mountain peaks, disappearing into deep gorges before joining the Var, which takes them to the sea. This natural route between the Alpine peaks and the Mediterranean offers a range of climates.

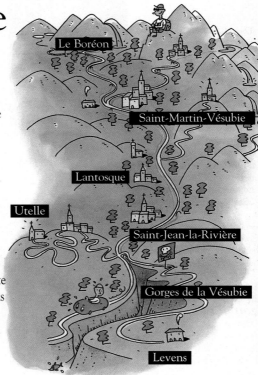

Le Boréon

Saint-Martin-Vésubie

Lantosque

Utelle

Saint-Jean-la-Rivière

Gorges de la Vésubie

Levens

and collecting the snow in winter. The 17th C. church contains a 14th C. black wooden Madonna, dressed in lace, who is traditionally taken up to her mountain sanctuary every summer. This is the Madonna of Fenestre.

Nearby
Vale of the Madonna de Fenestre
8 miles (13 km) NE of Saint-Martin-de-Vésubie via D94.

Saint-Martin-Vésubie

Medieval village
40 miles (60 km) N of Nice.
This village at 3,200 ft (960 m), serves as the ideal starting point for summer excursions into the mountains (*see following pages*). Some of the houses are Gothic, and the Rue du Docteur-Cagnoli has a central canal which is used for washing the street in summer

Emblem over the town hall, Saint-Martin-de-Vésubie

Spotcheck
F2

Alpes-Maritimes

Things to do

Hiking round the lakes
Canyoning and mountain-climbing
See the waterfalls
Artists' workshops

Within easy reach

Nice, p. 270.
Parc du Mercantour, p. 306.

Tourist Office

Saint-Martin-Vésubie:
☎ 04 93 03 21 28

Here, at 6,300 ft (1,900 m) the Madonna of Saint-Martin-de-Vésubie takes up her summer quarters between the last Saturday in June and the second Sunday in September.

THE PRALS LAKES

This easy 4-hour circular walk starts from the Vale of the Madonna de Fenestre. It is best attempted between May and November. Follow signposts 361 to 367, then 359 to 361. You go deep into Mercantour park, skirting the lakes. A rushing torrent pours through the Alpine meadows which you follow upwards for 1,700 ft (500 m). The water temperature is 55°F (13°C). Stop before you get to the sanctuary at signpost 361, and take the large horizontal path leading into the larch forest. Don't forget to buy local cheese from the Fenestre dairies on the way!

Drive to the sanctuary, then leave on foot to climb to the **Gélas summit** (10,500 ft (3,143 m). The climb will take around four hours and is really only recommended for experienced climbers with the correct equipment (Information and mountain guides are available from the Guides de la Vésubie, ☎ 04 93 03 26 60, or Guides du Mercantour, ☎ 04 93 03 31 32). If you do not have the right footwear, just walk as far as the meadows encircling the peak. This road will be full of pilgrims on 15 August and 8 September.

The forest of Boréon

5 miles (8 km) N of Saint-Martin-Vésubie via D89.
This Alpine forest of pines, firs, spruce and larches is even

higher at 4,900 ft (1,473 m) A **waterfall** drops 130 ft (40 m) into a narrow gorge, and the little lake at the bottom reflects the colour of the sky. The varied flora comprises many rare plants. This is a good place for longer hikes (*see following pages*).

Hiking around the Besson lakes

From the upper-level parking area at Boréon, via D189.
Time: 5½ hrs round trip.
Best season: Jun.-Nov.
Follow signposts 420 to 424 (outward leg).
A fairly strenuous, but unforgettable hike. Drive up to a height of more than 8,300 ft (2,500 m) to the 'twin' lakes (*bessons*), whose clear waters contain trout. At the end of the D189, east of Boréon, park your car (signpost 420) and take the wide path that follows the left bank of the vale. If you leave early in the morning, take a good pair of binoculars to be able to spot chamois and mouflons.

Musée des Traditions

Z. A. du Pra d'Agout,
Saint-Martin-Vésubie,
☎ 04 93 03 32 72.
Open in summer and
school holidays, except
Tue., 2.30pm-6.30pm;
w.e. and public holidays,
3pm-6pm.
Paid admission.
Leaf through the pages of
local history in this commu-
nal mill, which was
also the first elec-
tric power station
in the region. Pick
up facts and infor-
mation about daily
life in the highlands in
the 19th C., religious
beliefs, the rural environment, agricultural produce
and the arrival of the tram.
One of the mill's grindstones
still works in this living museum and the electric turbines
have recently been restored.

*Roquebillière and
Belvédère*

Waterfalls

The Gothic church of
Roquebillière (1533), on the
right bank of the river, contains rich furnishings and two
18th C. sculpted altar screens.
Further up, on the opposite
bank, the aptly named village
of Belvédère stands on both
banks and overlooks the

Valley of Gordolasque.
Take the scenic D171 to the
Ray waterfall, 4 miles (7 km)
further on, and at the end of
the road walk along the
½ mile (1 km) footpath
to the spectacular **Estrech
waterfall**.

The
grocery in
Lantosque
*sells the dried meat
and cheeses for which the
region is famous*

Lantosque

Souvenirs of Austria

Below 1,700 ft (500 m), the
valley becomes more
accessible, richer and lusher.
Many of the villagers are
called Otto, a name first
imported by the Austrian
soldiers who came here in the
18th C., then again by
Austrian workmen who came
to dig the Vésubie canal in
the 19th C. The 17th C.
Church of Saint-Sulpice
contains a piece of repoussé
leather depicting the birth of
the Virgin, an extremely rare
and precious item.

CANYONING AND MOUNTAIN-CLIMBING

**Bureau des guides
professionnels, rue
Cagnoli, Saint-Martin-
Vésubie
☎ 04 93 03 26 60
or 04 93 03 51 60.
If you want to discover
the region most like
Switzerland closest to
Nice, go with a guide.
In season, guides and
companions of the
Haute Vésubie will
design a personalised
hiking route for you,
and will teach you rock-
climbing and glacier-
climbing, or discover
canyoning with them. In
winter, they will take
you cross-country on
skis or snow-shoes.
Every level and every
distance is catered for.
Basic daily rate: 850 F
with a companion or
1,200 F with a guide.**

*The Gorges of
the Vésubie*

Magnificent sight

When a torrent encounters
limestone rock, it digs into
it. Follow the D2565
between Saint-Jean-la-
Rivière and Pont-Durandy,
which follows the bottom of
these extraordinary gorges,

and look up. The colour of the sides of the gorge varies over hundreds of feet, between pure white and a thousand and one shades of grey, streaked with green vegetation which turns red in the autumn. Drivers, however, shouldn't take their eyes off the road, or at least they should stop before doing so, as the road is dangerously narrow in places.

Utelle
In the footsteps of Masséna
6 miles (9 km) W of Saint-Jean-la-Rivière via D32. Altitude: 2,700 ft (800 m).
This medieval mountain village has been wonderfully preserved due to its isolation. Count the very tight bends on the access road and admire the wonderful view of the valley. Not far from the **Church of Saint-Véran** (17th C. sculpted altar screens), the GR5 joins the **Brec d'Utelle** at 5,300 ft (1,606 m), a slope of 1,700 ft (500 m). The 1½ hour walk follows in the footsteps of Masséna as he pursued the Austrian army. Hiking boots should be worn.

Utelle sanctuary
4 miles (6 km) SW of Utelle via D132.
For more than 1,000 years, Notre-Dame-des-Miracles has been used as a place of worship in this beautiful setting. Don't miss the incredible views from the chapel of the snow-covered Alps to the north, the Esterel in the south-west and the Mediterranean in the far distance. Drivers beware, as the access road is very narrow and full of hairpin bends.

Duranus
Le Saut-des-Français
3 miles (5 km) S of Saint-Jean-la-Rivière by D19.
At the place called Le Saut-des-Français, a plaque marks the actions of the *barbets* in 1793. The *barbets* were young men who refused to be conscripted into the Revolutionary army who threw the Republican soldiers they captured into the ravine 1,000 ft (300 m) below.

Levens
Artists' tools
8 miles (13 km) S of Saint-Jean-la-Rivière by D19. Workshop, ☎ 04 93 79 73 62 (visits by appointment). Showroom at the Maison du Portal, 1, Pl. V.-Masseglia, ☎ 04 93 79 85 84.
Open daily in summer, 10am-noon, 2.30pm-6.30pm; out of season, Sat.-Sun. and public holidays, 2.30pm-5.30pm. Jean-Pierre Augier has been collecting Provençal farm implements for 25 years and turns them into attractive figurative sculptures. This gives recycling a whole new meaning.

The Haute Vallée de la Roya the road to Italy

The Upper Valley of the Roya, on the eastern side of the Nice hinterland, did not become French until 1947. When the county of Nice was attached to France in 1860, Napoleon III did not want to deprive the king of Italy of his favourite hunting ground! The medieval architecture, religious paintings and rock engravings of this unspoiled landscape will be a revelation, and the highlight will be the Vallée des Merveilles.

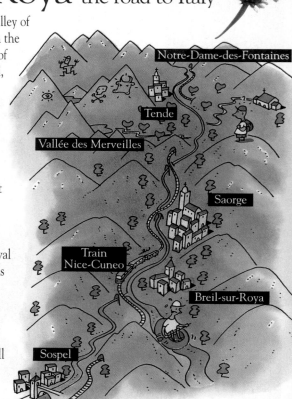

Notre-Dame-des-Fontaines

Tende

Vallée des Merveilles

Saorge

Train Nice-Cuneo

Breil-sur-Roya

Sospel

The medieval villages of Saorge and Tende

The medieval fortified villages overlooking the river Roya are built on such steep slopes that their flat stone roofs are stepped. Climb the flights of steps which replace streets and note the houses with their ornate lintels in green Tende stone. Also worth a visit are the various religious buildings: the Church of Saint-Sauveur in Saorge, the Franciscan convent or the Madonna del Poggio, and the Collegiate Church of Sainte-Marie-des-Bois in Tende.

The frescoes of Notre-Dame-des-Fontaines

A Sistine chapel in miniature in the mountains: behind the door of this little church, which stands in isolation over a mountain stream, contemplate one of the most beautiful series of 15th C. paintings. From ground to ceiling, the walls are covered with more than 2,150 sq. ft (200 m²) of frescoes on biblical themes.

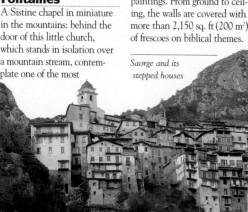

Saorge and its stepped houses

The Musée des Merveilles

Av. du 16-Septembre-1947, Tende,
☎ 04 93 04 32 50.
Open daily except Tue.,
10.30am-6.30pm (on
Sat., 9pm); 16 Oct.-30
Apr., 10.30am-5.30pm.
Paid admission.
Come to see artefacts, models,
replicas and exhibitions dem-
onstrating all that went on in
the valley 3,000 years ago. The
ultra-modern surroundings
enhance the exhibition.
Remember that Mont Bégo
was at the centre of all this
activity, as it was perceived to
be the incarnation of the gods
of thunder and rain and was
worshipped by the people.

❀ Canoeing, raft-ing and canyoning

Roya-Évasion, 1, Rue
Pasteur, Breil-sur-Royal,
☎ 04 93 04 91 46.

Be inspired by the Roya, and
leap into its pools to cool off.
If you want to try your hand
at canyoning, rafting or
canoeing and kayaking, you
will have to walk through
the forest for about an hour to
reach the starting point and
meet a professional guide.
The half-day rate is 80 F for
kayaking, up to 250 F for
canyoning.

Nice-Cuneo train (Italy)

Stations at Sospel,
Breil, Saorge, Saint-
Dalmas and Tende.
This quaint little train has
been running again since
1979. It clings to the

Spotcheck
F2

Alpes-Maritimes

Things to do

The Vallée des Merveilles
Canoeing, rafting and
canyoning
The Nice-Cuneo train

Within easy reach

Menton, 30 km S, p. 270.

Tourist Office

Tende: ☎ 04 93 04 73 71
Sospel: ☎ 04 93 04 15 80

mountainside and performs
incredible rail acrobatics.
Take it between Breil-sur-
Roya and the Col de Tende
where it passes through no
fewer than 50 tunnels, some
of which are at a steep gradient. Bridges and viaducts
span the peaks and gorges of
the Roya and every other
obstacle. (Trains run daily.
Information at Nice station,
☎ 04 36 35 35 35; Nice-
Tende single 2nd class fare
for one adult is approx. 59 F.).

Roya coffee

An ersatz coffee was once
made in the region based on
the principal forest crop –
the acorn. Here's how it's
made: after harvesting the
acorns in the autumn, place
them in a pot and leave
them to stew in their own
juice, stirring frequently.
When they have turned
dark brown, grill them until
they are perfectly dry, then
grind them in a coffee mill
and use it in the same way
as coffee.

THE VALLÉE DES MERVEILLES

*Access: 2½ hours on foot, horseback or 4x4 vehicle
(Jun.-Oct. only).*
**Park at the Mesches and follow the path to the
refuge des Merveilles. ☎ 04 93 04 77 73.**
Daily guided tours in summer (visits at 7.30am,
11am and 3pm), weekends in Jun. and Sep., Sun. in
Oct. *Paid admission.*
**Allow at least one day to explore this amazing
open-air museum. In a landscape of red and
green glacial rocks and sparkling lakes, prehistoric peoples produced tens of thousands of
rock engravings. Only guided tours provide
access to the most interesting areas, and there
is a signposted path through this enchanting
valley which is classified as a historic monument.
(See also p. 70.)**

Digne-les-Bains
capital of lavender country

Digne-les-Bains is situated at the meeting-point of three valleys and is famous for its spa, specialising in treating ailments of the respiratory tract and rheumatism. This ancient city, which was known to the Romans in the 1st C. BC, is also an attraction for lovers of the exotic, as well as amateur astronomers.

The old city

The old city centres on the Cathedral of Saint-Jérôme, and is a lovely place for a **walk.** Explore the old passageways such as Rue Pied-de-Ville and the old sloping, narrow lanes with peculiar names, such as the Rue Prête-à-Partir ('ready to leave'), so named because it was so often flooded. The **Cathedral of Saint-Jérôme,** built in 1490, was restored and rebuilt in the neo-Gothic style in the 19th C. On the right, there is a square 16th C. tower which serves as belfry and belltower, with a wrought iron campanile. It is an excellent spot from which to get a comprehensive view of the whole town.

Notre-Dame-du-Bourg Cathedral

A few ruins of the Roman city are still visible in the old Bourg district, which is dominated by the beautiful, late 13th C., Romanesque Cathedral of Notre-Dame. The nave is rather austere with an attractive barrel-vaulted roof. The southern wall has large windows to let in the light and is covered with a fresco of the Last Judgement. The north wall has a depiction of the Annunciation and the Crucifixion.

The Alexandra-David-Neel foundation

27, Av. du Maréchal-Juin,
☎ **04 92 31 32 38.**
Guided tours Jul.-Sep. daily at 10.30am, 2pm, 3.30pm and 5pm; Oct.-Jun. at 10.30am, 2pm and 4pm. Open daily.
Time: 1¼ hours.
Free admission.
Alexandra David Neel was a traveller and orientalist, who visited every country in the Far East and crossed

Tibet on foot. She bought this house in 1928 and lived in it from 1946 until her death in 1969. The collection contains many maps, photographs and illustrations accumulated over her 30 years of travel, as well as oriental objects and artefacts (Buddhas, bowls, tankas), including those presented to the first European

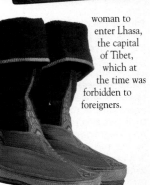

woman to enter Lhasa, the capital of Tibet, which at the time was forbidden to foreigners.

Spotcheck
D2

Alpes-de-Haute-Provence

Things to do

Train des Pignes
Geological reserve
Gassendi Observatory

Within easy reach

Sisteron, 30 km NW,
p. 186.
Route Napoléon, p. 238.

Tourist Office

Dignes:
☎ 04 92 42 36 62 62

Train des Pignes

Av. Pierre-Sémard,
☎ 04 92 31 01 58.
The train is nicknamed 'the pine-cone train' in memory of the pine cones burned for fuel instead of coal during World War II. The Train des Pignes links Digne to Nice. The locomotive was built in 1909 and is a historic monument, but it only runs on certain sections of the line and only on certain days. Leaving from Digne, you will arrive at Saint-André-les-Alpes, a distance of 27$\frac{1}{2}$ miles (44 km) in just over 2 hours, but **the trip is exceptionally picturesque.** Return journey is by autorail. Daily departures at 7am and 10.30am (p. 302).

GASSENDI OBSERVATORY

The great French astronomer Pierre Gassendi was born at Champtercier, 6 miles (10 km) from Digne. The Observatory that bears his name (☎ 04 92 31 91 45) in his home town organises special sessions about the changing skies (the moon, galaxies and so on), and invites visitors to watch the night sky after sunset (all year round by appointment, on Tue. and Sat., in summer at 9.30pm, cost: 40 F).

Geological reserve of Haute-Provence

Parc Saint-Benoît,
☎ 04 92 36 70 70.
Open daily, 9am-noon

and 2pm-5.30pm (4.30pm on Fri.). Closed at weekends, Nov.-Apr.
The *reserve géologique* covers a massive 370,650 acres (150,000 ha), and opened in 1984. It has 18 sites and 29 communes, where the last hundreds of millions of years of the earth's history are preserved. The exhibition centre is in a woodland park and offers a guided tour through the ages, including fossilised animals. There is also a room with 10 tanks containing 70 live species of fish and invertebrates.

Museum for an ichthyosaurus

At **La Robine**, 6 miles (10 km) from Digne, there is a museum under a Plexiglass dome which contains the remains of an ichthyosaurus, a reptile dating from the Secondary Era. The Office de Tourisme at Digne organises excursions to the reserve from July to late August. Reservations ☎ 04 92 36 62 62. 90 F a day, 50 F half-day; a car is essential. You will also be able to visit the ammonite platform: 1,700 sq. ft (160 m^2), containing 500 fossil shells.

The Hautes Vallées of the Var and the Verdon

right next to the Alps

At the foot of Mercantour, the Roudoule district is one of the most impressive gorges. The raging torrents have gouged deeply into the red shale. Meanwhile, the historic cities of Entrevaux and Puget-Théniers, on the banks of the Var, retain the atmosphere of this district which was once the frontier between France and the county of Nice, when the latter belonged to Italy.

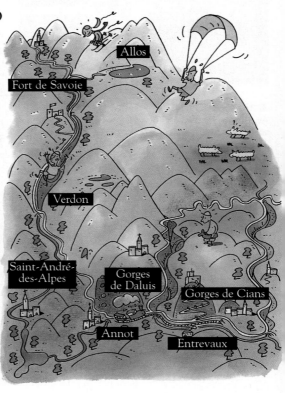

Entrevaux

The impregnable Château

68 km NW of Nice by N 202.

Perched on top of the rock, this fortified city is crowned by a precariously balanced citadel. The town is predominantly 18th C. though the cathedral dates from the 17th C. The curtain wall has slits for firing arrows. Several of the streets (Rue du Marché, Rue Basse) are medieval and the castle is right at the top. It is a pretty steep climb, but the view over the Var, 650 ft (200 m) below, is totally unforgettable.

Oil-press and flour mill

Pl. Moreau, extra-muros. Information at the Office de Tourisme.
Open daily., 9am-noon and 1pm-7pm.
This 15th C. mill is still used by growers who come every February to press their olives. Once they have filled 12 large baskets with the fruit, they press them down gently in order to obtain the

extra-virgin,
cold-pressed olive
oil. At the end,
they keep the
grignon (the skin
and stones) for
making soap.
In another
part of the
mill, grain
is ground
into flour.

Secca
**Robert
Lovera,
Pl.
Charles-Panier,
☎ 04 93 05 40 08.**
This is similar to carpaccio –
wind-dried paper-thin slices of
meat – but the speciality of
Entrevaux is much finer.
Secca enjoys a high repu-
tation locally and it is
the brainchild of Robert
Lovera, who runs his own
butcher's shop, and will
explain how the little muscle

in the beef rump, which is
known in French as the *rond
de gîte,* is sliced paper-thin
then degreased, salted and
dried slowly for 90 days. It
should be eaten with just a
slice of toast.

Daluis
Shale gorges
15 km N d'Entrevaux.
These are called Gorges de
Schiste and Gorges Rouges
because of the red shale rock
which is a **magnificent sight.**
After the village of Daluis,
perched at 2,660 ft (800 m)
above the Var, take the D2202
which hugs the red rocks like
a corniche.

After the
Berthéon
bridge, note the
so called Woman's

Spotcheck
D2-E2

Alpes-de-Haute-Provence

Things to do
Daluis gorges
Cians gorges
Canyoning
The cave of Méailles
Learning to para-glide
Walks around the Allos
lake.

Tourist Offices
Allos: ☎ 04 92 83 02 81
Annot: ☎ 04 92 83 23 03
Entrevaux:
☎ 04 93 05 46 73
Saint-André-des-Alpes:
☎ 04 92 89 02 39

Head (Tête-de-Femme), who
seems to have chosen the
gorges as her cleavage, enhanced about a mile (3 km) further
on by a string of diamonds
(the mountain stream).

Annot
Picturesque
houses
13 km W of Entrevaux.
This semi-alpine village, at an
altitude of 2,330 ft (700 m), is
frequently bombarded by huge
blocks of sandstone which
break off from the nearby cliff.
Take a closer look at them.
They all have nicknames such
as the 'King's Bedchamber' ('La
Chambre du Roi') (signposted,
behind the station), or the

CANYONING AS A FAMILY OUTING

**Access from the D28
to Guillaumes, then
take the Route de Tire-
Bœuf, a turning on the
right (parking).
Arrive at the Durandy
Bridge (parking), 3
miles (5 km) below.
Time: 3 hours.
If you are a beginner,
ask for information on
☎ 04 93 02 51 20
(Valberg Pulsion).
Open 15 Jun.-15 Sep.,
reservations required.
The Daluis gorges are
an ideal place to go canyoning for the first time.
The professionals don't consider that a neoprene
suit is required here. Take advantage of this. The
route is signposted, the gradient is gentle and you
will cross the bed of the stream about 30 times;
half-way down you can bathe in the pool of the
Clue d'Amen waterfall. This is a heavenly trip in the
canyon country of Nice; listen out for the song of
the bluebird, a bird unique to the area.**

'Camel of Lights' (on Route du Fugeret). At the entrance to the village there are cave dwellings, and the village contains some handsome 16th- and 17th-C. houses, and a Romano-Gothic church.

The cave of Méailles

6¼ miles (10 km) NW of Annot. Access by car to the Louvrettes ravine 1,660 yards (1,500 m) N of Méailles, then a 2 mile (3 km) footpath with a 1,266 ft (380 m) gradient. 2½ hour round trip.
Free admission.

The cave is reached on foot. A gallery 1,330 ft (400 m) long runs deep into the limestone cliff. The opening is very low but it broadens out quite quickly and becomes higher. Inside there are plenty of stalactites and a thick layer of limestone tufa. The interior is cool, damp – and pitch black! Reserved for brave souls equipped with a torch.

Puget-Théniers
Medieval district

4 miles (7 km) E of Entrevaux.

At the foot of the ruins of an old château which once belonged to the Grimaldis, this pretty village has alpine features combined with those of Provence. Wander through the medieval district, with its old houses and contemplate the treasures of the 13th C. **Gothic church.** There is an extraordinary **altar screen depicting the Passion** at the entrance, and an altarpiece depicting **Notre-Dame de Secours** in the apse.

The little Train des Pignes

Between Puget-Théniers and Annot, via Entrevaux, occasionally as far as Nice or Digne. ☎ 04 93 88 18 78 or 04 93 82 10 17. May to October only.

This historic little train pulled by a 1909 steam locomotive, classified as a historic monument, operates at incredible altitudes (for a train) running through the Provençal hinterland. You are sure to enjoy yourself as the train rocks and sways, bumps and grinds and stops at every station. But it offers a unique opportunity to see the loveliest landscapes in the southern Alps, which can't be seen from the road. The trip between Annot and Puget, some 12½ miles (20 km) takes just over an hour. Round trip ticket: 110 F. (*See also p. 299*).

Beuil
Cians gorges

18¾ miles (30 km) NE of Puget-Théniers.

The foaming torrent drops 4,333 feet (1300 m) in less than 15½ miles (25 km). Follow its mad rush from Beuil (D28). The scenery is magnificent, and the red rock even encloses the road entirely at two points (very impressive). Take the turning to Pierlas, then the winding road up to the village of Lieuche, whose church contains a painting which is worthy of the Louvre, the **polyptych of the Annunciation** by Louis Bréa (late 15th C.).

Colmars
Le fort de Savoie
25 miles (40 km) NE of Barrême. Altitude: 4,233 ft (1,270 m)
☎ 04 92 83 41 92.
Open daily in summer, guided tours 10am-11.30am; out of season at 10am, by arrangement with the Office de Tourisme,
☎ 04 92 83 46 88.
Exhibitions in Jul.-Aug. in the fort, open daily 2.30pm-7pm.

The fort stands north of the village. Imagine the atmosphere that must have prevailed in the fort in the 17th C., when it had to protect Savoie from Piedmontese invasions. The low vaulted passages between the rooms were designed to stop the enemy from advancing, should they manage to get inside.

The watchtower has a larchwood frame and the path on the outside leads down to the Verdon.

Lac d'Allos
Various walks
22½ miles (36 km) N of Saint-André-des-Alpes.

Access to the lake via the D226, then ¾ mile (1 km) following the footpath.
This mountain village, at an altitude of 4,733 feet (1,420 m), becomes a ski resort in winter. Climb up to the vast lake 7,416 ft (2,225 m), from which there are some lovely walks in summer. You can either walk right round the lake or hike up to Mont Pelat at 10,170 ft (3,051 m), a trip that will take just over 2 hours. The view is breathtaking.

Learning to paraglide
☎ 04 92 83 02 81 or
☎ 04 92 83 80 70
(Allos Office de Tourisme).
Open Jul.-Aug. and Dec.-Mar. *Beginner's rate: 200 F.*
Launch yourself from the heights of the Haute Vallée of the Verdon, which is used by world champion hang-gliders and paragliders. For your paragliding maiden voyage, a professional skydiver will teach you the joys of taking off as a duo – and landing, of course! Then do it all over again. With a bit of luck the folded parachute silk will open out as you glide down …

SAINT-ANDRÉ-DES-ALPES: FLOATING DOWN THE RIVER
Pro-Verdon activités, J. Raoust, rue Basse,
☎ 04 92 89 04 19 or 07 19. May-Oct.
Canyon down the gorges de Fontgaillarde by floating on the Verdon, using the routes formerly reserved for coarse fishermen. Just don a neoprene suit and a lifejacket and let yourself be carried along by the water of the mountain stream which are quite calm in summer. Throughout the two-hour descent, enjoy the pleasure of diving in the deep water pools. You can walk along the banks and watch the water-ouzels diving for their food. You must be a good swimmer and be at least 14 years of age.

Barcelonnette and the Vallée de l'Ubaye

The Vallée de l'Ubaye in the southern Alps has an eventful history. For a long time, it was the battlefield in numerous conflicts between the European powers. This has given the inhabitants a rather restless nature. In the 19th C. many even went to seek their fortunes in Mexico. Today, they devote themselves to enhancing and promoting their natural and historic heritage.

Barcelonnette

Mexican villas

Barcelonnette is the capital of the Ubaye. The Cardinalis tower, a 14th C. bell-tower, is a remnant of the Dominican convent which occupied the city centre until the French Revolution (in the Place Manuel). A few elegant villas are reminders of the emigration to Mexico of some of the citizens of Barcelonnette in the 19th C. On their return to France they built the Church of Saint-Pierre (1928) in Romanesque-Provençal style.

Jazz Festival

Info. and reservations at the Office de Tourisme. In mid-July, jazz musicians give performances in the lovely setting of the Parc de la Sapinière, and give master classes for a fortnight to budding jazz musicians (enrolment, ☎ 04 43 58 98 50). The atmosphere is really buzzing, and there are impromptu street performances and displays.

The sundial route

Complete route available at the Office de Tourisme. Enjoy the dedications inscribed into the sundials in the Ubaye Valley. That of **Paul Reynaud's birthplace** (Rue Béraud) offers the advice: 'Pray that the hour does not catch you unaware.' At Faucon, ¾ mile (2 km) E of Barcelonnette, the

church sundial proclaims: 'By using the present moment appropriately, prepare for a happy end'. But that of the neighbouring monastery is more cautious: 'At every hour, believe and hope'.

Vallée de l'Ubaye
Fortifications

10-14 miles (16-22 km) NE of Barcelonnette via the D900,
☎ **04 92 81 04 71.**
Open during the school holidays. Guided tours lasting 1½ hours at 4pm. Daily 10am-11.30am and 2.30pm-6pm. *Paid admission.*
The valley marks the border with Italy and has retained an impressive array of defences, built between the 17th and 20th C. The **forteresse de Tournoux,** clinging to the mountainside, the **batteries de Roche-la-Croix,** used during the Italian offensive in June 1940, and the **ouvrage de Saint-Ours-Haut,** an impressive underground earthworks, are just some examples.

Museums of daily life in the 19th C.

Open daily in summer; out of season, ask for information.
These three museums are like a jigsaw puzzle which, when completed, gives you a picture of the inhabitants of the Ubaye. What was it like farming this stony soil in the 19th C.? Visit **Saint-Paul-sur-**

Ubaye (grange de la maison Arnaud, ☎ 04 92 84 32 36). How did state schooling enable the town to develop? Take a trip to **Pontis** (town hall, old schoolhouse, ☎ 04 92 44 26 94). What were these people doing in Mexico? The answer is in **Barcelonnette** (La Sapinière, Av. de la Libération, ☎ 04 92 81 27 15, a villa built in the late 19th C. by Alexandre Raynard on his return from Mexico, which is now a museum about the history of the Valley. Open all year round.

Soap works and wooden toys

Take a trip through the valley to discover the special products it has to offer. At La Bréole, visit the **Savonnerie de l'Ubaye** soapworks, with its mountain fragrances. (☎ 04 92 85 54 73). At Serennes, 17½ miles (28 km) E of Barcelonnette, you will find a delightful workshop making wooden toys, the **atelier de la Marmotte** (a wooden train costs 145 F; ☎ 04 92 84 35 01, open all year, every day in summer; Mon. and Sat. out of season). In Barcelonnette, in the Rue

Grenette, discover how the local yarrow-flavoured liqueur **génépy** is made in the **Marie-France Martin-Charpenel** factory (☎ 04 92 81 44 07), 708 F for a 6-pack. After 4pm in summer: guided tour and free samplings. For all the rest, make your purchases at the **Maison des produits de pays de Jausiers,** Route de Barcelonnette, à Jausiers, 4¾ miles (7 km) NE of Barcelonnette (☎ 04 92 84 63 88).

Spotcheck
D1
Alpes-de-Haute-Provence

Things to do
Jazz Festival
Visit to a soap works
Whitewater sports

Tourist Office
Barcelonnette :
☎ 04 92 81 04 71

WHITEWATER SPORTS

AN Rafting, Pont du Martinet, Méolans-Revel, ☎ **04 92 85 54 90.**
Open Mar.-Nov.
In whitewater rafting, you skim over the foam. The hot-dog, however, is a two-man canoe which requires careful team-work to avoid you both ending up in the water. From the 1 hour introduction (160/200 F) to whole day trips, when you finish you'll be washed out. If you plan to try canyoning you will be asked to wear flippers and a wetsuit and be careful to avoid the rocks.

Parc du Mercantour
a nature park in wolf country

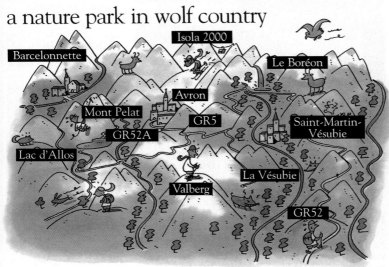

Isola 2000
Barcelonnette
Le Boréon
Avron
Mont Pelat
GR5
Saint-Martin-Vésubie
GR52A
Lac d'Allos
La Vésubie
Valberg
GR52

The Parc du Mercantour is a country park and nature reserve covering an area where the Alpine landscape meets the gentle Mediterranean climate. It is a land of enchantment, of rushing streams, brooks, bubbling waterfalls, cool crystal-clear lakes and high mountains. But beware of the Big Bad Wolf, about a dozen of them also take their holidays here ...

The village of Lantosque, in the Vallée de la Vésubie

to come quite close, and there are also marmots, hares and weasels.

Pretty mountain villages

The park covers seven wild river valleys which, listed from south to north, are the valleys

Wildlife

Mercantour covers an area of about 62 miles (100 km) along the Italian frontier, between the Hautes Vallées of the Ubaye and the Verdon in the north (p. 300), and the Valleys of the Var, the Vésubie and the Roya in the south (p. 296). Nature-lovers can enjoy some 163,200 acres (68,000 ha) of lakes, forests, rocky outcrops and meadows. The flora is abundant and varied (more than 2,000 species of which 40 are unique to the area). The animals (chamois, ibex, moufflons) are typical of the high mountain ranges and are fairly tame, allowing you

RAMBLING AND HIKING

With more than 375 miles (600 km) of hiking and walking trails, the park is a favourite with ramblers, especially as this is a nature reserve and has hardly been touched by man. The GR5 and the GR52 cross Mercantour, and the GR52A skirts it from village to village to the south. If you want to map out a suitable route, ask for a guide from the Bureau des Guides du Mercantour, ☎ 04 93 03 31 32. Open 10.30am-noon and 4.30pm -8pm in summer; 5pm-7pm out of season.

of the Roya, Bevera, Vésubie, Tinée, Upper Var, Upper Verdon and Ubaye. There are several mountain villages in the park. All have **Romanesque churches** and houses with thick stone walls. They include Rimplas, Breil, Saorge, Entrevaux, Saint-Martin-Vésubie and Roubion where you can stock up on honey and various soft cheeses, including goat's cheese, to sustain you on your ramble or hike.

The wolves of Mercantour

At the last count, there were between 8 and 12 wolves, who had wandered over from Italy and chosen to take up residence in the Tinée Valley. Shepherds taking their flocks to the high pastures have had several encounters with them, but they are elusive creatures. However, old superstitions die hard and there are plenty of locals who 'cry wolf'. Even when damage has clearly been done by an unruly dog, the wolf is a convenient scapegoat.

Mountain biking or skiing?

It should not be forgotten that Mercantour is a high mountain park and altitudes range from 1,500 to 10,476 ft (500-3,143 m). The highest point is the summit of Mont Gélas. The topography, consisting as it does of cirques, glacial valleys, deep gorges, raging torrents and permanent snow, enables you to enjoy the pleasures of a long hike or mountain bike ride. In winter there is skiing at the resorts of Valberg, Isola 2000 and Auron. (Information ☎ 04 93 02 41 96.)

Picnicking by the waterfalls

Le Boréon (above Saint-Martin-Vésubie) is the starting-point for many hikes in the forests or around the lakes. One hiking trail leads to the magnificent waterfall called **Cascade du Boréon**, which has a fall of 133 ft (40 m) at an altitude of more than 5,000 ft (1,500 m). Much further to the east (a few miles from Barcelonnette on the D909), the azure **Allos Lake** is the largest in Europe.

Spotcheck
E2

Alpes-de-Haute-Provence

Things to do
Mountain biking or skiing
Rambling and hiking

Within easy reach
Valley of the Vésubie, p. 292.

Walking in the national park

It is possible to hire a guide to show you the sights that the Mercantour has to offer. You can book a guide in **Barcelonnette** (☎ 04 92 81 21 31) and **Saint-Étienne-de-Tinée** (☎ 04 93 02 42 27). Book 2 or 3 days in advance. A half-day tour costs 50 F;

you must wear hiking boots, take rations and carry a water-bottle. The guides also offer themed walks on such topics as local wildlife and flora. These can be booked at **Entraunes** (☎ 04 93 05 53 07), which organises week-long hikes or day-long walks for 110 F. A special children's event is organised at **Saint-Sauveur-de-Tinée** (☎ 04 93 02 01 63).

A

Agay, 226.
Aix (district), 180.
Aix-en-Provence, 174.
  Calissons, 177.
  Cézanne's footsteps, 175.
  Cours Mirabeau, 174.
  Festivals, 175.
  Markets, 176.
  Musée Granet, 177.
  Musée Vieil-Aix, 176.
  Muséum d'histoire naturelle
    (Natural History museum),
    176.
  Painted furniture, 178.
  Quartier Mazarin, 177.
  Saint-Sauveur Cathedral,
    176.
  Santon figures, 178.
Allos, 303, 307.
Alpilles (les), 134.
ANIMAL WATCHING (see also
  AQUASCOPES, PARKS,
  ZOOS).
  Butterfly house, 217.
  Sainte-Anne Cathedral, 160.
  La Londe-les-Maures park,
    207.
  Ornithological observatory,
    130, 158-159.
  Pont-de-Gau ornithological
    park, 130.
  Paul-Ricard oceanographi-
    cal museum, 201.
  Tortoise village, 223.
  Undersea footpath, 212.
  Whales and dolphins, 100.
  Zoo, 208.
Annot, 301.
Ansouis, 156.
  Castle, 156.
  Musée extraordinaire, 157.
Antibes, 252.
  Grimaldi castle, 252.
  Immaculée-Conception
    Church, 252.
  Markets, 252.
  Musée Peynet, 253.
  Vauban harbour, 252.
ANTIQUES: map 18-19.
  Aix-en-Provence, 176.
  Antibes, 253.
  Apt, 60.
  (Marseille) Flea market,
    194.
  Forcalquier, 184.
  L'Isle-sur-la-Sorgue, 166.
  Menton, 291.
  Montauroux, 247.
  Nice, 271.
  Roquemaure, 143.
  Saint-Tropez, 216.
Apt, 160.
  Antique dealers, 60.
  Crystallised fruits, 160.
  Earthenware, 160.
  Festivals, 160.
  Maison du parc du Luberon,
    160.
  Market, 160.

AQUASCOPES, 100.
  Agay, 226.
  Cap d'Antibes, 255.
  Giens, 207.
  Le Lavandou, 215.
  Nice, 272.
  Port-Cros, 212.
  Sainte-Maxime, 218.
Argens (valley), 232.
Arles, 126.
  Alyscamps, 126.
  Boulevard des Lices, 128.
  Ferias, 128.
  Festivals, 128.
  Gardens, 128.
  Musée Réattu, 127.
  Museon Arlaten, 129.
  Rencontres internationales
    de la photographie
    (photography conference),
    128.
  Saint-Trophime, 126.
  Sausage, 129.
  Van Gogh foundation, 127-
    128.
ART, ROMAN: map 68-69.
  Breil, 307.
  Entrevaux, 307.
  Ganagobie, 74, 184.
  Grimaud, 220.
  Lérins, 74, 242.
  Mons, 251.
  Montmajour, 75, 134.
  Notre-Dame-des-Pommiers,
    186.
  Rimplas, 307.
  Roubion, 307.
  Saint-Gilles-du-Gard, 75.
  Saint-Martin-Vésubie, 307.
  Saint-Michel-de-Frigolet,
    75, 145.
  Saint-Paul-de-Mausole,
    139.
  Saint-Trophime, 126.
  Saint-Sauveur, 182.
  Saint-Véran, 164.
  Saorge, 307.
  Sénanque, 74, 163.
  Senez, 238.
  Silvacane, 75, 159.
  Thoronet (Le), 74, 233.
  Vaison, 148.
Aubagne, 197.
Aups, 230.
  Market, 230.
  Musée Simon-Ségal, 230.
  Villecroze caves, 230.
Auribeau-sur-Siagne, 246.
Avignon, 140.
  Angladon-Dubrujeaud
    foundation, 142.
  Chartreuse du Val-de-
    Bénédiction, 143.
  Festival, 141.
  Hike, 143.
  Musée Calvet, 142.
  Musée du Petit Palais, 142.
  Musée lapidaire, 142.
  Notre-Dame-des-Doms,
    142.
  Palais des Papes (Palace
    of the Popes), 141.

  Ramparts, 140.
  Rocher des Doms, 142.
  Saint-Bénezet bridge, 141.
  Tours in town, 140.

B

Bagnols-en-Forêt, 251.
Bandol, 200.
Banon, 186.
Barbentane, 143.
Barcelonnette, 304, 307.
  Festival, 304.
  Paul Reynaud's birthplace,
    304.
  Museums, 305.
  Mexican villas, 304.
Barjols, 232.
Bar-sur-Loup (Le), 268.
Barroux, 173.
Baux-de-Provence (Les), 136.
  Citadel, 136.
  Musée Brayet, 136.
  Musée de l'olivier, 137.
  Musée des Santons, 136.
  Sporting activities, 137.
  Val d'Enfer and cathedral of
    images, 137.
BEACHES: map 98-99.
  Arène (l'), 196.
  Argent, 211.
  Ayguade, 211.
  Beauduc, 130.
  Bergerie, 206.
  Blanche, 211.
  Bora-Bora, 216.
  Bouillabaisse, 216.
  Canadel-sur-Mer, 223.
  Canebiers, 216.
  Capte, 206.
  Cavalière, 223.
  Courtade, 211.
  Grand Radeau, 130.
  Graniers, 216.
  Grottes, 213.
  Lavandou, le 214.
  Moorea, 216.
  Mourillon, 203.
  Noire, 211.
  Notre-Dame, 211.
  Pertuis-de-la-Comtesse,
    130.
  Piémançon, 130.
  Prado, 191.
  Pramousquier, 223.
  Tahiti, 216.
Beausoleil, 289.
Beausset-Vieux (Le), 199.
Belvédère, 294.
Berre (étang de), 150.
Beuil, 302.
Biot, 264.
  Fougasse breads, 265.
  Glassworks, 265.
  Musée Bonsaï Arboretum,
    264.
  Musée d'Histoire et de
    Céramique, 264.
  Musée national Fernand-
    Léger, 265.
Bonnieux, 154.

Bories: *map 62-63*.
  Gordes, 163.
Bormes-les-Mimosas, 214.
Bouc-Bel-Air, 178.
Boulbon, 145.
Boulouris, 226.
Breeding
  Llamas, 173.
  Ostriches, 171.
Breil, 307.
Bréole (La), 305.
Brignoles, 232.
  Mini-France park, 233.
  Musée du pays brignolais
    (folk museum), 232.

C

Cadenet, 156.
  Musée de la vannerie
    (Wickerwork and basketry
    museum), 156.
  Sporting activities, 157.
  Saint-Étienne Church, 156.
Cadière-d'Azur (La), 198.
Cagnes-sur-Mer, 258.
  Château-museum, 258.
  Marina, 259.
  Race course, 259.
  Renoir museum, 258.
  Sporting activities, 259.
  Vaugrenier park, 259.
Calanques (les), 195, 197.
Callelongue, 195.
Camargue, 130.
  Beaches, 130.
  Boat trips, 130.
  Camargue museum, 130.
  Ornithological park, 130.
  Race for the cocarde, 131.
  Rice museum, 131.
  Regional park, 130.
  Sporting activities, 131.
Cannes, 240.
  Canolive, 241.
  Carlton, 241.
  Ciné-Folies, 240.
  Croisette, 240.
  Festival, 114.
  Markets, 241.
  Musée de la Castre, 240.
  Palais des Festivals, 240.
Cap Canaille, 196.
Cap d'Antibes, 254.
  Coastal footpath, 254.
  Eden Roc (L'), 255.
  Gardens, 254, 255.
  Garoupe lighthouse, 254.
  Naval and napoleonic
    museum, 254.
Capitou (Le), 225.
Cap-Roux (pic du), 225, 226.
Carmes (valley), 233.
Carpentras, 170.
  Crystallised fruits, 171.
  Markets, 171.
  Porte Juive, 170.
  Porte d'Orange, 171.
  Synagogue, 170.
Carry-le-Rouet, 153.
Casinos: *map 104-105*.

Cassis, 196.
  Bar de la Marine, 196.
  Calanques, 197.
  Cosquer's cave, 71, 196.
  Musée des Arts et
    Traditions populaires (folk
    museum), 196.
  Route des Crêtes, 197.
  Wine, 197.
Castellane, 238-239.
Castellet (Le), 198.
Castles: *map 62-63*.
  Ansouis, 156.
  Château-Arnoux, 187.
  Comtes de Toulouse, 144.
  Entrecasteaux, 233.
  Entrevaux, 300.
  Gordes, 162.
  Gourdon, 268.
  Grimaud, 220.
  If, 192.
  La Tour-d'Aigues, 157.
  Lourmarin, 155.
  du Masque de fer, 243.
  Roquebrune, 288.
  de Sade, 154.
  Tholonet, 180.
  Vallauris, 256.
Caussols (plateau de), 269.
Cavaillon, 164.
  Market, 165.
  Melon festival, 165.
  Saint-Jacques hill, 164.
  Saint-Véran Cathedral, 164.
  Sporting activities, 164.
  Synagogue, 164.
Caves
  Baume Obscure, 238.
  Cosquer, 196.
  Méailles, 302.
  Saint-Cézaire-sur-Siagne,
    245.
  Sainte-Marie-Madeleine,
    204.
  Thouzon, 167.
  Villecreuze, 230.
Cengle (plateau de), 180.
Céreste, 157.
Château-Arnoux, 187.
Châteaudouble, 229.
Châteauneuf-du-Pape, 146.
Châteauneuf-les-Martigues,
  195.
Coaraze, 280.
Cogolin, 220.
  Carpets, 221.
  Musée Raimu, 221.
  Pipes, 220.
Colle-sur-Loup (La), 268.
Collobrières, 222.
Colmars, 303.
Commercial interest (sites):
  map120-121.
  Barcelonnette: Ubaye soap
    factory, 305.
  Castellane: Chaudanne, 239.
  Èze: soap factory, 279.
  Giens: mine, 207.
  Grasse: perfume industry,
    248.
  Isle-sur-la-Sorgue (l'): paper
    mill, 167.

Marseille: soap factory,
  194.
Martigues: power station,
  152.
Sainte-Croix-du-Verdon:
  hydroelectric power station,
  237.
Salon-de-Provence: soap
  factory, steel and iron
  industry, and authority port,
  151.
Contes, 281.
Cookery lessons, 178, 245.
Cotignac, 233.
Coursegoules, 263.
Crafts (see Shopping)
Crau (pays de la), 150.
Cuges-les-Pins, 205.

D

Daluis, 301.
Digne-les-Bains, 238, 298.
  Alexandra-David-Neel
    foundation, 298.
  Gassendi observatory, 299.
  Notre-Dame-du-Bourg
    Cathedral, 298.
  Saint-Jérôme Cathedral, 298.
  Geological reserve, 299.
  Train des pignes, 299.
Draguignan, 228.
  Flayosquet oil mill, 229.
  Musée des Arts et
    Traditions populaires (folk
    museum), 228.
  Musée du Canon et des
    Artilleurs, 229.
  Musée municipal, 228.
  Nartuby gorges, 229.
  Pierre de la Fée, 229.
Dramont (Le), 226.
Drinks
  Génépy, 305.
  Melon liqueur, 165.
  Monk's liqueur, 243.
  Origan du Comtat, 147.
  Pastis, 26, 185.
  Orange wine, 268.
Durance (valley), 158.
Duranus, 295.

E

Entraunes, 307.
Entrecasteaux, 233.
Entremont (plateau d'), 179.
Entrevaux, 300, 307.
  Castle, 300.
  Delicatessen, 301.
  Mill, 300.
Escarène (L'), 272, 280.
Esquillon (headland), 227.
Eyguières, 135.
Èze, 278.
  Exotic garden, 279.
  Path, 278.
  Soap works, 279.
Èze (peak), 278.
  Astrorama, 278.
  Walk, 278.

F

FAUNA (see ANIMAL WATCHING)
Fayence (district), 250.
FEASTS
　Abrivado, 128, 135, 139.
　Baguettes, 281.
　Carreto Ramado, 111, 135.
　Cheese, 187.
　Ferrade, 111, 131.
　Festo Vierginenco, 133.
　Gardians, 127.
　Journées gourmandes, 149.
　Journées médiévales, 183.
　Joutes nautiques, 153, 166.
　Lavender, 81, 173.
　Lemon, 291.
　May tree, 111.
　Olive, 134, 288.
　Olive oil, 134.
　Oursinades, 111, 153.
　Pastorale, 149.
　Pastrage, 145.
　Pegoulade, 128, 135.
　Potters', 257.
　Procession of bottles, 111, 145.
　Procession of snails, 281.
　Provençal, 200.
　Saint-Jean, 295.
　Sainte Marie-Salomé, 132.
　Sainte Sarah, 132.
　Sardinades, 153.
　Transhumance, 111, 139.
　Tripettes, 232.
　Violettes, 265.
FERIA
　Arles, 111, 128.
　Saint-Rémy-de-Provence, 139.
　Saintes-Marie-de-la-Mer (Les), 133.
Ferrat (cape), 276.
　Botanical garden, 277.
　Grand Hôtel, 277.
　Sporting activities, 277.
　Villa houses, 276.
　Zoo, 277.
FESTIVALS: map 106-107.
　Avignon, 141.
　Baroque, 272.
　Big-bands, 175.
　Chœurs lauréats, 149.
　Chorégies, 147.
　Cinema, 114, 127, 183.
　Été de l'orgue historique, 204.
　Festival of Marseille, 195.
　Folk, 153, 183.
　Font-Robert, 187.
　Gospel, 151.
　International Photography Conference, 128.
　Jazz, 151, 160, 183, 195, 253, 272, 304.
　Jean Giono celebration days, 183.
　Lyrical art, 147, 149, 175.
　Manosque festival, 183.
　Mediaeval music, 233.
　Modern dance, 175.

Mosaïque gitan (gipsy mosaic), 129.
Nights in the citadel, 187.
Organa, 138.
Piano, 159.
String quartet, 154.
Summer, 171.
Rencontres du Sud, 129.
Rencontres internationales de Lurs, 184.
Rencontres musicales de Haute-Provence, 195.
Soirées d'Été, 163.
Sud-Luberon, 157.
Tréteaux de Nuit, 161.
Vues sur les docs (documentary film festival), 195.
FLORA (see also GARDENS, PARKS).
　Bamboos, 247.
　Bonsaïs, 264.
　Botanical conservatory, 210.
　Botanical garden of Coa, 149.
　Cactus, 284.
　Carnations, 79.
　Jasmine, 249.
　Orange blossom, 79, 257.
　Orchids, 143.
　Lavender, 78, 80-82, 161, 173.
　Mimosa, 78, 214.
　Palm trees, 207.
　Plantes aromatiques, 22-23.
　Rose, 79, 249, 255.
　Tulips, 79.
　Violets, 79, 266.
FOOTPATHS (see also GARDENS, HIKING): map 92-93.
　Botanical, 181, 213, 263.
　Calanques, 197.
　Cave, 204.
　Coastal, 206, 216, 226, 254.
　Cavaillon, 164.
　along the Durance River, 158.
　Ecological, 243.
　Friedrich-Nietzsche, 278.
　Harmas, 147.
　Lavender, 81.
　Maquis, 224.
　Martel, 236.
　Mont Ventoux, 172.
　of the Nesque gorges, 173.
　Point Sublime, 236.
　Route des Crêtes, 197, 236.
　Saint-Eutrope hill, 146.
　Saint-Paul-de-Vence, 261.
　Themed, 215.
　Tour of Cézanne, 175, 180-181.
　Tour of dolmens, 251.
　Tour of Ochres, 59.
Fontaine-de-Vaucluse, 167.
　Paper mill, 167.
　Pétrarque museum, 167.
　Resistance museum, 167.
Fontvieille, 134.
Forcalquier, 184.
　Citadel, 184.
　Market, 184.

　Notre-Dame-du-Bourguet Cathedral, 184.
FORESTS
　Boréon, 293.
　Cedar trees, 155.
　Trees, 96-97.
Fréjus, 224.
　Aquatica, 224.
　Archeological museum, 224.
　Hiking, 224.
　Missiri mosque, 225.

G

Ganagobie, 184.
Garavan, 291.
Garde-Freinet (La), 223.
GARDENS (see also FLORA, PARKS): map 76-77.
　Albertas, 178.
　Biovès, 291.
　Botanical, 277.
　Box tree, 179.
　Château de Gourdon, 269.
　Cimiez, 274.
　Colombières, 291.
　d'Été, 128.
　Domaine de Manon, 249.
　Entrecasteaux, 233.
　Ethnobotanical, 195.
　Exotic, 201, 279, 291, 294.
　Hill top, 165.
　Japanese, 287.
　Lavender, 173.
　L'Harmas, 147.
　Mont-Boron, 274.
　Notre-Dame-des-Fleurs, 262.
　Prieuré de Salagon, 185.
　Rayol-Canadel, 215.
　Saint-Martin, 209.
　Scents, 161.
　Thuret, 254.
　Val Rameh, 291.
　Villa Eilenroc, 255.
　Villa Île-de-France, 276.
Gassin, 217.
GASTRONOMY: map 24-25.
　Bakery museum, 154.
　Berlingots (humbugs), 30, 171.
　Bézuquette, 145.
　Biscotin, 177.
　Café, 297.
　Calissons, 30, 177.
　Cheese, 186, 263, 293.
　Chocolate, 179.
　Chichi-frégis, 203.
　Clou de Cézanne, 177.
　Crespeou, 42.
　Crystallised fruits, 30, 139, 160, 171, 275.
　Esprit blanchard cake, 169.
　Farm lamb, 186.
　Fougasse bread, 265, 291.
　Honey 31, 145, 172, 241, 251.
　Jams, 206, 217, 222, 275.
　Lemon, 20, 290.

Melon, 21, 41, 165.
Musée de l'Art culinaire, 259.
Navettes biscuits, 191.
Nougat, 30, 173, 205.
Olive oil, 28-29, 135, 219, 231, 241, 271, 274.
Panisse, 291.
Papalines, 30, 143.
Pastas, 270.
Patiences, 223.
Pichade, 291.
Pichoulines, 151.
Pignatines, 257.
Pignolats, 139.
Quince preserve, 233.
Sausage, 129.
Sea-urchins, 153, 200.
Secca, 301.
Socca, 291.
Soleil pernois, 169.
Tapenade, 135, 231.
Tarasque, 145.
Tarte tropézienne, 216.
Walnut oil, 186.
Gaude (La), 179.
Gélas (peak), 293, 307.
Giens, 206.
Beaches, 206.
Footpaths, 206.
Tree nursery, 207.
Wrecks, 207.
Gigondas, 149.
Glanum, 149.
GOING OUT
La Civette, 143.
La Marine, 196.
Pam-Pam, 253.
Sénéquier, 216.
Voom-Voom, 253.
Gonfaron, 223.
Cork Écomusée, 223.
Tortoise village, 223.
Gordes, 162.
Castle, 162.
Festival, 163.
Moulins des Bouillons, 162.
Vitrail museum, 163.
GORGES
Blavet, 251.
Cians, 95, 302.
Daluis, 95, 301.
Loup, 94, 267.
Nartuby, 229.
Nesque, 95, 172-173.
Régalon, 159.
Rouges, 94.
Siagne, 246.
Verdon, 94, 234.
Vésubie, 94, 294.
Goult, 161.
Gourdon, 268.
Castle, 269.
Grasse, 238, 248.
Domaine de Manon, 249.
Fragonard villa, 249.
Perfume indutries, 248.
Musée d'Art et d'Histoire de Provence, 248.
Musée international de la Parfumerie, 248.
Sporting activities, 249.

Graveson, 145.
Gréolières, 269.
Grette (La), 250.
Grimaud, 220.

H

Hauts-de-Cagnes (Les), 258.
HIKING: map 92-93.
canyoning, 263, 303.
on foot, 130, 137, 143, 157, 180-181, 186, 195, 197, 199, 204, 213, 214, 223, 224, 226, 233, 243, 249, 267, 274., 278, 289, 293-295, 303, 307.
HORSE RIDING, 57, 183, 231, 247, 274.
Hyères, 208.
Architecture, 209.
Castel Sainte-Claire, 209.
Market, 209.
Mild garden, 208.
Noailles villa, 209.
Saint-Paul Collegiate Church, 208.
Templiers tower, 208.

I

ISLANDS
Bagaud, 213.
Barthelasse, 141.
Bendor, 47, 201.
Embiez, 201.
Frioul, 195.
Lérins, 241, 242 (see also Lérins).
Levant, 213.
of Marseille (Pomergue, Ratonneau, If), 192.
Or, 212.
Porquerolles, 210.
Port-Cros, 212.
Rascas, 213.
Sainte-Marguerite, 242.
Saint-Honorat, 242.
Isle-sur-la-Sorgue (L'), 166.
Issambres (Les), 219.
Istres, 151.

J

Juan-les-Pins, 253.
Festival, 253.
Marineland, 253.

L

La Ciotat, 199.
Lacoste, 154.
LAKES
Allos, 303, 307.
Besson, 293.
Prals, 293.
Sainte-Croix, 235.
Lantosque, 294.
Lauris, 157.
Lavandou (Le), 214.

LEISURE PARKS: map 102-103.
Aqualand, 203.
Aquatica, 224.
El Dorado City, 195.
Marineland, 253.
Mini-France, 233.
OK Corral, 205.
Parc nautique du Niagara, 221.
Phoenix, 273.
Lérins (islands), 242.
Ecological, 243.
Fort, 242.
Masque de fer castle, 243.
Monastary, 242.
Sporting activities, 243.
Levens, 295.
Londe-les-Maures (La), 207.
Lorgues, 231.
Loup (valley), 266.
Lourmarin, 155.
Luberon (Grand), 156.
Luberon (Petit), 154.
Lucéram, 280.
Lure (mountain), 186.
Lurs, 184.

M

Madone-de-Fenestre, 292, 293.
Mane, 195.
Manosque, 182.
Jean-Giono center, 183.
Feats, 183.
Carzou foundation, 183.
Saint-Sauveur, 182.
MARKETS: map 18-19.
Craft, 128, 146, 172, 214, 218.
Exceptional, Cannes, 131, 160, 166, 171, 184, 202, 270.
Farm, 160, 207.
Fish, 153, 189, 216, 241, 270.
Flea markets (see ANTIQUES).
Flower, 140, 176, 189, 241, 248, 252.
Truffles, 171, 230.
Marseille, 188.
Arcenaulx, 189.
Balaboum Theatre, 192.
Calanques, 194.
Cantini museum, 193.
Carré Thiars, 191.
Cité radieuse, 194.
Corniche, 191.
Cours d'Estienne-d'Orves, 191.
Cours Julien, 194.
Festivals, 195.
Frioul islands, 192.
Garden of Remains, 192.
Hydrocycle, 193.
If castle, 192.
Markets, 189, 194.
Miramar, 190.
Mirros, 195.
Musée d'Archéologie méditerranéenne, 190.
Musée d'Art contemporain, 193.

Musée des Arts africain, amérindien et océanien, 190.
Musée des Beaux-Arts, 193.
Musée d'Histoire de Marseille, 193.
Musée du terroir marseillais, 192.
Museum shop of the OM, 195.
Navettes biscuits, 191.
Notre-Dame-de-la-Garde, 191.
Palais Longchamps, 193.
Prado beach, 191.
Quartier du Panier, 189.
Saint-Victor Abbey, 191.
Santons, 193.
Soap, 194.
Stade vélodrome, 194.
Tarot, 194.
Vieille Charité, 190.
Vieux-Port, 188.
Martigues, 152.
Folk festival, 153.
Markets, 153.
Power station, 152.
Ziem museum, 152.
Martin (cape), 289.
MASSIF
Esterel, 226.
Maures, 222.
Sainte-Baume, 204.
Maubec, 165.
Maussane-les-Alpilles, 135.
Mées (Les), 187.
Ménerbes, 154.
Menton, 290.
Biovès garden, 291.
Carnolès palace, 291.
Cocteau museum, 290.
Garavan, 291.
Lemon festival, 291.
Market, 291.
Saint-Michel church, 290.
Mérindol, 158.
Ornithological observatory, 158.
Régalon gorges, 159.
Meyreuil, 179.
MILLS
Alziari, 274.
des Bouillons, 162.
de Contes, 281.
Cornille, 135.
de Daudet, 134.
d'Entrevaux, 300.
de Flayosquet, 229.
paper, 167.
Monaco, 279, 282.
Cathedral, 283.
Exotic garden, 284.
Musée d'Anthropologie préhistorique, 284.
Oceanographical museum, 284.
Prince palace, 283.
Saint-Jean feast, 295.
Sporting activities, 295.
Wax museum, 285.
MONASTERIES (see ART, ROMAN).

Cimiez, 75, 274.
Ganagobie, 75, 184.
Lérins, 74, 242.
Le Thoronet, 74, 233.
Saint-Michel-de-Frigolet, 75, 145.
Sénanque, 74, 163.
Silvacane, 75, 159.
Verne (la), 74, 222.
Mons, 251.
Aqueduc de la Roche-Taillée, 251.
Musée Marine et Montagne, 251.
Tour of the dolmens, 251.
MONT
Agel, 281.
Mules, 289.
Faron, 202.
Gros, 289.
Rouge, 161.
Ventoux, 172.
Vinaigre, 213, 223.
MOUNTAINS
Lure, 186.
Sainte-Victoire, 180.
Montagnette (la), 144.
Montauroux, 247.
Monte-Carlo, 286.
Casino, 286.
Japanese garden, 287.
L'Hermitage, 287.
Salle Garnier, 286.
Prince Rainier's cars, 286.
Sports events, 287.
Montmajour, 134.
Monmirail (lace), 149.
Mougins, 244.
Cookery lessons, 245.
Musée de l'Automobile, 244.
Notre-Dame-de-Vie, 244.
Photography museum, 245.
Picasso's house, 245.
Valmasque park, 246.
Mouriès, 134.
Moustiers-Sainte-Marie, 234.
Ceramics, 237.
China museum, 234.

N

Nartuby (waterfall), 95, 229.
Nice, 270.
Carnival, 118, 275.
Cimiez monastery, 274.
Crystallised fruits, 275.
Côte d'Azur observatory, 275.
Festivals, 272.
Forest park, 274.
Marc-Chagall museum, 274.
Markets, 270.
Masséna museum, 273.
Matisse museum, 274.
Modern Art museum, 275.
Musée des Beaux-Arts, 273.
Negresco, 272.
Oil factories, 271, 274.
Phoeni park, 273.
Promenade des Anglais, 272.

Sainte-Réparate Cathedral, 271.
Saint-Martin-Saint-Augustin Church, 271.
Sporting activities, 274.
Notre-Dame-de-Pépiole, 200.
Notre-Dame-des-Fontaines, 296.

O

OCHRE
Conservatory, 59, 161.
Tour, 161.
Feasts, 59.
Maison Chauvin, 59.
OLIVE/OLIVE TREE, 28-29.
Oil (see GASTRONOMY and MILLS).
Olive tree museum, 137.
Oppède-le-Vieux, 165.
Orange, 146.
Arc de triomphe, 146.
Chorégies, 147.
Musée municipal, 146.
Saint-Eutrope hill, 146.

P

Paillons (bassin des), 280.
PALACES: map 104-105.
PARKS (see also FLORA, GARDENS): map 76-77.
Caillenco, 247.
Camargue regional park, 130.
Floral tropical de Provence, 143.
Mercantour, 306.
Mont-Boron forest park, 274.
Moulin-Blanc, 205.
Mugel, 199.
Port-Cros national park, 213.
Saint-Pons, 205.
Valmasque, 245.
Vaugrenier, 259.
PEAKS
Babaou, 223.
Canadel, 223.
Èze, 278.
Peille, 281.
Peillon, 281.
PERFUMES
Making, 80-83, 249.
Musée des Arômes, 138.
Musée des Arômes et du Parfum, 145.
Musée international de la Parfumerie, 248.
Perfumed source, 269.
Pernes-les-Fontaines, 168.
Cycling 168.
Horloge tower, 168.
Musée du Costume comtadin, 169.
Ostrich breeding, 169.
Pertuis, 157.
PÉTANQUE, 90, 226.
Pont-de-Gau, 130.
Pont-de-Siagne, 247.

Pont-du-Loup, 267.
Pont-Julien (Le), 155.
Pontis, 305.
Porquerolles, 210.
  Beaches, 211.
  Botanical conservatory, 210.
  Sainte-Agathe fort, 210.
  Light house, 211.
  Mountain biking, 211.
Port-Cros, 212.
  National park
  Palud beach, 212.
  Port-Man bay, 213.
  Tour of the forts, 213.
  Undersea footpath, 212.
  Vallon de la Solitude, 213.
Port-Grimaud, 221.
Pradet (Le), 207.
PREHISTORY: map 68-69.
  Caves (see CAVE).
  Dinosaurs, 180.
  Merveilles valley, map 68-69, 70, 297.
  Mules mount, 289.
  Musée d'Anthropologie préhistorique, 284.
  Musée d'Archéologie méditerranéenne, 190.
  Prehistoric Audides caves, 239.
  Robine (La), 299.
Puget-Théniers, 302.
Puyricard, 179.
Puy-Sainte-Réparade (Le), 178.

R

Ramatuelle, 217.
Racecourse, 259.
Rayol-Canadel, 215.
RECIPES
  Aïgo boulido, 42.
  Berlingots, 31.
  Melon sorbet, 21.
  Raïto, 43.
  Salade niçoise, 43.
REMAINS, ROMAN: map 68-69 and 72-73.
  Alyscamps, 126.
  Aqueduc, 251.
  Arc de triomphe, 138, 146, 151, 170.
  Glanum, 139.
  Maison des Messii, 148.
  Mausoleum, 139.
  Musée archéologique, 151.
  Musée lapidaire, 142.
  Oppidum, 179.
  Pont-Julien (Le), 154.
  Sarcophage de la Gayole, 232.
  Theatre, 146, 148.
  Trophée des Alpes, 279.
RESTAURANTS (FOR LOCAL DISHES): map 36-37.
RESTAURANTS (GOURMET): map 32-33.
Rimplas, 307.
Robine (La), 299.
Robion, 165.

Roquebillière, 294.
Roquebrune, 286.
  Castle, 288.
  Procession, 288.
  Sainte-Marguerite church, 288.
Roque-d'Anthéron (La), 159.
  Abbaye de Silvacane, 159.
  Festival de piano, 159.
Roquemaure, 143.
Roquette-sur-Siagne (La), 247.
Roubion, 307.
Rougon, 236.
Roussillon, 161.
Route Napoléon, 238.
Rustrel, 59, 161.
  Ochre festival, 59.
  Tour of ochres, 59, 161.

S

Sablet, 149.
Saint-André-des-Alpes, 303.
Saint-Antonin-sur-Bayon, 181.
Saint-Césaire-sur-Siagne, 245.
  Caves, 71, 245.
Saint-Chamas, 151.
Saint-Cyr-sur-Mer, 203.
Saint-Étienne-de-Tinée, 307.
Saint-Gilles-du-Gard, 75.
Saint-Jean-Cap-Ferrat (see Ferrat).
Saint-Martin-Vésubie, 292, 307.
  Musée des Traditions, 294.
Saint-Maximin-la-Sainte Baume, 204.
Saint-Michel-de-Frigolet, 145.
Saint-Michel-de-l'Observatoire, 195.
Saint-Paul-de-Mausole, 139.
Saint-Paul-de-Vence, 260.
  Collegial Church, 260.
  La Colombe d'Or inn, 261.
  History Museum, 260.
  Maeght foundation , 261.
  Ramparts, 260.
  Walks, 261.
Saint-Paul-sur-Ubaye, 305.
Saint-Pilon (le), 204.
Saint-Raphaël, 225.
Saint-Rémy-de-Provence, 138.
  Aéroclub, 138.
  Alpilles museum, 138.
  Feria, 139.
  Glanum, 139.
  Mario-Prassinos foundation, 138.
  Mas de la Pyramide, 139.
  Mausoleum, 139.
  Musée des Aromes, 138.
  Notre-Dame-de-Pitié Chapel, 138.
  Organa, 138.
  Présence-Van Gogh art centre, 138.
  Saint-Martin Collegial Church, 138.
Saint-Roman, 287.
Saint-Sauveur-de-Tinée, 307.
Saint-Tropez, 216.

  Citadel, 216.
  Beaches, 216.
  Le Byblos, 217.
  Footpath, 216.
  Maison des papillons, 217.
  Market, 216.
  Musée de l'Annonciade, 216.
  Musée naval, 216.
  Sandals, 217.
  Sénéquier, 217.
Saint-Vallier-de-Thiey, 238.
Saint-Zacharie, 205.
Sainte-Baume (massif), 204.
Sainte-Cécile, 165.
Sainte-Croix-du-Verdon, 237.
Sainte-Maxime, 218.
  Aquascope, 218.
  Fishing, 219.
  Market, 218.
  Musée des Traditions locales (folk museum), 218.
  Musée du Phonographe et de la Musique mécanique, 219.
  Themed walks, 219.
  Wood, 219.
Saintes-Maries-de-la-Mer (Les), 133.
  Baroncelli museum, 132.
  Church, 132.
  Gipsy pilgrimage, 132.
  Horse féria, 133.
  Kayaking, 133.
  Panorama du voyage, 133.
  Virgin celebration, 133.
Sainte-Victoire, 181.
Salernes, 231.
Salin-de-Giraud, 129.
Salon-de-Provence, 150.
  Iron and steel industry, 151.
  Energy museum, 151.
  Festivals, 151.
  Musée de Salon et de la Crau, 150.
  Nostradamus museum, 150.
  Port authority, 151.
  Refinery, 151.
  Saint-Laurent Collegial Church, 150.
  Soap factories, 150.
Sanary-sur-Mer, 200.
  Eastern promise, 200.
  Festival, 200.
  Notre-Dame-de-Pépiole, 200.
Saorge, 296, 307.
Sault, 172.
  Lavender fair, 172.
  Lavender garden, 173.
  Market, 172.
Sausset-les-Pins, 153.
SCIENTIFIC SITES: map 120-121.
  Caussols: observatory, 269.
  Digne-les-Bains: observatory and geological reserve, 299.
  Èze: astrorama, 278.
  Forcalquier: observatory and geological reserve, 185.
  Nice: observatory, 275.

SEA CRUISES, 100, 131, 151, 195, 197, 202, 207, 214, 219, 221, 226, 241, 243, 272.
Séguret, 149.
Seillans, 251.
Sénanque (Abbey), 163.
Senez, 238.
Sérignan-du-Comtat, 147.
Servanes, 129.
SHOPPING
  Artist's tools, 295
  Books
    Abécédaire (l'), 61.
    Arcenaulx (les), 40, 189.
    La Roumanille, 143.
    Librairie de Sénanque, 163.
    Librairie Dumas, 61.
    Rue des Bouquinistes Obscurs, 61.
  Carpets, 221.
  Equipment
    for herdsman, 133.
    for pétanque, 91.
  Fabrics: map 50-51.
    Aux Jardins de Provence, 143.
    in Nice, 270.
    La Maison des Lices, 52.
    Les Olivades, 52.
    Souleïado, 52, 155.
  Furniture: map 50-51.
    Ateliers Laffanour, 53.
    Mélodie Mauve, 178.
  Glassworks: map 50-51.
    Biot glassworks, 265.
    Stained glass windows, 27.
  Ironworks: map 50-51.
    Art of metalwork, 135.
  Mirrors, 195.
  Musée boutique de l'O.M., 195.
  Pipes, 220.
  Sandals, 217.
  Santons: map 50-51.
    in Nice, 270.
    Canolive, 241.
    Carbonel, 193.
    Chave 197.
    Daniel Scaturro, 197.
    Driades, 219.
    Fouque, 178.
    Jacques Flore, 193.
  Terracotta and earthenware: map 50-51.
    Atelier Basset, 231.
    Atelier Bernard, 160.
    Atelier Ségriès, 235.
    Atelier Vagh, 231.
    Auge-Laribe, 265.
    Boutal, 231.
    Michel Coquet, 56.
    Ravel, 197.
    Terracotta of Launes, 231.
    Vernin, 155.
  Wax, 246.
  Wooden objects, 219, 250.
  Wooden toys, 305.
Signes, 205.
Silvacane (Abbey), 75, 154, 159.

Sisteron, 186.
  Citadel, 186-187.
  Farm lamb, 186.
  Notre-Dame-des-Pommiers, 186.
  Sporting activities, 186.
SPORTS: map 84-85.
  Archery, 137.
  Baloon, 184.
  Canoeing and kayaking, 133, 151, 167, 236, 297, 301.
  Canyoning, 87, 249, 268, 274, 297.
  Climbing, 86, 137, 149, 164, 181, 226, 269.
  Cycling, 101, 131, 143, 157, 169, 181, 193, 206, 211, 249, 274, 289, 307.
  Deltaplaning, 199.
  Diving, 88, 199, 201, 207, 212, 227, 241, 295.
  Fishing, 87, 207, 232.
  Free gliding, 138.
  Hiking (see HIKING).
  Gliding, 181, 186, 199, 289, 303.
  Golf, 89, 129, 225, 281.
  Hang-gliding, 186, 251.
  Horse riding (see HORSE RIDING).
  Hydrocycle trip, 193.
  Karting, 89, 268.
  Parachuting, 89, 144, 221, 287.
  Piloting, 199.
  Pot holing, 86, 232, 249.
  Rafting, 87, 236, 249, 274, 297, 305.
  Rowing, 151.
  Sailing, 151, 206, 221, 235, 259, 274, 277, 289.
  Skiing, 86, 307.
  Squash, 179.
  Tennis, 89, 179, 274, 287.
  Waterskiing, 88, 221, 259, 287.
  Whitewater sports, 305.

Tarascon, 144.
  Castle, 144.
  Fabrics museum, 145.
  Gliding, 145.
  Maison de Tartarin, 144.
  Sainte-Marthe Collegial Church, 144.
TAROT, 194.
Tende, 296.
Théoule-sur-Mer, 226.
Tholonet (Le), 181.
Thoronet (abbey), 233.
Toulon, 202.
  Chichi-frégis, 203.
  Creeks, 202.
  Market, 202.
  Mont-Faron, 202.
  Musée de la Marine, 203.
  Musée municipal, 203.
Tour-d'Aigues (La), 157.

Musée des Faïences, 157.
Musée de l'Histoire du pays, 157.
Tourrettes-sur-Loup, 266.
Tourtour, 231.
TRAIN, TOURIST
  des pignes, 299, 302.
  des plages, 214.
  Nice-Cuneo, 297.
Trinquetaille, 129.
Turbie (La), 278, 279.

U

Utelle, 295.
  Notre-Dame des Miracles, 295.
  Saint-Véran Church, 295.

V

Vacqueyras, 149.
Vaison-la-Romaine, 148.
  Chœurs lauréats festival, 149.
  Journées gourmandes, 149.
  Notre-Dame-de-Nazareth, 148.
  Roman remains, 148.
  Théo-Desplans museum, 148.
Vallauris, 256.
  Alberto Magnelli museum, 256.
  Castle, 256.
  Earthenware museum, 256.
  Flowers, 257.
  Madoura collection, 257.
  National Picasso museum, 256.
  Pottery, 257.
  Pottery museum, 257.
VALLEYS
  Argens, 232.
  Bevera, 306.
  Durance, 158.
  Gordolasque, 294.
  Loup, 266.
  Merveilles, 70, 297.
  Roya, 296, 306.
  Siagne, 244.
  Tinée, 307.
  Ubaye, 304, 307.
  Var, 300, 307.
  Verdon, 300, 307.
  Vésubie, 292, 307.
Venasque, 169.
Vence, 262.
  Émile-Hugues foundation, 262.
  Footpaths, 263.
  Guided tour, 263.
  Notre-Dame-des-Fleurs, 262.
  Rosary chapel, 262.
Ventoux (mount), 172.
Verdon (gorges), 234.
Verne (Chartreuse de la), 222.
Vernègues, 56.
Vésubie (vallée de la), 292.

VILLAGES, HILL TOP: *map 62-63.*
in the Alpes-de-Haute-
Provence:
Banon, 286.
Entrevaux, 300.
Lurs, 184.
Moustiers-Sainte-Marie,
234.
in the Alpes-Maritimes :
Auribeau-sur-Siagne,
246.
Coaraze, 280.
Gourdon, 268.
Lucéram, 280.
Peillon, 281.
Saorge, 296.
Tourettes-sur-Loup, 266.
in the Bouches-du-Rhône:
Les Baux-de-Provence,
136.
in the Var:
Barjols, 232.
Collobrières, 222.
Cotignac, 233.
Gassin, 216.
Grimaud, 220.
La Cadière-d'Azur, 198.
La Garde-Freinet, 223.
Le Beausset, 199.
Le Castellet, 198.
Mons, 251.
Ramatuelle, 217.
Seillans, 251.
in the Vaucluse:
villages in the Luberon,
154-157.
Gordes, 162.
Goult, 161.
Roussillon, 161.
Venasque, 169.
Villecrozes, 231.
Villefranche-sur-Mer, 277.
Saint-Pierre Chapel, 277.
Saint-Elme citadel, 277.
Villeneuve-lès-Avignon, 143.
Villeneuve-Loubet, 259.

W

WINES: *map 44-45 and 46-49.*
Bandol, 201.
Château de l'Isolette, 49.
Châteauneuf-du-Pape,
146.
Château Sainte-Roseline,
228.
Château de Selle, 228.
Château Simone, 179.
Clos Sainte-Magdeleine,
197.
Domaine de l'Angueiroun,
215.
Domaine Ott, 198.
Écomusée du liège (cork),
53, 223.
Gigondas, 149.
Maison des vins de Bandol,
201.
Mas de Rey, 129.
Musée du Père Anselme,
147.
Musée du Tire-Bouchons,
154.
Musée du Vin, 47.
Palette, 48.
Porquerolles, 210.
Sablet et Séguret, 149.
de la Sainte-Victoire, 181.
Vacqueyras, 149.

Z

ZOOS: *map 102-103.* 201, 202,
224, 277.

This guide was written by Jeanne Barzilaï, Catherine Bézard, Éva Cantavenera, Pascal de Cugnac and Virgine Motte, with additional help from Jackie Baldwin, Marie Barbelet, Denis Hill, Bernadette Massin, Frédéric Olivier, Françoise Picon and Isabelle Romain.

Illustrations: François Lachèze

Illustrated maps: Philippe Doro

Cartography: © Idé-Infographie (Thomas Grollier)

Translation and adaptation: Chanterelle Translations, London (Josephine Bacon)

Additional design and editorial assistance: Christine Bell, Cecilia Walters, Rachel Leyshon and Emma Baxter

Project manager: Liz Coghill

We have done our best to ensure the accuracy of the information contained in this guide. However, addresses, phone numbers, opening times etc. inevitably do change from time to time, so if you find a discrepancy please do let us know. You can contact us at: hachetteuk@orionbooks.co.uk or write to us at Hachette UK, address below.

Hachette UK guides provide independent advice. The authors and compilers do not accept any remuneration for the inclusion of any addresses in these guides.

Please note that we cannot accept any responsibility for any loss, injury or inconvenience sustained by anyone as a result of any information or advice contained in this guide.

First published in the United Kingdom in 2000 by Hachette UK

Distributed in the United States of America by Sterling Publishing Co., Inc. 387 Park Avenue South, New York, NY 10016-8810

A CIP catalogue for this book is available from the British Library

ISBN 1 84202 006 4

Hachette UK, Cassell & Co., The Orion Publishing Group, Wellington House, 125 Strand, London WC2R 0BB

Printed in Spain by Graficas Estella

Voucher section

Wherever you see this symbol ✿ in the guide, you will find a voucher in this section which will entitle you to a discount or special offer. If you find a voucher here you want to use, the corresponding page number in the guide is there for your reference.

On presentation of this Vacances guide

La Cathédrale d'Images

(Cathedral of Images)

p.137

Buy 5 entry tickets and get 1 free
Offre une entrée gratuite
pour cinq entrées achetées

La Cathédrale d'Images
Chemin Départemental 27
13520 LES-BAUX-DE-PROVENCE
☎ 04 90 54 38 65

On presentation of this Vacances guide

La Fondation Angladon Dubrujeaud - Musée

(Angladon Dubrujeaud Foundation)

p.142

Reduced entry prices for students and families and a free entry ticket for children under 12 years. Also offering group tours.

Propose l'entrée au tarif réduit pour les étudiants et les familles, l'entrée gratuite pour les enfants de moins de douze ans et offre un parcours-découverte du musée

Fondation Angladon Dubrujeaud - Musée
5, rue Laboureur – 84000 AVIGNON
☎ 04 90 82 29 03

On presentation of this Vacances guide

L'Étoile du Délice

(confectioners)

p.165

10% discount when you buy small packets of chocolates

Offre 10% de réduction sur l'achat de ballotins de chocolats

L'Étoile du Délice
57, place Castil-Blaze
84300 CAVAILLON
☎ 04 90 78 07 51

On presentation of this Vacances guide

Le Musée du Vieil Aix

(Museum of Old Aix)

p.176

A free postcard

Offre une carte postale

Musée du Vieil-Aix
17, rue Gaston-de-Saporta
13100 AIX-EN-PROVENCE
☎ 04 42 21 43 55

On presentation of this Vacances guide

La Fondation Carzou

(Carzou Foundation)

p.183

Reduced price entry tickets

Propose l'entrée au tarif réduit

Fondation Carzou
9, boulevard Elemir-Bourges
04100 MANOSQUE
☎ 04 92 87 40 49

On presentation of this Vacances guide

El Dorado City

(Wild West town)

p.195

Free entry ticket for one child

Offer valid when the child is accompanied by 2 adults paying the normal entry fee (not available with any other promotions)

Offre une entrée gratuite pour un enfant

Offre valable pour un enfant accompagné de deux adultes payant le tarif normal (non cumulable avec d'autres promotions)

El Dorado City
13220 CHATEAUNEUF-LES-MARTIGUES
☎ 04 42 79 86 90

Le Jardin Exotique-Zoo
(Exotic Garden and Zoo)
p.201

10% discount on an entry ticket
Offre 10% de réduction sur le billet d'entrée

Jardin Exotique-Zoo
Quartier Pont-d'Aran
83110 SANARY-BANDOL
☎ 04 94 29 40 38

Le Jardin d'Oiseaux Tropicaux
(Tropical Bird Garden)
p.207

Children's tickets at group rates
Propose l'entrée des enfants au tarif de groupe

Le Jardin d'Oiseaux Tropicaux
Quartier St-Honoré
83250 LA-LONDE-LES-MAURES
☎ 04 94 35 02 15

La Maison Courrieu
(pipe maker)
p.220

15% discount on all purchases made
Offre 15% de réduction sur les achats

La Maison Courrieu
58, avenue Georges-Clemenceau
83310 COGOLIN
☎ 04 94 54 63 82

Le Musée Espace Raimu
(Raimu Museum)
p.221

15% discount on all purchases made
Propose une réduction de 15%
sur tous vos achats

Musée Espace Raimu
18, avenue Georges-Clemenceau
83310 COGOLIN
☎ 04 94 54 18 00

Aquatica
(water park)
p.224

Buy three entry tickets and get one free

Not available with any other offer

**Offre une entrée gratuite
pour trois personnes payantes**

Offre non cumulable avec d'autres promotions

Aquatica
RN98
Quartier le Capou
83600 FRÉJUS
☎ 04 94 51 82 51

Aquavision
(sea trips)
p.226

**10% discount on tickets
and offers group rates to individuals**

**Offre 10% de réduction et propose les entrées
individuelles au tarif groupe**

Aquavision
Boulevard de la Plage
83530 AGAY
☎ 04 94 82 75 40

Le Musée des Arts et Traditions
(Folk Museum)

p.228

Group rates for individual entry tickets

Propose l'entrée au tarif de groupe

Musée des Arts et Traditions Populaires
15, rue Roumanille
83300 DRAGUIGNAN
☎ 04 94 47 05 72

Le Musée du Pays Brignolais
(Brignolais Folk Museum)

p.232

Reduced price entry fee for adults (15F) and children (5F)

Propose l'entrée à 15F pour les adultes
et à 5F pour les enfants

Musée du Pays Brignolais
Place des Comtes de Provence
83170 BRIGNOLES
☎ 04 94 69 45 18

On presentation of this Vacances guide

Grotte de Baume Obscure

(stalagmite caves)

p.238

Group rates for individual entry tickets

Propose l'entrée au tarif de groupe

Grotte de Baume Obscure
Chemin Sainte-Anne
06460 ST-VALLIER-DE-THIEY
☎ 04 93 42 61 63

On presentation of this Vacances guide

La Grotte des Audides

(prehistoric caves)

p.239

20% discount on an entry ticket

Offre 20% de réduction sur le billet d'entrée

Grotte des Audides
Parc Préhistorique
1606, route de Cabris
06460 ST-VALLIER-DE-THIEY
☎ 04 93 42 64 15

La Parfumerie Galimard
(Galimard Perfumery)
p.249

**10% discount on purchases
or perfume creation workshops**

*Offer valid at all the Galimard factories and workshops
in Grasse and Èze-Village*

**Offre 10% de réduction sur les achats ou sur
les stages de création de son propre parfum**

*Offre valable pour toute visite des usines Galimard
de Grasse ou d'Èze-Village*

Parfumerie Galimard
Route de Pégomas B.P. 65
06332 GRASSE
☎ 04 93 09 20 00

Le Domaine de Manon
(rose grower)
p.249

**10% discount on entry fees,
plus 10% discount on·fresh flower petals**

**Offre 10% de réduction sur les prix des visites
et des pétales de fleurs fraîches**

Le Domaine de Manon
36, chemin du Servan
Plascassier
06130 GRASSE
☎ 04 93 60 12 76

On presentation of this Vacances guide

Le Musée Peynet

(Peynet Museum)

p.253

Half-price entry tickets

Propose l'entrée à demi tarif

Musée Peynet
Place Nationale
06600 ANTIBES
☎ 04 92 90 54 30

On presentation of this Vacances guide

Roya Évasion

(canoeing and rafting)

p.297

10% discount for individual entry tickets and for groups of less than 10 people

Offre 10% de réduction sur les entrées individuelles et aux groupes de moins de dix participants

Roya Évasion
1, rue Pasteur
06540 BREIL-SUR-ROYA
☎ 04 93 04 91 46

Aqua Viva Est
(Municipal swimming pool)
(not featured in guide)

10% discount on entry tickets
Offre 10% de réduction

Aqua Viva Est
Piscine Municipale
Route de Grasse
04120 CASTELLANE
☎ 04 92 83 75 74

---

*All these promotional offers are exclusive
to our readers, and are valid until 31st March 2002*

*Ces offres promotionnelles sont reservées
à nos lecteurs, et sont valables jusqu'au 31 mars 2002*

NOTES

NOTES